THE BRITISH TAR

IN FACT AND FICTION

THE POETRY, PATHOS, AND HUMOUR
OF THE SAILOR'S LIFE

BY

CHARLES NAPIER ROBINSON
COMMANDER, ROYAL NAVY
AUTHOR OF "THE BRITISH FLEET"

WITH INTRODUCTORY CHAPTERS ON
THE PLACE OF THE SEA OFFICER AND SEAMAN
IN NAVAL HISTORY AND HISTORICAL LITERATURE
BY

JOHN LEYLAND
AUTHOR OF "THE BLOCKADE OF BREST," ETC. ETC.

ILLUSTRATED WITH
FRONTISPIECE IN COLOUR AND ABOUT ONE HUNDRED AND THIRTY
REPRODUCTIONS OF OLD PRINTS, ENGRAVINGS, AND WOODCUTS
DEPICTING THE CHARACTER, COSTUME, AND CUSTOMS OF
THE SAILOR AFLOAT AND ASHORE, AS DESCRIBED BY
THE HISTORIANS, THE POETS, THE NOVELISTS
AND THE PLAYWRIGHTS

LONDON AND NEW YORK
HARPER AND BROTHERS
45 ALBEMARLE STREET, W.
1909

Publishing Statement:

This important reprint was made from an old and scarce book.

Therefore, it may have defects such as missing pages, erroneous pagination, blurred pages, missing text, poor pictures, markings, marginalia and other issues beyond our control.

Because this is such an important and rare work, we believe it is best to reproduce this book regardless of its original condition.

Thank you for your understanding and enjoy this unique book!

TO THE
BROTHERHOOD OF THE SEA

PREFACE

THIS volume originated in the wish of many friends that I would reproduce a further series of the pictures in my collection, some of which were published in " The British Fleet," illustrating the social side of the sailor's life. In almost all naval histories and biographies, certainly in those of later days, there are pictures of battle scenes and portraits, while drawings of the ships and their equipment may be found in most of the books on seamanship and the like. For some unexplained reason, however, although there exist many paintings, engravings, and prints depicting sailors afloat and ashore, these have seldom been used to illustrate works dealing with the achievements of the seaman or the development of the sea service. It has always seemed to me, therefore, a pity that this wealth of pictorial art, always curious and sometimes beautiful, should not be rescued from its state of comparative obscurity, and by means of the admirable methods of reproduction now in vogue be placed at the disposition of that larger public which cannot afford the leisure to search for, or the means to purchase, the originals. Many of the prints reproduced are exceedingly scarce, and in the natural course of all perishable things tend to disappear, or to be locked up in the collections of wealthy people, which comes to pretty much the same thing.

To accompany the pictures which I had selected for reproduction I prepared the two sections of this volume dealing with the seaman on the stage and sea songs, because many of the illustrations were connected with those subjects and were originally published as embellishments to songs and plays. Then came the idea of dealing in the same work with the seaman as he is found in history and in fiction, for which purpose I had already gathered a large quantity of material. To attempt such an undertaking single-handed within a moderate period I felt to be impossible, and I therefore appealed with confidence to my old friend and colleague, Mr. John Leyland, to give me his assistance. Very readily he acquiesced in my request, devoting much care and research to these sections, and making many helpful suggestions.

In order to illustrate the personality of the seaman as described in successive periods by his contemporaries, we have ransacked a whole literature, pursuing our researches through many curious by-paths in order to reach new sources of information. In so doing we have both of us learned a great deal about the sea service of a kind not to be found in any ordinary History of the Navy. Indeed, it may truly be said that no one has yet produced an adequate and wholly satisfactory work on the subject which we mapped out before us. We have enjoyed many advantages, and not least of them to find our labours lightened by the volumes of the Navy Records Society, that admirable library for which we are indebted in the main to Professor Sir John Knox Laughton, R.N., to whose exertions in the field of naval literature every writer on the subject in the future, as well as those for many years past, must owe a deep debt of gratitude.

When the work as originally projected had been completed, and the proofs read, Mr. Leyland was happily inspired to propose two introductory chapters, in which, by the light of what follows, he has described the place of the sea officer and the seaman in naval history and literature. If this volume is admitted to have any value as a serious contribution to naval history, I feel that it will be mainly because of the inclusion of those chapters. Mr. Leyland disclaims any direct didactic purpose, but the lesson is there manifest to every one, and it is not only for the youngsters who are entering naval life, but for all who realise the importance to the British Empire of the Navy which protects its communications and guards its heart.

A few words about the contents of the various sections will not be out of place in the Preface. In the first part, that which deals with the sailor as he is pictured in the literature of the sea written with a serious intention, the ordinary naval histories prove to contain less information than might have been expected. It is from the less accessible works of the diarists, the pamphleteers, and the satirical writers that we have been able to construct our character of the sailor. Pepys, for his period, gave us little assistance, what he has to say on the subject being only in a very general way, except where he describes some incident that came under his own observation, or where he makes some humorous or epigrammatic remark, as where he says : " A purser would not have twice what he got unless he cheated." Pepys's little-known narrative of his voyage to Tangier in 1683, printed in the Rev. J. Smith's edition of his " Life and Correspondence " (1841), is, however, very instructive. The inner life of the Navy was not, indeed, unknown to the literary workers, but they were, as a

rule, unattracted by it, and, moreover, it was obscured
by the greater political activities which resulted in some
measure from the seamen's efforts. It is chiefly, then,
from out-of-the-way sources, like the sober pages of
Captain Boteler, Braithwaite's clever sketches, and
Lurting's ingenuous narrative, or the lurid and sensa-
tional pictures of Ned Ward, and later on of Jack Nasty-
face, that, by collation and elimination, we get the most
useful kind of illumination. From these and similar
sources I think it is clearly shown that in all times the
sea influenced those who lived upon it, and assisted in
the formation of their character. The object has been
to describe the seaman on his proper background of
hardship and privation, often of cold and misery, and
to discover his sturdy, honest, loyal character and realise
the true personality of the man. His professional keenness and devotion to duty earn our respect and compel
our admiration no less than his personal qualities excite
our sympathy and win our affection.

In the section dealing with the sailor on the stage
and the work of the dramatists a different method has
been followed. The field, from the point of view
taken in this volume, was practically unfurrowed. So
far as I am aware, no one had hitherto attempted to
point out the extent to which the sailor figured on the
stage in the Tudor and Jacobean eras. " Hicke Scorner "
was a revelation. " Captain Sym Suresby " in " Ralph
Roister Doister " is the type of an early seaman, though,
with the exception of Hazlitt, in his edition of Dodsley,
most of the commentators have followed one another in
describing him as a servant. Hazlitt accepts him clearly
as the master of a vessel, and there appears to have been
an evident intention on the part of the playwright to
exhibit the honesty and the candour of the rough sailor.

The apt knowledge of sea terms displayed by Shakespeare has been referred to by others, but the extent to which all the poet-dramatists used the sea language has not been elucidated in any popular work. No better proof is needed of the extent to which the Elizabethan audiences were similarly acquainted with the technical terms of the sailor's art. " Ben Legend," in Congreve's " Love for Love," has been described as the " first of a long line of stage sailors " ; but Davenant, Wycherley, D'Urfey, and others had drawn characteristic seamen long before ; and " Captain Durzo " is unmistakably intended by Ravenscroft as a typical seaman. The fact seems to be that the stage sailor and the nautical play are British products, home-grown, and enjoying a popularity absolutely unique in the annals of the theatre. Molière's " Misanthrope " suggested to Wycherley the idea of " The Plain Dealer," and it is particularly instructive to find the English counterpart of " Alceste " appearing as the sea officer " Captain Manly," because the author says that he has made him choose a sea life in order to avoid the world. The professional aloofness of a captain of a man-of-war, with which, of course, Wycherley was well acquainted, was one singularly fitted to enable a man to cut himself off from his fellows. Byron, it will be remembered, called him " the lone chieftain." But the subject in all its branches will be found to be most fruitful of discovery by those who may be at the trouble of exploring it. What, for example, was the connection between the sailor's hornpipe of 1795 and the " Jig of the Ship " referred to by a writer just two hundred years before ? Indeed, I trust that this section will be found interesting by all students of the British drama and theatrical literature.

The section on the sailor of fiction pivoted naturally

around the three great writers—Defoe, Smollett, and
Marryat. But long before the eighteenth century the
age of discovery had brought the mariner into the beginnings of the English novel. The romance of the sea
stirred the imagination or set a-dreaming the scholars of
the spacious times of Elizabeth; some it actually sent
a-venturing, like Lodge; others it led, like Sir Thomas
More, to picture ideal states; while even John Lyly
could not resist the inspiration, but must introduce us
to a sailor who spouts euphuisms. That the national
literature would have been the poorer without the
characters of Robinson Crusoe, Tom Bowling, and Peter
Simple goes without saying. What has been done here
is to show that these seafarers had a very large number
of less well-known shipmates. The maritime life which
Defoe depicts is characteristic of the age in which he
lived, when the adventures of Dampier and Shelvocke,
the exploits of Captains Avery and Kidd, made more
noise in the world than the achievements of the Navy.
But the nautical setting which Smollett gave to his
novels was that of many other stories of the eighteenth
century, even to the extent of utilising the voyage of a
ship and the character of her company as an allegory
to explain a particular theory of Christianity. In later
times Marryat's contemporaries, many of whom had
also served afloat, assist materially in the discovery of
the personality of the seaman. Quite recently Admiral
Moresby, who entered the service in the first half of the
last century, describing his youthful experiences, remarks
of James Hannay: "A truly remarkable man—editor,
essayist, scholar, and novelist; no better picture of the
Navy at this time can be found than in his books."

Since the section on sea songs was prepared three
important anthologies of naval poetry have appeared,

those of Messrs. John Masefield and Christopher Stone, the latter with an introduction by Admiral Sir Cyprian Bridge, and that of Professor C. H. Firth, published by the Navy Records Society. In the scholarly introduction to the last-named work I have fortunately had an excellent standard against which to compare my chapter on naval historical verse. In my researches I believe I have omitted very few ballads of importance, my illustrative selections being from the best authorities—the Halliwell, Roxburghe, Bagford, and other collections, as well as from the many garlands and slip songs in my own possession. It is most satisfactory to know that I have the support of Professor Firth for my contention that these ballads have at least some historical value. "They tell historians what was felt and what was believed by those who wrote the ballads and those who bought them, show how public opinion was formed, and help to explain the growth of popular traditions." It has been assumed by some writers that the elder Dibdin's songs were very rarely sung on board ship, and that there were no chanties in the Navy, but I have here quoted the evidence of contemporary seamen that both were heard afloat in the ships of the old Navy. As to the chanty, neither men-of-war's-men nor merchant seamen can claim it as peculiarly their own, for both have used it in the days gone by. It is, indeed, the earliest form of sea song, adapted to the needs of the mariners. It was used by all the old sailors before they carried music to sea with them, it was known in the Mediterranean in classic times, and I have myself heard Dyaks on the coast of Borneo and Hawaiians under the shadow of Mauna Loa chantying in primitive fashion aboard their native craft. Some writers appear to have attributed much too gloomy a view of nautical life to the poets, but the attitude of any one towards the sea is largely a matter of individual experience. To the seaman it is fickle, strong, and cruel. To the poet maybe it presents something of beauty or of terror. Addison was able to contemplate a storm with " agreeable horror." To some it brings restlessness, and to others it is restful. By a mercy of Providence in this island generation after generation have been eager to dare its dangers and to face its discomforts in preference to staying at home.

The chapters on Naval Art were originally written at much greater length, but have been reduced to keep the volume of a reasonable size. As all descriptions of portraits, battle pieces, etc., must be more or less of a catalogue, perhaps the reduction of this section will not be found a fault by the general reader. Although no longer merely a picture book, the illustrations were its *raison d'être*. They have been chosen from among a great many more of a similar kind which are not to be easily found elsewhere. Moreover, two or three equally attractive groups of naval genre have been left untouched, as satire and caricature. This is not to say that those who will may not find more than a suggestion of both in the pictorial contents of this volume, but it was not primarily to either of these aspects they owed their inclusion. They have been selected from the point of view of a seaman and a lover of the Navy, for humour or pathos in the representation of the sailor first, for illustration of the letterpress secondly, and lastly for some suggestion to collectors like himself.

It is chiefly the picturesque side of sea life which we find reflected in fiction and on the stage. The glory, the romance, and the humour have been laid on with lavish hand, while the other and less attractive aspects are merely utilised as a contrast, and to bring into greater prominence the brighter colouring. The converse is the rule with those writers whose purpose was more serious, more didactic, or more commonplace. Here we get the darker side, the grievances, the troubles, and the dangers of the sea calling. In these pages an attempt has been made to contrast the real with the ideal; to place, as it were, in parallel columns the descriptions handed down to us of the seaman in various periods of our history, and to deduce from the characters, as we find them drawn for us by pen and graver, the typical sailor himself, his qualities, and his environment.

CHARLES N. ROBINSON.

January, 1909.

CONTENTS

THE PLACE OF THE SEA OFFICER AND SEAMAN IN NAVAL HISTORY

The personal element—Influence for success or failure—Moral ascendancy and the capacity and energy to win exemplified by the war with Spain—Foredoomed failure of the Spaniards—Land armies and naval preparations—Councils of war—Antagonisms—The Dutch Wars; balance of naval force; strength and weakness of officers and men of both fleets—Character of French officers—De Tourville—Rooke and Shovell—Fighting instinct—Benbow, Mathews, Byng—Formalism—Want of inspiration, and jealousies—Conduct of the captains—Failure—The new spirit—Hawke, Boscawen, Rodney, Hood, Howe, Nelson, and Jervis—Fresh impulse and higher training—The "Band of Brothers"—Influence on the fleet—The makers of Victory.

THE BRITISH TAR

PART I

HISTORICAL LITERATURE, BIOGRAPHY, PAMPHLET, AND SATIRE

PART II

MYSTERY, PAGEANT, COMEDY, AND DRAMATIC LITERATURE

PART III

SEA STORIES, NOVELS, MAGAZINES, AND CHAP-BOOKS

PART IV

POEMS, BALLADS, SONGS, AND DOGGEREL

NAVAL ICONOGRAPHY

THE SEAMAN AND SEA LIFE IN PICTORIAL ART

Early vestiges of the seaman—Tapestry, illumination, and sculpture—Costume and equipments—Tudor and Stuart representations—Pictures of the Dutch Wars—Portraits of sea officers—Battle pieces—Holbein, Kneller, and Zoffany—Hollar, Van de Velde, and Monamy—The school of Hogarth—Satire: Sandby, Gillray, and Rowlandson—Humorous art: Collet, Bunbury, and George Cruikshank—Pictures of the seaman's social life—The engravers in line, mezzotint, and stipple—The byways of Art—The book illustrators, frontispieces, song-heads, broadsheets, lottery tickets, lodge summonses, trade prospectuses, and valentines.

LIST OF ILLUSTRATIONS

THE PLACE OF THE SEA OFFICER AND SEAMAN IN NAVAL HISTORY

CHAPTER I

THE INFLUENCE OF PERSONALITY
1217-1702

A MONG the several causes that lead to success, or, in the absence of them, to failure, in naval warfare is one which stands pre-eminent over all the others. It is that personal element which creates, rules, and directs the material, and which triumphs over material obstacles when these lie in the way. The object of this book is to discover the personal element in naval operations and engagements, the individuality of seamen, as revealed in the pages of literature, historical, biographical and other. We have nothing to do with material considerations, nor with fighting, except when battles may disclose the personalities of those who have taken part in them, and may show us the underlying causes of success or failure in the action of those individuals. The purpose is purely historical. There is no intention of dealing with the Navy of steam and steel, of submarine and wireless telegraphy. Doubtless, in these times, as in all others, the man is more than the machine, but this volume will neither point a moral nor adorn a tale. The lessons, such as they are, will take shape for themselves, and the reader may apply them if he will.

At the outset, it seems desirable to devote a section to an analysis of cause and effect in this matter, upon the evidence of naval history. To survey the whole of that history for this purpose would be a vast and difficult business, and there can be given here but a slight sketch with the object of adding significance and

value to the fuller illustrations of life and character that
follow. The influence of personality is found in every
department of naval activity—where there is success, in
the statesmen who shape aright the course of national
policy, in the administrators who create and maintain
the necessary elements of the Navy, in the admirals
who direct with professional skill the employment of
naval forces, and the officers and men who with united
effort give living vigour to masses of dead material.
We may discover the causes of naval failure in the un-
wisdom of rulers, the paralysing influence of long and
inert peace, dissensions which destroy unity of effort,
or insufficient training, inexperience, or intellectual or
moral inferiority, or slackness of officers and unfitness
of men. When Howard wrote to Walsingham, in July,
1588, that neither sickness nor death should make them
yield until the service in hand was ended, and when he
added that he never knew nobler minds than those
then in the fleet, he was expressing the two things which
are primordial factors in success—the moral ascendancy
over all discouragements, and the capacity and energy
that fit men to win. We may say that with these two
elements, acting in all spheres of naval activity, success
is not only possible, but certain. They are the informing
spirit and power of professional competence, of determined
action, and of mastery over the enemy. They were
the thing that mattered in all early seafaring, when the
frail craft which navigated the seas were proof and evidence of the qualities of those who manned them.

These two qualities of moral ascendancy and mental
force which give strength and direction to endeavour,
were seen when Hubert de Burgh encountered Eustace
the Monk in the Strait of Dover in 1217, disclosing his
professional skill in the master-stroke of so handling the
fleet that the weather-gage was gained, whereby he was
enabled to send the cloth-yard shafts of the archers
down upon the foe on the wings of the wind, and afterwards to get to close quarters for grappling and boarding.
They were evident not less in the courage and fighting

prowess of the men of the Cinque Ports who completed
the victory.　Hubert de Burgh belonged to the race of
the Drakes and the Blakes, the Hawkes and Rodneys,
the Hoods and Nelsons, and the stout fellows who manned
his ships were kinsmen of the seafaring and fighting men
who manned our ships in later days.　In the ever-
growing importance of the Navy and the widening of
maritime knowledge through the great discoveries, the
compelling influences towards higher professional skill
were at work.　The soldiers who held naval command
in earlier times necessarily became seamen, or were
displaced by seamen.　Seamen and soldiers fought side
by side in the incredibly murderous battle of Sluys in
1340, and in the action known as Les Espagnols sur Mer
ten years later, both being won by the superior fighting
power of the English.　As soon as the ocean became
a pathway to the new-found lands, there was no room
on board, if things were to be done well, for any but
seamen.*

The qualities and powers of seamen in the great age
of world discovery which brought us into mortal conflict
with Spain, and for ever decided the destinies of the
nations, will be described by illustrative quotation
subsequently.　Here it is enough to remark that the
mariners who battled with many a North-Atlantic
gale, who fought with ice and fog, and all the Arctic
horrors, who doubled the North Cape, and navigated
the frozen seas of Lapland and the further East, who
sought to break the icy barriers of the North-West,
in unspeakable suffering, and often the direst misfortune, who struck at the monopolies of Spain in the
West Indies and Central America, who brought home
the treasures of silver mules and plate fleets, who
widened the bounds of the known world and circumnavigated it—men such as Willoughby, Burrough, Gilbert,

---

* The English side may be read in Nicolas's " History of the Royal Navy,"
and the French in De la Roncière's " Histoire de la Marine Française."
" The Black Book of the Admiralty " (Rolls Series) gives the earliest code of
maritime laws.

Drake, the Hawkinses, Frobisher, Davis, Fenner, and a hundred more,—that it was they who laid the foundation of English sea power.

It was generally held, wrote the Venetian ambassador at Madrid, in April, 1588, that Englishmen were of a different quality from Spaniards, " bearing a name above all the West for being expert and enterprising in all maritime affairs, and the finest fighters upon the sea." This was the temper of the men who had circumnavigated the world with Drake and sailed with the great explorers. When Winter took alarm in the long cruise, and turned back from the Strait of Magellan, we are told that he did so " against the mariners' will." Religious bitterness sharpened the quarrel. Tales of San Juan de Ulloa and of Spanish dungeons were common amongst the men. The Venetian ambassador wrote that the battle would in any case be very bloody ; " for the English never yield, and although they be put to flight and broken, they ever return, athirst for revenge, to renew the attack, so long as they have a breath of life." The impatient urgency with which Drake pleaded that he might again be sent out to strike another blow at the Spaniards on their own coasts, and the anger with which he bore the bonds that held him back, supported by Hawkins, Frobisher, Fenner, and all seamen of experience, were proof enough of their qualities. " If we stand at this point," wrote Hawkins to Walsingham, " in a mammering and at a stay, we consume." The undaunted spirit of Howard, who, though no great seaman, knew how to defer to seamen, was typical of the spirit of all. " The advantage of time and place in all martial actions is half a victory, which being lost is irrecoverable," wrote Drake to the Queen. The other English leaders were all cast in the same mould, and as to the quality of the ships' companies, we have ample testimony in the letters both of Howard and Drake.

Very different was the temper of the Spaniards, though this was unknown except to the seamen who had encountered them. Spanish soldiers were numerous, well-disciplined, and inured to war, and Spanish galleons traversed every sea, and brought to the treasury of Spain the riches of the Indies and Peru. But the ordinary Spaniard disliked the sea, and military success on land had exercised a harmful influence, because, in conjunction with hereditary tendencies, it induced the government to put more trust in soldiers than in the Navy. Captain Fernandez Duro thought that Philip II disliked the sea owing to his suffering from sea-sickness, and that his treatment of seamen and the Navy was influenced thereby. The crews of Spanish ships were made up of many nationalities brought into the fleet, who served often unwillingly, and always without patriotism. English seamen had measured the quality of their opponents. Fenner expressed it very clearly. They had met them irregularly in every sea, and had realised most thoroughly that they had little fighting power. We shall gain nothing by ignoring the fact that the Armada was almost beaten before it sailed, and that all men of judgment knew it. Its inherent weaknesses are revealed in the despatches of the Venetian ambassadors, and the strong qualities of the force opposed to it speak aloud from the pages of our naval history.

It was a misfortune for the Spaniards when the Marquis de Santa Cruz died in February, 1588, but the task of bringing the fleet from Spain through the Channel to the Low Countries, there to embark an army to be landed in England, would have been much beyond his powers. The Duke of Medina Sidonia, who succeeded to the command, accepted it reluctantly, pleading—like Morard de Galles in 1796—his unfitness for the task. He was a small, rather bandy-legged man, who pitifully confessed to the King that he knew nothing of war by sea or land, that he was always sea-sick when he embarked, and that he never failed to catch cold. The gallantry of men like Recalde and Oquendo could not avail to avert a catastrophe, which faulty strategy and the want of sea instinct had made inevitable. As Ubaldini, whom Drake instructed to write an account

of the Armada, says, the whole business had " rested
upon the sagacity and technical grasp of the naval art
possessed by the English officers." *

In the great enterprises of the time there were displayed unity of sentiment and energy of execution
which produced success in the main, but we have to
observe that in the operations subsequent to the defeat
of the Armada, rivalry grew up between commanders
seeking for court favour, and that there was also rivalry
between classes, the soldier being impatient when over-
borne by appeals to seamanship, and the seaman discontented when he thought himself sacrificed to the
soldier.   Philip had learned the lesson, and had regenerated his Navy on the English plan, and we had no
Army to enforce naval successes, nor any means of co-
ordinating the work of naval and military forces. Drake's
successors, Essex, Vere and Mountjoy were all soldiers,
and the expeditions of 1596 and 1597, rich as they were
in lessons regarding the interdependence of naval and
military forces, were embittered and spoiled by the
rivalries and dissensions of commanders.   Conditions
were thus exemplified, which, in the eighteenth century,
led to miscarriage and disaster.† Decadence was foreshadowed, and in the time of James I new antagonisms
were springing into life, which developed apace under
his successor. The low-water mark of English seamanship
was reached.   Never was there a greater contrast than
that between the Navy ably directed, vigorously and
energetically handled, and fighting as a Navy should
fight, under Drake and his comrades, and the Navy
deplorably disorganised, ineptly commanded, internally

* For the war with Spain read Laughton, " Defeat of the Spanish Armada "
(Navy Records Soc.) ; Corbett, " Drake and the Tudor Navy," and " Suc-
cessors of Drake " ; " Naval Tracts of Sir William Monson " (Navy Records
Soc.). The Spanish side is told in Duro, " La Armada Invencible."

† In Lord Wimbledon's expedition against Cadiz, 1625, every flag officer
was a soldier, and there was an instruction that no sea captain should meddle
with the punishment of land soldiers, nor any land commander with that of
seamen. The record was one of divided counsels, vacillation, and inevitable
failure. Of the deplorable conditions that resulted some particulars are given
in a subsequent chapter.

demoralised and mutinous, which failed so lamentably in the time of Charles I, when the ship-money fleet was flouted by Tromp, and the Spanish squadron, which had sought our help, was destroyed under its very nose in the Downs.

The regeneration of the Navy under the Commonwealth, and the excellence of its general administration at the time of the first Dutch War, cannot be described here.* In the three wars with the Dutch we fought in new conditions altogether. Their seafaring was of ancient date, and they were world-explorers like ourselves, but as an organised force their fleet came into existence later than our own. Raleigh could remember the time when they did not " dispute *de Mari Libero*, and acknowledged the English to be *Domini Maris Britannici*." One of Elizabeth's ships, he said, would have " made forty Hollanders strike sail and come to an anchor." But the Dutch were as much seamen as ourselves, and in the East had preceded us in enterprise. They had supplanted the Portuguese, and in 1623 had driven us out from Amboyna to the mainland by a massacre, and thus had led to the foundation of the East India Company. Their merchants existed by their over-sea commerce and carrying trade, while a vast population lived by the herring fisheries, so that it was said Amsterdam was built upon herrings. They had shown their sea supremacy over Spain, and rejected our claim to the *Mare Clausum*. As a world power they could not have done anything else. Their very existence as such depended upon the safety of their commerce at sea.

Nor were the Dutch in any way inferior to us in the qualities of their admirals. Blake had been an Oxford scholar, a merchant, a politician, and a colonel in the Army, and there is no evidence that he ever served at sea before the age of fifty. Tromp was his match at Dungeness in November, 1652, and in the Three Days' Battle in February, 1653. In the Four Days' Battle of

* See Oppenheim, "The Administration of the Royal Navy, 1509–1660."

1666, De Ruyter, Evertszoon, and the younger Tromp inflicted a defeat upon Monk, Rupert, and Ayscue. Nothing was wanting in the valour, sagacity and seamanlike knowledge of the British admirals, as they proved in these and other actions. Nor did De Ruyter's appearance in the Thames, and his destruction of shipping in the Medway in 1667, disgraceful as it was to England, and those who had the care of England's Navy, cast any reflection upon them, proof though it was of the courage, resource and good seamanship of De Ruyter and Van Ghent. At Solebay, May 28th, 1672, De Ruyter once more showed the qualities of a great sea commander, and we failed in our purpose against his bold defensive action. All we could claim was that Spragge, that most energetic of sea officers, had destroyed the enemy's fishing fleet. In the final battle of the Texel, De Ruyter displayed tactical skill which was new in naval warfare, and showed qualities in his defence against a superior enemy that perhaps have never been equalled. By this it must not be understood that the English officers were not able tacticians also, for the Duke of York's Fighting Instructions of 1673, providing for a dividing and containing operation, anticipated in a measure the principle embodied in Nelson's memorandum. But the history of the Dutch wars is proof enough that Blake, Monk, Ayscue, Penn, Myngs, Lawson, Spragge, and the others met in the Dutch admirals skilled fighting seamen not inferior to themselves.

We must, therefore, look elsewhere for the causes of the Dutch decline. Some of them lie outside the sphere of this book. They may be found in the superior strategical situation of this country, the more weatherly character of the ships we were able to build owing to our deeper harbours, and the virtues of a single direction of naval affairs, as compared with the divided system that was imposed by the very nature of the government of the United Netherlands. A still greater factor was the drain upon the Dutch national resources, owing to the necessity of maintaining a land army of nearly

60,000 men, and the opposition of a powerful military party, which found some favour with those great soldiers, the princes of the House of Orange. One Richard Gibson, a seaman who sailed in the *Tiger* with Captain Peacock, has left a narrative of a discourse between an English sea captain and a Dutch skipper—"how the English came to beat the Dutch at Sea"—with reference to the misfortunes of the Dutch in the first war, drawing from De With the outspoken confession that the English were masters of "us and the sea." The Dutch skipper said that the States General, remembering the arbitrary proceedings of William II, Prince of Orange, turned out his friends from the sea and land services, when he was dead, and "put in gentlemen creatures of their own." And the English parliament, by a like jealousy, "put out all the King's captains that were gentlemen, and put in seamen to be captains that were creatures of their own." Thus it happened, said the skipper, that the Dutch went to war with gentlemen-commanders at sea, and the English with seamen-commanders, and so it was that the English beat the Dutch. But, he added, if thereafter the conditions should be reversed, "we should beat you." There was sound sense in these remarks, and many of the reverses we suffered later may be traced to the gentlemen intruded into the fleet and the evil effect of their counsels at Whitehall. Gibson himself in a later discourse deplored the power placed in the hands of gentlemen-commanders in British ships, and, as a tarpaulin seaman, objected to gentlemen-lieutenants being set over the seamen. Further light is thrown upon this matter in a later chapter.

The English sea captains were mostly men of very daring character, and fine types of good seamanhood. Sir William Berkeley, who cut the Dutch line on June 1st, 1666, and was killed in an heroic struggle against great odds, lacked nothing of bravery. Sir John Harman, who was with him, and who was Vice-Admiral of the Red in the battle of the Texel, was a real seaman, as

were Sir Richard Haddock and many more. Gibson
gives instances of the signal gallantry of some English
captains. He speaks of his own captain, James Peacock
of the *Tiger*, who was mortally wounded in the battle
off Scheveningen, 1653, when Admiral of the Red.
Dutch prizes he brought into port by the dozen, and a
stirring account is given of how he had captured a
Portuguese ship, by good seamanship, under the very
guns of the coast, lashing ship to ship, bringing them to
anchor, boarding with the utmost gallantry, and then
by a ruse deceiving the gunners on shore, and so getting
his prize to sea. The *Tiger's* boatswain, afterwards
commander of the *Greyhound*, 18, to avoid being captured,
blew up his ship, and perished with many of his men, and
a hundred Dutchmen who had boarded her. Another
captain of the same mettle was Sir Christopher Myngs,
the same whose death the seamen so deeply mourned,
as Pepys records. When captain of the *Elizabeth*, in
1652, Myngs captured, unassisted, three Dutch men-
of-war, none of them much inferior to his own vessel,
and brought them as prizes into the fleet at Spithead.
Blake received him with a significant censure, which
Gibson records. "You believe you have done a fine
act to take three Dutch ships singly, but what if they
had carried you to Holland? What could you have
then given the State for the loss of their ship? I do
not love a foolhardy captain; therefore hereafter temper
your courage with discretion, and undertake nothing
hazardous if you can avoid it. So you may come to
preferment."

Captain Owen Cox, a fighting sailor, who recaptured
the *Phœnix* which Badiley had lost at Leghorn; Captain
Edward Spragge, afterwards the famous admiral; Captain
Nicholas Heaton, who had risen from being a trumpeter's
mate, and was a tried seaman—these were types of the
captains who were engaged in the Dutch wars, and to
their resolute qualities and good seamanship our successes were mainly due. Allin, Kempthorne, Spragge,
Narborough, and many of their captains gave proof of

the finest seamanship and the hardest fighting qualities in the desperate engagements with the Barbary pirates. Where there was failure, as in the earlier actions of the first Dutch war, it may be attributed in part to the half-hearted behaviour of certain of the captains, some of whom were called upon to account for the " miscarriage." After the battle of Dungeness, November 30th, 1652, Blake complained to the Admiralty Commissioners of a certain " baseness of spirit, not among the merchantmen only, but many of the State's ships." Probably, however, if all the captains had been as headlong as Axon and Batten, who by their over-daring lost their ships to the enemy, more of them would have shared the same fate, and the misconduct does not seem to have been grave, for three of the captains were punished merely by fines. The seamen were mostly of a good class, many of them " with some conscience in what they did," seriously-minded and trustworthy. They had many complaints, chiefly on the ground of want of pay, and many of them preferred the licence of the privateer, and the opportunities for plunder which it presented, to the discipline of the man-of-war.

The Dutch also had brave captains, who were real fighting seamen, like Douwe Aukes, a Frieslander, who commanded the *Struisvogel* in Ayscue's action with De Ruyter in August, 1652. This brave man, who was surrounded by English ships, inflamed the courage of his men, which was flagging, by going to the powder magazine with a linstock in his hand, and calling out at the top of his voice, " Take courage, my children, take courage. I will show you the way, and as we can no longer withstand our enemies, I will free you from imprisonment with the help of the stick in my hand." But there were too many Dutch captains like those reproached by De Ruyter after the same action for having forgotten their duty by reason of cowardice. A mutinous spirit existed in the fleet, and the people in the *Brederode* in the battle of the Kentish Knock, September 16th, 1652, refused to receive De With on board.

Some of the captains acted with what he thought brutality and outrage, by firing at the English over and through other Dutch ships. He implored the captains " with clasped hands " to devote themselves to the service of their country. In Opdam's fleet, in 1665, the spirit of some of the captains was not good, and four who deserted their posts in the line of battle were shot for cowardice, while others less guilty were cashiered. There were occasions also on which the men were mutinous, being demoralised by privateering, and in 1652 a riot took place in which a number of seamen and others were killed. These are facts not to be lost sight of in an inquiry into the personal and moral elements conducing to victory and defeat.*

A study of the Dutch wars leads to certain conclusions. Neither side could claim any final victory. The English had proved on the whole the better fighting men, but not in skill, nor bravery, nor conduct had we any great advantage over our adversaries. On both sides there was misconduct on the part of captains, but the evil was more widespread in the Dutch fleet than in our own, and to strained relations between admirals and captains and the cowardice or defection of the latter, many of the misfortunes of the Dutch were due. The furious controversy between Appleton and Badiley arising out of the episode at Leghorn, and the riotous conduct of Badiley's crew, show that all was not well in our own Navy in the first Dutch war.† In the second war the enemy appeared in the Thames, not through any fault of the seamen, but the Navy Office was greatly dismayed. The third Dutch war ended in deserved failure, though the seamen were sound, and we had many tarpaulin captains of the best stamp. Wherever there was success,

* For the Dutch wars, Colliber's "Columna Rostrata" is an arid narrative. For the period consult Pepys, "Diary"; Selden, "Mare Clausum"; Granville Penn, "Life of Penn"; Gardiner, "First Dutch War"; Hollond, "Discourses of the Navy"; Tanner, "Catalogue of the Pepysian Manuscripts" (the last three issued by the Navy Records Soc.).
† Appleton, "A Remonstrance of the Fight in Leghorn Road"; Badiley, "Reply to Certain Declarations, &c." (Radstock Coll., R.U.S.I.).

it may be traced to sound naval direction from the shore, to capable leading afloat, and to the loyalty and skill of captains, and the prowess and daring of the crews. The ultimate decline of the naval power of the Netherlands was due to many causes, and chiefest among them to the exhausting nature of the demand for land defence, and the steady growth of our own naval influence and commerce in every part of the world. In the quality of their navies there was little to choose between the English and Dutch. Sir Cloudesley Shovell, writing half a century later, said : " Experience has taught me that where men are equally inured and disciplined in war, 'tis, without a miracle, number that gives the victory. . . . To fight, beat, and chase an enemy, I have sometimes seen, but have rarely seen at sea any victory worth boasting where the strength has been nearly equal." And Jervis expressed the same opinion writing of Keppel's action with D'Orvilliers, 1778.*

The French had been our allies in the last Dutch war, but it was the firm belief of the Navy from Rupert downward that they had not supported us, if they had not betrayed us. Their failure may be attributed with greater probability to the internal condition of the French fleet, and the dissensions that divided it. Its history had not been unlike that of our own fleet. Beginning with a coast defence organisation, and developing with the help of mercenaries, many of them Genoese, with galleys in the Mediterranean, commanded by aristocratic officers and manned by the *chiourme*, consisting of freemen adventurers—the *bonnes-voglies*— and slaves, captives, and criminals released from gaol, it had been reorganised by Richelieu, who had laid the foundation of the system that Colbert developed. The story is told of Mazarin that when he lay on his deathbed, he told the young king that he owed everything to his Majesty, but that he had in some sort repaid

* Shovell, to the Earl of Nottingham, July 18th, 1702. Brenton, "Life of the Earl of St. Vincent," ii. 80.

the debt by giving him Colbert. The work of that great minister is not to be recorded here, but not even Colbert, within the ten years which had elapsed since he had assumed office, could give the fleet officers trained for ocean and Channel service, and instinct with the long deposit of experience and the sea tradition. The Navy was an aristocratic profession directed by courtiers and soldiers. D'Estrées, who was in command of the French fleet allied with us in 1673, was a soldier by training and experience, a man of presumption and excessive pride, and many of his captains were of the same class. Some good captains there were, like Tourville, afterwards the famous admiral, and Forant and Gabaret, most of them adherents of Duquesne; but Duquesne, upon the report of D'Estrées, with whom he had had an embittered quarrel, was disgraced, and his successor, De Martel, was sent to the Bastille. So deficient was the French fleet of sea experience, that it was necessary in 1672 to impress officers out of the merchant navy.

But the institutions of Colbert were yielding fruit, and Tourville's fleet which met Torrington at Beachy Head in the much-disputed action, was better officered and manned than any fleet the French had sent to sea before. Tourville was a great seaman, a man with a stout heart, and an honest man, and there were others like him. The English fleet had been almost destroyed by fraud and incapacity under the rule of Buckingham and Northumberland, but had been partly regenerated by James II. Russell was Tourville's inferior, eager fighter as he was. His "Fighting Instructions," which hold a remarkable place in tactical history, were in all probability the work of Torrington. Pontchartrain, the most incompetent of all French Ministers of Marine, the feeble successor of Colbert and Seignelay, who had indeed deliberately proposed to Louis to destroy the fleet, had done immense evil to the French Navy. He had a strong prejudice against Tourville, whom he forced to sea a month before the intended concentration of force could

take place, which was the real cause of the great disaster suffered by the French off Cape Barfleur. Tourville was a brave man, and his fleet fought well, but
we won because, as good seamen, we could endure, and
when the wind went round our numerical superiority
triumphed over the incapacity of Russell. Fortunately,
the captain and master of the fleet, David Mitchell and
John Benbow, were both men who had followed the sea
from boyhood to middle age, and were well acquainted
with the tides and half-tides round Cape Barfleur and
Cape de la Hague. As to the destruction of the French
ships in the battle of La Hogue, which did more than
anything else to break the spirit of the French Navy, it
was determined by Marshal de Bellefonds, the soldier
superior of Tourville. The views of experienced seamen
were flouted, the minister heeded the counsel of landsmen, and the disaster was organised on shore.

It was otherwise with the British naval forces. Ably
directed, they were for the first time made an effective
instrument of power in the Mediterranean. A winter
squadron was kept in the Straits in 1694–5, the fleet
being ready at Cadiz. Russell did not like the winter
work, which was new to him, but he, and afterwards
Rooke, and the captains, astonished the French by the
admirable seamanship they displayed. War was formally
declared against France and Spain in May, 1702, and
Marlborough, who ruled the strategy of the campaign,
desired to strike at Spanish maritime power at its heart
at Cadiz, to hold the Straits and the Western Mediterranean, and afterwards to proceed against Toulon.
Rooke was ill and unwilling, and the expedition to Cadiz
was a fiasco. The old evil of quarrel and jealousy
between the services and between commanders was the
root and origin of the failure. It was not incapacity,
naval or military. " We are here," wrote Colonel
Stanhope, " not only divided sea against land, but land
against land, and sea against sea. Now if it be true
that a house divided cannot stand, I am afraid that it is
still more true that an army and fleet each divided

c

against itself, and each against the other, can make no conquests." From this cause, and this alone, the attack upon Cadiz was ignominiously abandoned. Rooke had not behaved well, and it was not he, but that brave man Hopsonn, and the bolder spirits in the fleet who retrieved our fame by attacking Châteaurenault, in a wild season and on a wild coast, in the sheltered harbour of Vigo, in October, 1702. By prompt enterprise and daring in breaking the boom and attacking in circumstances which would have daunted all but the stoutest hearts, they gained one of the most complete victories recorded in our naval annals. The same spirit was displayed at Malaga, two years later. Without going into the question of the tactics employed, we recognise the success to have been due to the brave hearts, stubborn fighting and good gunnery of the Englishmen, which excited the admiration of their Dutch colleagues. The downright spirit was in them, and on the way to Gibraltar, every captain was prepared to fight his way through, and if that was impossible, there were some at least who agreed to burn their ships rather than surrender. The heart was taken out of the French. As seamen we were uncontested superiors, and Minorca fell into our hands through the vigorous action of Leake. "The English have taught us," wrote Marshal Tessé to Pontchartrain, "that the sea can be kept in all weathers, for they promenade it like the swans in your river at Chantilly." The qualities of our seamen had made us, for the first time, a great Mediterranean power.*

* Corbett, "England in the Mediterranean, 1603–1713"; Chevalier, "Hist. de la Marine Française, jusqu'au traité de paix de 1763"; Browning, "Journal of Sir George Rooke" (Navy Records Soc.).

THE DEATH OF LORD ROBERT MANNERS,
Poland,—Hamilton,
The Captain mortally wounded on board the "Resolution,"
April 12, 1782.

THE CAPTURE OF JUDGE JEFFREYS,
Grichton,—Male,
The Judge seized in the disguise of a sailor at Wapping,
December 12, 1688.

The failure of Mathews in 1744 may be ascribed to various causes. He was a good officer and no coward, but a disciplinarian and a slave to forms, somewhat eccentric, and described as " Il Furibondo " in Horace Mann's correspondence with Walpole. His greater defect was that his age was sixty-seven, and that he had not been at sea between 1724 and 1742. Lestock was more prone to enforce his own orders than to obey the orders of others. He also was of senior years, possibly older than Mathews. He had expected to be appointed to the command in the Mediterranean, and when Mathews came out he did not disguise his resentment. Charnock says he was unconciliatory in bearing, austere in command, and restless as a subordinate, with fewer friends than most men, and with a manner that did not enable him to recruit their depleting numbers. Campbell says of him that he apparently wanted both honour and honesty, and that he was " an artful, vindictive disciplinarian." Beatson asserts that the two officers " bore each other a most rancorous hatred." Thus want of co-operation, due to hostility of feeling, led to the failure. The Sailing Instructions gave sanction to Lestock's aloofness during the night preceding the action, and the Fighting Instructions enabled him to make no effort to support his admiral. He stuck to the dead letter of the rule. The signal for the line of battle was flying when the signal to engage was made, and he could not obey the latter without disobeying the former.

Lestock's captains, chafe as they might and did, had no choice but to obey his orders, and the inaction of his division weakened the nerve of Captain Burrish of the *Dorsetshire*, who was with Mathews in the centre, and his inaction not improbably influenced the captains astern of him. Fortunately for the credit of the Navy there were brave men commanding some of the ships. Captain James Cornwall of the *Marlborough* bore down to assist the flagship *Namur* in engaging the *Real Felipe* and *Hercules*, and fighting most manfully he was killed with 42 of his men, while 120 were wounded. Many of the captains with Mathews fought well, and Cornwall's conduct was glorious. There were brave captains in the van, also, with Rear-Admiral Rowley, and amongst them Edward Hawke in the *Berwick*, afterwards the famous admiral. Lestock, having obeyed the letter of the Instructions, was absolved, but Burrish and three other captains were punished. Mathews had blundered, but if he had been supported by such loyalty and courage as Cornwall and Hawke displayed, the result would have been different. Campbell declares his belief that Lestock ought to have been shot. " The misfortune originated in a continued misunderstanding between Mathews and Lestock, the latter of whom sacrificed his own reputation in the hope of ruining the former." * Yet there was no lack of capacity or courage in the Navy at large in the war of the Austrian Succession. Captains like Philip Saumarez and Charles Saunders, who accompanied Anson with his brilliant band in the circumnavigation of the globe, were types, and Anson's victory over La Jonquière (May 3rd, 1747), and that of Hawke over L'Etenduère (Oct. 14th, 1747) were examples of the effect of sound dispositions and fighting skill.

Captain Mahan has pointed out, as significant, that the men at the head of the Navy at the time of Mathews's failure had no record of fitness, or else had become superannuated, so that reputation came to be associated with age.† Hawke in 1747, at the age of forty-two, when he was two years older than Nelson at the Nile, was thought young to be entrusted with a squadron of a dozen ships of the line. There were symptoms of perplexity and perversion of standards, which often work disastrously when war succeeds to a prolonged period of inert peace. Byng was a younger man, his age being fifty-two in the fight off Minorca in 1756, when he met that brave and skilful officer, the Marquis de la Galissonière. But he was one of those

* The proceedings of the courts martial that followed the action are very voluminous, as is the pamphlet literature that ensued.
† "Types of Naval Officers."

men who anticipate difficulties, and he went far on the way to meet them, being more than half defeated before he began. Byng, it is true, had to deal with a situation which his government had not foreseen. It cannot be said of him that he failed in courage, nor that he was a man without tactical insight. He endeavoured to observe while modifying the old Instructions, in order to engage his enemy with advantage, but his captains, 'less alert, mistook his meaning. His force was not adequate to enable him to make a general chase, and the action was inconclusive. Byng was really punished for what followed, involving the loss of Minorca. Gibraltar was the lodestone, Blakeney and his forces at Mahon were abandoned, and a council of war reached the conclusion that Byng himself had desired. We have to notice also the estrangement, or even hostility, between the naval and military services, which may have induced, though it did not dictate, the action that Byng adopted. There was no spirit of co-operation nor any large conception of the interdependence of sea and land forces in operations such as those in which Byng was engaged.* Another matter which deserves attention is that success or failure depended upon the officers, and not upon the men. As will be seen in a succeeding chapter, there were gross abuses affecting the physique and fitness of the men, in bad and scanty food, cold and hardship, but when the battle was engaged it was not the men of the lower deck, but the tone and quality of the officers that decided the course of the action. Not in any record of fighting in this period do we find any failure in the seamen.

Byng's withdrawal to Gibraltar after the engagement with La Galissonière was decided upon the deliberation

---

* In relation to this matter, reference may be made to what has been said above concerning the Cadiz expedition of 1702. In 1706 there was bitter jealousy during Peterborough's operations in Catalonia. The relations between Vernon and Wentworth in 1741 are an illustration of the same state of feeling. A mark of a great change may be seen in Boscawen's relations with Amherst and Wolfe, and St. Vincent's with Monckton and Grey.

of a council of war, which, by leading questions, reached the conclusion to which Byng's own fears had prompted him. The cumulative effect of the answers was that Minorca must be abandoned because the fleet could not save it, while the fleet was required at Gibraltar, because it alone could save that endangered possession. Faulty views of strategy dictated this melancholy conclusion The evil influence of a council of war in the hands of a weak man was thus exemplified, and there was always the danger that such councils, by giving opportunity for the expression of antagonistic views, might impair the judgment of a chief. But the council of war was an ancient institution in the Navy, often employed, and the " flag of council " is one of the earliest signals known.* Where men realised their object with clear discernment and resolute purpose to attain it, knowing their own minds, as in 1588, such councils strengthened their confidence and shaped their endeavours. Byng's council of war in 1756 cast discredit upon the institution, and in the very next year, when Captain Arthur Forrest in the *Augusta*, with the *Dreadnought*, Captain Maurice Suckling, and the *Edinburgh*, Captain William Langdon, in company, defeated seven French ships of war off Cape François, there took place what came to be known as the " half-minute council of war," doubtless because of the contrast it presented to Byng's council. When the French came in sight, Forrest, as senior officer, made the usual signal for the other captains to come on board for a council of war. " Being all met on the quarter-deck, Captain Forrest said, ' Well, gentlemen, you see they are come out, to engage us.' Upon which Captain Suckling answered, ' I think it would be a pity to disappoint them.' Captain Langdon was of the same opinion. ' Very well,' replied Captain Forrest ; ' go on board of your ships again,' when he immediately made the signal to bear down and engage the enemy." † Within

* Perrin, "Nelson's Signals ; the Evolution of the Signal Flags" (Naval Intelligence Department, Historical, No. 1), 1908.

† Beatson, " Naval and Military Memoirs," ii. 43. For Hawke's view of Councils of War see his letter to the Admiralty, May 10th, 1758.

little more than half an hour the battle had begun. The day was always celebrated by Nelson, and a picture of the battle was painted by Swaine, and engraved.

The council of war, if the term may properly be applied to their deliberations, was seen at its best in Nelson's discussions with his "band of brothers." Here the admiral knew his own mind, and his officers entered heartily into his plans. Therefore councils of war, though there have been occasions on which they have wrought immense evil, have their value when they are composed of good and resolute sea officers.

It is now timely to say something of Anson and Hawke, and the regeneration of the Navy in their hands. It was Hawke's good fortune to wield a weapon which Anson had fashioned. An able officer of energy and indomitable resolution, Anson was also a fine disciplinarian, and his great voyage round the world had given him a profound knowledge of men and of the necessities of the naval career. His squadron had been a school of sea experience and training, and not a few of his comrades in that heroic circumnavigation afterwards added lustre to our naval annals, and foreshadowed the band of brothers of Nelson. It was a title to no small distinction for Anson that he appointed to high command such men as Hawke, Boscawen, Saunders, Rodney, Howe and Keppel. Hawke's reputation had been determined by the energetic and seamanlike course he had taken in Mathews's action. In his singleness of purpose he was like Nelson. But he had nothing of Nelson's mercurial temperament, and his captains were bound to him by his personal energy, direct force, impartiality and justice. With a sickly ship, and little time to train gunners in his miserable crew, he had captured the only ship taken in Mathews's action. In the engagement with L'Etenduère he had been thoroughly supported by his captains, with the exception of Fox of the *Kent*, who was deprived of his command, and the names of Robert Harland, of Charles Watson, who afterwards covered himself with glory in the East Indies, of Saunders,

who made the *Neptune* strike after a close action of
two hours, of Philip Saumarez, who was killed in the
attack on the *Tonnant*, and of Rodney, who bore an
honourable part, are an abiding proof of the new life
and new spirit in the service at the time. This was,
indeed, sufficiently shown by the refusal of eight
captains summoned to the council of war after the
engagement, to " rank with Captain Fox until his character should be cleared up with regard to the aspersions
cast upon it for his behaviour in the action." Beatson
recounts repeated acts of bravery of captains of the
period.

Brilliant, however, as was the work that had been
achieved, there was still more to be done. Anson was
not satisfied. When he went afloat in the grand fleet
off Brest in the summer of 1757 he wrote to the Lord
Chancellor Hardwicke, his father-in-law, " I do assure
your Lordship when I began to exercise my fleet I never
saw such awkwardness in going through the common
manœuvres necessary to make an attack upon an enemy's
fleet. What we now do in an hour, in the beginning
took eight. . . . Most of the captains declared they had
never seen a line of battle at all, and none of them more
than once." We cannot question the opinion of Anson
upon such a matter. Skill as well as bravery was required. The quality, however, was there, and perhaps
Anson, excellent judge as he was, had misjudged the
training power of Hawke, and with him, of Boscawen.

The brilliant action of Quiberon Bay was proof enough
of the new spirit, and in that signal triumph Hawke
and his officers gave proof of unsurpassed seamanship
in a most strenuous and admirable exhibition of professional skill. Administration, strategy, tactics, courage,
enterprise, and co-operation were all exemplified in
the qualities of the leader, and were matched in those
of his followers. Bompart's seasoned crews had been
turned over to the fleet of Conflans at Brest, and the
latter put to sea for his defensive position at Quiberon
Bay, believing that Hawke would not dare to follow

him, amid the formidable rocks and shallows of the
Cardinals. The French fleet was ill-fitted for the contest,
and its admiral could not measure the intrepidity and
seamanhood of the men he was to meet. There were
few pilots in the fleet, and the sailing master gave warning of the perils, but there was no hesitation in Hawke,
nor in Howe, nor in any of the captains. It was a lee
shore, fringed with little-known reefs, and a rising
winter wind and tide drove them on, with sails reefed,
in a wild career, where only good seamanship could have
saved and only unconquerable resolution could have
triumphed. But the story of that most dramatic fight
is not to be told here. All we will observe is the supreme
quality of the admiral, the skill, training and capacity of
his officers, and the endurance and hard fighting virtues
of the men. One of the grandest episodes in British
naval history, the action of Quiberon Bay was a super-
lative example of the supremacy of men over material
means and obstacles, measuring risks and daring all.
Conflans, and his officers, good as they were, were out-
matched. Crews, ships and stores, all were defective,
and most of all he had clamoured for seasoned men.

Boscawen's part in defeating the French plan of
invasion was scarcely less notable than Hawke's. The
boldness with which he allowed De la Clue to leave
Toulon, the splendid efficiency with which his own fleet
was got to sea—an example of skill not often surpassed
in naval annals—the fine decision with which he attacked,
and the determination he displayed in signalling to his
ships to make more sail in order to reach the enemy's
van—signals not well understood by his captains—are
all illustrative of the new quality in the fleet and the
results that were attained. A survey of the naval
events that led to the taking of Louisburg, Quebec and
Montreal, and brought about the fall of French power
in India, would reveal the same influences at work.*

* Corbett, "England in the Seven Years' War"; Waddington, "La
Guerre de Sept Ans"; Lacour-Gayet, "Marine Militaire sous Louis XV."
Beatson's "Naval and Military Memoirs" is excellent for all this period
(1727–83).

Nevertheless, like the tide that flows and ebbs, so has the Navy risen and fallen in its ideals, and consequently in the state in which it has been maintained. The period which elapsed between the Peace of Paris in 1763 and the outbreak of the war of American Independence worked little good for the Navy. The corruption of the House of Commons, the hatred which it aroused, the virulent bitterness of men like Wilkes, the resignation of Pitt, the weakness of the ministry of Rockingham, the cabinet torn with dissensions, the bitter factions in the country, and the spirit that led up to the outbreak of the war with the American colonists, were the things underlying the naval decline to which they led. Political strife, the buying of offices in the State, the giving of appointments as rewards for political service, wrought a great evil, and the Navy was rent by violent internal strife, so that it was said that " if a naval officer were to be roasted, another officer could always be found to turn the spit." Sandwich's corrupt administration profoundly affected the spirit of discipline in the Service. Howe came home from America weary, deceived and disappointed. That distinguished officer Barrington refused to accept a command, though he was willing to serve as second even under a junior. " Who would trust himself in chief command," he wrote, " with such a set of scoundrels as are now in office ? "

Keppel's failure in the action with D'Orvilliers (July, 1778) was partly the fruit of an evil tradition which condemned actions to be indecisive—the very opposite of the resolute conception of duty which inspired Nelson's whole life that nothing was done while anything remained undone—and partly it was the outcome of political broil. It led, as all the world knows, to courts martial, and to a pamphlet literature in which the last thing considered was the good of the State. The partisans of Keppel and Palliser knew little of moderation, and factious defection was at work in many departments of the fleet. " Sea officers in general," wrote Rodney, " are too apt to be censorious. It is their misfortune to know little of the

world and to be bred in seaport towns, where they keep
company with few but themselves. This makes them
so violent in party, so partial to those who have sailed
with them, and so grossly unjust to others."

But Rodney himself, great seaman and tactician
that he was, was no universal favourite. His unsparing
severity, his haughty censures, his scarcely disguised
contempt for many of his officers, deprived him of their
sympathy and made it difficult for some of them to
respond to his inspiration or to understand his ideas.
We now know how splendid those ideas were, because
Rodney was really the first of sea officers to grasp
thoroughly and apply efficiently the principle of concentration in attack, directing the onslaught of the whole
fleet upon the centre, van, or rear of the enemy. But
Rodney was not understood. Either he was ahead of
his time, or he had failed to school his officers in the
system he intended to pursue. It was Captain Robert
Carkett, stout, bull-dog seaman though he was, whose
stupidity had not been moved by the genius of his chief,
that frustrated Rodney's finest tactical inspiration in
the action with De Guichen off Martinique on April 17th,
1780. Rodney bitterly accused his subordinates of
deliberately wrecking the battle. Sir Hyde Parker,
commonly called " Vinegar Parker," came home in high
dudgeon, but if faction and arrogance had not divided
the fleet, there would have been no such consequences
as Rodney had to deplore.

Sandwich had to confess that it was no easy thing
to find a successor to Parker as second in command.
Some, he said, were unfit from their factious connec-
tions, others from inferiority or insufficiency, and it was
necessary to make a promotion in order to find the right
man. Samuel Hood, one of our ablest sea officers, was
selected, but he also was a caustic critic with a dislike
of Rodney which amounted almost to hatred.* He
passed many harsh judgments upon his fellow-officers.
Graves he thought cunning and incompetent, Rowley,

* Hannay, "Letters of Sir Samuel Hood" (Navy Records Soc.).

silly, Pigot, a nonentity, and Douglas, feeble to im-
becility. But his contempt was most bitter for his own
chief, who, in truth, seemed to be more solicitous about
the booty at Saint Eustatius than about the vastly
more important business of intercepting De Grasse
before he could get to Fort Royal, which he did in
April, 1781. Vacillation followed, and Graves failed
miserably at the Chesapeake, arousing afterwards the
contempt of Rodney for the half-begotten battle, in
which the principle of concentration had had no proper
part. Possibly judgments upon this matter may have
to be revised, and a higher place to be given to Graves in
the development of tactics than has hitherto been assigned
to him. Kempenfelt also, who is known to most readers
because of his tragic end in the *Royal George*, 1782, had
a noteworthy place in the development of naval signals
and tactics.

The great battle of April 12th, 1782, was the crowning
act of Rodney's career. It was incomplete, and its
incompleteness aroused the bitter scorn and resentment
of Hood and of some of the captains. " Come, we have
done very handsomely as it is," said Rodney, in a mood
strangely contrasting with Nelson's changeless resolve
to annihilate the enemy wherever they were found.
The fine officer who had given the new meaning to
tactics, had failed in the final extremity. A certain
irresolution, a want of will to carry the business through
in face of all risks, such as Hawke, Howe and Nelson
were willing to run, weakened his arm, and deprived
him of part of the fruit of victory. Rodney was in poor
health, and his age was sixty-three, which may account
for something, but not for all, and Cornwallis and many
of the captains shared the contemptuous regret felt
by Hood for the deplorable failure to follow up the victory.
Nelson afterwards expressed the same view of the action
to Cornwallis, though recognising the great obligation of
the country to Rodney.* We cannot, however, resist
the conclusion that if there had been harmony, and a

* "Blockade of Brest," Introduction (Navy Records Soc.).

right understanding in the fleet, there would have been
no failure to record.

It is necessary to remember that Rodney, Hughes
and others commanding the fleets at that time had
foemen worthy of themselves. The French Navy had
been reconstituted, strengthened and reorganised under
Louis XVI. Its officers were mostly drawn from the
petite noblesse of the provinces, and particularly of the
maritime provinces, who furnished an hereditary body
of solid, devoted officers, little dowered with wealth,
but having the instincts of seamen, and doing no discredit to themselves. The names of La Clocheterie,
Lamotte-Piquet, and Grimoard, to mention no others,
deserve to be remembered among officers of lesser note
than De Guichen and De Grasse, and Captain Chevalier
has vindicated the French officers of that period from
the charge of indiscipline often made against them.*
As to the men, they also were of good quality, and though
serving under a hard code they rarely failed in endurance
or skill. These are facts not to be overlooked when we
consider the outcome of the war of American Independence.

In the years that followed the conclusion of peace
in 1783, both the British and French navies were to
pass through terrible ordeals, the character and consequences of which are of vital interest to this inquiry.
The cumulative effect of immense wrongs and untold
hardships in both services, the inherited tradition of
suffering, and with it the simplicity of the seamen which
made them the tools of the unscrupulous, opened the
floodgates of a torrent of violence which swept with
mutiny, massacre and crime through the services of
the two countries. But here we are to observe a profound distinction between the effects and consequences
of mutiny and revolution in England and France. The
results for the French Navy were terrible and far-reaching,
shattering the whole organisation from base to summit,
and laying the foundation of the crowning disaster of

* "Hist. de la Marine Française."

1805. In the British Navy, the discontent was neither deep nor, except in such cases as that of the massacre of Pigot and the officers of the *Hermione*, violent. How little it really affected the Navy, and how temporary was the effect of the Mutiny, may be estimated by the fact that the year of the outburst at Spithead and the Nore, 1797, was the year also of Jervis's victory at St. Vincent, and Duncan's at Camperdown. Perhaps it was not without significance that the spirit of mutiny arose in a ship which, by taking the ground after leaving Lisbon, had no share in the February battle. How Jervis dealt with the mutineers of the *Marlborough*, and with the rather weak captain of that ship, is well known. The seamen of the fleet had tangible grievances, which were stated and remedied, the men at Spithead returning to their allegiance. The outbreak at the Nore was more serious and disquieting, and was characterised by greater political sedition, influenced by the French Revolution and the agents of Irish discontent, but it was quelled, and the mutinous spirit died down.

The fundamental difference between the mutiny and revolution which affected the navies of England and France was that in the British Navy the officers were unaffected, while in the French service they were swept away, and out of an incoherent and disorganised force a new race of officers had to be created. That feature which we have already noted is thus again brought to prominence. The seaman is of immense importance in the organisation, but it is the influence of the officer that matters most of all. The decay of the French Navy had its seat and origin in the failure of the directing power in the arsenals on shore and in the ships afloat. The naval establishments anticipated the Revolution. The profound misery of the men caused them to welcome the anarchical theories of the emissaries of sedition, and to band themselves together in clubs, with the result that conditions were set up in which a spark alone was sufficient to provoke the conflagration. Massacres at Toulon, pillage at Rochefort, and the worst excesses at

Brest indicated too clearly the gravity of the malady.
The fleet seethed with the fury of the Revolution, and
its material and moral situation became deplorable.
Far more grievous than the state of the ships' companies
was the fate of the officers, many of whom were hurried
to the scaffold, and executed with every circumstance
of barbarity, while hundreds of them were driven into
exile. Out of the incoherent disarray came men whose
civisme might be irreproachable, but whose qualities as
officers were in the lowest state of inferiority. Discipline
was overwhelmed, ignorance ruled supreme, and neglect
was evident in every department of the administration.

The glowing history of the war with the French Revolution and Empire cannot be told in this place. Howe's
famous victory, the Glorious First of June, 1794, was
one of our greatest triumphs, lustrous with many a
tale of gallantry. It was fought on Howe's principle
of concentrated attack in the old sledge-hammer
fashion, the battle raging furiously all along the line
in a great series of duels, and the French were beaten
by the sheer weight of English fighting power, while the
old Admiral—for he was old at sixty-eight—directed
the action, sometimes seated in an arm-chair. The
great struggle between the *Brunswick* and *Vengeur*
will ever live in our naval annals, and so with many
another fight in that battle. Perhaps if Howe had
been a younger man, the five ships which escaped might
have been captured, but the Admiral was worn out by
his exertions. He was a man of long-tried capacity,
cool, cautious, and imperturbable. Horace Walpole
said of him that he was " undaunted as a rock and as
silent." When he came home from North America in
1778, he had been spoken of as " the first sea officer of
the world." His squadrons were the school of tactics,
and the nursery of good officers and seamen. Not all
of them were as resolute as Captain John Harvey of the
Brunswick, but there were few of them who did not do
honour to the service to which they belonged. Some
of them were dissatisfied with the incompleteness of the

D

success, and we know that there were officers imbued
with the spirit of Nelson who spoke rather slightingly of
a " Lord Howe's victory."

Irresolution still clung to some of the admirals. There
was the inconclusive fighting of Hotham in the Mediterranean, arousing the profound discontent of Nelson in
the *Agamemnon*, whose soul abhorred anything less than
final completeness, and who had nothing but contempt
for timidity. The opportunity came again, but still
Hotham did not pursue his advantage, though Nelson
thought the French might have been destroyed on the
system which he afterwards employed at the Nile.
Bridport's action of June 23rd, 1795, had also been inconclusive, and when the abandonment of the Mediterranean was necessary in December, 1796, the depression
was felt both in the Navy and the country, deepened by
the spirit of mutiny which was then becoming rife.

But, in the action off Cape St. Vincent, the great opportunity came. A victory, as Jervis said, was very essential
at that time, and Nelson, by his independent action,
showed the qualities which were soon to dominate in
greater engagements. He wore out of the line, and took
the *Captain* straight down to attack the Spanish flagship,
supported by brave Troubridge in the *Culloden*, and how
he boarded the *San Nicolas* and *San Josef* is in all our
histories. It was an illustration of the high courage,
the gallantry and the spirit of the officers of the time,
and Jervis, like the great seaman he was, applauded
the " disobedience " which was the mark of the original
genius of Nelson.* Tucker, in his " Life of St. Vincent,"

* With regard to Nelson's "disobedience," it must be observed that some
difference of opinion exists. According to the log of the *Victory*, Jervis
made a general signal at 12.51 p.m. to "take suitable stations and engage as
arrive up in succession." The log of the *Excellent* says the signal was made
at 1.5 p.m., and that of the *Egmont* at 1.20 p.m. The log of the *Victory*
places the incident of Nelson's bearing down upon the Spanish line between
12.30 and 12.45 p.m. The log of the *Captain* places it at 12.50, or a little
later. That of the *Prince George* is confusing, mentions the wrong signal,
and implies that Nelson wore out of the line in execution of it. But if that
were so, Nelson gave a very liberal interpretation to the signal, and one that
was not expected ; and Collingwood wrote to Nelson on the next day : "You
formed the plan of attack ; we were only accessories to the Dons' ruin."

says of the fleet in the Mediterranean that its captains
were heroes of a hundred fights. " All this is proudly
true ; great captains they assuredly were ; bright they
have made our annals ; each ship was a perfect school."

It is not necessary here to say anything of the courage,
the tenacity, the high sense of duty, the professional
skill, or the fearlessness of responsibility which existed
in Nelson. It is more to the purpose to point out the
assiduous manner in which he applied himself to the
maintenance of the health and efficiency of his fleet.
Still more important is it to observe the keenness of his
sympathy, and the enthusiasm of his personality,
which inspired his officers. In these men the highest
elements of naval efficiency were found. They were the
flower and fruit of a great school of teaching, and the
strong qualities of Jervis, the high distinction of Hood,
and the lofty inspiration of Nelson were the force which
evoked all that was best in the officers of that splendid
time. No captain ever failed to support Nelson in
anything he undertook. The magnificent triumph of
the Nile was an example of his splendid thoroughness,
and of the skill and fearlessness of his officers. It was
the same at Copenhagen, where Nelson's independence
of character was again displayed. Not only the captains,
but officers of every rank were filled with the spirit
which glowed in the bosom of Nelson, and the men
were as hardy and good as officers could ever desire to
command.

The final triumph of Trafalgar was the crowning
episode of the great naval campaign. The Peace of
Amiens had been a truce only, and when war broke
out afresh the British Navy was prepared. Never
was there a more enduring and courageous officer than
Cornwallis, who held his grip upon the forces at Brest.
Rarely has there been a finer diplomatic seaman
than Pellew, and few more sterling characters have
there been than Collingwood. The spirit in which
Calder's inconclusive action was regarded was itself
proof of the high standard that was maintained. The

captains were, with few exceptions, men of equal character and resolution, though there were weaknesses in their theoretical training. Those who have read the histories of the blockades know the fearless bravery, the contempt of danger, and the will to conquer which were found in the younger officers, who executed a hundred intrepid enterprises against the French forces on the coast and in the ports. These men were prepared to run the peril of their lives in exploits of peculiar danger that they might serve their country well.

Thus it was that when the fleets met in October, 1805, all the elements of victory were on our side—well-found ships, highly trained officers, and trusty hard-fighting men. It was not so with the French fleet, which was demoralised from the beginning, and more than half beaten before the battle began. The reasons for that condition have been suggested. They cannot be further explained. Let it be noted that in unwise strategical dispositions, in administrative mismanagement, in the setting of impossible tasks, in the inevitable weakness of the admiral in command the seeds of disaster were sown.

But sustained victory in a long war brings revenges of its own. Followed by a long peace, if vigilance be relaxed, it may react in a paralysis of endeavour. In exaltation of spirit is begotten an easy confidence, which too often causes the sources of victory to be forgotten. Nelson and his officers were men of transcendent qualities, but their influence, though great, was not lasting, and there were men like Keith who regarded the originality of the great seaman as an evil and as inadmissible in other men. The immense weight of tradition partially regained its sway, and at the time there was little of higher training for officers, so that some of those who fought with Nelson never seemed to penetrate the greatness of his conceptions. Even Collingwood sought to distinguish the merits of Trafalgar by saying of it that there was " no dodging, no manœuvring." Few seamen of that time had Nelson's patient power of study and influence in training, which enabled him to handle his fleets with such daring and certainty of success. They perceived in his actions chiefly the principle of the headlong attack. Of courage and resolution there was no lack, but even so brilliant an officer as Lord Dundonald could say, " Never mind manœuvres ; always go at them."

After Trafalgar, the Navy stood at the height of its splendour, and its officers felt the fullest confidence in their prowess. They had despised their foes, and when they encountered the young American Navy they despised their new foes also. They had begun to pay less attention to gunnery, and the failure in this matter, resting partly upon too much pride and self-confidence, prepared the way for many discomfitures. When the war broke out with the United States in 1812 the old advantage was lost, and the qualities of a new adversary began to appear. The Americans were mostly dwellers on the sea coast, and their seamen were men of practical experience, who built the swift schooners of which so much has been written in maritime history. Along the coast from Maine to Maryland there was a hardy population of seafaring men, who had gained experience in the fishing fleet, and in the whalers of the North Atlantic and the South Seas. In the war of American Independence the officers and crews had been without the training of a regular service, but a war navy was established and brought to efficiency by many years of sea service. American officers were real sailormen, and Captain John Rodgers, Captain Stephen Decatur, Captain Isaac Hull and Captain William Bainbridge were the equals of Captain Philip Broke of the *Shannon* and his compeers. The Americans, moreover, had an advantage in the number of trained seamen on board their ships who had served in the British Navy, probably in some ships to the number of ten or fifteen per cent. of the total complement of the ships. But American seamen were also of prime quality. When the *Guerrière* was captured, the *Constitution* was handled by Hull with consummate

ability and seamanship, and his men gave proof of hardihood, discipline, readiness, and skill at the guns. We
had often captured vessels in which the difference in
force was far heavier against us than in this instance, but
now we were matched with officers and men of another
stamp. There was desperate fighting in several of the
single-ship actions, and generally something like equality
of character. When the *Java* was captured by the *Constitution* in 1813, the result was attributed to the more
careful training and efficient condition of the crew of the
American. But that the fighting power and character
of British seamen and the ability of British officers were
not diminished was shown in the brilliant victory of
the *Shannon* in the famous fight with the *Chesapeake*.
This was a new proof of the enormous value of good
organisation and training, shaped in the discipline of
several years of active service at sea. Broke had commanded the *Shannon* for nearly seven years, and his
crew were accustomed to long habits of discipline, and
thus the victory was decisive.

The lesson of the war is so clear that it should be
unnecessary to point it out. Two races had met in
conflict, each of them high in intelligence, and each of
them possessing the true fighting edge, and the victory
often went in the single-ship actions to that side which
had earned it by thoroughness of preparation. Here
we notice also that when equality of fighting power is
reached, and ships and squadrons are handled equally
well by their officers generally, it is the quality of the
gunnery officers and seamen gunners that tells most in
the deadly effect of the gun fire, and thus it was that
the seamen of the United States, in the war of 1812–15,
often with some advantage in the weight of their broadsides, exercised in many of these minor actions the de-
ciding influence for success.

THE BRITISH TAR

PART I

HISTORICAL LITERATURE, BIOGRAPHY, PAMPHLET, AND SATIRE

CHAPTER I

THE PRIME OF ENGLISH SEAMANHOOD

OUR subject being the personality of the British seaman, and its impression upon the national literature, we shall in this section endeavour to delineate him, first of all as he laboured at his vocation in the ages wherein he makes, as it were, but a ghostly appearance in historical narrative or chronicler's record. We shall picture him upon the background of his period, piecing together the few and scanty evidences that remain, until we have a recognisable portrait of the man. Then we shall observe him in the printed pages of the larger navigations, when the ocean had become a pathway instead of being a barrier, and follow him in some world-wide explorations, in much hardship and silent heroism. And, lastly, we shall describe him in the language of those who saw him in the time of the Commonwealth and the Restoration, and the great century of war which ended with Trafalgar, glancing also at his character in the later days of the sailing Navy.

Few subjects of inquiry should prove more fascinating to a race of islanders, who have always depended upon the exertions of seamen for their prosperity and safety, than an attempt to discover the personality and qualities of these men, as revealed in histories, chronicles, biographies, and in literature generally. With the passage of centuries the mariner remained unchanged in the temperament of courage, resource in danger and emergency, loyalty, devotion, cheerfulness, and hardihood, wherewith long contact with the sea, comradeship

in its dangers and responsibilities, and a life absorbed in
its occupations could not have failed to endow him.
There was something in his frank and breezy personality
which made him easily distinguishable from the man
whose life was passed on shore, and it was in relation to
this strongly marked individuality that Henry Fielding,
the novelist, made the apt remark, in his account of his
journey to Lisbon, that the truth and justice of the observation was established that " all human flesh is not the
same flesh, but that there is one kind of flesh of landsmen
and another of seamen."

Softening manners and the new graces of later times
have eliminated from the personality of the seaman
certain features of violence and cruelty which were
found in the medieval mariner, whose warfare was not
often distinguishable from piracy. It was a ruder age
than ours, but we may surmise that the fighting seaman
was not more cruel than the soldier who fought on shore,
and that his greatest excesses were tempered by the
boisterous humour of his temperament. He was, indeed,
a lineal descendant of the Saxon seafarers, of whom a
Roman poet sang that they were " fierce beyond other
foes, and cunning as they were fierce ; the sea is their
school of war, and the storm their friend ; they are sea-
wolves that live on the pillage of the world." But the
reflection may be suggested that this fierceness was a
form of courage, and that this cunning was fertility of
resource, wherein the sailor remained unchanged. We
must guard ourselves also against accepting too readily
the landsmen's estimate of the old sailor, more especially that of the later landsmen, who have been
inclined to judge him by modern standards.

Seamen spent their lives cut off in a large degree from
the life of the shore, while living in a fellowship and comradeship of their own. They could not thus be as other
men. Waging a tireless contest with the elements, often
in cruel hardship and deprivation, enjoying little of the
sweetness of life as landsmen knew it, punished under
hard and brutal codes, looking for their reward, in early

times, in the profits of piracy, later in the spoils which
they wrung from the weakening hand of Spain, and later
again in the sharing of other prize money, suffering often
the agony of parting and tasting seldom the joys of re-
union, prepared in daily readiness for the conflict with
adversaries, they became bound in a brotherhood of
peril, and penetrated, as it were, with the very salt of the
sea. Sometimes, they have been described as the salt
of the earth also—men to be trusted, good comrades,
because their lives were passed in helping others in that
wooden world of their own, and men of gay and joyous
temperament, because in rude health they had been
schooled to laugh at hardships, and had never learned the
guile of the shore. We are concerned here only with the
seaman under sail, but his successor who navigates under
steam is little changed, save in his environment. The
old mariners proved themselves men of resource and
decision, alert in observation and action, with an independence of character which impelled them to bold and
adventurous courses, and never bade them shrink from
enterprise or peril.

The sea career demanded much from those who engaged in it—many sacrifices, and an abstraction from
many enjoyments. It was an ancient verity that
mariners must live their lives with the sea. Thus
Pericles said of the Peloponnesians that they would
not easily acquire the art of seamanship. " How can
they, who are not sailors, but tillers of the soil, accomplish
much ? For not even have you, though exercising
since the time of the Median war, brought it to perfection yet." The skill of the sea is like skill of other kinds ;
it is not a thing to be cultivated merely by the way or at
chance times ; it is jealous of any other pursuit which
distracts the mind for an instant from itself. And
Sir Richard Hawkins, writing two thousand years later
of the " attribute of the mariner," said that " government
at sea hardly suffereth a head without exquisite experience." *

* "Observations of Sir Richard Hawkins," 1593.

Froissart gives many a vivid description of sea fighting in the fifteenth century. In his account of the battle of Sluys, 1340, he pictures for us the warlike spirit and gaiety of Edward III surrounded by his knights and companions. " Long have I wished to meet with them, and now please God and St. George we will fight with them, for much mischief have they done, and if possible I will be avenged." Then we are told how the fleet was skilfully manœuvred for the advantage of position, so that the sun might not be in the eyes of the archers. " This battle was very murderous and horrible," says Froissart ; " combats at sea are more destructive and obstinate than those upon land, for it is not possible to escape or flee. . . . The French were completely defeated, and all the Normans and others were killed or drowned, so that not one of them escaped." It was the same when the Spaniards were encountered off Winchelsea ten years later. We see Edward in the prow of his vessel, habited in a black velvet jacket, with a hat of beaver on his head, " which became him much," shortly to be exchanged for his helmet. He was as joyous on that day as ever he had been in his life, and ordered his minstrels to play before him a German dance which Sir John Chandos had lately introduced, and for his amusement, and that of the ship's company, he made that knight sing with the minstrels, which delighted them greatly. But the watch cried out, " Ho ! I spy a ship," and presently the horizon was crowded with sails, and when wine had been served round, the battle was soon engaged. " Lay me alongside that Spaniard who is bearing down on us, for I will have a tilt with him." In those days it was fighting at close quarters, and the ships were grappled to one another by chains. The Duke of Lancaster was in a vessel ready to sink, his men having all they could do to bale out the water, but they boarded the Spaniard just in time to be saved. We are irresistibly reminded of Nelson at St. Vincent, and of the thoroughness of Trafalgar, but at Trafalgar our sailors did all that was possible to save the enemy's wounded and shipwrecked men, while in the earlier actions described by Froissart, the beaten foes were thrown overboard, " not one being saved." The short range of the weapons used made boarding a constant practice in every age up to the end of the old war.

It was not until after the sixteenth century that the customs of naval warfare, in the treatment of enemies, were really changed. When the *Nuestra Señora del Rosario* was surrendered in 1588, it had been stipulated that the lives of the prisoners should be spared, and yet when the ship came into Torbay it was no sailor but the Sheriff of Devon who thought it a pity the men had not " been made water spaniels." It would have been quite in consonance with such fighting methods that the men captured at San Juan de Ulloa in 1568, or who were afterwards put on shore by Hawkins, should be slain. Smugglers, both in Spanish and English law, forcibly resisting the King's authority, were liable to be put to death without more ado.

From such aspects of the old seaman's character, it is pleasant to turn to those more human qualities which proved him to be the forefather of the seaman of later times. Absorption in his business gave him something of a reverent attitude, combined with his harder virtues as a fighter. Gaiety and joyousness of disposition, a temperament prone to sentiment and romance, and a nature not seldom inclined to quaint unconventionality were developed in him, and largeness of heart and tolerance of mind were elements in his personality. He was always an object of attraction and interest to his fellows when he returned from his voyages and told them his wondrous tales. Thus it was that the language of the sea descended into the speech of the people, being employed to describe nearly every vicissitude and condition to which human nature is heir. If a man progresses in the world, he goes " ahead "; if he meets with reverses he is " in shallow water," or he " goes to leeward "; if there is anything to which he can firmly hold it is his " sheet anchor "; if he is intoxicated he may be " half

seas over," or, in lighter mood, may have " three sheets
in the wind " ; if he suffers deprivation he may be on
" short allowance," or " run aground," or even experience
" banyan days "—the latter phrase is rare, in these
times, but has been heard from the lips of one who
had no kinship with the sea ; if he has resources or
expedients at hand he has " still a shot in the locker " ;
if his affairs are in order they are " ship-shape," with the
orderliness of a ship, or they may be all " a-taunto,"
and if he gets the best of an opponent in argument he
gives him " a broadside."

The first appearance of the seaman in literature, as
distinguished from the soldier who fought on shipboard,
is in the pages of Chaucer. The Shipman is a finished
portrait of the fifteenth-century seaman in his very habit
as he lived, a very human character who was welcomed
as a comrade by the pilgrims to Canterbury. He came
from the West Country, where so many fleets were
equipped for the King, and as Chaucer says, " for aught
I woot," from the then renowned port of Dartmouth,
which was much frequented by shipping. The Shipman
was a reverent man, in so far as this was testified by his
joining the goodly company on the Canterbury Pilgrimage. Like many seamen in those and much later times,
and like the seamen of some nations in these days, he
wished, perhaps, to make a votive offering at the shrine.
Such offerings were customary, and were given in gratitude for a prosperous voyage, and sometimes when
danger threatened, and if the donors were wealthy men,
silver nefs or painted windows were their offerings.

But the Shipman bound to Canterbury excited the
hilarity of his companions, and that he was a subject of
jest is known by the fact that he rode as well as he could
—" as he couthe "—upon a " rouncy," which was a
heavy horse, mostly used for draught purposes, and
therefore not able to keep up easily with the ambling
paces of the horses of " the verray parfight gentil knight,"
or of his brown-faced squire, or probably of the rest of
the company. Then the Shipman's attire was rough

and homely, being a gown of " falding " reaching to the knee. It was a sea gown, of a kind long continued to be worn by seamen, girt about the waist, and, though represented in the Ellesmere manuscripts as black, it was probably of a dark blue, or rusty brown colour, the material being a rough serge-like fabric, intended to stand hard usage. A dagger hung under the Shipman's arm attached to what seems to have been a leathern strap placed round his neck. It was a knife which he used for eating and other purposes, and very necessary on board ship. His complexion was browned by the hot summer, and not, be it marked, by the tanning of the salt winds of the sea, so that presumably he had been latterly on shore, and perhaps had ridden up all the way from Devonshire, though more probably he may have been awaiting the readiness of some ship in the Thames.

But though the seaman was rough, he was skilled in the essentials of his art. He understood navigation and pilotage, knew the tides and the currents well, and was acquainted with the harbours and dangers of the coast. He appears to have understood also some method of navigation by the moon, or, more probably, the pole star, while, as for his " lodemanage," or skill as a pilot,

Ther nas noon swich from Hulle to Cartage.

It was before the time of the famous globe of Martin Behaim, and of the " rutters," or sailing directions, but the seamen of Chaucer's time had their latitude and longi-tude from the system of Ptolemy and the Almagest, and the astrolabe, on which Chaucer himself wrote a treatise, was the instrument for celestial observations. The Ship-man had often done battle with the tempest, and knew where he could run for a safe haven, being acquainted with them all from " Gootland " in the Baltic to Cape Finis-terre, as well as every creek at home and on the coasts of the Peninsula, which he appears to have visited in his barque, the *Maudelayne*. Besides being thus a skilled mariner, Chaucer's Shipman was a jovial companion, and was welcome in the company of the pilgrims for his largeness of heart and genial tolerance—

> And, certeinly, he was a good felawe.

Rough he may have been of speech and manner, but he was a hearty comrade, little skilled in the ways of landsmen and not at all schooled in the manners of the Court. He would drink deeply at times, and had little scruple as to how he obtained his liquor. Full many a draught of wine had he drawn from the vintage of Bordeaux, while the "chapman," who was a merchant or supercargo, was asleep. The pirates of those days were not public offenders in the sense of later times. They were carrying on war, and if the liquor of a Frenchman was stolen, the Englishman would not think ill of the larceny. Hence Chaucer's Shipman was fit to keep the good company bound to Canterbury, though he may have scandalised them at times. At least, he appears not to have chosen his stories with the same nicety as some of his companions, and in the Prologue to his tale—which is sometimes misplaced—he gives fair warning in homely language that he is going to tell a "mery" story, which word in his mouth might mean a licentious one.

> And therefor, hoste, I warn thee biforn,
> My joly body shal a tale telle,
> And I shal clinken yow so mery a belle,
> That I shal waken al this companye;
> But it shal nat ben of philosophye,
> Ne physices, ne termes queinte of lawe;
> There is but litel Latin in my mawe.

Here, then, is the picture of a seaman of the fifteenth century, a man whom Chaucer had known, brave, hardy, ruthless in his dealing with enemies, a free liver and a man with few scruples, but withal true at heart, a good fellow and a prime seaman, skilled in his business and craft.

As the world was broadened by the great explorers in the centuries that followed, seamen grew larger in their experience, and became discoverers of distant regions, surveyors and pilots of the seas and coasts, and often scientific navigators and students of nautical astronomy. They opened up fresh regions in their quest for the riches of distant lands, and their knocking at the gates of the treasure house of the world. Sea officers become diplomatists, as well as fighters, and, if sometimes they plunged nations into war, there were occasions upon which they became intermediaries of peace. Not a few of them wrote professional works for the information of their comrades and successors, and treatises on navigation and nautical astronomy began to issue from the press in the sixteenth century.

It was inevitable that the high qualities demanded for success in great enterprises should develop a larger intelligence both in officers and men. The Portuguese and Spaniards led the way in exploration—we do not go back to the navigations of the Norsemen at the end of the tenth century—but the Bristol seamen had shown their hardy quality, buffeting the storms of the North Atlantic before Columbus made his first voyage, and before John Cabot made his great voyage in 1497. The maritime enterprises of the days of Henry VIII, and especially the three voyages of William Hawkins, of Plymouth, demanded the high qualifications of courage, perseverance, zeal, patience, sympathy, and understanding of men. These explorers waged their conflict with the ravages of scurvy, the execrable badness of food, and the inveterate hostility of rivals. It was nothing to their disparagement that they were seeking a new way to the riches of the world, to the Indies, to Cathay, and to the Spice Islands. Sir Hugh Willoughby, endeavouring to discover a North-East Passage, perished on the coast of Lapland ; Chancellor pursued the expedition ; Burrough discovered the strait between Nova Zembla and the mainland ; Pet penetrated the Kara Sea ; and Jackman never returned from his voyage. The successive efforts made to penetrate the North-West Passage hold a great place in our maritime history. The three voyages of Martin Frobisher were heroic at-

E

tempts to cleave a way into the frozen North; and
Sir Humphrey Gilbert later on lost his life in his effort
to penetrate the mysteries of those regions. Another
undaunted seaman of the times was John Davis, a man
of high and notable attainments, who became the real
father of Arctic exploration, and did much to develop
scientific seamanship.* His three northern voyages laid
a solid foundation for the navigators who followed.

Hakluyt, in his great collection of the voyages of the
navigators—his " Principal Navigations, Voyages, Traf-
fiques and Discoveries of the English Nation, 1599 "—
exclaims in his preface : " Did not Richard Chanceler
and his mates performe the like northward of Europe ?
Did not the valiant English knight, Sir Hugh Willoughby ;
did not the famous pilots, Stephen Burrough, Arthur Pet,
Charles Jackman, accoast Nova Zembla, Colgoieve and
Vaigatz to the North of Europe and Asia ? . . . But besides the foresaid uncertaintie, into what dangers and
difficulties they plunged themselves, *animus meminisse
horret*, I tremble to recount." Thus does the great re-
corder of voyages suggest the qualities that were found
in the seaman as a navigator and explorer in the Northern
Seas, making " triall of the swelling waves and boisterous
winds which commonly there do surge and blow."

The men who took part in these expeditions were cast
in no common mould. Sebastian Cabot, as governor of
the Mystery and Company of the Merchant Adventurers,
laid down instructions for the conduct of the expedition
of Willoughby and Chancellor, based on the ordinances
prepared for southern navigators by the Chief Pilot of
Spain, which show the orderly manner with which the
expedition was conducted. Willoughby was the general
commanding the expedition, and Chancellor its pilot
major, and it was enjoined upon them and the masters,
merchants, and other officers to be so knit and accorded
in unity, love, conformity, and obedience in every degree and on all sides, that no dissension, variance or

* Davis's "Seamen's Secrets," 1594; "The World's Hydro-
graphical Description," 1595.

contention might rise or spring betwixt them and the mariners of the company, to the damage or hindrance of the voyage. These mariners had a livery of watchet blue, which they wore upon great occasions or when they were paraded, but which otherwise remained in the charge of the merchants for its safe-keeping while the men were wearing their working clothes. There was to be no blaspheming of God, no detestable swearing, no communication of ribaldry, no filthy tales, nor ungodly talk amongst them. Neither were there to be dicing, carding, tabling, "nor other divilish games to be frequented." There were to be prayers in the morning and evening, and thus the "unruly mariners," of whom Henry Sidney had spoken when he visited the ships before they put out from the Thames, were ordered in obedience and propriety of behaviour. In the same way the expedition itself was disciplined, and the captain, pilot major, masters and masters' mates, these being the navigating officers of the vessel, with the assent of the councillors and the greater number of them, were to discuss the navigation of the expedition, the captain-general having a double voice in the decision. Many other instructions are laid down for the safe conduct of this great expedition, and it may be remarked that similar rules existed in all such cases, and that there was a strong effort to subdue any unruliness amongst the mariners who were employed.*

Sir John Hawkins, when he set sail on his slaving expedition in 1562, laid down a simple and direct rule: "Serve God duly; love one another; preserve your victuals; beware of fire, and keep good company." Full cargoes of negroes from Sierra Leone, sold to great profit in the Spanish possessions, were the guerdon of his endeavours, and, returning to Padstow in September, 1565, from his next expedition, he exclaimed: "God be thanked, in safety, with a loss of twenty persons in all

---

* Hakluyt, "Principal Navigations"; Beazley, "John and Sebastian Cabot." In the latter book is a remarkable bibliography of Cabot literature.

these voyages, and with great profit to the venturers of the said voyages, as also to the whole realm, in bringing home both gold, silver, pearls, and other jewels, great store—His name therefore be praised for evermore, Amen." *

Something of the spirit of seriousness and devotion appears in all the seamen of those times, and it was not confined to our own Navy. In the account of Frobisher's second voyage, which left Tilbury on 27th May, 1577, the narrator, Captain George Beste, states that they all received the Communion before their departure, " by the Minister of Gravesend, who prepared us, as good Christians towards God, and resolute men for all fortune." In a great storm amid the ice floes, whilst shrewdly trusting to the skill of the master and his mates, very "expert mariners," and the master gunner, with other "very careful sailors," they remembered that they had help from above, "God being our best Steersman." When they landed on the shore of Meta Incognita they knelt down and thanked God for his great goodness in bestowing hidden treasure upon his poor and unworthy servants, and besought the Holy Spirit to deliver them in safety into their own country. The orders for the voyages were similar in tone to those in the case of the expeditions of Willoughby and Hawkins. Swearing, dice, card playing, and filthy communications were to be banished, and there was to be a service to God twice a day, according to the usage in the Church of England, and to " cleare the glasse according to the old order of England." †

The seamen and navigators were enlarging the known world, penetrating its mysteries and breaking down the Spanish monopolies. In some of them was engendered greed for gold, but rarely in the sordid spirit, generally with a high ideal, and not seldom in the spirit of reverence and devotion. Sir Humphrey Gilbert's object in attempt-

* Hakluyt, "Principal Navigations," "The Hawkins' Voyages" (Hakluyt Soc.).

† Beste's narrative of the three voyages is in Hakluyt, also a narrative of the first voyage by Christopher Hall, master of the *Gabriel*, of the second by Dionese Settle, and of the third by Thomas Ellis.

ing the North-West Passage was to discover a route to
Cathay and the Spice Islands, and the same object inspired the efforts of Frobisher, Davis, and others. But
there is no more beautiful or touching picture in English
literature than that which tells us how Humphrey Gilbert
met his end. Can we ever forget how he sat abaft in
the *Squirrel* on that melancholy afternoon of the 9th
September, 1583, exhorting the seamen to courage and
resignation, the ship being near to foundering, water-
logged, and unmanageable? A book was in his hand,
and ever as the *Golden Hind*, which was in his wake,
neared him within hailing distance, he cried out in a
loud voice, " We are as near to heaven by sea as by
land," repeating which words, " well beseeming a soldier
resolute in Jesus Christ," he perished, the ship going
down with her company. Such is the striking incident
recounted by Edward Hayes.*

The voyages of Hawkins, Drake, and other navigators
of the time all showed the mettle of our hardy seamen. Intense religious fervour filled them, and they had
a comfortable creed which enabled them to regard the
Spaniards as Egyptians to be spoiled, and as Amalekites
to be destroyed. The Spaniards, on their part, had an
equal bitterness, and piracy and treachery were matched
in the conflicts. After the terrible and sanguinary affair
at San Juan de Ulloa, Sir John Hawkins made a voyage
to the coast of Spain in 1590, and returned well satisfied
with his crews and equipment, though others held a
different opinion and brought charges of knavery and incompetence all round. That particular expedition was a
failure, and Hawkins wrote to Burghley declaring the
sufficiency of the preparation and its want of success.
" Thus God's infallible word is performed, in that the
Holy Ghost, said Paul, does plant, Apollo doth water,
but God giveth the increase." Reading which letter
Elizabeth exclaimed: " God's death! This fool went
out a soldier, and is come home a divine ! " †

* Hakluyt, "Principal Navigations."
† State Papers, Domestic; Elizabeth, ccxxxiii. p. 118.

In a mixed community of seamen, forming the companies of ships both of war and discovery, suffering much hardship and often being wronged by self-seeking persons ashore, it was inevitable that at all times discipline could not be universally good. Thus when the *Mary Rose* capsized at Spithead in Henry VIII's reign, her commander, Sir Peter Carew, had described her company as " a sort of knaves whom he could not rule." They " soe maligned and disdayned one the other that, refusing to doe that which they should doe, they were careless to doe that they oughte to doe, and so contendinge in spite, perished in frowardnesse." The captains of Elizabeth also suffered much from the drafting on board their ships of men of the wrong class, and it was said that the ships were manned by a " loose rable " and a " vagrant, lewd and disorderly "—a " ragged regiment of common rogues." Perhaps it could scarcely have been otherwise in times when men were paid irregularly, when they were fed upon vile provisions, and when they were punished for every offence with remorseless savagery by flogging, keel-hauling, tongue-scraping, or hanging up with weights round the neck " till heart and back were ready to break." Privations were many in the fleet.

Great exertions were required to provision the ships in 1588, but the supplies were not sufficient and men had to be put more than four to a mess, which was the proper complement. Often five or six men had to be satisfied with the rations allowed for four, and there were times when " six upon four " became a matter of course. Loud complaints were raised as to the bad quality of the beer, which was always described as sour, and the men traced their disorders to it. These complaints of the seaman concerning the quality of his food continued long after this date.

Disorders arose mostly from men who had not the right spirit of the sea, and who, not having been brought up to it from boyhood, were drafted on board the ships and served only from greed for gain. Monson said that nothing bred such disorders in sailors as liberty and over-much clemency. Raleigh remarked upon their cupidity. "We find it in daily experience that all discourse of magnanimity, or national virtue, of religion, of liberty, and whatsoever else hath been wont to move and encourage virtuous men, hath no force at all with the common soldier in comparison of spoil and riches ; the rich ships are boarded upon all disadvantages, the rich towns are furiously assaulted, and the plentiful countries willingly invaded. Our English nations have attempted many places in the Indies, and run upon the Spanish headlong in hopes of their reals of plate and pistolets, which, had they been put to it on the like disadvantages in Ireland or in any poor country, they would have turned their pieces and pikes against their commanders." *

But this is merely a partial picture ; it does not show us the true seaman. Our mariners had been trained in the school of the sea, accustomed from boyhood to rough work in the fisheries, and in manhood in the voyages of Willoughby, Chancellor, and the others in the Northeast, or had cruised with Frobisher or Davis, or round the world with Drake, and had made semi-piratical cruises in the Bay of Biscay, or in the track of the homeward-bound treasure fleet—the famous Flota of Spain. It was this quality of seaman-like skill and long experience that was the real cause of the defeat of the Spanish Armada in 1588, manned as it was largely by soldiers and by fair-weather sailors, who had never experienced the rage of North-Atlantic gales. Drake, writing to the Queen on 13th April, 1588, with a seaman's and a diplomatist's tongue, assured Her Majesty in these words : " I have not in my lifetime known better men, and possessed with gallanter minds, than your Majesty's people are for the most part, which are here gathered together, voluntarily to put their hands to the finishing of this great piece of work, wherein we are all persuaded that God, the Giver of all victories, will in mercy look upon your most excellent Majesty, and us your poor

* "History of the World," IV, II, 4.

subjects, who for the defence of your Majesty, our religion and native country, have resolutely vowed the hazard of our lives." The seamen knew their own qualities, and Fenner, who was with Drake at the burning of the city of Cadiz, wrote that "twelve of her Majesty's ships were a match for all the galleys in the king's dominions."

Reference has been made above to the opinion of Sir Richard Hawkins that the seaman should be a man of knowledge shaped by "exquisite experience." He was referring to a distinction which still existed in his time, but which appears to have been gradually dying out, between the higher ratings of the mariners as prime seamen and the men who hauled and drew with the mariners, and were sea labourers merely. Indeed, he observed that "some ancient seamen" defined a mariner as a man who "is able to build his ship, to fit and provide her with all things necessary, and after to carry her about the world; the residue to be but sailors." In a return made after the death of Elizabeth, in 1603, this distinction is clearly marked, the men being divided into mariners, gunners, and sailors.

CHAPTER II

THE PERSONALITY OF THE TUDOR MARINERS

IN the sixteenth century professionalism increased among the seamen owing to the demands of war and the great expeditions which were undertaken in order to discover new lands and new approaches to the treasure house of the world. Active service throughout the year was becoming common, and the seaman learned to look with something of contempt upon the " gentlemen captains " who were intruded into the service. These were men who did not make the sea their occupation. The name did not imply that the professional captains rose from a lower rank in life, but indicated the presence of many men who came in mainly for purposes of profit, or embarked only for the voyage as " gentlemen volunteers " or soldiers. Though not as skilled as the real tarpaulins, they could often be trusted to work with a will in emergencies. Thus in the narrative of a great storm in Frobisher's second voyage we read of " the gentlemen and souldiers within borde taking great paynes at this pinche at the capstone." In Elizabeth's time many men who had entered the service as soldiers and courtiers ended by becoming really professional seamen. But generally the result of these changes was that those who had neither sea legs nor sea stomachs became objects of ridicule to men whose life business was the sea. In the expedition undertaken by Essex in 1597 soldiers and aristocratic volunteers were embarked to the number of some 500, including the Earls of Rutland and Southampton and other lords,

but a stiff gale took the courage out of them, and it is
stated that one or two actually died of sea-sickness.
When the fleet returned after an unsuccessful attempt
to pursue the voyage a number of these landsmen deserted, hastily and secretly, " forgetting either to bid
their friends farewell or to take leave of their general."
They were volunteers who had been drawn by the hope of
plunder, but Rowland White wrote to Sir Robert Sidney :
" This storm hath killed the hearts of many voluntary
gentlemen, who are returned already from Plymouth." *

These extracts show that the mariners were being
segregated into a more marked class by the increasing
demands which were made for seaman-like skill and
endurance on the part of those who undertook distant
expeditions or hazardous enterprises. Indeed, the complaints that were made about the " gentlemen captains "
indicated surely enough the growing professionalism of
the naval service. Pepys, the inimitable diarist and
vigilant naval administrator, knew the evil of officers
of this class in the fleet. Writing seventy years later,
he said: " The truth is the gentlemen captains will undo
us." They, and men taken green from the shore, were
the standing horror of the real seamen from Elizabeth's
days onward. †

Men were obtained mainly by the system of impressment, which was intended to bring in mariners from the
coast towns and fisheries who were acquainted with the
work of ships at sea. To a large extent this object was
attained, but not altogether, for in the voyage which
has been referred to (1597) Essex told the Privy Council
that men were taken up by the press-masters " in mariners' clothes but shall not know any one rope in the
ship." ‡ It was reported that the Queen's ships were so

---

* State Papers, Domestic, Elizabeth, cclxiv.; "Diary of Sir Henry
Slingsby," p. 250.
 † "A Satire on the Sea Officers," written after the battle of Beachy
Head, 1690, shows that the merits of tarpaulins and gentlemen officers
were still being discussed, as does "A Rough Draught of a New
Model at Sea," written by Lord Halifax about the year 1694.
 ‡ State Papers, Domestic, Elizabeth, cclxiv.

ill-manned that though they had men enough so far as
numbers went, not one ship in the fleet had half her
complement of good men. " We were furnished with
men of all occupations, that never knew any rope, many
of them, nor ever were at sea." It was the working of
the system that was at fault, and not the system itself,
for later on, when sea captains were supplied with press
warrants, they usually were careful to take up only
suitable men.

Sir Richard Hawkins speaks of the difficulties he encountered in obtaining and handling his mariners, and
shows quite clearly what were the conditions of life at
sea at that time. " Mariners are like to a stiff-necked
horse, which, taking the bridle betwixt his teeth, forceth
his rider to what him list, maugre his will ; so they
having once concluded and resolved are with great difficulty brought to the reign of reason." This was in 1593,
and he was speaking of his departure from Plymouth.
" For some would be ever taking their leave and never
depart ; some drink themselves so drunk that except
they were carried aboard they of themselves were not
able to go one step ; others, knowing the necessity of
the time, feigned themselves sick ; others to be indebted
to their hosts, and forced me to ransom them—one his
chest, another his sword, another his shirts, another his
card and instruments for sea ; and others, to benefit
themselves of the imprest given, absented themselves,
making a lewd living in deceiving all those whose money
they could lay hold of, which is a scandal too rife among
our seamen." The men who had thus grown stiff-necked,
knowing their value, were apt to enforce their demands
by mutinous behaviour. They would engage to embark
for an expedition, receive money, and then absent themselves. Cavendish was said to have lost much in this
way, and Hawkins was very angry when he saw the
varlets who had engaged with that navigator walking
about the streets of Plymouth after his departure. In
his own ship when he went to sea there were men who
" vaunted that they had cosoned the Earle of Cumber-

land, Master Cavendish, Master Reymond and others, some five pounds, some ten, some more and some less."

But Hawkins admits that many of the mutinies were due to thefts and frauds committed on the men in detaining wages and prize money. The seaman was generally of a trustful nature, and was often defrauded even until comparatively recent times. Hawkins encountered a mutinous spirit at sea, and there were occasions when the seamen demanded a voice in the conduct of the voyage, which indeed seems to have been traditional with them under the old laws of the sea. If they were not listened to, they became very unwilling. Such turbulence was perhaps the inevitable accompaniment of the conditions in which they served, the work of profit in which they engaged, and the vigorous maritime vitality, that was undoubtedly assuming a predatory character in the operations of the period, as was illustrated, notably towards the end of the war with Spain, when the Spanish flag had been swept from the sea, and there were few vessels to capture or despoil. There was one captain, returning from a cruise, in June, 1603, who told Cecil that he had not met a single Spanish merchantman, and that as a consequence the privateersmen were plundering French ships. He recounted how he had examined a French merchant ship and had released her, whereupon his company " grew into such a mutiny, by reason I would not rob them, that they would have stowed me under hatches." It is an indisputable fact that in many of these voyages neutral ships were seized on the supposition that they might be guilty, and thus heavy work was provided for the Admiralty Court, and many owners lost their profit and were despoiled. It is not, however, necessary to enter further into this mundane aspect of the question in this place, but it will suffice to point out that, from the Queen downward, all those who had any share in maritime enterprise were eager to profit by the spoil. Thus in 1585 Drake had brought home plunder to the value of £67,000, and other voyages were as profitable, or even more so.

Men would dare much for profit or adventure in those times, and the hard life of the seafarer on the ocean voyages has a large place in maritime history. In the account of Frobisher's third voyage in 1578—his most important in regard to the number of vessels engaged in it, and the hopes that were set upon it by the eager assayers and goldsmiths who had examined his glittering quartz from Meta Incognita—there is a picture of the misery of the scurvy-stricken men in the horror of the storm. The cold was so bitter that they could scarce open their eyes to handle ropes or sails. The month was July, but snow lay half a foot deep on the hatches, " which did so wette thorow oure poore mariners' clothes, that he that had five or six shifts of apparell, had scarce one drie threede to his backe, which kinde of wette and coldnesse, together with the over labouring of the poore menne amiddest the ise, breed no small sicknesse amongst the fleete, which somewhat discouraged some of the poor men who had not experience of the like before."

In addition to such hardships the food was often insufficient and of the vilest, more especially in the active fighting service of the Queen. Monson's tracts are full of complaints of the victualling and of the frauds on gunner's and boatswain's stores in Elizabeth's time. The faults in victualling were probably mostly due to ignorance, and it is recorded that the seaman insisted on his gallon of beer a day in the tropics. The ale supplied to him was undoubtedly pestilential stuff. Scurvy was rife, for the men fed on salt beef, salt fish, and cheese, and the food was cooked in salt water. The ships also were badly ventilated, and their holds foul with bilge water and drainage, while the cooking galley, which was built of bricks and mortar, contributed to render the food on board unfit to be eaten.* But the men who lived in these conditions became inured to hardships, and the history of the times shows that they never failed, when demands were made upon their courage and endurance.

It must not be supposed, moreover, that the interests

* Men were buried in the ballast in foreign ships.

of the mariner were neglected by the real sea officers who prepared the expeditions of the sixteenth and seventeenth centuries, and shared all the perils while bearing all the responsibilities. Nor must it be imagined that either dire hardships or sober counsels served to diminish the high spirits of the sailor when the immediate cause of his trouble or depression disappeared. Musicians were always carried, and song and dance broke the monotony and aroused the spirits of the dejected. It is recorded of Drake's great expedition that his vessels were plentifully furnished with all manner of provisions and necessaries for so long a voyage, and that such as served only for ornament or delight were not forgotten. For this purpose he took with him very expert musicians for several instruments, and the furniture and fittings of the ship were rich and sumptuous. John Davis, in his first voyage, in 1585, for the discovery of the North-West Passage, had musicians with him, and a jovial company, and John James, who narrates the events of the voyage, says that they made friends of the Eskimos by playing and dancing to amuse and attract them, the Englishmen over-leaping the Eskimos, but good wrestlers getting the worst of it in some bouts with the hardy northerners. Sir Richard Hawkins, in his voyage in 1593, had also musicians on board, and with the sound of trumpets, " waytes," and other music, as well as the salute of his guns, did he bid farewell to the Devon men gathered to wish him God speed on Plymouth Hoe.

Incidentally we gain an insight into the amusements and diversions of mariners in those times—song with a note of melancholy and sentiment in its tone, carousal with hearty jollity, sport with some callousness to suffering inflicted, which must not surprise us in men who saw all the brutalities of the slave trade. Thus Sir Richard Hawkins, in his observations on his voyage into the South Seas, describes how his men made sport of the sufferings of the sharks they captured. Let us not think harshly of them, for high-spirited men even in modern times have found diversion from monotony in the same or similar ways. " Every day my company tooke more or less of them, (the sharks) not for what they did eat of them (for they are not held wholesome ; though the Spaniards, as I have seene doe eate them), but to recreate themselves, and in revenge of the injuries received by them ; for they live long, and suffer much after they bee taken, before they dye. At the tayle of one they tyed a great logge of wood, at another an empty batizia (a small cask) well strapped ; one they yoked like a hogge ; from another they plucked his eyes out and so threw them into the sea. In catching two together, they bound them tayle to tayle, and so set them swimming ; another with his belly slit, and his bowels hanging out, which his fellows would have every one a snatch at; with other infinite inventions to entertayne the time, and to avenge themselves, for that they deprived them of swimming, and fed on their flesh, being dead." *

But before we proceed to the later periods of naval history in our quest for the personality of the seaman, some reference must be made to his professional character as a navigator. The great explorers of the days of Elizabeth did not choose raw countrymen or worthless persons to man their ships. They knew well that prime seamen, experienced navigators, and pilots were essential for the success of their operations, and in the accounts of their voyages we hear few complaints of the seamen, except occasionally, when they suffered the direst hardships, and some expressions of discontent were wrung from them. The expert mariners had advanced far in their skill in navigation. Their scientific knowledge was based largely upon the researches of foreigners. Johann Müller, known as Regiomontanus, had published his " Epheme-rides," with tables of the sun's declination calculated for the years from 1475 to 1566 ; and his pupil, Behaim, had constructed his famous globe, the most important

* "Observations of Sir Richard Hawkins in his Voyage unto the South Sea, 1593," 1622. A similar story is told relating to compara-tively recent times in the " United Service Journal," 1833.

geographical instrument which had appeared up to the
beginning of the sixteenth century. Globes, and not
charts, were chiefly used, and all the navigators began to
be supplied with instruments. John Davis translated in
1561 the " Compendium " of Cortes, and Bourne's
" Regiment of the Sea," the earliest original work on
navigation, appeared in 1573. Davis wrote his " Seamen's Secrets " in 1594, and invented the backstaff,
which has been called the " Davis quadrant " ; and in
many other ways scientific navigation made great and
notable progress.

But the hard, practical seaman did not always welcome
these scientific advances, doubting whether any book
could take the place of practical experience. He looked
askance at all theory, being himself a man of bone and
sinew, trusting much to the skill born of experience from
boyhood—the class of man of whom it was said later
that " every hair was a rope yarn, every tooth a marline
spike, every finger a fish-hook, and his blood right good
Stockhollum tar ! " Thus between science and practice
arose a controversy, which has had its parallel in comparatively recent times, the practical school questioning
the qualities of the seaman whose knowledge they assumed to be mostly theoretical. Amongst these was
Captain Luke Foxe, of Hull, who, as a collector of voyages, trod in the footsteps of Richard Eden and Hakluyt,
and as a practical navigator did notable things at sea.
His volume, bearing the whimsical title of " North-West
Fox ; or Fox from the North-West Passage," was published in 1635. It includes a collection of voyages from
the earliest times down to Baffin and later discoverers,
and is a singularly interesting book, because it presents
to us, with much dry humour and uncommon freshness,
the character and outlook of a seaman who had spent his
whole life in the business of the sea. " Gentle Reader,"
he says in his preface, " expect not heere florishing Phrases
or Eloquent tearmes ; for this child of mine, begot in the
North-West's cold Clime (where they breed no Schollers),
is not able to digest the sweet milke of Rhethorick, that's

food for them." Many had inquired " as what hath Foxe
done ? " Others, "how farre hath hee beene ? hath he
beene as farre as any man ? if there be a Passage, how
chance hee hath not found it ? if not, why doe they
search after it ? and, in fine, hath hee made a voyage
or no ? The meaning of this last query I know not,
nor, I think, they neither ; but for that the most desire
to know what I have done, and how farre I have bin,
I answer, as the old women tells tales, Further and
further than I can tell ; and for the rest I referre them
to mine owne Journall."

Foxe goes on to deride the " Mathematicall sea-men,"
who would fail in their contest with " the ruffe and
boisterous Ocean." " Being deprived of Sun, Moone
and Starres for long season, they will then thinke that
they onely dreamed before, when they imagined of the
course of the seas, and that their Bookes were but weake
Schoolemasters ; that the talke of art were farre short
of the Practice, when, at beholding the Starres, which
they thought to have used as guides and directions,
seeme now as they threatened their ruine and destruction ; nay, when they shall looke forth and tremble at
the rising of every wave, and shall be agast with feare
to refraine those Rockes and dangers which lye hid
within the sea's fairest bosome, together with the great-
nesse of the Ocean, and smalnesse of their ship ; for want
of experience to handle, not knowing how to shun, they
will then thinke that the least gale is of force to over-
throw them, and know that art must be taught to practice by long and industrious use. For it is not enough
to be a Sea-man, but it is necessary to be a painefull
Sea-man ; for a Sea-bred man of reasonable capacity
may attaine to so much art as may serve to circle the
Earth's Globe about ; but the other, wanting the ex-
perimentall part, cannot ; for I doe not allow any to be
a good Sea-man that hath not undergone the most
Offices about a Ship, and that hath not in his youth bin
both taught and inured to all labours ; for to keepe a
warme cabbin and lye in sheets is the most ignoble part

F

of a Seaman ; but to endure and suffer, as a hard cabbin, cold and salte meate, broken sleepes, mouldy bread, dead beere, wet cloathes, want of fire, all these are within board ;   besides   Boate,   Lead,   Top-yarder,   Anchor-morings and the like."

Captain Foxe had been a seaman from boyhood, and, while expressing the views of many old salts who de-spised men of theory, he appears to have had the special object of depreciating Captain Thomas James, who was engaged in the same sphere of discovery in the same year as himself, 1631. The narratives of these two navigators are remarkable as being almost, if not quite, the earliest separately published English works describing voyages in search of a North-West Passage. When Foxe met James there were discussions as to their several navigations, and various festivities broke the monotony of the cruise. But a certain acrimony seems to have tinged the discourse. Foxe was entertained on board James's ship, with sea provisions and some partridges. They dined between decks, the great cabin not being large enough to accommodate the full company, and much water came on board, " as we could not have wanted sause if wee had had roast mutton." In his own mind Foxe pondered whether it was better for James's company " to bee impounded amongst Ice, where they might be kept from putrifaction by the piercing ayre ; or in open sea, to be kept sweet by being thus daily pickled." However, he said, they were to be pitied, their " ship taking her liquor as kindly as our selves, for her nose was no sooner out of the pitcher, but her nebe, like the Ducks, was in't againe." Foxe found James a " prac-titioner in the Mathematicks," and regarded with dis-favour also his practice of keeping his flag flying in those icy regions. He says : " My ambition was more Aethe-riall, and my thoughts not so ayerie, so to set my sight towards the skie, but when I eyther call'd to God or made Celestiall observation."

In manning and equipping his expedition Foxe had taken great care to secure men " of Godly conversation," not exceeding thirty-five years of age, and, if possible, with experience of Arctic navigation. He was completely victualled for eighteen months, though whether the baker, brewer, butcher, and others were masters of their calling he said he knew not. However, he indicates a plenteous store—excellent fat beef, strong beer, good wheaten bread, good Iceland ling, butter and cheese of the best, " admirable sacke and aqua vitæ," pease, oatmeal, oil, spice, sugar, fruit, and rice, " with chyrargerie, as sirrups, julips, condits, trechissis, antidotes, balsoms, gummes, unguents, implaisters, oyles, potions, suppositories, and purging Pils ; and, if I wanted instruments, my chyrurgian was enough." As to equipments, the carpenter was " fitted from the thickest bolt to the pumpnayle or tacket, the Gunner from the Sacor to the Pistoll, the Boatswaine, from the Cable to the Sayle-twine, the Steward and Cooke from the Caldron to the Spoone." Touching books, Foxe confessed his deficiencies at length, seeming to imply that if he had not had knowledge in his head, printed volumes would have been of little use to him.

The incisive and humorous remarks of Captain Luke Foxe are proof enough of the rise of that school of professional seamanship already referred to, of which the spirit has never been lost—a school in which the traditions of the storm-bitten mariners of Elizabeth, trained in adventure and discovery, and in piracy under the Careys and Killigrews, Oglanders, Champernownes, and others, were progressively more and more influenced by the scientific developments of the seaman's art. The mariner of those times rarely spoke in literature, though when he did it was very much to the point, and mostly from the conditions of his life and the things he did have we discovered what manner of man he was. Of his seaman-like skill, and of the honest work of the shipwrights also, we have brilliant proof in the fact that in Elizabeth's reign not a single ship was lost by stress of weather, by grounding, or by fire ; while only two ships were captured from us, and then only after desperate fighting and against outnumbering odds. Meanwhile, in battle and tempest, the whole Spanish navy had disappeared.

But in the reign of James I a decline set in, and under his successor things went from bad to worse. More mariners were required, but there was little money, so that the leaky ships went to sea with men discontented, mutinous and half-clothed, provided with food whose very savour was corruption It was still the same old story. Professional officers were profoundly discouraged, landsmen were given command. and the King's vessels were ravaged by disease. When the miserable expedition returned from Cadiz in 1625 Sir John Pennington wrote from Plymouth that " the greatest part of the seamen being sick or dead, so few of them have sufficient sound men to bring their ships about " ; and St. Leger wrote that it would not be possible to move the men until they recovered strength ; " they stink as they go, and the poor rags they have are rotten and ready to fall off," while many of the officers were nearly in as bad a plight. In 1629 Sir Henry Mervyn, commanding in the Narrow Seas, wrote to Buckingham's secretary a pitiable account of the miserable condition of the men, who had neither shoes, stockings, nor rags to cover their nakedness. " I have used my best cunning to make the *Vanguard* wholesome. I have caused her to be washed all over, fore and aft, every second day ; to be perfumed with tar burnt and frankincense ; to be aired 'twixt decks with pans of charcoal ; to be twice a week washed with vinegar—yet if to-day we get together 200 men, within four days afterwards we have not one hundred." And again he says, " foul weather, naked bodies, and empty bellies make the men voice the King's service worse than galley slavery." They clamoured for food and clothing in mid winter, and Sir John Watts at Portsmouth ordered " shot " to be used against them when they showed their tattered garments and made " scandalous speeches." *

* In 1623, in order "to avoyd nastie beastlyness by diseases and unwholesome ill smells in every ship," the issue of slop clothing by the Crown was ordered, and has continued with more or less regularity ever since. Swinburne, "The Royal Navy," 1907, p. 345.

John Hollond, in his second discourse on the Navy —" The Navy Ript and Ransackt," written about the year 1659—speaks of the victualling in his time : " For the men will, and do run away rather than eat it, and those that do or are forced to stay contract diseases, sickness, and ofttimes death by eating it, whereby they are either thrown overboard, or turned ashore, to the great disservice of the State." * And, again, to anticipate the period we are approaching, and to give another illustration of the internal condition on board warships, showing the long-standing hardship, it was said in 1703 that " a hot country, stinking meat, maggoty bread, noisome and poisonous scent of the bilge-water have made many a brave sailor food for crabs and sharks." Even at that time it was stated that for one man who died by shot, ten died by bad provisions. But there is not space here to give any account of the victualling of the Navy, one of the most interesting subjects that any one can pursue, and one that played no small part in giving its character to the seaman's life and thus to his own personality.†

Before we go any further in this voyage of discovery in quest of the true and the much-suffering seaman, something more must be said about the system of impressment for the fleet, which affected his life so greatly, and has played so large a part in our naval history. Already we have alluded to it, and we shall refer to it again. Even at this day, impressment for the Navy has never been declared illegal, but, on the contrary, has been frequently sanctioned by Parliament, as in 1378, 1555, 1562, 1696, 1703, 1740, 1810, and even as recently as 1836. Few officers doubted that impressment was indispensable for providing seamen for the Navy, and it

* " Hollond's Discourses " (Navy Records Society), Second Discourse, chap. iii.

† Hodges, " Great Britain's Groans ; or an account of the oppression, ruin, and destruction of the loyal seamen of England, in the fatal loss of their pay, health, and lives, and dreadful ruin of their families," 1695; Robinson, " The British Fleet," Part II, chap. iii.; Oppenheim, " Naval Administration."

was not until the war of 1854-5 that a fleet was manned
without recourse to it. The law only allowed seafaring
men to be pressed, but the press-gangs seized artisans,
apprentices, and labourers, and great hardships and oppression were the result. At all times impressment was
a cruel visitation upon the seafaring population, bitterly
experienced and deeply resented, but its greatest severi-
ties were not felt until the eighteenth century. Attempts
were made to encourage volunteers, but in the stress of
war the supply was altogether inadequate. The fleet of
1666 was well manned by means of the press, but Pepys
wrote that in the City of London men were pressed contrary to all course of law, some of them " poor patient
labouring men and housekeepers." He wrote on 1st July
in that year : " But, Lord ! how some poor women did
cry ; and in my life I never did see such natural expression of passion as I did hear in some women's bewailing themselves, and running to every parcel of men that
were brought, one after another, to look for their husbands, and wept over every vessel that went off, thinking
they might be there, and looking after the ship as far as
they could by moon-light, that it grieved me to the
heart to hear them."

Captain George St. Lo, who was captured by the
French in 1690, after a desperate conflict, in which he
was severely wounded, wrote during his detention in
France several pamphlets on naval subjects, and made
suggestions for doing away with impressment. It was
want of pay, not the hardship of serving, that the men
resented ; and St. Lo defends the captains, against whom
many harsh things had been said, amongst others in a
pamphlet by one Henry Maydman, a purser, and says
the men never fared better than when the captain and
purser disagreed. In his pamphlet, entitled " England's
Safety, or a Bridle to the French King," 1693, he expresses the opinion that sufficient men could be raised
without the impress, if they were properly paid. In a
later pamphlet, 1694, he explains a plan of registration
for English seamen, and says that by it the fleet would

be supplied with able and daring " haulbolings," as he calls seamen, instead of raw lads and persons who had never been to sea, without the great charge caused by impressment. He speaks of the sort of men the press-gangs brought on board as " shacome-filthies," " ragga-muffings," and " scrovies." Defoe, in his " Essay on Projects," 1697, expressed similar ideas with regard to impressment, and also proposed a system of registration. He said that men would be willing to serve if assured of a fair wage, " for it is not the fear of danger which makes our seamen lurk and hide and hang back in time of war, but it is wages is the matter : 24s. per month in the King's service, and 40s. to 50s. per month from the merchant is the true cause ; and the seamen is in the right, too ; for who would serve his King and country, and fight and be knocked on the head at 24s. a month, that can have 50s. without that hazard ? " In a rare and interesting book, " The Life and Adventures of Matthew Bishop," recounting his experiences from 1701 onward, he tells how at Waterford he got together a number of young men for a game of football, and induced many of them to join voluntarily. He played a similar trick at Dublin, getting up a cudgel match between six sailors and others, and then induced the competitors to go on board.

In that scarce tract " The Navy Royal, or A Sea Cook turn'd Projector," printed in 1709, wherein the writer, Barnaby Slush, states that very seldom did his thoughts " soar one inch higher than the steam of my burgoo kettle," he says much in favour of the seaman and a good deal against the officers. But he shows himself no opponent of the system of impressment. " Mistake me not, Sir, I am not such a blind zealot against pressing as to cry it down to all intents and purposes, or to say with a certain Oliverean captain that in itself it is the most horrid thing in nature, and inconsistent with the rights and liberty of the subject. For he who in time of peace follows the sea as his proper vocation, does and ought as naturally and justly expect being pressed when a war

breaks out, as a blacksmith or any other craftsman does
to bear a musket in the trained band when summoned
to the defence of his country. Our island would be just
as no island were the authority of impressing abolished
or reputed tyrannical."

There was also the serious complaint that men newly
returned were sometimes seized again by the press, and
carried once more to sea. The "London Spy," 1699,
presents to us an exaggerated picture of men coming
ashore in such a condition as would make them the easy
victims of these practices. They enter a public-house,
short pipes in their mouths, oaken truncheons in their
hands, thrum-caps upon their heads, and wearing canvas
trousers. "Presently in steps another of the tarpaulin
fraternity, with his hat under his arm half full of money,
which he hugged as close as a school-boy does a bird's-
nest. 'Ounds, mother,' says our marine Crœsus to the
landlady, 'where are you?' She, hearing his tongue,
thought, by his lively expressing himself, he had brought
good news, and came running with all speed to meet
him, crying—'Here I am, son Bartholomew, you're
welcome ashore: I hope your captain and ship's crew
are all well?' 'By fire and gunpowder! I don't care if
they be all sick; why, we are paid off in the Downs,
and I am just come up in a hoy. Come, mother, let's
have a bucket-full of punch, that we may swim and toss
in an ocean of good liquor, like a couple of little junks in
the Bay of Biscay.'"

CHAPTER III

THE CHARACTER OF THE SEA OFFICERS

WE have now reached a point at which we are able to enter with greater knowledge into the lives and occupations of the seamen of former times, and to bring before ourselves pictures, as it were, of the officers and men in their character as they lived. We are in the golden age of pamphleteers, diarists, essayists, and satirists, who depict in vivid colours the men they had seen and known. Bad food, pestilence, and want of pay were, after all, but the background upon which these old seamen moved. They are not to be detached from it, for they were influenced by it, but their character came from their kinship with the sea. Inimitable Pepys describes some of the things that went to the making of them. That kindly humorist and observer, with a touch of malevolent wit, Richard Braithwaite; that thinking seaman, Captain Nathaniel Boteler; the lower-deck secretary, Thomas Lurting; writing naval chaplains, like Henry Teonge; the facetious, cheery, and irreverent satirist, scurrilous Ned Ward, whose gibes and witticisms are alive with the slang of the tavern; Barnaby Slush, the sea-cook, his brother pamphleteer; with the more serious writers, Robert Crosfield, Captain St. Lo, William Hodges, and others—these are the men who bring the sailors once more upon quarter-deck and fore-castle. Braithwaite's " Whimzies " was dated 1631; Boteler wrote about the year 1635; Lurting was a sea-man with Blake in 1667; Teonge's Diary refers to 1675-9; and Ned Ward's scandalous witticisms were

73

dated 1706. But Braithwaite's "sayler" is the enduring
type of two centuries or more ; Boteler's "Dialogues"
were thought timely to be published in 1685 ; and Ned
Ward's satires obviously refer to a period not much later.
All these were very different men. Braithwaite was the
humorous scourge and anatomist of the society of his
time. Of Boteler we know little, but he was an officer
of good service and a serious thinker with a vein of wit,
who described the duties and qualities of officers and
men for the benefit of persons in authority. Lurting was
a Quaker of strong convictions. Teonge was a penniless
parson, who left his Warwickshire rectory to escape his
creditors, and was chaplain of the *Assistance* in Narborough's expedition to punish the Barbary pirates.
His diary throws a flood of light upon naval life in the
reign of Charles II, and even more curious is "The
Straights Voyage," 1671, a narrative poem by John
Baltharpe, who was serving on board Sir John Harman's
flagship in the Mediterranean. Ward, it is worth
remembering, was for his libellous attack on the
Government in his "Hudibras Redivivus" condemned
to stand in the stocks at the Royal Exchange and
Charing Cross in 1705, the year before he dated the
preface of his "Wooden World Dissected," and received
rough usage at the hands of the mob. "As thick as
eggs at Ward in pillory," says Pope in the "Dunciad."
There is also the so-styled "sea-cook" and brother
scribe, Barnaby Slush, whose "Navy Royal," published
in 1709, has already been alluded to.

From the pages of these several writers we shall now
endeavour to delineate the personalities of the officers
and men of ships of war in a period which may be taken
to run from about the year 1630 to the end of the seventeenth century, making note of what has been said by
some writers a little later. Our diarists, commentators,
and satirists will give us some account of the personalities
we are in search of. In this chapter we shall deal only
with the captain, the lieutenant, and the midshipman,
these being the officers for whom uniform was provided

THE CHARACTER OF THE SEA OFFICERS 75

when it was first given in 1748. In the seventeenth
century there were many other classes of officers, fore-
runners of the modern warrant officer, of whom we shall
have much to say in the succeeding chapter. The captain
was, of course, the chief officer in a ship of war. In him
was centred all authority, and he was the despotic chief
of the community, sometimes exerting his authority
harshly, and sometimes acting as the friend and true
leader of his officers and men. As we have seen, he might
be a gentleman captain, serving for pride and profit, or
he might be a tarpaulin captain, bred from boyhood to
the sea, or, again, he might be a soldier, chosen for qualities of rectitude and command.

There is no intention here of dealing with the politics
of the time or the naval operations that were so important
in the shaping of events. But it may be remarked
parenthetically that, notwithstanding a clear understanding of the conditions which made for efficiency
possessed by the Stuart kings, their navy was, as has
indeed been seen, always ill-supplied, ill-fitted, and
manned by discontented men, with no proper body of
sea officers. The men, starved and robbed, ended by
blaming the King, and went solid for the Parliament,
which removed the cavalier officers. The chiefs who
served the Parliament best at sea—Deane, Montagu,
Blake, and Monk—were land officers by training, but
were men of character and honesty whom the seamen would follow, and sea officers were their advisers.
Some of the "tarpaulins," promoted rapidly by the
Parliament, either for professional worth or their poli-
tically safe character, were probably not fitted for
high command, and men of the serious temper disclosed in 1642, and later during the Commonwealth,
could least of all tolerate the so-called "gentlemen
captains," who received their places for reasons of court
or as offices of profit. Such officers "alienated the
hearts of the Puritan seaman," and Pepys, after the
Restoration, writing on 2nd June, 1663, when the old
influences were at work again, tells us that Mr. (after-

wards Sir William) Coventry, who was accused of selling
offices, confessed that " the more the Cavaliers are put
in, the less of discipline hath followed in the fleet." In
Charnock's " Marine Architecture " there is printed a
remarkable attack upon officers of this class, made in
what Charnock calls " vulgar terms." The writer says
the " gentlemen " have had " the honour to bring drinking, gaming, whoring, swearing, and all impiety into the
Navy, and banish all order out of the ships." Their lack
of seaman-like skill had caused ships to be lost, and they
would often remain in port when they ought to be at
sea. A captain of this class would bring " near twenty
landmen into the ship, as his footmen, tailor, barber,
fiddlers, decayed kindred, volunteer gentlemen or ac-
quaintances as companions," and all to the " great discouragement of tarpaulins of Wapping and Blackwall,
from whence the good commanders of old were all used
to be chosen." These gentlemen were evidently fore-
runners of Smollett's pink-coated, white-vested, crimson-
breeched dandy, Captain Whiffle, and probably they
were as much exaggerations of the actual personages.
What the seamen really disliked was the man of no
proper sea knowledge or aptitude, who, in defiance of
regulations, would sleep on shore and run up to London
on every possible occasion. Pepys records how he
" spied " the captain of the *Lark* in 1675 sauntering
about Covent Garden, when the King's service required
his presence on shipboard, and remarks that the custom
grew and that ill example impaired discipline.*

How the mariners loved and appreciated a good sea
officer is shown by their grief at the death of Sir Christopher Myngs, who had died of his wounds received in
the Four Days' Battle, as recorded by Pepys, and it
must be remembered that this occurred at a time when
men were clamouring for pay, and in a state of great
distress. Pepys describes the episode as " one of the
most romantique that ever I heard in my life, and could

* See also "A Rough Draught of a New Model at Sea," by Lord
Halifax, c. 1694.

not have believed, but that I did see it." He was in a coach with Sir William Coventry. " About a dozen able, lusty, proper men come to the coach-side with tears in their eyes, and one of them that spoke for the rest begun and said to Sir W. Coventry, ' We are here a dozen of us, that have long known and loved, and served our dead commander, Sir Christopher Myngs, and have now done the last office of laying him in the ground. We would be glad we had any other to offer after him, and in revenge of him. All we have is our lives ; if you will please to get his Royal Highness to give us a fire-ship among us all, here are a dozen of us, out of all which choose you one to be commander, and the rest of us, whoever he is, will serve him ; and if possible, do that which shall show our memory of our dead commander, and our revenge.' " * Captains then and earlier came from various classes of society. Sir Christopher Myngs is said to have boasted that he was a shoemaker's son, but the story is probably apocryphal. Edward Montagu, Earl of Sandwich, represented the aristocracy. Generally they were comparatively poor men who carved their fortunes in the Navy, sometimes by prize money and sometimes by private trade, some of them, says Pepys, " giving up their whole care to profit them- selves and not the King's service." They were not all of that disposition, and we read of Captain John Leake, afterwards the well-known admiral, looking for some- thing higher. " Being of a brave and generous disposi- tion he did not consider so much to raise his fortune as his reputation. Contrary-wise, he whose mind is turned to get money can hardly do a brave action, and such an one may make an excellent trader, but can never make a good officer."

Entick, the naval historian, who helps us singularly little in this inquiry, enables us to give a picture of Sir John Leake at a later period of his life. " Sir John Leake was of middle stature, well-set, and strong, a little inclined to corpulency, but not so as to incommode him

* "Diary," 13th June, 1666.

in the least. His complexion was florid, his countenance
open, his eyes sharp and piercing, and his address both
graceful and manly, denoting both the military man and
the gentleman. As he had a good person, he had also a
good constitution, hardly ever knowing what it was to
be sick; and though he took his bottle freely, as was
the custom in his time in the fleet, yet he was never
disgraced or impaired his health by it. . . . In short, as
to his personal and natural qualities, he was what phy-
sicians define as a perfect man, namely, he had a sound
mind in a sound body. . . . He was certainly one of the
best seamen the island has produced." Cast in the same
mould, and inspired with the same ideas, was Leake's
brother-in-law, Captain Stephen Martin-Leake, who was
a fine type of a naval captain, to be contrasted with men
of a less humane and sometimes even of a brutal class.

Boteler remarks that the captain had as high a charge
as any colonel on land, for he commanded as many
men, and was answerable for the ship and all her
ordnance, which might be worth £40,000 or upwards.
" And for the point of honour," he adds, " what greater
honour hath our nation in martial matters than in his
Majestie's Navy ? " Thus must the captain be " of un-
suspected loyalty, approved valour, full experience and
sufficient skill." For was he not responsible for the conduct of the ship and for all that concerned her officers
and men, including discipline and the ordering of punishments ? That there were brave and capable captains
who fought in the Dutch wars and under Rooke and
Shovell is known ; while others, like those who were with
Benbow, merited all the hard things that could be said
of them. Teonge has nothing to say to the disparagement of Captain Holden, of the *Assistance*, in 1675, who,
with the lieutenant, welcomed the threadbare chaplain
on his arrival in London " with bottels of claret, etc.",
and proved throughout to be a very genial and even
convivial person, so that the chaplain indited a poem
in his honour, each line beginning with successive letters
of his name. We may certainly conclude that the great

majority of captains in the Navy were not any less
gentlemen because they were seamen. The fact is, indeed,
capable of proof, and it was perhaps only natural that
scurrilous writers should choose their examples from the
exceptions and exaggerate the worst features of them.

Ned Ward—who slandered the Army, in his " Mars
stript of his Armour," as he did the Navy—has no word
in praise of the captain, whom he describes as " a levia-
than, or rather a kind of sea-god, which the poor Tars
worship as the Indians do the devil, more through fear
than affection ; nay, some will have it that he is more
a Devil than the Devil himself." He lived in the great
cabin at the stern, his "sanctum sanctorum," guarded
by a marine, with a drawn sword, at the door. The lam-
poonist says that he rarely issued forth, lest his authority
should be weakened by his being seen too much. Upon
his appearance the lieutenants sheered off to the other
side, " for 'tis impudence for anyone to approach within
the length of a boathook." Perhaps Ward had in his
mind certain of Benbow's captains when he characterised
the subject of his denunciation as a coward. " He has
no mortal aversion for the French ; it is not their blood
he thirsts after, but their claret ; 'tis involuntary, to be
sure, if he spill the one or the other. He has a rare hand
at playing away his lieutenants upon hair-brained enterprises, for he is as prodigal as the devil of other men's
blood, when money is in the way, and always makes use
of a lieutenant's paw to draw it out of danger, for though
it is mighty common for him to quit the ship without
leave for a good dinner, yet he makes it an indisputable
law never to step forth when danger calls him. So he
deputes for his proxy some numbskulled officer, whom
he most esteems, and to demonstrate this kind love the
more, he strips him of all when the prey is took, that
the world may not think that the young squire's courage
was mercenary. Thus the wretched ship's crew that
sweat and fight for bread, get scarce the very husk,
while he runs away with the flower of the cargo, and
epicurises his pocky carcass for ever after."

In a publication entitled " Satirical Reflections on the
Vices and Follies of the Age," 1707, the sea captain is
described as " Bluff as the winds that on the ocean
roar." Barnaby Slush, like Ned Ward, depicts the captain as the oppressor of the seamen, who suffer all the
toils of the service, while their leaders all the while sit
gorging their pampered carcasses or lie battening in ease
and luxury, regardless of the sailor's wants, and bent on
nothing but how to circumvent them of the very necessaries of life. This harsh judgment would seem to
apply better to some greedy purser than to the captain,
of whom, however, with the other officers, it is alleged
by Slush that he was the chief and essential cause of the
bitter and invincible aversion which the best and choicest
of mariners had for the service.

We seem to get a glimpse of a mercenary-minded
captain, such as Ward and Slush had in view, in the
story told of Sir John Balchen, Admiral of the White,
lost in 1742, who, when he was a captain, arriving at the
Nore from the West Indies in 1716, had some discussion
with the surveyor of customs. His own account of what
happened shows that when he returned on board his
ship—and the incident throws light on the manners of
the times—he found the surveyor of customs sitting on
the quarter-deck, in company with the surgeon and sailing
master, discussing a bowl of punch, and they invited him
to join them and " to bouse his own personal jib." The
surveyor suspected Balchen of smuggling Jesuit's bark,
whereupon Balchen demanded his authority to act.
Not being able to produce this, the surveyor was denounced as an impostor, and one of his legs was fastened
in the bilboes, while Balchen walked about in a towering
rage. The surveyor jeered at the captain, saying, " There
is £100 on that leg, captain," to which Balchen replied,
" Is there ? Then you shall have two," and his other
leg was also clapped into the bilboes. It is, perhaps, safe
to assume that a small transaction settled the business
between them.

Ned Ward's biting sarcasms were, as from his pen

they could not but have been, a libellous exaggeration
of a certain class of captains, and the Navy was not at
so low an ebb in his time as when Smollett saw it forty
years later. Ward painted every officer in colours more
or less dark, his object being to bring into bright light
the sterling qualities of the much-suffering seamen.
Burchett, whose " Memoirs of Transactions at Sea "
refer to about the same period (1688–97), remarks that
it was of no little consequence for the good of the service
that the captains should take " a fatherly care of the
men under their command by seeing that right be done
them in every particular." They must treat the men
humanely, and cause the other officers to do the like,
because the seamen were too liable to follow ill example,
and the officers themselves must set the good example.

Ward's " Wooden World Dissected " went through
several editions, the fourth appearing in 1749, and
the book was almost certainly read by Henry Fielding, the novelist, who also much later gives a portrait of a naval captain, writing probably more from the
impression that he had received from Ned Ward's book
than from actual knowledge. In the " Journal of a
Voyage to Lisbon," published after Fielding's death in
1755, he tells us that he was made angry by a certain captain at Dover. He had written to this officer, whose ship
was lying near that in which he had arrived, to ask him
if he would send him and his party ashore in the war-
ship's longboat. The request was met with a verbal
refusal. " He might have sent a written answer, as it
was the part of a gentleman so to have done ; but this
is a character seldom maintained on the watery element,
especially by those who exercise any power on it. Every
commander of a vessel here seems to think himself entirely free from all those rules of decency and civility
which direct and restrain the conduct of the members
of a society on shore ; and, each claiming absolute
dominion in his little wooden world, rules by his own
law and his own discretion. I do not, indeed, know so
pregnant an instance of the dangerous consequences of

G

absolute power, and its aptitude to intoxicate the mind, as that of these petty tyrants."

The lieutenant came next after the captain in the sea hierarchy, and was indeed his deputy and heir-apparent to his office. Lieutenants first appear in the sixteenth century.* There were officers of the rank in Armada days, and Monson says that the employment was "for a gentleman well bred, who knows how to entertain ambassadors, gentlemen and strangers when they come aboard, either in the presence or absence of the captain." It would appear that some of these young gentlemen became filled with an idea of their own importance, and Boteler notices the fact. "Only he is admonished that he be not too fierce in his way at the first (which is an humour whereto young men are much addicted), but to carry himself with moderation and respect to the master, gunner, boatswain, and the other officers, that so he may not be despised but beloved and obeyed ; and when experience hath taught him more fully to understand his place he may grow to an higher strain, and at last attain to his affected port, a captainship." This admonishing did not altogether chasten the spirit of the lieutenants, for Pepys, writing to Sir John Kempthorne in December, 1677, described them as dull and ignorant, having gained their offices by favour, and he questioned what sort of captains the honour and safety of the crown and government would depend upon, "when the few commanders (for God knows they are but few) that are surviving of the true breed shall be worn out." Accordingly an examination and test of the qualifications of lieutenants was instituted, and in the next year Pepys wrote : "I thank God we have not half the throng of those of the bastard breed pressing for employment which we heretofore used to be troubled with, they being conscious of their inability to pass their examination, and know it to be to no purpose now to solicit for employment till they have done it."

* State Papers, Dom. Eliz. ccxiii., Nos. 64, 67 and 89 ; the narrative of Ric. Tomson, Lieutenant of the *Margaret and Joan*, throws a light on the character of the officers of this rank.

The improvement was continued, but there were lieutenants of many characteristics in the fleet, and Ned
Ward, as usual, fixes upon the worst types and satirises
them. There were three classes of them, he says—the
" captain's vicegerent," the " kind of spare topmast
that lies idle while the first is standing," and " the hoble-
dehoy, or boy in man's clothes." Of the senior lieutenant
he speaks thus : " Often in his sleep he fancies himself
actually in possession, to the no small wonder of the
quarter-deck, when in the dead of night they hear him
cuff the bed and bedposts, and crying out, in a cold
sweat, ' Zounds, mind your Hand, you Dog at the Helm,
and bear away ; Bear up round, you Slave, for the
Enemy you see edge down upon us ' ; so offering at the
Quartier's Chops in his dream, he strikes his fist against
the ship-side, and streight that awakes him, to his no
little comfort, in finding he has been all this while sleeping in a whole skin. . . . Of all the officers of the ship he
rails the most against the captains, tho' he is the first
of any that hopes to be one." The lieutenant was the
officer who was charged with the business of impressing
men. " He and his Bandogs together, make a woeful
noise in all the sea port towns round the Kingdom ; he
beats up all quarters, and rummages all the Wapping ale-
houses as narrowly as he would a prize from the Indies.
. . . In fine, he's a perfect hurricane in a little town, and
drives the laggard dog along the streets with as much
noise and bustle as butchers do swine to Smithfield."
It is ill fortune that we have no genial diarist to tell us
of the better class of lieutenants ; but Teonge and Wit-
cherley suggest men of a different mould, and we may
be sure there were many like Smollett's honest Lieutenant
Bowling at a later date—" as good a seaman he is as
ever stepped upon forecastle, and as brave a fellow as
ever cracked biscuit." The lieutenant was not for ever
railing at his captain, nor puffed up with senseless envy.
Often they tossed the flowing bowl together, and chaplain
Teonge was as merry as any of them. They would " end
the day and week with drinking to our wives in punch-

bowls "—the " sweethearts and wives " of the seaman's
Saturday night.

In those times the lieutenant was usually a man of
sea experience, often brought into the service ; while
the midshipman, who was originally a foremast hand,
being generally a youth whose duty lay amidships,
employed in the transmission of messages between the
quarter - deck and the forecastle, rose to the dignity
of the quarter-deck, and solved the problem of how
" to breed up officers and gentlemen, who should be
also seamen, skilled to manage a ship, and maintain a sea fight judiciously, of discretion and courage,
and able to speak to the seamen in their own language."
The midshipmen learnt their work under the supervision
of mates and quartermasters, but had much to do to
keep their position of quarter-deck officers, although
scurrilous Ward says that the midshipman of his time
was " in the first-rate line in a ship towards the top-mast-
head of preference, for all admirals as well as captains
are obliged to begin their rise here."

Barnaby Slush has some trenchant remarks upon the
situation and the discouragement of the volunteers, or
as he styles them, Reformadoes—gentlemen of birth and
liberal education, who were invited into the fleet to be
sharers in its dangers and partakers in its posts of trust
and honour, some of them under the title of midshipmen
or letter-men—the " King's letter boys "—who came
under the cognisance and jurisdiction of the captain.
According to Slush, the captain seldom failed to make
them uneasy under his rule, for it was the nature of
" these mighty Czars " to take a great deal of satisfaction in humbling these generous spirits. " And yet such
is the whimsy of some bloated chiefs that to try the
utmost extent of a gentleman's patience, will at every
turn be commanding them with a ' God dam ye, Sir,'
upon pitiful concerns, or errands, rather, very unbecoming
their birth and character, and which might much better
be effected by any common blunt tar." He goes on to
point out that the entertainment of the midshipmen and

the letter-men was not such as it should be—that they ought at least to have had cleanly accommodation for their bed and board, since it was not pay that brought them into the Navy. " It must needs strike a damp upon their spirits when they find that the captain's tailor, footman or valet has more conveniences and better accommodation, and that they are themselves reduced to the necessity of fetching their own peas, or pork, or burgoo, of swabbing their own platters, and of herding at nights among a gang of sorry scabs, the very outcasts of a parish." It was not surprising, he adds, that gentlemen of estate refused to abandon their children to such an entertainment, and " to swing most vilely in some louzy berth, surrounded with the noise and stink of rotte-ye-dogs and blackguard boys." " What reformadoes then can we expect can launch forth into the deep when there's so very uninviting a scene before 'em ; a youth of any tolerable hopes and good parts must have a wonderful stock of christian stoicism to choose to abandon the secure and standing advantages which law, physic, divinity, trade, nay, agriculture itself, does propose to its followers, and venture his all in so uncertain and fluctuating a bottom as the navy, which at best affords no better annuity even to a lieutenant than any of the other professions can pick up in a month perhaps."

What impression do we receive from this attempt to characterise the principal officers of ships of war in Commonwealth days ; in the years when we were fighting with the Dutch ; under the Restoration, with its Spanish, Dutch, French, Danish, and Algerian wars ; and in the time of William III and Anne, which saw the real beginning of the long struggle with France, and the victories of Russell, Rooke, and Shovell ? Of fighting capacity there was no lack at any time, though a grave malady afflicted the fleet both before the Commonwealth and after. We must, however, guard ourselves against regarding as absolutely veracious all the things which lampoonists and lower-deck advocates have said to the disadvantage of superior officers. They painted them in dark and savage colours, sometimes almost as fiends in human shape, the despots and self-seekers of a decadent age, and they did so partly for the sake of contrast, and partly to emphasise the more their advocacy of the seamen's cause. In an age of shamelessness and brutality, foulness and cynicism, when courtly divines smiled at frivolities and excesses and at the humours of men who fought, gambled, swore, drank, and ended days of debauchery by nights in the gutter, the envenomed scribe had excuse for the bitterness of his satires. We may suspect that sometimes he ascribed to sea officers, of whom he may have known little, certain of the dark features which idle report attached to them, and which he observed in the degenerate frequenters of the court. Heartless commanders there were who tortured crews almost to mutiny, but they were the exception, and, if in those days there were brutal captains, such as the pamphleteers have described, there were others of a finer and higher type, men with hearts and sympathies, zealous seamen and navigators, as the whole history of the Navy proves. Of men of the latter class the diarists have little to say. They have left to the political satirist and the embittered scribe the opportunity to defame, and we must therefore recognise that, if they have given us the truth, the whole truth is not presented in their pages.

CHAPTER IV

THE SAILORS OF THE STATE

DESCENDING through the ranks and ratings of the sea hierarchy, in this middle period selected for the exposition of character, we are now brought to the standing officers, the inferior officers, and the seamen themselves. It was a period in which officers of the classes referred to were losing their ancient powers. The doubling of lieutenants on board ship, and the later increase in the number of those officers, diminished the privileges of the standing officers, who, instead of being the captain's advisers in emergency, and responsible with him for the well-being of the ship, now became subject to the orders of the lieutenants. Nay, even, as one writer said, the boatswain who was the agent for visiting the wrath of the captain upon misdemeanants, became himself, with other standing officers, liable to be " caned, bilboed, and despitefully treated " ; whereas formerly the masters, their mates, boatswains, gunners, and carpenters had had as much command over the men and were better obeyed than the lieutenants afterwards, " as they deserved, for most of them were fit to command, and very often did, with great reputation when their superior officers were killed or disabled in a fight."

First of all we come to the master, who, with his mates and quartermasters (or quartiers, as the old phrase has it), and the gang who attended upon them, looked to the navigation of the ship, her compasses, steering apparatus, and so on. The very salt ran in the veins of the master of a ship of war. He was a man of authority,

responsible for much, and upon his skill the safety of the
ship depended. He and his mates were, says Boteler, the
guides to lead the ship her right way, and the scouts to
look out that she took no harm anywhere. These masters
were real seamen, and the " Captain " in Boteler's " Dialogues " says that they could not abide gentlemen
commanders. " These masters undergo the command
of a captain with a great deal of repining and sullenness,
and the rather in regard that many times they meet
with weak captains." Ward gives an amusing caricature
of the master which is worth quoting. " His station is
the meridian altitude of the lower kind of midshipmen ;
his mates make him the great planet of their observation ; when their exaltation is risen thus high, it is noon-
day with them, and they look no further. He is a seaman
every bit of him, and can no more live any while on dry
land than a lobster, and but for that he is obliged sometimes to make a step ashore to new-rig and lay in a
cargo of fresh peck and tipple, he cares not tho' he never
see it. . . . His very conversation is so salt that he cannot have a tooth drawn ashore without carrying his
interpreter. ' It is that aft-most grinder aloft on the
starboard quarter,' will he cry to the all-wondering
operator." When he chanced to take a trip on land he
would hoist himself upon a horse as if he were astride a
yard-arm, and would haul on the reins as if they were
main-sheets. Hauling aft upon one rein only, " about
ship goes the beast and tosses my gentleman overboard ;
but up he ships upon his legs, as manfully as a tailor
upon a shopboard, and, finding that a horse will neither
answer the helm nor his expectations, he e'en orders him
back to his moorings, and straight takes a berth in the
stage coach, which always makes her way as good as she
looks."

We may now pass on to the purser, chief among the
" standing officers," who was always an important man
on shipboard. Boteler places him lower in the scale, but
he rapidly rose to a position of dignity and profit. He
was generally a man with friends, and it was essential

that he should have some capital or supporters with money. Even his position might be a matter of purchase. It was his duty to account for disbursements made for the ship and for moneys defrayed from funds entrusted to him or by bills. It was his business also to account for and take charge of the slops and provisions placed on board the ship for issue, and the greater part of his wages consisted of percentages on the value of articles which passed through his hands. Some stores were supplied, but he himself became a private purveyor of many things, and public and private interests often clashed. He would draw stores for men who were dead, run, or discharged by keeping their names on the books, and would make profit in sundry other ways, the vilest of all procedures being probably the tricking of men into leaving the ship, either to visit the shore or to join some other vessel. The unfortunate man then lost the whole of his wages, which the purser or his accomplices could draw with a forged ticket. Thus it is not surprising to find the "Admiral" in Boteler's "Dialogues" remarking upon the importance of having pursers of integrity and sufficiency. "The purser might purse up roundly for himself, and that without all discovery." Unfortunately they were not all persons of integrity, and Ward says that they went through many transmigrations, the last generally "from being a poor knave in the Fleet near the Old Bailey to be a substantial gentleman in the Fleet at Spithead." "He is the most excellent alchemist in Nature, for he can transmute rotten pease and mouldy oatmeal into pure gold and silver with very little expence in that operation. In him miracles are not ceased, for he oft-times turns water into wine and wine into water with one mere fiat to his steward; but all this is no great wonder in a man that has to do with the devil." The purser was denounced and lampooned by many satirists and ballad-writers.

The boatswain was another of the "standing officers," and a man often much feared on board. His real charge was that of all ropes belonging to the rigging of the ship, cables, anchors, and other gear, and he was especially responsible for the longboat and her furniture, and was able to steer her.   But in addition to his charge and administration of stores and his direction of work on board ship among the seamen, who ran like hares at the shrill sound of his pipe, we read in Boteler's " Dialogues " that the last duty of the boatswain was to see all offenders duly punished as they are censured by the captain or by the " marshal court " of the whole fleet.

Naval punishments, which had a large place in the lives of seamen, present a very curious and important study, and some reference shall be made to the subject here.   The " Admiral " of the " Dialogues " asks particulars of the punishments inflicted, and the " Captain " describes them.   " The punishment at the capstein is when a capstein bar being thrust through the hole of the barrel, the offendor's arms are extended at the full length cross-wise, and so tied unto the bar, having sometimes, a basket of bullets, or some other the like weight hanging by his neck ; in which posture he continueth till he be either brought to confess some plot or crime, whereof he is frequently suspected ; or that he hath received such suffering as he is censured to undergo at the discretion of the captain. The punishment by the bilboes, is when a delinquent is laid in irons, or in a kind of stocks that they use for that purpose ; and which are more or less ponderous, as the quality of the offence is, that is proved against the offending patient. The ducking at the main yard arm is when a malefactor, by having a rope fastened under his arms, and about his middle, and under his breech, is thus hoisted up to the end of the yard, from whence he is violently let fall into the sea, sometimes twice, sometimes three several times one after another ; and if the offence be foul, he is also drawn underneath the very keel of the ship, the which they tearm keel-raking, and being thus under water, a great piece is given fire unto right over his head, as well to astonish him the more with the thunder thereof, which proveth much more offensive to him, as to give warning to all others

THE TARS' RECREATION.
CARINGTON BOWLES, 1782.

THE JOLLY TARS OF OLD ENGLAND ON A LAND CRUISE.
I. PLAYER.—J. C. IBBETSON, 1802.

To face page 90.

But were his call, stick and cat, too, all thrown over board he yet would distinguish himself by his throat, for no ass in Christendom brays like himself."

In this survey of the characteristic figures in ships of war, we now come to the master gunner, who also was an important standing officer. He had charge of ordnance and gun-mountings and of everything that concerned ordnance stores, including charge of the powder rooms. Sir John Leake, the admiral, like his father before him, had himself been a gunner, and the position was at that time thought to be one of great credit. The gunner afterwards became chief of the warrant officers, and lived aft, while the boatswain and carpenter lived forward, his armoury being below the officers' quarters. The gunroom thus became the living-room of the junior officers, who, to some extent, were then under the gunner's charge. Sometimes gunners were selected by favour, and Ward tells us that the gunner was "commonly a spawn of the captain's own projection."

The carpenter, with whom a joiner might be associated, had charge of the ship's stores generally, in regard to repair and maintenance, and exercised important duties on board, though sometimes he might be " the tool the captain makes use of to cut the King's timber to his own service." The cook was often remarkable for his inability to cook. In 1704, in appointing these men to his Majesty's ships, the Lord High Admiral directed the Navy Board " to give the preference to such cripples and maimed persons as are pensioners of the chest at Chatham," and Lord Nottingham, when Lord High Admiral, gave a patent to his own cook to appoint all the cooks in the Navy. That the cook's position was sometimes an office of profit is evident from remarks made by the " Admiral " in Boteler's discourses. " I doubt not but these cooks know well enough how to lick their own fingers, and I assume myself that their fat fees make them savers, whosoever else loseth by the voyage." Ward can say nothing better for the sea cook than that his knowledge extended not to half a dozen dishes, but that he was such a pretty fellow at what he undertook " that the bare sight of his cooking gives you a bellyful." Slush was himself a cook, or describes himself as such, with thoughts no higher than the steam of his burgoo-kettle, and " his contentment in a small chirping can of flip and a pipe of tobacco."

We shall pass over the surgeon and his mates, the quartermaster, sail-maker, and other personages who exercised some authority in the old Navy, in order that we may reach the seamen class. And here all are agreed that there was a blunt honesty of character in the men that made them beloved and respected. Rough and brutal they might be, but they gave proof of qualities of endurance and courage, as well as of resource, that were found in few other men. Simplicity and openness of mind characterised them beyond their fellows, and they were often the victims of unscrupulous land sharks of sharper wits than their own. Let Captain Boteler speak of them as he knew them in the ships of Charles I. Something had been done to improve their condition, which he noted with pleasure. " For these people, when they are left to themselves, are generally found to make more of their bellies than their backs." They revelled in opportunities of pillage, but knew little of the value of what they seized. " There is nothing that bewitcheth so much, nor anything wherein they promise to themselves so loudly, and delight in so greatly ; insomuch that I have known some of them, who thought they might look for a hanging from their own commanders at their return for their irregular going out, and adventured the cutting of their throats, by the enemy, in their going out ; yet stuck not to rove into an enemy's quarter two or three miles, in hope only to pillage some rotten house-hold stuff ; and I saw one of them returning with a feather-bed on his back, all that way, in the extremity of hot weather, that was not worth ten shillings when he had it home." The " Admiral," upon hearing this, says he thinks these good fellows should have some allowance of pillage granted while they are in his Ma-

jesty's service, and the " Captain " replies, " I would so
indeed, for I am sure that it would not only whet their
stomachs to the service, but to the fighting that belongs
to the service." He explains that the pillage he advocates would extend only to properties found " betwixt
the decks."

A strong characteristic of the sailor was noted both
by Pepys and Boteler. It was the very conservative
liking which he commonly displayed for any good things
he had been accustomed to, and his suspicion of changes
which he thought might deprive him of any fancied
advantage he enjoyed. These were things that touched
him very narrowly. He had no love for new-fangled
inventions, and resented anything that might diminish
his rights or privileges in the way of good beef or pork, or
" Poor John," deep potations of beer, and later on liberal
allowances of undiluted rum. The King's service might be
reckoned worse than galley slavery by some, but set the
seaman ashore, and it was seldom long before he was found
turning to the salt sea once more. He was no epicure,
and sad experience had taught him both the value of
substantial food and that they did not pipe to dinner on
land. The victualling question was always with him.
Even want of pay affected him less. Famine did not
reign in all the King's ships at all times, and there was
generally enough of salt beef, pork, and fish, to be
washed down with ample potations of small beer. The
excessive eating of salt food was known to be a chief
cause of disease, but the men were not to be deprived
of what they liked, and in these matters were much
opposed to change. Monson had noted the fact, and
Pepys, writing in his minute book many years later,
said, " Englishmen, and more especially seamen, love
their bellies above everything else, and therefore it must
always be remembered, in the management of the victualling of the navy, that to make any abatement from
them in the quantity or agreeableness of the victuals,
is to discourage and provoke them in the tenderest point,
and will sooner render them disgusted with the King's

service than any other hardship that could be put
upon them." The "Admiral" who, in Boteler's Dialogues, discusses this matter with the "Sea Captain,"
propounds the notion that the feeding of the mariners
might be assimilated "to the manner of foreign parts."
The "Captain" assents, saying that excessive eating of
salt meats at sea "is questionless one main cause that our
English are so subject to calentures, scarbots, and the like
contagious diseases above all other nations." He would
have them imitate the Dutch by consuming less flesh
and fish, and more "pease, beans, wheat, flour, butter,
cheese, and those white meats (as they are called)."
But the "Admiral" remarks that "the difficulty con-
sisteth in that the common seamen with us are so bessotted
on their beef and pork as they had rather adventure on all
the calentures and scarbots in the world than to be weaned
from their customary diet, or so much as to lose the least
bit of it."

We are indebted to Richard Braithwaite, the satirical
author of "Drunken Barnaby's Journal," "A Strappado
for the Devil," and other literary slashes at society,
for a very remarkable character sketch of the sailor,
which appears in his volume entitled "Whimzies,"
1631, wherein, under an alphabetical arrangement, all
manner of persons are described with wit and significance.*
He tells us of the mariner's carelessness of danger, or
rather his insensibility to it. "The bredth of an inch-
boord is betwixt him and drowning, yet hee swears and
drinks as deeply as if hee were a fathom from it. His
familiarity with death and danger hath armed him with
a kind of dissolute security against any encounter."
Braithwaite had seen the seaman ashore, more often
than afloat, and he depicts him as a deep drinker. "The
sea cannot roar more abroad than hee within, fire him but
with liquor. He is as watchfull as a crane in a storme,

* This is an exceedingly rare volume, not to be found in the
British Museum, the London Library, or the Guildhall Collection. It
has been sought for in the Cambridge University Library and elsewhere, but we are indebted for a sight of it to Messrs. Pickering and
Chatto, of the Haymarket.

and as secure as a dormouse in a calme." Again he
says, " He must feede his valour with the liquid spirit
of some piercing elixir, and thus hee ducks and dives
out of his time like a true didapper." * To this character
of the seaman Braithwaite recurs a few sentences further
on. " He ever takes worst rest when hee goes to bed
most sober. Hee will domineere furiously in the height
of his potation, but hee is quickly cudgell'd out of that
humour by the master of the house of correction. Hee
has coasted many countreys, arrived in sundry havens,
sojourned in flourishing cities, and conversed with various
sorts of people ; yet call him to account, and you shall
find him the most unfruitfull'st navigatour that ere you
conversed with." Evidently Braithwaite had not heard
many of those travellers' tales, for which seamen then
and afterwards have been famed, and he proceeds :
" Deepe drinkers have ever shallow memories ; hee can
remember nothing more precisely than the great vessel
at Heidelberg ; affairs of state are above his sconce.
It is his best arithmetick to remember his month's pay ;
and if necessitie urge him not, he would scarcely thinke
on that either."

In another place Braithwaite refers to the hardihood
of the seaman, which has attracted the attention of
other writers. " Hee makes small or no choice of his
pallet ; he can sleepe as well on a sacke of pumice as a
pillow of doune." And then attention is drawn to his
roughness : " He was never acquainted with much
civilitie ; the sea has taught him other rhetoriche.
Compassionate himselfe he could never much and much
less another. He has condition'd with the sea not to
make him sicke ; and it is the best of his conceite to
jeere at a queasie stomache. He is more active than
contemplative, unless he turn astronomer, and that is
only in cases of extremity. Hee is most constant to his
shirt, and other his seldome wash'd linnen. Hee has
been so long acquainted with surges of the sea, as too
long a calme distempers him. He cannot speake low,

* Didapper, the Little Grebe or other small diving bird.

the sea talks so loud. His advice is seldom taken in naval affaires; though his hand is strong, his head-peece is stupid." But Braithwaite knew the value of the man. " He is used therefore as a necessary instrument of action; for hee can spinne up a rope like a spider and down again like lightning. The rope is his roade, and the top-mast his beacon. One would think his body were wounded, for he weares pitch-cloath upon it; but that is invulnerable, unlesse a bullet casually finds out a loope-hole and that quite ripps up his saile-cloath. He partakes much of the chameleon, when hee is mounted the top-mast, where the ayre is his diet-bread. His visage is an unchangable varnish; neither can winde pierce it, nor sunne parch it. . . . What a starveling hee is in a frosty morning with his sea frocke, which seemes as it were shrunke from him and groune too short, but it will be long enough ere hee get another."

Braithwaite also tells us of the seaman as a fighter and some of the things that impelled him to fight. " Hee loves to fish in troubled waters, have an oare in any man's boate, and to breake the tenth commandment is the conclusion of his luke warme prayer. Hey for a rich prize ! . . . He is of a phlegmatick, watry constitution; very little sanguine, unless it bee in a sea fight, wherein, though he expect no honour, he expresseth some flying sparkes of valour, in hope to become sharer in a pyraticall treasure." We have heard a great deal of the vile food of the seamen, and how much store they set upon their beef, pork, and " Poor John." Braithwaite remarks of the seaman : " He hath an invincible stomach, which ostridge-like could well-neare digest iron. Hee is very seldome subject to surfet, or shortens the dayes of his watry pilgrimage with excesse, unless it fall out upon rifling of wines, that he endanger his top-saile with an over-charge."

We are told also of the brotherhood of the sea, and the strong bond of its comradeship. " Hee is many times so long on sea, as hee forgets his friends by land. Associats hee has, and those so constantly cleaving,

H

as one voice commands all. Starres cannot bee more
faithfull in their society than these Hans-kins in their
fraternity. They will brave it valiantly when they
are ranked together, and relate their adventures with
wonderfull terror. Yet these relations ever halt through
want of learning, which defect abridgeth the story of
their deserving. Necessary instruments they are, and
agents of maine importance in that Hydrarchy wherein
they live ; for the walles of their State could not subsist
without them ; but least usefull they are to themselves,
and most needfull of others supportance. They taste
of all waters and all weathers ; onely the gale of pros-
peritie seldome breathes on their sailes ; neither care
they much for any such companion."

It is not without regret that we find Braithwaite—
who evidently wrote with deep sympathy for the sailor's
suffering, and his little reward for his labours—unable to
discern earnestness in the mariner's devotion. " In
a tempest you shall heare him pray, but so amethodically,
as it argues that hee is seldome vers'd in that practice.
Feare is the principall motive of his devotion ; yet I am
pursuaded, for forme sake, he shews more than hee
feeles." And the following is the characteristic conclusion of this sketch of the mariners as Braithwaite
saw them. " They sleepe without feare of losing what
they enjoy ; and in enjoying little, they share in the
lesse burden of cares. Yet it is much to be wondered
at, that our sayler should have such frequent occasions
to erect his eye upward, and retain such servile dejected
thoughts inward. He converseth with the starres,
observes their motions, and by them directs his com-
passe. Singular notions derives hee from them ; meane
time he is blind to Him that made them. He sliceth
the depths, and is ignorant of Him that confines them ;
he cutteth the surging swelling waves, and thinks not of
Him that restraines them ; hee coasteth by the shelfes,
and forgets Him that secures him. True is that maxime ;
Custome takes away the apprehension of passion. In
the infancy of his profession, there appeared not a

billow before his eyes which conveyed not a feare unto
his heart. Numerous perils has hee now passed, hourely
objects of approaching danger are presented. Yet
these as well as those equally sleighted. Death hee has
seene in so many shapes, as it cannot amaze him, appear
it never so terrible unto him. Yet needs must that
enemy affright him against whom hee comes, for whom
hee was never provided before hee came. Well : suppose
him now drawing towards the port where all mortalities
must land. He has tugged long enough upon the maine,
he must now gather up his vessel within the haven. He
has drawne in his sayles, and taken adew of the sea ;
unlesse she shew him so much kindnesse, as to receive
him into her briny bosome, and intombe him dying,
whome she entertained living ; which courtesie if she
tender him, the wormes are deceived by him, for hee
goes not the way of all flesh, but the way of all fish,
whose fry feedes on him, as their forefathers fed him."
Such is the seaman as presented to us by one who had
penetrated at least one side of the seaman's individuality,
describing it in a whimsical manner, and closing with the
pathetic end of his ill-rewarded labours.

These remarks upon the seaman's hard lot and the end
to which it tended, bring us to the consideration of
another remarkable characteristic of the old mariners,
which is to be noted in their conduct and in the pages
of literature. It is a certain political earnestness which
they displayed upon some occasions, combined with
strong religious fervour, which was spread abroad through
the fleet, though it certainly was not universal. Puritanism, which had so deeply affected the life of the people,
did not leave the Navy unchanged, and the civil antagonisms which divided the nation into two camps
awoke controversies in the King's ships also, both in
the ports and at sea. Batten, surveyor of the Navy,
described as an " obscure fellow " by Clarendon, did
much to bring over the Navy to the Parliament, and
Warwick, appointed commander-in-chief, busied himself
in removing the Royalist officers in 1642. There were

some seamen who conceived a high dignity in their duties to the King, and afterwards to the Commonwealth and the State, or who attempted to reconcile the realities of rebellion with protestations of loyalty to the " Lord's anointed." Many of them were from the Eastern Counties, and being of serious purpose and devout mind, brought a new temper into the ships akin to the temper of Cromwell. Prayer was said twice daily—before dinner, and again the after psalm sung at setting the evening watch, and any man absent was liable to spend twenty-four hours in irons. Swearing was punished by three knocks on the forehead with the boatswain's whistle, and smoking was forbidden anywhere but on the upper deck, and that sparingly, by the bilboes.

Seamen played a conspicuous part in the political changes of the Civil War, the Commonwealth, and the Restoration. Those who came forward to protest were probably not representative, in a strict sense, of their comrades, but undoubtedly there were in the Navy many men who felt that they had some conscience in what they did. They were of a " new model " also, and knew well the importance of their service. When Charles attempted to arrest the Five Members in 1642 many of them came " above bridge," and appeared amongst the excited crowds at Westminster. Their action was afterwards misconstrued, and the " Seamen's Protestation," which was printed in explanation, was a remarkable document, showing political zeal combined with a devout tone of mind. They said that their protest was against the arbitrary power of the Crown, and in loyal defence of King and Parliament. " In vain it is for us to keep the narrow seas, if some go the way to lose the land. . . . Be pleased to understand, although we have no churches, we say our prayers as well as you, and the same God you have at shore is ours at sea ; Whom we will serve, though not so decentlie as we would, being for the most part of our days restrained from a church, to dwell upon the seas for your better securitie. For, be it well known, your safety consists in ours ;

your churches, aye, and houses too, would quickly
fall and be in the dust, should we let pass those who long
to prey upon your lives and fortunes. But, for our
religion, king, and country, we do, and will, advance
our colours against the world." The concluding words
are remarkable : " Now what remains, but that on our
knees we send up our prayers to that great Pilot of
Heaven and Earth, who steers the world with his finger,
that he would protect and defend her to His own glory
and our comfort; so shall our King be safe and firm in
his throne while his religion flourishes and his subjects
peacefully live smiling under his sceptre: to the eternell
disgrace and shame of those who would intend to sub-
vert our proceedings." *

So much, then, for the seriously minded seaman ashore.
Now let us, about the year 1657, go on board the *Bristol*,
frigate, a 56-gun fourth-rate, in which Teonge, twenty
years later, was chaplain. We do so in company with
Thomas Lurting, whose " Fighting Sailor turn'd Peace-
able Christian, manifested in the Convincement and Con-
version of Thomas Lurting, with a short relation of
many great Dangers and wonderful Deliverances he
met withal," was published in 1710, and again in 1713.
This Lurting, after serving for some time, joined the
much-persecuted sect of the Quakers, who then commonly
refused to bear arms, and when conviction grew strong
upon him and his associates, they were in a strange place
on board a ship of war. Lurting tells us that in 1646,
being then of the age of fourteen, he was impressed, and
carried to Ireland, where he served two years in the time
of the Long Parliament, after which he arrived in London,
and then engaged in the wars with the Dutch and
Spaniards. He was turned over to the *Bristol*, in which

* "The Seamen's Protestation, concerning their Ebbing and
Flowing to and from the Parliament House at Westminster upon
Tuesday, the 11th January, 1642. Ordered by the Vice-Admiral to
be published and set forth through the whole Kingdom, as a manifestation of the Seamen's Loyaltie to their King and love to their
country." London, printed by B. A. 1642. In Granville Penn's
" Life of Sir William Penn," the " Protestation " is printed in full.

ship, he says, in process of time, it pleased God to convert him. He was a boatswain's mate, and was responsible for about two hundred men. It was his business to see that they were present at time of worship, and he was very diligent in that duty, compelling them by force when they refused to obey. Lurting gives a striking description of Blake's action at Santa Cruz, and records four several deliverances from peril within the space of six hours, for which he thanks God.

There came on board the *Bristol* a certain soldier who had been at a Quakers' meeting in Scotland, and two young men, who conversed with him, were converted to his belief, so that very soon there was a little band of Quakers on board, who suffered much at the hands of their comrades, including Lurting himself. The boatswain's mate avers that the captain of the *Bristol* was a Baptist preacher, and was much troubled by the increase in the number of Quakers in the ship. The chaplain, whom Lurting speaks of as the priest, called out to him, " O, Thomas, an honest man and a good Christian ! Here is a dangerous people on board, a blasphemous people, denying the ordinances and word of God." Thus exhorted, Lurting gave many a buffet to the offending sectaries. But his own conscience was greatly troubled, and soon he, too, listened to the converse of these men, and joined their meetings, whereupon a great noise was heard in the ship, with much bustle, and the captain was informed that Lurting was among the Quakers. The chaplain, he says, reproached him bitterly, while the captain turned over the Bible from end to end to prove that the Quakers were no Christians. Others became convinced, nevertheless, and in less than six months the little band of Quakers comprised twelve men and two boys. A serious distemper broke out on board, which led to an interchange of good offices, and Lurting says that the captain was very kind to him and ordered him a hammock. " And now all was very quiet, no persecution, but a general love amongst all sorts of perswasions that were on board, and truth had great dominion and several were convinced." Such was the atmosphere on board the *Bristol* under the command of Blake.

Up to this time the Quakers had not manifested any objection to fighting, though they had refused all share of plunder, and the captain told a brother captain that he would not care if all his men were Quakers, "for they were the hardiest men in his ship." But this state of contentment soon gave place to a good deal of wrangling, and there were clearly scoffers in the ship's company who had no liking for their Quaker shipmates. The *Bristol* was ordered from Leghorn to Barcelona to take or burn a Spanish man-of-war which was lying there, and Lurting says the Quakers fought with as much courage as any. "But He that hath all men's hearts in His hand, can turn them at His pleasure; yea, He in a minute's time so chang'd my heart, that in a minute before, I setting my whole strength and rigor to kill and destroy men's lives, in a minute after I could not kill or destroy a man, if it were to gain the whole world; for as I was coming out of the fore-castle door, to see where the shot fell, the word of the Lord ran through me, How if I had killed a man!" Upon this, serious doubt fell upon the Quakers on board, and they deliberated what they should do. At last one of them, taking his courage in his hands, went to the captain, saying he could fight no longer. "Then," exclaimed the captain decisively, "he that denies to fight in time of engagement I will put my sword in his guts." "Then," said the Friends, "thou wilt be a manslayer, and guilty of shedding blood." Upon which the captain beat the offending man sorely with his cane and fist, and, says Lurting, bitterly or sarcastically, "he was Baptist preacher!"

Thereafter the captain became the enemy of the Quakers, and left it open for any other man to kill them, for Lurting tells us a printed order was fixed up in the ship, saying, "If any man flinch from his quarters in time of engagement, any may kill him." Not long afterwards the *Bristol* was cruising off Leghorn, and a ship was sighted which was thought to be a Spanish man-of-war. Orders were immediately issued to make sail and clear for action, much to the consternation of the Quakers, who debated amongst themselves what they should do, and again a man went to the captain and said, " I can fight no more." At this the captain became greatly enraged, and seizing the Quaker's cap threw it overboard, grasped the man by his collar, beat him with his heavy cane, and dragged him down to his quarters. Overcome with passion, he called for his sword, apparently with intent to kill the man, but Lurting went towards him, and the captain, relenting, turned away. According to Lurting's account, before night the captain sent the priest to him, and desired him not to be angry, and from this time forward was very kind to him. Fortunately for the Quakers, the ship in sight proved not to be an enemy. It is worth while to observe that Philemon Bacon, captain of the *Bristol*, was killed in the Four Days' Battle in 1666. After the trouble on board Lurting left the fleet, but has several other episodes to recount of being pressed, and of the things he said to the captains and officers as to his unwillingness either to fight or do anything that might conduce to fighting. He seems to have served no more.

Before we leave the seaman, with all his character of hardihood, sentiment, superstition, and intermittent fervour, we shall extract from the pages of Ned Ward and Barnaby Slush what they had to say about him. Both of them were in keen sympathy with his sufferings, and were loud exponents of his deserts, and in proclaiming his virtues, rude and rough as they were, they undoubtedly did some wrong to many officers who were not so black as they were painted. Ned Ward avowedly wrote his book " to draw the picture of the most Glorious Piece of the Creation called a Tar," and now, at last, we may quote the scurrilous writer with some measure of satisfaction. He describes the seaman as a " sharp blade," if kept whetted with good diet, but bad usage made him dull and lazy. " But his laziness does not so

much proceed from his disposition as his disgust, for he
has been a pretty active fellow, and would be so still,
were he but fairly dealt with ; but a pox on't, cries he,
the useful cur's made to turn the spit, while my lady's
lap-dog runs away with the roast meat. . . . He can no
more sleep in sheets than in a horse pond, and put him
into a feather-bed, he shall fancy he's sinking streight,
and fall to swimming all weathers, but sling him up in
a hammock, and he shall lie a whole night as dormant as
Mahomet hanging betwixt two load-stones. His chief
station is that hill of Parnassus, the forecastle ; here he
and his brother jacks lie pelting each other with sea wit,
and toss jests and oaths about as thick and fast as boys
do squibs on a coronation day." Ward goes on to speak
of his bravery. " He looks the most formidable when
others appear most drooping ; for see him in bad weather,
in his fur-cap and Wapping large watch-coat, and you'd
swear the Czar was returned once more from Muscovy ;
and yet he is never in his true figure but within a pitch't
jacket, and then he's as invulnerable to a cudgel as a
hog in armour." The liquor he most loved was " flip,"
and he thought of the pay-day more than of the day of
judgment. At last it came, and brought him a whole
hatful of money. " If he be sober at that juncture he
is damnably puzzled in contriving the ways and means
how to spend it, but if, as he commonly is, deviled with
flip, he scorns to spend one thought upon the matter,
but straight while 'tis yet warm in his cap, fairly sits
down to the cards or hazard, and generally throws it all
away before sunset." His qualities, the satirist says,
were evoked by honest commanders, but he often received more knocks than money. He did not know
right from left, but he would always answer to starboard or port, and he was stiff-necked, loving his honour
" like roast beef," and was ready to spend his blood upon
any quarrelsome occasion. " In fine, take this same
blunt sea-animal, by and large, in his tar-jacket, and
wide-kneed trowzers, and you'll find him of more in-
trinsick value to the nation than the most fluttering

beau in it ; and yet he is infinitely short of what he has
been in days of yore, when partiality and self-interest
were less in fashion."

Barnaby Slush tells us that the true and active mariners
were not to be decoyed by bounty, for "it's not money
so much as fair usage that has the strongest influence
over them." He says they were men of spirit, ready to
throw up two or three years' pay because of an unhand-
some drubbing, and were the very life and soul of the
Navy. They are men of independent character, setting
little store by what they earned, that he brings before
us, " for ships, like animate bodies, are more or less
strong, vigorous and nimble just in proportion to the
goodness or vivacity of the internal agent. A stout,
hearty, and active crew give life and spirit to the ship,
to the guns, to everything ; it is these strike terror in an
enemy and baffle the united force of the seas and tempests." The man is truly more than the machine, and
this old writer, satirist as he was, spoke well when he
enforced the value of the man behind the gun. He added
that it was a task worthy of the best inquiries to discover the most proper, just, and conducive ways of
manning ships of war, and made some suggestions with
that object. He spoke of the discouragement and indifferent prospects of the seaman in ships of war, who
rather than remain subject to bad usage, would " choose
to fall in with the merchant service, where it is not barely
the freedom or the good peck met with there that draws
'em, but 'tis mainly the charming prospect of becoming
in a short period mate or gunner, or the like officer aboard
these vessels, by which they stand fair in rising to be
commander." The expectations of those who were attracted to the Navy were dashed by those who tried the
experiment, and who cried, " 'Tis all castles in the air,
Jack ; thou must go three years apprentice to the
keeper of Newgate, and be a tolerable proficient in
Legerdemain and Wheedle before ever thou canst worm
thyself into anything there, Bo ! "

With regard to severity of punishments, Barnaby

Slush did not harangue against the cat or attempt to prove the cudgel an unlawful weapon, saying severity was reasonable when it was just, for it was the very life of discipline, but he charges the officers with injustice. " Pique, revenge, rage, drink, everything but reason, shall again and again hurry on a young hair-brain'd Jack-Pudding to a-thrashing the fellows like dogs or stock-fish." The men detested partiality in punishment. " No one grumbles at his lot in an engagement nor curseth the bullet that unlegs him, because all on board were alike exposed to misfortune." Next Barnaby Slush has a thrust at the doctors. " Where one jolly tar has been cut off by a cannon ball, at least two have been swept away by ignorant or infamous practices."

But the note we like to find in this sea-cook is that of real admiration for the jolly tar, who was not to be reduced to water drinking so long as other liquors could be had for credit or money, " for liquor is the very cement that keeps the mariner's body and soul together." However the seaman might suffer, " yet bring him but once into play again, his native warmth and resolution shall, in spite of all past vows, hurry him on to action, and he shall fall to and with that eager ardour and hearty goodwill, as if all was to be his own that he fought for." But this is not all. " There is a certain daringness of spirit in a British mariner, proper and natural, as is that of our mastiffs, a kind of natural haughtiness which eminently distinguishes him from the rest of men. A courage so inherent, so strongly seated, that I have actually seen a ship's crew, though notoriously wronged the preceding day, yet one and all run and beg and stickle to make one of the number to go upon a skirmish in the boats, and those that were excluded have appeared more nettled at this undesigned affront (as they thought) than ever they seemed to be for the most palpable injustice." He adds significantly : " But good mariners grow not up like mushrooms, without care or culture. It is morally impossible, nay, and it's naturally impossible, too, to have a brave, active, skilful, resolute, body of sailors without just and generous as well as understanding officers." So convinced was this old writer of the influence of good officers that he said it wholly lay in a captain's power " to have alway his complement, nay, and double his complement, without ever a pressed man among 'em."

To this account of the seaman we may append some notes upon the seaman's friend, the chaplain, who occupied a somewhat uncertain place in the ship's hierarchy. Something depended, no doubt, upon the chaplains themselves, and Pocock, chaplain of the *Ranelagh*, in 1704, says he had a cabin, or at least that he slept in the master's cabin, and again that he removed out of the admiral's cabin and hung up a hammock in that of the lieutenant. Chaplains at one time were paid like surgeons out of deductions made from the monthly wage of seamen, the chaplain receiving a groat and the surgeon twopence in respect of each man. Teonge had been in a very impoverished condition when he joined the *Assistance* in 1675, with a poor wardrobe, part of which he had had to pawn in order to get himself a small sea bed, pillow, blanket, and rug, and he thanks Providence in his diary for having put into his hands a ragged towel, which he found on the quarter-deck, " a piece of an old sayle, and an earthen chamber pott." We thus see that Pocock was in a better position than Teonge had been, and no doubt the conditions of life on board had improved within the thirty years that had elapsed between the dates of their service.

In company with naval chaplains of this period we shall now go on board certain ships of war in order to witness some characteristic features of naval life at the time. When Chaplain Teonge dropped down the Thames in the *Assistance* in 1675, he pictured a good deal of drunkenness and suggested immorality on board. The seamen's wives and sweethearts were there, for it was no uncommon thing for women to be carried in ships—at least, in coastwise passages. Teonge tells us that punch and brandy were drunk, and that the song " Loath

to depart " was sung, * the result of the excesses being
that " our ship was that night well furnished, but ill-
man'd, few of them being able to keepe watch, had there
beene occasion." The chaplain preached his first sermon
on shipboard in a rolling sea, and remarks that " all our
women and olde seamen were sick this day." Arriving
at Dover, the last of the women were sent on shore,
saluted by " 3 cheares, 7 gunns, and our trumpetts
sounding." The captain was something of a fire-eater,
for it was the custom to make Dutch men-of-war " vail
their bonnets," but he was not well pleased when they
did so, and Teonge could not forget his words : " I wish
I could meete with one that would not vaile his bonnett,
that I might make worke for my brethren at White
Hall "—meaning officers out of employment who would
find service in war. The chaplain tells us of bowls of
punch being drunk round the ship, and on one occasion
remarks : " Nothing to-day, but drinke to our friends
in England in racckee at night." He describes punishments that have been referred to, and others, but generally we find a note of jollity contrasted with the grim
consequences of famine and disease. On Christmas Day,
in 1675, Teonge records as follows : " At 4 in the morning
our trumpeters all doe flatt their trumpetts and begin at
our captain's cabin, and thence to all the officers' and
gentlemen's cabins, playing a levite at each cabine doore,
and bidding good-morrow, wishing a merry Christmas."
Then they went to the poop and sounded three " levites "
in honour of the morning, and after prayers the captain
and officers went to dinner, " where wee had excellent
good fayre ; a ribb of beife, plumb puddings, minct pyes,
etc., and plenty of good wines of severall sorts ; dranke
healths to the King, to our wives and friends, and ended
the day with much civill myrth."

Contrasted with this enjoyment there are frequent
entries in the diary of men buried at sea, generally several
in each month. One was " little better than starved to
death with cold weather," and another " 'tis said eaten

* See page 430.

to death with lyce." Men were sent on shore, " pittifull creatures," and there was great hardship in bad weather. These latter notes refer to Teonge's service in the *Royal Oak*, 1679.

Another chaplain, the Rev. Richard Allyn, of the *Centurion*, 1691–2, describes the terrible conditions on board in a gale of wind. He tells us how the men, whom he calls " puggs," were variously affected, some praying, but more of them cursing and swearing louder than wind and weather. George, the caulker, fell upon his marrow-bones and cried for mercy, while another man rated him soundly for his cowardice. " Poor George, thus disturbed at his devotion, would look over his shoulder, and, at the end of every petition, would make answer to old Robin with a ' God d—n you, you old dog ! can't you let a body pray at quiet for you, ha ? A plague rot you ! Let me alone, can't ye ? ' Thus the one kept praying and cursing, and t'other railing for half an hour, when a great log of wood, by the rowling of the ship, tumbled upon George's legs, and bruised him a little ; which George, taking up into his hands, and thinking it had been thrown at him by old Robin, let fly at the old fellow, together with an whole broadside of oaths and curses, and so they fell to boxing." Parson Allyn tells us he mentions this incident only to show " the incorrigible senselessness of such tarpawlin wretches in the greatest extremity of danger."

CHAPTER V

THE EIGHTEENTH CENTURY

FROM ROOKE TO NELSON

IN the two chapters which precede this we have made acquaintance with the officers of the King's ships as they walked the quarter-deck, and with the men of the same ships as they worked on the forecastle and the lower deck, under the Commonwealth, in the Restoration period and a little later. We have found the seamen of bold and independent temperament, never failing in courage, never shrinking from peril or hardship, but resenting unfair treatment and the cruelties of which they were the victims. How they broke the boom and burnt the galleons at Vigo in one of the hottest fights ever fought, and what were their services with Rooke and Shovell in the capture of Gibraltar and the defeat of the French off Malaga we know. What they thought of the captains who deserted Benbow we can imagine. How they perished in hundreds in the great storm of 1707 is one of the saddest passages in our naval history. Combined with a quality of earnestness in these men there was a carelessness of many things that others set great store upon. The mariner was a guileless being, and often the prey of men less honest than himself. He was a good comrade, and never forsook a friend in distress. Regardless of his sufferings, he was a gay and jovial soul, spoken of as the jolly tar, fond of his glass, indulging too much, and often pictured to us as a dissolute person by those who saw him ashore, in his

worst moments, when he was but newly arrived from
long absence at sea, and who never knew his qualities
afloat.

We shall now see how these characteristics, or at least
some of them, were manifested by the men of certain
privateers in 1708-9. Captain Woodes Rogers, who made
a voyage round the world in those years, was a notable
seaman and a man of skill, character, and resolution—
the same who discovered Alexander Selkirk on the island
of Juan Fernandez, thus suggesting to Defoe the character of Robinson Crusoe, which will ever live in our
literature. The Journal of Woodes Rogers, Master
Mariner, was published in 1712, and has been made
known more recently in a volume entitled " Life Aboard
a British Privateer in the Reign of Queen Anne," by
Robert C. Leslie, of which a second edition appeared in
1894. The *Duke* and *Duchess*, privateer ships, set out
from Bristol on 2nd August, 1708, with other vessels
bound for the Cove of Cork. Arrived at that place to
victual and ship additional mariners, Woodes Rogers
notes the strange behaviour of his men in the fact " that
they were continually marrying while we stayed there
though expected to sail immediately." They were not
all Englishmen. A Dane who was on board was united
by an Irish priest to an Irish woman, though neither
understood a word of the other's language, and they had
to use an interpreter. " Yet I perceived this pair seem'd
more afflict'd at separation than any of the rest. The
fellow continu'd melancholy for several days after we
went to sea." When the time came later on for parting
company with certain men-of-war, it became necessary
to acquaint the men with the fact, in order that, while
in company with one of his Majesty's ships, any mal-
contents might be exchanged into her. But, says Rogers,
confirming what Barnaby Slush said at about the same
period, with the exception of one fellow " who expected
to have been made tithing man in his parish that year,"
all hands were satisfied, and even the discontented
tithing man became reconciled when asked to join hands

at the grog tub in drinking to a good voyage. They did not like the King's ships, because in them were more hardships, less pay, and fewer prospects of loot. When they approached Cape Horn it was observed that there was but a slender stock of liquor on board, and that the men were meanly clad. "Yet good liquor to sailors," says Woodes Rogers, "is preferable to clothing." The jollity of the men was displayed when they "passed the tropick," and took tribute according to custom of those who had not done so before. Rogers describes what happened. The men were hoisted half-way up to the yard by a rope running through a block on the main yard, and thence they were let fall into the water, "having a thick cross thro' their legs, and well fastened to the rope, that they might not be surprised and let go their hold." He humorously remarks that this ducking proved of great use to his fresh-water sailors "to recover the colour of their skins, which were grown very black and nasty." About sixty were ducked after this manner three times, while others paid a half-crown fine.

When the circumnavigators under Woodes Rogers were at Angre de Reys they attended an important religious function or, as he calls it, an "entertainment." We are bidden to see them in a very gay and sprightly mood, where the spirit of the seaman came out predominantly. The Governor desired them to take part in the ceremony, whatever it may have been. Accordingly ten of them, with two trumpets and a hautboy, were present at the church music, the singing being performed by the fathers. "Our musick played 'Hey, boys, up go we!' and all manner of noisy paltry tunes." By this time the musicians were more than half drunk, and we are told that they marched at the head of the company. After them came the religious procession, followed by certain dignitaries, including the Governor of the town, Captain Woodes Rogers, and Captain Courtney, "with each of us a long wax candle lighted." They were splendidly entertained by the fathers, whom they afterwards welcomed on board the *Duke*. Thus Woode

Rogers describes what happened: "They were very merry, and in their cups propos'd the Pope's health. But we were quits with 'em by toasting the Archbishop of Canterbury; and to keep up the humour, we also proposed William Penn's health, and they liked the liquor so well that they refused neither." The weather becoming rather bad, the whole company remained on board for the night, not being landed until the next morning, when, says Rogers, " we saluted 'em with a huzza from each ship."

Unfortunately, we have few vigorous eye-witnesses to describe for us the life and the actions of seamen in those times. No brilliant pen brings before us the gallant fellows who fought with Commodore Wager, with Whitaker and Norris, with Dursley and Riddell, all officers who knew how to lead the bold men who followed them. After the Peace of Utrecht in 1713 the Navy fell to what is commonly regarded as its lowest ebb. The early part of the century was characterised by much brutality, by a lowering of the standard of conduct, and by a stronger tendency to the setting of private interest above public duty. The discipline was still barbarous, but the captains, brutal as some of them were, were mostly real seamen. Nevertheless, there was little upon which the Navy could congratulate itself, and, with the exception of Anson's great voyage, it did little that was worthy of its history in the seventeenth century until after the middle of the eighteenth. It was in that strange world that Smollett found several of its most extraordinary characters, and in fiction, as we shall see, throws vivid light upon the personal and social life of the Navy at the time. Captain Stephen Martin-Leake, writing to a friend in January, 1729, suggests a picture of the seaman ashore in a description of Portsmouth and the vicinity, referring to houses of entertainment for seamen, of which many were at Portsmouth Point. " It (the Point) has one good street through the middle, from the Point Gate to the water side, is full built, and very populous and thriving, being the Wapping of Portsmouth. Here the Johns carouse, not being confined to hours, and spend their money for the good of the public, which makes ale houses and shops thrive mightily upon this spot. Some have compared it with the Point at Jamaica, that was swallowed up by an earthquake, and think, if that was Sodom, this is Gomorrah ; but it is by no means so bad as some would make it, though bad enough."

There were, of course, men of honour and credit in the service then, as at all other times, and Anson himself, Sir Chaloner Ogle, Lord Aubrey Beauclerc and Captain James Cornwall, who was killed in Mathews's action, are types of the best. Great professional jealousy existed, and there were many quarrels with the soldiers. Smollett, in his sober account of the expedition against Cartagena, has drawn a dreadful picture of the sufferings of the seamen that resulted. " They were destitute of surgeons, nurses, cooks, and proper provisions ; they were pent upon between decks in small vessels, where they had not room to sit upright ; they wallowed in filth, myriads of maggots were hatched in the putrefaction of their sores, which had no other dressing than that of being washed by themselves with their own allowance of brandy ; and nothing was heard but groans, lamentations, and the language of despair invoking death to deliver them from their misery."

It is not surprising to find at such a period a surgeon of the Navy, John Atkins, who was the author of a book entitled " The Navy-Surgeon ; or a Practical System of Surgery," 1737, offering some reflections upon the disadvantages of the naval career. This he does in a volume which describes events and observations made during " A Voyage to Guiana, Brasil and the West Indies in his Majesty's ships the *Swallow* and *Weymouth*," published in 1735. Thus he writes : " The man whose means of subsistence irreversibly depends on the sea, is unhappy, because he forsakes his proper element, his wife, children, country and friends, all that can be called pleasant (and of necessity, not choice) to tempt unknown dangers on that unknown, deceitful, trackless path ; lee shores, tempests, wants of some kind or other, bad winds, or the rougher passions of ourselves, are continually molesting ; and if common danger under one adopted parent (Neptune) does not always unite us, yet we are still cooped up like fowls to the same diet and associates. And to compleat our ill luck, while we are contending with sinister Fate, the rogues at home perhaps are stealing away the hearts of our mistresses and wives. Are not these a hapless race thus doomed ? " Nevertheless, we may observe that Atkins was only expressing one aspect of naval life in these reflections, for in his descriptions we find " the bowl unflung," and hear the clinking of glasses and the echoes of song. " How happy were we when the wind blew abaft ! " When they left Spithead, he tells us they saw those appearances in the sky which were called *capræ saltantes*, and by the sailors morris dancers. We seem to perceive that the Navy surgeon was inclined, like Captain Luke Foxe at an earlier time, to cast on occasions a sly shaft at the scientific seaman. On one " cheerful evening " off the coast of Brazil, they were surprised by an unexpected event, the moon becoming totally eclipsed, but when she recovered her light, he says humorously, " we repeated our sacrifice in bowls, and fell into reflections and admiration of that Power which supports the regularity of the planetary motions, and the sublimity of that art which can so exactly calculate them ! "

The Navy did not then stand apart from other elements of sea life as it does in these days. Officers and men passed from the Navy to the merchant service, or came from the merchant service to the fleet. Often they took part in smuggling, and not seldom served in privateers. Smollett has given a gloomy picture of the sufferings of seamen on active service ; Atkins suggests their loneliness and echoes their gaiety. Now we may contrast the melancholy account given by the sea novelist, as serious historian, with the narrative of another great novelist when he, too, was recording facts Fielding makes many. allusions to the sea in his novels, but he never showed any

real knowledge of what seamen were until he wrote his
" Account of a Voyage to Lisbon," 1754, and we have
seen that he therein gibes at the naval captain as an
arrogant autocrat. But, in the same book, the author
of " Tom Jones " presents a far more pleasing picture
of one Richard Veal, who was master of the *Queen of
Portugal*, the vessel in which the novelist voyaged to
Lisbon in declining health at the close of his life.

Veal was a man of thirty years' experience, part of it
in command of a privateer, and was such a man, we may
be sure, as would often be found in ships of war. " He
acted the part of a father to his sailors ; he expressed
great tenderness for any of them when ill, and never
suffered the least work of supererogation to go un-
rewarded by a glass of gin. He even extended his
humanity, if I may so call it, to animals, and even his
cats and kittens had large shares in his affections."
Nevertheless, his knowledge of the sea service had given
Veal an insight into the character of seamen, and when
wind-bound in harbour, he had the greatest reluctance
to sending a boat ashore, because he knew it was easier
to land his men than recall them. When he was off the
coast of Devon, he " dressed himself in scarlet in order
to pay a visit to a Devonshire squire, to whom a captain
of a ship is a guest of no ordinary consequence, as he is
a stranger and a gentleman who hath seen a good deal
of the world in foreign parts, and knows all the news of
the times." The squire was to send off a boat, but the
weather was too bad, and the captain saw his hopes of
venison disappear, for he would not risk taking a boat's
crew of his own ashore.

Fielding thus speaks of the men, and presents the same
character in the mariner which earlier writers had noticed.
" They acknowledged him (the captain) to be their
master, while they remained on shipboard, but did not
allow his power to extend to the shore, where they had
no sooner set foot than every man became *sui juris*,
and thought himself at full liberty to return when he
pleased. Now it is not any delight that these fellows

have in the fresh air or verdant fields on the land. Every one of them would prefer his ship or his hammock to all the sweets of Arabia the Happy; but, unluckily for them, there are in every seaport in England certain houses whose chief livelihood depends on providing entertainment for the gentlemen of the jacket. For this purpose they are always well furnished with those cordial liquors which do immediately inspire the heart with gladness, banishing all careful thoughts, and indeed all others, from the mind, and opening the mouth with songs of cheerfulness and thanksgiving for the many wonderful blessings with which a seafaring life overflows." It is in relation to this character of the seaman that Fielding makes the apt remark that all human flesh is not the same flesh, but that there is one kind of flesh of landsmen, and another of seamen.

He saw that the mariner was not a drunkard only, but that he had a saving virtue in him that ennobled him beyond his fellows. The captain was accustomed to summon all hands to prayers on a Sunday morning, " which were read by a common sailor upon deck with more devout force and address than they are commonly read by a country curate, and received with more decency and attention by the sailors than are usually observed in a city congregation. I am, indeed, assured that if any such affected disregard of the solemn office in which they were engaged, as I have seen practised by fine gentlemen and ladies, expressing a kind of apprehension lest they should be suspected of being really in earnest in their devotions, had been shown here, they would have contracted the contempt of the whole audience. To say the truth, from what I observed in the behaviour of the sailors in this voyage, and in comparing with what I have formerly seen of them at sea and on shore, I am convinced that on land there is nothing more idle and dissolute ; in their own element there are no persons near the level of their degree who live in the constant practice of half so many good qualities. They are, for much the greater part, perfect masters of their

business, and always extremely alert and ready in
executing it, without any regard to fatigue or hazard.
The soldiers themselves are not better disciplined nor
more obedient to orders than these while aboard; they
submit to every difficulty which attends their calling
with cheerfulness, and no less virtues than patience and
fortitude are exercised by them every day of their lives.
All these good qualities, however, they always leave
behind them on shipboard; the sailor out of water is,
indeed, as wretched an animal as the fish out of water;
for, though the former hath, in common with amphibious
animals, the bare power of existing on land, yet if he be
kept there any time, he never fails to become a nuisance."

Fielding was describing seamen in the very period
of the outbreak of the Seven Years' War, in which we
showed that we had mastered again the lesson which
had almost been forgotten in the previous half-century.
The scarlet coats, breastplates, and flowing wigs of the
Restoration period had given place to the blue and white
uniform of George II. These were the times of the
victories of Boscawen and Hawke, of the capture of
Louisburg, Quebec, and Montreal, whereby our rule
was established in Canada, and of the downfall of the
French dominion in India.

The life of the sea in those days is brought before us
by Captain Edward Thompson, commonly spoken of as
"Poet Thompson," because of his love for breaking
out into verse in his writings in sentimental and descriptive poetical effusions. In him we trace that love for
the drama which manifested itself in seamen later on,
and made them familiar to landsmen on the stage.
As we shall see presently, being on half-pay, in 1773,
Thompson adopted and altered for the theatre Shadwell's old nautical play, "The Fair Quaker of Deal."
In his "Sailor's Letters, written for his Select Friends in
England," of which a second edition appeared in 1767,
the letters having been written between 1754 and 1759,
he shows the sentimental and hilarious sides of the
sailors' disposition. "Nothing can load them with

that dejection of spirit as a still calm"; their hopes
hung on the wings of the wind. Thompson himself
was of a gay and humorous temperament, and in his
mind a particular glory seemed to settle on the island
of St. Helena, which he thought had been placed where
it was for the recreation of seamen. At St. Helena he
wrote: " If a man can be intoxicated without liquor,
I am, and am as much over head and ears in love as ever
swimming Leander was with his fair Hero. I believe
the philtrum operates so strongly to make a rhymer of
me, to make me even attempt a sonnet to my mistress'
eyebrow."

> Tell her I'll love her while the clouds drop rain,
> Or while there's water in the pathless main ;
> Tell her I'll love her 'till this life is o'er,
> And then my ghost shall visit this sweet shore ;
> Tell her I only ask—she'll think of me,
> I'll love her while there's salt within the sea ;
> Tell her all this, tell her it o'er and o'er ;
> The anchor's weigh'd, or I would tell her more.

Thompson loved the sea, but he loved the land also.
He knew the sufferings and disappointments of a sea
life, and exerted his eloquence, in a letter to his uncle,
to prevent his cousin, who was attracted by the glamour
of the sea, from entering upon the naval career. " Youth
and good spirits will conquer the greatest difficulties ;
but the sea life is so opposite to human nature, that
I am astonished so many engage in the pursuit, when
so few approve it. If I have ever met with one Tar who
was uneasy on shore, I have found thousands in a worse
situation at sea. Besides, the disagreeable circumstances
and situations attending a subaltern officer in the Navy
are so many and so hard, that had not the first men in
the service passed the dirty road to preferment to encourage the rest, they would renounce it to a man."
Here it is obvious that Thompson is using the language
of hyperbole with the object of dissuading his cousin.
He continues : " It is a mistaken notion that a youth
will not make a good officer unless he stoops to the most

menial offices; to be bedded worse than hogs, and eat less delicacies. In short, from having experienced such scenes of filth and infamy, such fatigues and hardships, they are sufficient to disgust the stoutest and the bravest —for, alas! there is only a little hope of promotion sprinkled in the cup to make a man swallow more than he digests for the rest of his life." He proceeds to describe the state of inferior officers in the service, and remarks that all commanders are not gentlemen or men of education. "I know a great part are brave men, but a much greater seamen. . . . The last war, a chaw of tobacco, a rattan and a rope of oaths were sufficient qualifications to make a lieutenant, but now, education and good manners are a study of all; and so far from effeminacy that I am of opinion the present race of officers will as much eclipse the veterans of 1692 as the polite the vulgar."

Another letter is addressed to the cousin himself, giving a somewhat exaggerated picture, though one full of essential truth. "It will be thought an indulgence to let you sleep where day ne'er enters, and where fresh air only comes when forced. The two first rules I would have you observe are these: first, avoid low company; secondly, Hold-fast! one is material for the preservation of the soul, the other of the body." He tells his cousin that nothing but a necessary pride will preserve him from the former of these evils, and he says that not a vice is committed on shore that is not practised afloat, wherein he differs from some other observers. But Thompson did not decry his profession. There was in him a knowledge of its importance and its requirements. "It is a mistaken notion that any blockhead will make a seaman—yet, I confess, there are as many men of illiberal parts who call themselves seamen, as any other occupation can boast of. In short, it is so diametrically opposite that I don't know one situation in life that requires so accomplished an education as a sea officer. To shine in the character (which we hope every man has ambition enough to wish) he should be a man of letters and languages, a mathematician, and an accomplished gentleman."

Evidently a new spirit was abroad in the Navy and a better and more distinguished class of officers was springing up who concerned themselves with the higher duties of their profession. Hawke, a few years before, when a young rear-admiral, writing to Warren, in 1747, had said: " I have nothing so much at heart as the faithful discharge of my duty, and in such manner as will give satisfaction both to the Lords of the Admiralty and yourself. This shall ever be my utmost ambition, and no lucre of profit, or other views, shall induce me to act otherwise." Warren had his eye upon the Spanish galleons for profit, and Anson had captured the great galleon five years before, to his own enrichment. But the spirit of Hawke took hold upon his followers, and the officers in the King's ships were many of them of high character, increasingly so as time went on, and they devoted themselves to promoting the health and happiness of the seaman. As John Paul Jones wrote in 1777, breathing the spirit of his own service as well as of the British Navy, "None other than a gentleman as well as a seaman both in theory and practice, is qualified to support the character of a commissioned officer in the Navy; nor is any man fit to command a ship of war who is not also capable of communicating his ideas on paper in language that becomes his rank."

Sir Gilbert Blane, physician to the fleet, in a most instructive and thoughtful volume entitled " A Short Account of the most efficacious means of preserving the Health of Seamen, particularly in the Royal Navy," dedicated to the officers and captains on the West Indies station in 1780, remarked that more might be done for the men than was commonly supposed, and this was not only the office of humanity and duty, but of interest and policy also. " The formation of a seaman depends upon a long habit, and a practical education from an early period of life. If our stock of mariners were exhausted or diminished, neither treasure nor any other means could soon repair the loss." He enforced the value of the seaman from the peculiar dependence of Britain upon that order of men, and pointed out, apart from motives of humanity, the great importance of maintaining them in the fleet. He showed how maladies were introduced, and gave curious particulars of the methods adopted by some officers when men were brought on board to enter the service. " Those who have strictly put the methods in practice—of stripping and washing their bodies, cutting off their hair, and destroying all their clothes before allowing them to mix with the ship's company—know how effectual and infallible they are." But Blane remarks that a true seaman was always cleanly, and those who required a degree of compulsion, far from considering it a hardship, expected it, " and it is the duty of officers, as it is of parents to children, to constrain those entrusted to them to perform what is for their good."

In the same author's " Observations on the Diseases Incident to Seamen," 1785, are many interesting re- marks upon the good health preserved in Rodney's fleet, to which Blane was appointed physician in 1780. There was still room for improvement, but the Navy was on a better footing with regard to the health and comfort of seamen than it appeared to have been in former times. The victuals were in general of excellent quality. " And most of the commanders whom I have the honour to know are humane attentive and intelligent." Rodney's fleet was in a much better state than Vernon's in 1741, which sent 11,000 men to hospital in the course of that and the preceding year, of whom one in seven died. Blane's remarks upon the sea life may be quoted here. " To conclude, there is no situation of life in which there is room for more virtues, more conduct, and more address, than that of a sea officer. The men are thrown upon his humanity and attention in more views than one ; they are subject to a more arbitrary exertion of power than the constitution of the State authorises

in civil life, Englishmen giving up into his hands that
which they hold most dear, and of which they are most
jealous, their liberty. It is the character of seamen
to be thoughtless and neglectful of their own interests
and welfare, requiring to be tended like children ; but,
from their bravery, utility, and other good qualities,
they seem entitled to a degree of parental tenderness
and attention from the state they protect and the officers
they obey."

The life on board ships of war at about this time is
pictured for us in a very entertaining manner in the
"Journal of Rear-Admiral Bartholomew James, 1752–
1828" (Navy Records Society, 1896). James introduces us to the humours and tribulations of what he
calls his "orlopian days in the midshipmen's berth"
in his earlier days in the service. He first went to sea
in the *Folkstone* cutter in 1764. A little later, in 1771,
he has much that is amusing to say of the entry of midshipmen, when with two others he joined the *Torbay*.
Never, he says, should he forget the joy of his messmate
Richard Marsingall's mother, when she communicated
the news of his appointment to that young gentleman.
"Richard," said she, "my dear son Richard, get up,
thou art made for ever." "What am I made, mother?"
he asked in surprise and astonishment. "Oh ! Richard,
my tender life, thou art made a midshipman," and
James adds the comment, "Alas ! little, my good lady,
didst thou know what a sea of trouble thy son had to
go through ; little didst thou conjecture what innumerable
difficulties he was about to encounter, and 'the snubs
that patient mids from their superiors take,' or thou
wouldst not have supposed by his being a midshipman
that he was made for ever ; though literally it was the
case, for, poor fellow, he never was made anything else,
but died before he had served his time."

The tailors were set to work to make uniforms of
fashionable type for these young midshipmen, and James
draws an amusing picture of the extraordinary figures
they cut, and their precipitate retreat after being sur-

veyed by the captain. His picture of them deserves to rank with Michael Scott's sketches of Captain Deadeye and Sir Oliver Oakplank. "This great circumnavigator circumambulated us, and with a stamp of his foot, bid us begone and instantly get cut down, reduced and made decent by the Plymouth tailors." This was the beginning of his tribulations, but he was very soon perfected in all the knowing tricks of a midshipman, and completed his examinations by composing "bowls of punch by the rules of trigonometry and proving the purser a rogue by Gunter's scale." He exercised his fascination upon the ladies in the West Indies, thereby getting himself into many scrapes, and has much to say about the events in which he was engaged, and of terrible hardships by storms and bad food. Then, in 1776, he arrived at New York and secured the prizes he had brought alongside the wharf, where others were already tied up, and here, he says, commenced the most agreeable time he ever experienced during his "servitude" as a midshipman, for he had almost every luxury of life, without an anxious care or an unhappy moment; he and his messmates were free from the snubs they had been accustomed to. "Among the innumerable good things I was in possession of there was on board one of the prizes three cases of the best Bordeaux claret, which Captain Hudson had directed to be sent to him and Captain Chinnery, of the *Daphne*. We were keeping as usual Christmas Day, and were desirous to drink good wine; we therefore drank the three cases out, and the following day filled them with claret of a very inferior sort out of the casks, corking them with the same long corks, and sealing them all over with a deal of attention and care; which answered every purpose, as the captains, on drinking the wine, observed, 'It might be very good claret, but for their parts they found very little difference in that and the cask claret.'" There are many other anecdotes in the Journal illustrating the humours of the midshipman's berth.

James was accustomed to keep his birthday hilariously,

or as he says, " with some degree of spirit, and being
merry and happy on the occasion is as great a hobby-
horse of mine as Uncle Toby's fortifications ever could
be to him." He has much to tell us of jovial days spent
even in tempestuous gales, on short commons and with
little water, when a buoyant temperament was necessary to keep up the spirits of the men. Later on, in
1796, he entertained Prince Frederick Augustus at
Naples, with Sir William and Lady Hamilton, and he
records that " the loyalty of that exquisite and charmingly
lovely woman outshone, for in the ecstasy of singing
' God Save the King,' in full chorus with the whole
ship's company, she tore her fan to pieces and threw
herself into such bewitching attitudes that no mortal
soul could refrain from believing her to be an enthusiastic
angel from heaven purposely sent down to celebrate
this pleasant, happy, festival." In the same year,
James's birthday party included Nelson, Fremantle,
Isaac Coffin, and many other naval officers. The whole
book is full of amusement, as affording an insight into
life on board ships in his time. He took command of
the *Maria*, a merchant ship, when he was on half-pay,
and in 1797 he describes the reduction of bread to a
quarter-pound per day, the coals and wood all expended
and the last butt of water in broach. Experience
had taught James to say to himself " Patience ! "
" But to some of the most notorious of the crew the
consolation was not acceptable, and seditious tumult
began to rear its head, which I appeased by administering
a few doses of the oil of cat, which soon restored the most
cordial intimacy between our unavoidable distress and
the vile disposition of our mutineers."

In a whimsical volume entitled " The Story of the
Learned Pig, by an Officer of the Royal Navy," printed
by R. Jameson, signed " Transmigratus," and dated
from " Woolwich, June 16. 1786," is a picture of
the disconsolate state of officers after the Peace
of 1783. A one-armed lieutenant, clad in a shabby
blue coat, with facings which once had been white,

enters the great man's apartment and tells the tale
of want of employment and of the claims of officers
upon the country. "Who, I ask, are more proper objects for her attention ? If a generous sacrifice of the
ease and comforts of life ; if a cheerful exchange of a
healthy and happy air for the contagion of foreign and
inhospitable climes ; if watching and starving, and
gallantly venturing life, to secure her safety and prosperity, can give a claim to her favour ; then we have a
great title to her protection. O publick virtue, whither
art thou flown ? A favourite (only because he is a
favourite) without one earthly pretension to distinction—
a very drone in the commonwealth—a fellow ; who, to
use a vulgar phrase, has never been out of the smoke of
his mother's chimney, shall enjoy a sinecure of hundreds,
—nay, thousands a year; whilst he who has been mutilated
in fighting for his country (here he held out his stump)
shall be daily put to his shifts how to get a dinner !
Is this justice ? is this reward ? . . . A subaltern officer
in the army is soon made up : he has little more to learn
than the exercise of a musket and the manœuvring of a
company, which are both to be acquired in three months.
But the case differs widely with the naval officer. It
requires years of experience, service, and application to
fit him for his duty; and, when it is considered that our
empire by sea is the sole security of our liberty, what
can be a more important object of the nation's care
than the cultivation of his abilities, and the reward of
his services ? " The outbreak of the French Revolutionary
War soon put an end to the evils against which the lieutenant declaimed.

CHAPTER VI

FROM TRAFALGAR TO LATER TIMES

WITH the mention of Nelson and his comrades at Bartholomew James's birthday party in the previous chapter, we find ourselves in the full splendour of the spacious days of the British Navy. From the pages of history, biography, diaries, and pamphlets a good deal might have been gleaned concerning the grievances of seamen, out of which arose the mutinies at the Nore, Spithead, and some other places. It may, however, be observed that the discontent of the mutineers was nearly always intermixed with a disposition to deal gently with the officers against whom the mutiny was directed. There has been preserved a letter written by Miss Mary Boger, a relative of Captain, afterwards Admiral, Boger, which illustrates this particular character of the risings. The Captain, who then commanded the *Cambridge*, 80, the guardship at Plymouth, was superseded by the mutineers, but, as he was a great favourite with the sailors, he had no fear for his personal safety, and two delegates were despatched from the ship every morning to Mrs. Boger and her daughter, " to let their ladyships know that their late captain was well and had nothing to fear." Meanwhile he was a prisoner in his own cabin. Sir John Colpoys had a narrow escape. He had ordered the marines to fire over the heads of the mutineers, and sailors belonging to the other ships judged this action worthy of death. They therefore issued instructions to the officer who executed the captain's commands to prepare for execution. " Captain

Colpoys immediately stepped forward, and like a brave
and good man, as he was, told them that if any one was
to die, he would be that man, as the officer had done
his duty." The rope was placed round his neck, but
the mutineers were moved by a better spirit when one
of their leaders set forth his many good qualities, declaring that he himself was under particular obligations
to him, and that his late captain should not be put to
death while he had a drop of blood in his veins. Colpoys,
however, was put into a boat with another officer and
landed, while the fifes and drums played the "Rogue's
March." " At last a day was set apart to commemorate
the sailors' return to their duty, having gained their
point, which the best informed officers were of opinion
ought to have been granted them long before. It was
a strange sight. The whole fleet walked in procession,
hand in hand, and their favourite officers were put into
open carriages. I shall never forget our old relative
Admiral Boger, in an open carriage drawn by four horses,
exposed to a scorching sun in the middle of a very hot
July, without a hat, but with his hair full dressed and
powdered, and in his full uniform, with a face as red as
scarlet from heat and excitement. In vain did he constantly request to have a glass of water. The sailors,
horrified at the request, told him that ' his Honour might
have any sort of grog, but that as for water, they would
not suffer his Honour to drink it.' He was paraded
round Dock, Stonehouse, and Plymouth, and they set
him down at his own door, gave him three tremendous
cheers, and took their leave."

It is pleasant to turn from the evidence of mutiny to
the brilliant and glorious features of our naval history
at the time. Unfortunately no great portrait painter
like Smollett takes us on board the ships of Rodney,
Hood, Howe, Jervis, or even Nelson. It was the noblest
age of English seamanhood, in which we were victorious
on every sea. A picture might be drawn of the fighting
seaman, of his hardihood, gallantry and endurance,
the man who buffeted the ocean in the great blockades,

K

the bold fighting fellow who took part in many a cutting-
out expedition, and the destruction of the enemy's
vessels in his ports or upon his coasts, the man also who
followed his officers in many a boarding operation.
There is the imperishable sketch of Nelson standing on
the quarter-deck of the *San Josef*, after he had boarded
her, and receiving the swords of vanquished Spaniards,
which he gave into the charge of William Fearney,
" one of my bargemen, who put them with the greatest
sang-froid under his arm."

Of the qualities of officers of Nelson's time, the pages
of History are full.   There was among them such a
spirit as the Navy had scarcely known before. They
were like Nelson himself, the incomparable leader of
men.   After the affair at Santa Cruz he declared " that
not a scrap of that ardour with which I served our
King has been shot away."   In the smoke of these
battle pictures we see the sturdy form of Jervis, a master
of men, severe, but kindly and a great naval administrator. We think of Collingwood, going into action at
Trafalgar, and saying to his captain, " Rotheram, what
would Nelson give to be here," and we do not forget
that Nelson, too, when he led the weather line, said to
Hardy, " What would poor Sir Robert Calder give to be
with us now."   Then there is Cornwallis, the tireless
watcher in the blockades, and there are many more
almost comparable to him. Nelson stood among his
compeers and comrades—Berry, the renowned captain ;
Blackwood, whose fame, said Nelson, was " beyond the
reach of envy " ; Troubridge, of whom Jervis said that
he tacked his ship to battle " as if the eyes of all England
were on him, and would to God they were ! " ; that
" brave fellow Hallowell," so described by Hood ; and
that placid seaman Ball. Nelson was always proud of
his ship and of his men. When he was in the *Albemarle*
he wrote, " Not a man or officer in her I would wish to
change," and of the *Agamemnon* he said that nobody
could be ill " in my ship's company, they are so fine a
set," while in the Mediterranean, in 1803, he declared his

ships were " the best commanded, and the best manned
afloat " and his captains at the Nile he proclaimed as
a " band of brothers." Under these influences the lives
of seamen became much more pleasant, though no doubt
a good deal of the old roughness still remained. Jervis
and Nelson, Cornwallis, Collingwood, and the others,
were constantly assiduous to procure fresh water, and
ample provisions, including fruit and vegetables, and
many amusements were provided for men on board.

The seamen of Nelson's time had in them the mettle
of courage and enterprise, the hardy virtues of audacity
and fearlessness. They were strong in their sentiment
of home life, and we catch many a glimpse of the officer
and seaman as a man of fine and human qualities. The
letters of Nelson's captains reveal their personal and
domestic virtues. Above all, they were great seamen,
and their powers were developed in the constant influence
of the salt element of their environment. The history
of the time is full of instances of signal hardihood and
daring, and withal there was the same devout strain of
thought, inarticulate sometimes, perhaps, which we have
observed in earlier time. Seamen lived much in contact
with the elemental forces of Nature, and being engaged
in service against the enemies of their country, qualities
were evoked which may be read between the lines of
many a commonplace narrative of events.

In " The Naval Guardian," by Charles Fletcher, M.D.,
which was dedicated to the Lords of the Admiralty in
1800, and of which a second edition, in two volumes,
appeared in 1805, we learn a good deal about the seamen
of that period. The author, who also wrote " A Maritime
State considered as to the Health of Seamen," was an
ardent advocate of the men who fought our battles in
the great war. The ships of the Navy aroused his enthusiasm, " and yet," he says, " how do these argosies,
these bulwarks of safety, sink like bubbles in the deep,
when unactuated by that which, under Providence, can
alone give them energy ! When we behold those heroes
embarking on board that Navy in defence of whatever

is dear to them, and opposing themselves to almost all
the Naval Powers at once of Europe, such spirit, accompanied with such success, is truly astonishing."

Fletcher's book consists of a series of letters supposed
to have been written by a captain, a naval surgeon,
and a chaplain, and interspersed with poetical allusions
and some dramatic pieces. These characters are no
doubt used to express Fletcher's own ideas upon the
subject dealt with, and they are particularly instructive.
There is a certain Lady B. who has a positive enthusiasm
for seamen, but whose scruples have to be overcome
by the surgeon and chaplain before she will allow her
son to enter the service. She learns that Sir Edward
Hughes has allowed the seamen to have tea, and thinks
it has been withheld " from an apprehension that it
might presently be the means of refining them into a
degree of politeness incompatible with the character of
a seaman." " No, Lady B.," replies the surgeon, " there
is no danger of that. . . . Politeness is a quality that a
British seaman has no pretension to ; there he would
be out of his element, and leaves it for his superiors, his
officers." To which the lady replies, " I know a great
many well-bred officers, Sir, in the Navy, but a much
greater number whose honest bluntness, not to call it
by an harsher name, would better suit the foremast-
man." What particular interpretation Fletcher set
upon the word politeness does not appear, but he seems
to have regarded it as subversive of valour. On another
occasion the same lady makes a proposal to inquire
into the means of ameliorating the situation of seamen.
" Sir, there can be no period unseasonable for such an
investigation ; for are they not those on whom our
liberties and lives depend ! Can anything be too good
for them ? . . . Ah, Sir, it is not from the vital source of
public weal that savings should be made. The constitution of seamen is the public constitution ; sap that,
and then place, pension, property, and all would, perhaps, when too late, be thought too slight a purchase
to redeem it." Whereat, the surgeon sees that Lady B.

is a superior person ; he thinks a ray of divinity beams from her eye, and he hails her as the patroness of seamen ! On another occasion she says, " I protest, Sir, I never sit down to dinner, but I wish them a share."

Touching the character of seamen, Fletcher tells us that if there should be mutinous conduct on board there would be more on shore. " Nay, I shall go further, and repeat what I have advanced in my preface to the book, that the *Royal George*, with a complement of one thousand men (provided she be well disciplined) abounds less in vice, if not more in virtue, than most villages in England with the same number of souls. . . . If they get drunk, it can only be when on shore upon leave ; and should they appear on board in that state, they are punished." He goes on to remark that he cannot bear to hear seamen spoken of with disparagement or contempt, whether they be officers or men. " It was only a captain of a man-of-war who was killed ! " " You shall be sent, sirrah, into a man-of-war, says a mother to her child, for there you'll be whipp'd into good manners ! And again, of the men,—a set of rascals !—the scum of the earth !— the sweepings of gaols !—the excrescences of the people ! with such like epithets." Such sneers made the writer's gorge rise, and he speaks scornfully of those who uttered them.

The hilarity of the seaman, his zest for life, and his high spirits, occupy a large space in Fletcher's pages. He gives us the humours of the midshipmen's berth. A young Irish gentleman, a native of Tipperary, comes to his captain with a complaint that he has been contumeliously treated by his shipmates. They had said the Irish were a nation of Hottentots and supplied two-thirds of the Newgate calendar, and that there never was a Tipperary man who had not a piece of potato in his brain ! The skipper regards this complaint from a double point of view. He knows that to make a butt of a comrade leads to much quarrel and dissension, and the young Irishman is bidden to enter into the spirit of the pleasantry. To which he replies that his shipmates might reflect upon his brogue, if they liked, but not upon his country! On board the ship, however, ridicule is not discountenanced. On the contrary, it has its utility, "and has been implanted in human nature for the best purpose." "But, however the punishment of Coventry may be thought necessary on shore, I do not think it ought to be practised on board."

Fletcher was incensed at a certain Parker, author of a book entitled "Life's Painter of Variegated Characters," wherein he had cast a slur upon the characteristic language of seamen, which, however, had been immortalised by Shakespeare and illustrated by Smollett. The captain of the letters has a great belief in the advantages of cheerfulness of spirit, and works much for the diversion of his men ; and Fletcher interpolates some dramatic pieces based in part upon the writings of Smollett. The remarks upon the amusements of seamen are singularly interesting. "In order then to improve the spirits of seamen to the best advantage, we would do well to mark with attention those in which they are most naturally disposed to indulge. Buffoonery, we find, they take singular delight in. We seldom see a ship without one or more droll fellows, who, sensible of this matter, make themselves voluntary laughing-stocks to their shipmates. There was in a certain ship I belonged to a humourist of his kind, whose name was Webb ; who, previous to his entering on board, had fitted himself out in Monmouth street, with a three-tail'd wig of an enormous size. When thus equipped, he had the art of assuming an uncommon solemnity of countenance, and which, added to the remainder of his appearance as a sailor, rendered him perfectly grotesque, and truly ridiculous ; consequently a subject of mirth. The 'Miller of Mansfield,' another of their sports, argues likewise their taste for low comedy. There is evidently something dramatic in this little pasttime. 'Stormy Castle,' 'Follow the Leader,' etc., are of the same stamp. Another sport, if such it can be termed, called 'Cobbing,' has been in common use amongst them, 'till of late that, from fatal consequences having some-

times attended, it has been justly discountenanced." The
conclusion is as follows: "As low spirits and indolence
have such an unfavourable effect upon health, it would be
wise, as well as benevolent, to provide whatever produces
jollity, contentment, and good humour, so far as is con-
sistent with sobriety and industry." The sailor, he tells
us, loves dramatic pieces of a comic kind, with music
and dancing, the whole to conclude with some song,
perhaps "God save the King," "Rule Britannia," or
the "Wandering Sailor," with full chorus.

We are brought into touch with naval life from another
point of view by the sketches of service which were published by Sir Robert Steele under the title of "The
Marine Officer." These appeared in 1840, but take us
back to the time of Nelson and Trafalgar. The young
officer had his commission in the Royal Marines at the
outbreak of the war in 1803, when he was a boy of
fourteen. At Portsmouth he says he could hardly walk
for the groups of officers in beautiful and rich uniforms,
Army and Navy, horse and foot, Hanoverian and British,
who were to be seen singly and together, arm in arm,
loitering, laughing, and quizzing, while every non-
commissioned officer or soldier who met or passed an
officer stopped, turned, and saluted, by bringing his
hand with a sort of flourish to his cap. Steele describes
a scene on board the *Puissant*, where men impressed
were being received. Says the captain: "Brown, don't
look so blue; how long have you been at sea, and how
old are you?" "Twenty years at sea, your Honour,
and I am thirty-two years old." "You can hand,
splice, reeve, steer, and heave the lead, eh, Brown?"
"Why yes, I doubt I ought, your Honour." But Brown
would not take the King's bounty. "Then you'll go
without bounty, that's all, and so march off." Another
man is brought up. "Jennings, how long have you
been at sea?" "Four years, your Honour." "Where
have you served?" "Nowhere, your Honour." "Come,
Sir, no slang, or I'll marry you to the gunner's daughter.
Send the boatswain's mate aft with the cat." "Beg

pardon, your Honour, I meant I had never served on board a man-of-war." "Time you should, sir, and amongst other things to learn manners." A third man is brought on deck. "Baker, who are you?" "A tailor, your Worship." "Don't worship me, merchant tailor; what brought you here?" "That are lifetenant and his gang, sir, took I just as I was going home last night." On which the lieutenant interpolates, "Tell the truth, sir; you were guzzling and cackling like a goose at the Magpie at the bowling green outside Gosport gates." The captain enters the man. "Well, Mr., for all that, you are just going aboard instead. We want tailors on board as well as ashore, and so you'll drive your needle, and be an idler on board one of his Majesty's ships."

Steele had an utter horror of the system of impressment, in its methods, and he gives a very graphic account of some incidents and brutalities, which he says were a blot on the service. It is particularly interesting to find in his pages a picture of the young officers of the Trafalgar time. He said he should never forget the first lieutenant of the ship in which he joined Cornwallis in the blockade of Brest at the outbreak of war. He preserved towards him the greatest respect and affection, for he said there were few such men to be met with either in the service or outside it. Independently of being a thorough seaman, and a first-rate officer, he was an elegant and accomplished gentleman, speaking French and Italian fluently, and being a good draftsman, as well. Moreover—

> He was stately, young and tall,
> Dreaded in battle, and loved in hall.

The second lieutenant was a regular tar, famous at boat sailing and the very man in a squall, with an eye eternally to windward. He was sure to clew up and reef in time, and was fond of his girl and his glass, and of a Saturday night, whether at sea or in port, used the toast—

> The wind that blows,
> The ship that goes,
> And the lass that loves a sailor.

The third lieutenant was the son of a poet, and said his father's translation of the Georgics was equal to the original; while the fourth lieutenant had a fancy for poring over Blackstone's "Commentaries." The junior lieutenant was a great economist, and was accustomed to talk of "the tottle of the whole." The captain of Marines was a perfect bantam, and had served with Nelson on board the *Vanguard* at the Nile. One of the subs, a youth from Devon, who used to fish from the stern windows, showed himself as cool as a cucumber at Trafalgar, and was the admiration of all his comrades. The chaplain was from Wales. "To tell the truth our Cambrian was better in the bottle than in the wood." The master was a droll fellow; and the purser used to spend his spare time abaft reading Shakespeare.

From this particularly interesting glimpse of life and character on board one of the ships which buffeted the gales in the ocean blockade we turn to some of the things said by Captain Basil Hall, who wrote three series of "Fragments of Voyages and Travels," nine volumes in all, and was a favourite and popular author with our grandfathers for his racy style, his descriptions of sea life, of the places he visited, and of the things he observed. Hall was destined from boyhood for the sea, for which he had a passionate love, and his interest in the service was boundless. Of the sailor he says: "His range of duties includes the whole world; he may be lost in the wilderness of a three-decker, or be wedged into a cock-boat of a cutter; he may be half fried in Jamaica, or wholly frozen in Spitzbergen; he may be cruising during six days of the week in the midst of a hundred sail, and flounder in solitude on the seventh; he may be peaceably riding at anchor in the morning, and be in hot action before sunset." Hall joined the *Leander* in May, 1802, and went to the Halifax station, she being the flagship of Sir Andrew Mitchell. He never lost his love for the ship, and often refers to the happy days spent on board and the men who were his comrades. In his company we visit the midshipmen's berth, and he describes for us many of its humours. Like the Tipperary man, he did not escape jesting shafts at his nationality. " Eh, Saunders, where are ye gaun ? " they would call out to him. His messmates were always frolicsome, light-hearted, and careless of all things, " up to any mischief or any business, and gradually forming themselves, by an involuntary process, for the right performance of those varied duties which belong to their calling." Some had a turn for mechanics, some for navigation ; others devoted much time to rigging and different branches of seamanship, their hands being constantly in the tar bucket. A few applied themselves to reading and drawing ; several desperate hands stuck resolutely to the flute ; one or two thought of nothing but dress ; a few swore a pretty steady friendship for the grog bottle ; while every now and then a sentimental youth deemed himself inspired and wrote execrable verse. They were always playing practical jokes, and evidently got a good deal of enjoyment out of life. " Speaking of the midshipmen's berth and of the occasional ruggedness of manners, I shall be doing wrong to leave an impression that they were a mere lawless set of harum-scarum scamps. Quite the contrary, for we had a code of laws for our government, which, for precision and directness of purpose, might have rivalled many of those promulgated by the newest born states of the world in these teeming days of political parturition."

Captain Hall recognised the existence of two methods of discipline and control in his time, the one severe and exacting, the other calculated to evoke the better qualities of men. " Nothing ever does or can go well, unless, over and above the mere legal authority possessed by the head, he shall carry with him a certain amount of good will, and the confidence of those under him, for it is material, in order to balance as it were the technical power with which the chief of such establishment is armed, that there should be some heartiness, some real cheerfulness, between him and those he commands." Captain Hall goes on to show how well disciplined in work and efficiency is a ship under a good officer, and he adds, " It has been well observed that the simple fact of Lord Nelson's joining the fleet off Trafalgar, double-manned every ship in the line."

And now, from this contemplation of the officers of the Nelson time, let us glance at the remarks of a pamphleteer—a sailor who, as he says on his title-page, was " politely called by the officers of the Navy, Jack Nasty-Face." His " Nautical Economy, or Forecastle Recollections of Events during the last War," was not published until 1836, but it relates to the period of Trafalgar, and was dedicated " To the Brave Tars of Old England," and addressed to " My Brother Seamen and Old Shipmates." It gives what may be described as a plain, unvarnished story—a story with a purpose, being a protest against the old but necessary evil of impressment, of which so much has been said, and against the punishments, of which a good deal of the severity still remained.

Jack Nasty-Face was himself impressed, and seems to have been sent on board the receiving ship, in the Thames, in May, 1805, with some of the Lord Mayor's men, who had been committed by magistrates for their offences, and therefore he met with rather rough treatment. He was sent round to Portsmouth and drafted on board a line-of-battle ship, fitting out to join Nelson's flag. Here he says he met with discipline " with all its horrors." He describes the daily routine on board, beginning with the cleaning of the deck, " with holy-stones or hand-bibles, as they are called by the crew." He tells us that the breakfast usually consisted of " burgoo," made of coarse oatmeal and water. There was also " Scotch coffee," made by boiling burnt bread in water and adding sugar, and generally cooked in a hook-pot in the galley. Usually eight persons formed a mess, in a berth between two guns on the lower deck, where a board swung which served for a table. Jack asserts that men were flogged for most trifling offences. At eight bells, or twelve o'clock, came the most pleasant part of the day, when the fiddlers played " Nancy Dawson " or some other

lively tune, being the signal that the grog was ready to
be served out. Jack says he became inured to the life,
made up his mind to be obedient, and soon began to
pick up a knowledge of seamanship.

His account of Trafalgar has many interesting points,
and he describes the behaviour of men as the ships were
bearing down upon the allied line.* " During this time
each ship was making the usual preparations, such as
breaking away the captain and officers' cabins, and sending the lumber below—the doctors, parson, purser, and
loblolly men were also busy, getting the medicine chests
and bandages and sails prepared for the wounded to be
placed on, that they might be dressed in rotation as they
were taken down to the after-cockpit. In such bustling,
and, it may be said, trying as well as serious time, it is
curious to notice the different dispositions of the British
sailor. Some would be offering a guinea for a glass of
grog, whilst others were making a sort of mutual verbal
will, such as, if one of Johnny Crapeau's shots (a term
given to the French) knocks my head off, you will take
all my effects ; and if you are killed, and I am not, why,
I will have yours, and this is generally agreed to. During
this momentous preparation the human mind had ample
time for meditation and conjecture, for it was evident
that the fate of England rested on the battle ; therefore
well might Lord Nelson make the signal ' England expects each man will do his duty.' " †

Jack speaks of a tyrannical midshipman, who delighted to torture the men, and who was killed in the
battle, and not lamented. He gives incidents which
show the humanity of the seaman. A young French-
woman, he says, unwilling to leave her husband at Cadiz,
disguised herself as a seaman, remained on board his
ship, and was engaged in the battle. Her husband was

* Jack Nasty-Face says the ship he was in cut off the five stern-
most ships of the allied line, meaning that she passed between the
fifth and sixth ships from the tail of the line. She was thus probably
the *Revenge* of the lee line.

† The signal really was "England expects that every man will do
his duty."

killed, the ship took fire, and a few survivors, among
them the unfortunate woman, stripped themselves naked
and swam for their lives. She was picked up half dead
in this condition, taken on board, provided with material
for clothing, and officers and men vied with one another
in doing all they could for her. Finally, the unfortunate
woman was sent across from Gibraltar to Algeciras.
The pamphleteer shows the pride the men had in their
ships. Nelson had painted the sides of his vessels in
chequers, and they became famous, so that it would be
said of a ship, " Oh ! she is one of Nelson's chequer-.
players." A new captain came and replaced the chequers
with stripes, whereat the men were indignant, thinking
they were robbed of the badge of their glory. They were
proportionately gratified, therefore, when a new captain
came who " Nelsonified " them again.

" What," says Jack of his ship, homeward bound from
Cadiz, after eighteen months' hard service, " what could
be more tormenting than to be homeward-bound, hearts
panting with the anticipated happiness of meeting wives
and sweethearts, or other relatives and friends, and a
lubberly head-wind playing with your distress ; could
anything more distressing be imagined ? But a sailor's
mind is not to be overcome by accidents or disappointments ; he meets them as he would an enemy, by facing
them, and merrily sings, ' Grieving's a folly, boys ! '
Every plan is resorted to, to keep up the spirits, and
nautical wit on these occasions generally displays itself."

Our pamphleteer had a high ideal of the seaman's profession. " If anything can lower the spirit of the British
sailor," he says of certain unfortunate episodes, " it is
that of not being able to speak triumphantly of any
enterprise he may have been upon." We shall conclude
our notice of the book by quoting the postscript of
Jack Nasty-Face's description, where he speaks of the
sailor's life. " To a youth possessing anything of a roving
disposition, it is attractive, nay, it is seductive ; for it
has its allurements, and when steadily pursued with
success it ennobles the mind, and the seaman feels him-

self a man. There is, indeed, no profession that can vie
with it ; and a British seaman has a right to be proud,
for he is incomparable when placed alongside those of
any other nation. Great Britain can truly boast of her
hearts of oak, the floating sinews of her existence, and
the high station she holds in the political world ; and if
she could but once rub out those stains of wanton and
torturing punishments, so often unnecessarily resorted
to, and abandon the unnatural and uncivilised custom of
impressment, then, and not till then, can her Navy be
said to have got to the truck of perfection."

From this time forward the situation of seamen rapidly
improved both in health and comfort. In " An Essay
addressed to the Captains of the Royal Navy and those
of the Merchants' Service," Robert Finlayson, M.D.,
surgeon in the Royal Navy, makes some observations
upon this subject. His book was published in 1824. He
shows how, in former wars, sea scurvy made such dreadful ravages as to enervate the arm of power, and it was
not uncommon to find three hundred men at once on
the sick list of a line-of-battle ship. It was justly observed
by some of the most experienced officers, says Finlayson, " that the blockading system of warfare, which
annihilated the naval power of France, could never have
been carried on, unless sea scurvy had been subdued ;
and more than one hundred thousand of British seamen
have been saved to the country by as many thousand
pounds." Finlayson pays a high tribute to the British
seaman and to his services to the state. " Is there a
Briton who can for a moment forget the blessings that
have been enjoyed for centuries under the safeguard of
our brave tars ?—and who can look with apathy on a
class of men to whom we are indebted for our riches and
commerce in war and peace, and who are our only safe
and permanent bulwarks in the trying hours of invading
hostility ? Can we neglect a body of men whose energy
increases with the raving of the storm, and whose constant practice and highest pride is to show the greatest
dexterity in the most imminent danger ? Never shall

we abandon the brave tar who mounts with alacrity on
the quivering shroud, when,

O'er his head the rolling billows sweep.

" Besides, our gallant ' sons of the wave ' have not
been less celebrated in human than in ' elemental war ' ;
for when the united powers of Europe were in league
against us, British seamen stood forward to wield our
naval thunderbolts and hurl destruction on our most
malignant enemy." Finlayson goes on to deplore that
this humorous and thoughtless class of persons were too
often seen from the most unfavourable point of view,
spending their holidays on shore. " They commonly
indulge in drinking, and make use of loose and indecorous
language, leaving the worst possible impression on the
public respecting their general character, and rendering
themselves an easier prey to a gang of harpies who
lurk in all our seaports." But, says Finlayson, however
they may be described, British seamen " have long
and justly been esteemed for a disinterested generosity
towards others in distress ; and self-interest and personal
safety have always been thrown aside when wanted by
their country."

Another writer—and the last we shall quote in this
place—is Captain Anselm John Griffiths, who published
in 1826 a treatise entitled " Impressment fully considered
with a view to its gradual abolition." He remarks that
Great Britain would have been subjugated by Bonaparte
if the Navy had not withstood the European world,
annihilated their fleets, and taken nearly all their foreign
possessions. In view of their services, he remarks that
seamen have every claim to gratitude and consideration.
" Let us purchase their affection and freedom, and no
longer have hundreds of these fine, open-hearted fellows
(for such they intrinsically are) skulking about during
the impress as helpers in stables, disguised as hod carriers,
labourers, etc., living in perpetual dread, degraded as
well as disguised, in spirit as well as in habits, and become
the object and marketable property of crimps, and on

whose head a price was set. Remember that by carrying the war into every country, every clime, every quarter of the globe, they kept you free."

Our description of the seaman as discovered in the pages of the historians (which have served us but little) and of biographers, pamphleteers, and writers of naval sketches is at an end. The men who fought at Algiers, at Navarino, in the Burmese, Chinese, and New Zealand wars, in the Russian war and the Indian Mutiny, as well as in later campaigns, had all the character of their predecessors of the earlier times, though they lived and served under a happier and milder dispensation. We shall find some of them described in the pages of fiction by Glascock, Marryat, Chamier, Michael Scott, and others, and brought before us by nautical dramatists and poets, full of the spirit bred of the comradeship of the sea, of hearty good humour and hilarity, and of the bravery and self-sacrifice which have ever distinguished the British seamen in all places and at all times.

PART II

MYSTERY, PAGEANT, COMEDY, AND DRAMATIC LITERATURE

L

CHAPTER VII

THE SEAMAN OF THE MYSTERY PLAYS

IN days of yore it was believed that between the older —and the better-known—world and the yet to be fully discovered Terra Incognita there existed an island, around which fabled land were woven many legends. Replete with brilliant colouring, of poetic beauty, this birthright of the mirage was thronged with all the fairy people—mysterious, quaint, and fantastic—imagined by the dreamers and the superstitious of the age. So, too, it may be said that between the real matter-of-fact world, as depicted in the histories, chronicles, and records of all time, and that other world of fiction, with its character-isation and incident, based on realities, but tinctured with the personal experiences or visual imagination of the writers, there exists another region, the life in which partakes both of the real and the ideal, the inhabitants—their manners, customs, and language—being invested with a halo of romance and attributes quite as mythical and extravagant as any ascribed to the fabulous denizens of Atlantis. Yet, just as in their descriptions of the imaginary island, where, as in the country of the lotus-eaters, it was " for ever afternoon," the ancient writers were limited in their drafts upon the imagination by their knowledge of what was, or traditionally had been, so, too, on the mystical world of the stage, in the miracle plays, the moralities, and even in the dramatic develop-ment of more recent times, we have the mirror held up to nature, or to the supernatural of terrestrial origin.

Hitherto it has been our endeavour in this volume to

discover the seaman as he is to be found depicted in the
pages of the serious writers of his era. We have traced
his character in historical narrative as a very real personage, and from Chaucer's Shipman, the mariner who
fought our medieval naval battles, we have followed the
same good fellow in that transitional stage when, as the
explorer of the Tudor period, he added to his professional
experiences those of extended travel and adventure. In
his next phase, the naval writers and diarists have shown
us the effect upon the seaman of discipline and the process of a stricter organisation working upon his mettle-
some disposition, with results as exhibited in his behaviour
under stress, whether of storm or of battle. As by turns,
pirate and merchant, raider or trader, with a very easy
estimate of human life, giving carelessly what was come
by easily, yet suffering untold hardships and enduring
incredible sufferings, or, as in later days, the frank and
breezy personality, made familiar to us by the annalists
and satirists of the great war, we have ever found him
loyal to his sovereign, his country, and to the brotherhood of the sea.

If this is the seaman of history, then also it should be
the seaman of the dramatist, and the sailor on the stage
should be—and, indeed, we find he is to a very large
extent—the replica of the sailor afloat. But in the vista
thus opened up to us we must expect to find behind the
footlights, sea life and seamen exhibited as in the mirage,
and some of their qualities and characteristics as sailors
exaggerated and distorted ; in a word, surrounded by an
atmosphere created for the purpose, which, if unreal, had
an influence which was not only good for the nation, but
helpful to the mariner himself, so far as it contributed to
raise him nearer to the best ideal of healthy manhood.

When there was merely a miracle play to be enacted,
and the nautical pageant was confined to scenes representing Noah's voyage in the Ark, Jonah's catastrophe,
and similar Old Testament episodes, the sailors were
presented as rude, boisterous characters, with little
regard for the sanctity of other men's property, addicted

to " a choice selection of expletives," their language characterised by a coarse humour which seems to have appealed to the audiences of the time. But when we come to Shakespeare's seaman, whether with a homely or marvellous environment, the nautical expressions which occur in the dramatic poet's writings and those of other playwrights of the period, with that larger view they seemed to take of the possibilities of Sea Power, we find they give us a reflection of the wider experience which the sailor explorers had acquired amid surprising events and turns of fortune, and the influence they were exerting upon our literature. Coming down a little later, if, on the one hand, we discover in some of the sailors of the Restoration dramatists the character and sentiments of that type of gentleman volunteer who wrote " To all you ladies now at land we men at sea indite," on the other, among the seamen of Davenant and Wycherley, Shadwell and Congreve, and their contemporaries, we shall find a manifest effort to reach much higher and finer examples of the Tarpaulin. Towards the end of the eighteenth century the dramas and dramatic pieces of a nautical character were of two kinds; the one commemorated and glorified the victorious tars winning their country's battles ; while the other, mainly with music, depicted the loves of the sailor, his return from sea, and the rescue of his sweetheart from the maw of the land shark. Then came the end of our fighting in the great war, and in the last days of the seaman trained under sails an exaggerated ideal took shape in the melodrama indelibly associated with the names of Douglas Jerrold and T. P. Cooke. This was romance run riot, where only the New River was real, and the British seaman, with sentiment on his lips, and a cutlass in his hand, flourished amid wrecks, smugglers, and the like. It is a little outside the limit we have set ourselves, but may it not be added that in the comic operas of Gilbert and other writers we have seen a not altogether unsuccessful attempt to reproduce the officers and men of a later Navy, not always in their

workaday hours, but in their playtime also, with William
Terriss as the exponent of the heart-breaking, gallant
tar ?

It may be said of our quest that, like the Elizabethan
seamen, we have set out upon a little-known and im-
perfectly explored sea, yet like them too, we shall hope
that the emprise will be successful, and that our discoveries may not be without value, in view of the novelty
and interest of the matters brought to light. In using
this metaphor, it must not be assumed that we do not
fully recognise the good work of the pioneers, and the
pilots who have driven their prows in the same waters.
To them we are indebted for many a sea mark and beacon
directing our course aright, and by them the difficulties
of exploration have been lessened and made easier.
But the object of our voyage is altogether different in
scope and purpose from those of any of the adventurers who have preceded us. We are to endeavour,
first of all, to seek the seaman in dramatic literature and
on the stage, to reproduce his appearance, character,
and achievements, as mirrored in the theatre of his era,
and, at the same time, to trace the evolution and development of the nautical play. The end will be reached
when those who have cared to accompany us shall
recognise on our canvas the sailor who in blue jacket,
white " slacks," and flowing ringlets, delighted the
audiences of the early eighteenth century.

At the outset of our inquiry it seems necessary to
say something about the beginning of the drama and
the growth of the dramatic art. In all the early civili-
sations we find, as in the Dionysiac festivals, that
singing, music, and dancing, with dramatic action,
formed a religious service. Originally, therefore, drama
partook partly of a mystical and solemn character,
but still more of the dithyrambic gaiety of chorus singers
and dancers. The early Christians did not depart from
many extinct practices of the pagans, but converted
them, and processions, spectacles, and representations
of events in Scriptural history were common, until

ultimately, as more topical subjects of local interest were introduced, acting as a profession was evolved. When Christianity became general its ministers favoured dramatic religious representations as rivals to gladiatorial displays, pantomimes, and more artistic comedies and tragedies of the pagan world. Thus miracle plays and mysteries came into being, and the primitive drama was employed by the Church. All the early entertainments of this nature were intended to serve an educational purpose, to point a moral, or make an appeal to the higher sympathies. They were intended to influence and instruct the ignorant people, to induce them to realise the meaning of the living pictures thus presented better than they otherwise could. But at the time when we take up the story the guilds and trading corporations had either undertaken the performance of the moralities themselves or supported and maintained professional actors for the purpose. As a result, the Christian liturgical drama degenerated, and the Mystery play became overlaid with comic interludes for the gross and vulgar enjoyment of the common people. To dancing and singing were added juggling and pantomime. The miracle plays, with dramatic representations of the Nativity, Death, and Resurrection, with other scenes from Christian history and the lives of the saints, had now undergone a secular development, and comprised the whole history of the world, from the Old Testament, blended with other forms of entertainment. It was toward the end of the twelfth century that the control of the plays and the pageants passed out of the hands of ecclesiastics, and became an adjunct of the festivals of the guilds. They were no longer performed in the churchyards, but in the streets and market places, and strolling players travelled over the country-side giving performances.

In a world peopled with the credulous and superstitious there was none more superstitious and credulous than the early mariner. As the seamen pushed the beaks of their queer-shaped vessels into the teeming solitudes of the vast oceans they were brought face to face with unfamiliar aspects of nature, with strange birds and still stranger fishes.   Unlearned, save in the technical duties of their calling, endowed with an enormous capacity for self-deception, having a child's eyes for the marvellous, with an abiding faith in the miraculous, it is not surprising that they gave a free rein to the imagination, and regarded all the uncommon things that amazed or scared them as of supernatural origin. Strange sights or sounds were of good or evil omen; these harboured or portended beneficent spirits to be propitiated or devils to be exorcised.   The corposant, that electric spark which, in form like the will-o'-the-wisp, glows and glitters at the yardarms or hovers a brilliant globule above the masthead, was the spirit of a saint — St. Elmo, which when the companions of Columbus saw, they sang litanies and offered up thanks, affirming that now all dangers were past.   The appearance of certain birds, particularly if they alighted on the ship, was an unfavourable omen;   the stormy petrel, Mother Carey's chicken, possessed the power of raising tempests, and most land fowl, unless they were black as a crow — an unexplained exception — brought ill luck to sea with them, while every one knows the dire consequences which followed the wanton destruction of an albatross.   It was permissible, indeed, to catch these noble birds as day after day they hovered in the wake of the ship, a familiar and beautiful spectacle amid the grey skies and wild waves of the Southern Seas, and to attach under the wing or round the neck messages for home or to other voyagers.   But to harm them surely presaged misfortune to the old-time seamen, and brought more than one promising expedition to grief and failure.

Then think of the prodigies in the way of the fishy denizens of the ocean, from the sea serpent to the mermaid, which have been made the source of endless traditional lore and legendary myth.   Olaus Magnus tells us that all the sailors of his day believed in a sea serpent two hundred feet long and twenty feet thick, with long black hair on its head, flaming eyes, and a scaly body. And from that time to our own some old floating log covered with barnacles, or a half-tide rock, with the seaweed rising and falling upon it, has been pictured as some marine monster, with horrible attributes, by seafarers innumerable. As if it were not sufficient that the mysterious habitants of the ocean should be of terrible aspect, we have the mermaid, of bewitching shape and entrancing loveliness, to tempt the unwary navigator into danger by her tricksy wiles and sweet melody. Have we not the authority of Hendrick Hudson for the fact that the skin of these syrens of the rocks is milk-white, and their tails " speckled like a mackerel " ? It were absurd, then, to talk about dugong, manatee, or seal ; these may be the originals of the ugly mermen, but the mermaidens, who sit upon the coral strand, dressing their hair with combs of pearl, are too lovable to be cast into the same category, even though the motives of these lovely creatures have ever been regarded by seamen as deceitful, and their purpose to lure the reckless and infatuated to destruction.

The unusual sounds of the sea, expressed to the credulous and perturbed mariners messages fraught with weal or woe, while to carry a priest as passenger, or even to talk about women, was a sure way of raising the devil. Any one who has heard at nightfall the doleful wailing and weird shrieks that arise from the birds on an unfrequented part of the coast, or a lonely islet in the ocean, will easily understand how the superstitious fears of the seamen were aroused, and how their imaginative nature gave rise to the amazing yarns which, with extreme circumstantiality, are set forth in the old books of travel, and have been perpetuated by many generations of tars. Sailors have seen and done strange things, like to nothing that happens on shore. They pass their time on a wild and wonderful element, remarkable for its strength, its capriciousness, and its cruelty, and their story teems with astounding perils and marvellous escapes. Tinged with an abiding respect

for the unseen Powers, whether of benevolent or diabolic
origin, their religious feelings and sentiments were deeply
ingrained by a superstitious reverence for the more
material representation of the supernatural, and this
strain in their character has added not a little to the
romantic aspect of nautical life, making the truth as
seen through their salt-washed eyes incomparably more
fascinating than any fictitious seascape drawn from the
landsman's imagination.

There can be little doubt, then, that in the shows
and processions which formed so prominent a feature
in medieval life the audience always contained its due
proportion of simple, open-mouthed seafarers, ready
to swallow the stories of marvels or new wonders, or
to attest their veracity from the store of similar experiences which had been their own lot. As already remarked, when in peril the sailors were in the habit of
offering candles and votive gifts to their patron saints,
and those that resorted to the Port of London regarded
St. Bartholomew, whose Priory had been established in
West Smithfield in the reign of Henry I, as their own
particular patron, a belief fostered by legends of the
assistance which the saint had given to those at sea.
Thus we read in the annals of the priory that eleven
ships from a port in Flanders being separated in a storm,
one of them ran aground and was buried half its depth in
sand. On board this vessel among the wailing crowd of
seamen and passengers, was one of riper age, who, turning
to them, said, " I have heard specially of one saint and
heavenly citizen, I have heard of Saint Barthilmewe,
that, among the knights of the heavenly king, is worthy
to be called upon, who pleasantly condescendeth to
the prayers of devout askers. Let us, therefore, lift
up our hands to Heaven, and avow, with clear devotion,
that, when we come whither we purpose, to London, we
shall bear thither, in the honour of Saint Barthilmewe, a
Ship of Silver, after the form of our ship, made at our
costs, offering to that church in mind of our deliverance."
It is recorded that upon the vow being made the saint

" with his holy hand, drew forth the ship by the fore-end," and that the thankful seafarers presented their offering to the priory. There are many legends of this nature, in some of which the saints actually appear and present those they have assisted with some token of their appreciation of the trust placed in them, which token would be carried to the church and there preserved as a relic, and a tangible piece of evidence to the miracle. A less reverent picture is presented in one story, where we are told of a sailor who promised St. Christopher a wax candle as big as himself. When he made the offer a bystander said : " Have a care what you promise; though you make an auction of all your goods you'll not be able to pay." " Hold your tongue," whispered the other, " you fool ! Do you think I speak from my heart ? If once I touch land I'll not give him a tallow candle ! " But at many famous shrines, where sailors and others went to make their thank-offerings, or, like Chaucer's Shipman, wipe out their sins by a pilgrimage, the concourse of people led at certain seasons to popular festivals. At some places, where by royal grant or prescription there was the right to hold fairs, mysteries and morality plays were exhibited for the entertainment of the strangers and all who congregated there, either for business or pleasure. Sometimes in the churchyard, and later on in convenient open spaces as the crowds of spectators increased, on gaudily decorated scaffolds, and sometimes on movable vans which could be drawn from one place to another, the miracle plays were presented, and in a later day the moralities from which, by various stages of development, the modern drama was evolved.

It was when the members of the trade guilds had succeeded the clergy in the management of the moralities, that we find the seamen playing a part upon the stage. Thus in the order of the pageants of the play of Corpus Christi, in the time of the mayoralty of William Alne, in the reign of King Henry V, A.D. 1415, the subject chosen for representation by the shipwrights was

"God warning Noah to make an Ark of floatable
wood," and that of the fishermen and mariners, "Noah
in the Ark, with his wife, the three sons of Noah with
their wives ; with divers animals." In the presentation
of this play of the building of the Ark, with its mixture
of coarse realism, profane buffoonery, and reverent
sentiment, the strong contrasts reflect and illustrate
the conceptions, occupations, and workaday life of the
mariners of the time. Noah having gathered his family
together, bids them "Leste this watter fall, To worche
this shippe, Chamber and hall, As God has bedden us
doe." And one of the other characters says : " I will goe
gaither sliche, The shippe for to caulke and pyche;
Anoynte yt muste be every stiche, Borde, tree, and
pynne." Then they began to build the ark, and Noah
said that the boards must be pinned together, that
he would make the mast of a tree, "tyed with cab-
belles that will laste," with a sail-yard, a top-castle and
bowsprit, and cords and ropes. Then they pretended
to build the ship, and on the boards which formed its
sides the beasts and fowls were painted. One can
picture the curious birds and animals which the imagination of the seamen would lead them to depict in this way
as entering the ark. After this, as a change, there was
a comic interlude in which Noah's wife, as a typical
woman of the seaports, with a ready fist and a shrewish
tongue, objected to accompany her husband and sons
unless her gossips went with her. "They love me well,"
she cries, "and I would save their life, if you will not that
they come into thy chest, then you had better go and get
a new wife." Then the sons try their hand, Shem points
out that the wind is fair, and after some further squabbling
the sons employ force and carry her into the ship. Whereupon Noah triumphantly remarks, "Welcome, wife,
into this boat," to which his wife replies, "Then have
thou that for thy note " (nut). The slap in the face
that follows elicits from the patient Noah the ex-
clamation, "Ah, Ha, marye, this is hotte ! " Apparently
the three sons carried their obstinate mother into the ark,

and when her husband gave her sarcastic greeting she
retaliated with a blow on his nob. In another collection
of plays Noah is not pictured as so long-suffering, and
when his wife taunts him with being afraid his attempts
to beat her end in a regular fight. Noah admonishes
husbands to chastise their wives while they are young,
meaning, we may take it, when newly married. There is
an evident reference to a nagging tongue, and it is only
the interference of their children that brings the tussle
to a conclusion. The greater part of the stage directions
is obviously paraphrased from the Bible, but the
fitting out of the ark, and its equipment, was that of the
ships of the period, while the coarse jokes and the horse-
play indulged in could only appeal to those who led a
hard and rough life.

It may be admitted as true that no sample can ade-
quately represent the complete work, but we have in
these quotations from one of the morality plays a sufficient indication of the kind of entertainment which
the country-folk appreciated. In this particular play,
too, the association between the calling of the performers and the subject represented is the more significant that it was not customary. The seamen were, it
appears, clearly recognised as of a different character from
the landsmen, and their rude and boisterous humour, ill-
disguised contempt for the softer habits of those who
lived ashore, the quaint expressions of their profession,
with their wider knowledge of the globe, all appealed to
the people, or enforced and emphasised the distinctive
attributes of the sailor, with manners, customs, and a
language of his own.

As we shall presently find, the sailor has always exhibited an aptitude for the histrionic art, and the presentation of the elementary passions and feelings on
the stage. Some of the actors and dramatic writers
who have got most nearly to the hearts of the people
began their lives as seamen. We need not be surprised,
therefore, if the medieval sailors took the notion of their
morality plays to sea with them, or if we find in the oft-

described ceremony enacted on crossing the line a lingering reminiscence and survival of the institutions which, overlaid with strange fancies and beliefs, furnished dramatic spectacles to the mariners when the art of navigation was in its infancy. It was not only on crossing the Equator that such performances took place, for a Dutch writer tells us that when a ship entered the thirty-ninth parallel all those on board who had not passed before were ducked overboard from the bowsprit, unless they were prepared to redeem themselves by some kind of payment to the seamen. The ceremony took place in the bows of the ship, where some kind of stage had been erected, and where the principal mariners, attired suitably for the occasion, made use of a set ritual with dramatic words and action. Other writers state that the sailors were dressed as judges, and that the mummery took the character of a trial, at which the victims of the seamen's facetiousness were on evidence found guilty and sentenced to death. It was very rough humour, however, for if the sentence was not redeemed with money, wine, provisions, or the like, flogging was the least of the punishments to which they became liable. None were exempt from punishment or fine, not even the captain, much less the unfortunate passengers, and one author mentions a case in which a man was drowned while being keel-hauled for refusing to pay forfeit. In the Spanish ships it was the custom to preface the trial of the offenders against Neptune's laws with an imitation bull fight, while in the Portuguese ships the forfeits, instead of being divided among the seamen, were regarded as contributions to the Church. These customs, it seems, were also practised when passing the Straits of Gibraltar and the Cape of Good Hope. Doubtless they had their origin, like the mystery plays, in religious rites, or in propitiatory offerings to the unknown deities of the ocean, and upon them extravagant buffoonery had been engrafted, until in time little remained but the rough and often cruel horse-play which tradition has associated with the ceremony.

In other ways, as the voyages became of longer duration, methods were devised in order to provide amusement for the mariners. As the instructions for the conduct of an expedition prohibited dicing, carding, and every kind of gambling, something else was needed in the shape of entertainment, and musicians were carried in the ships and the seamen encouraged to divert themselves with song and dance. There are references as early as the thirteenth century to mummeries which may have been something like the Christmas play and pageant of St. George which is still to be seen enacted at Yuletide in country places; doubtless there were Lords of Misrule and Abbots of Unreason afloat as well as ashore. The sailor is not only an enthusiastic playgoer, he is absorbed in the enchantment of the drama, and is never so pleased as when he can have his own show. It is only natural to suppose that those responsible for the success of the adventurers' undertakings would take advantage of this circumstance. In the accounts of the attempts to find the North-West Passage we may get some idea of the efforts made to amuse the sailors and their pastimes. Hawkins took "waytes" to sea with him, and the movements of the vessels when the pipes were playing were an invitation to dance. Certain it is that among the earliest of English ballets known to us there was "The Jig of the Ship," which appears to have been a characteristic dance by sailors given at the conclusion of a play. These jigs may have been ballet or pantomime or both, but it is noteworthy that in all the principal nautical dramas, which will be presently mentioned, a dance of sailors was introduced. Pepys mentions in 1668 how after dinner he went to the Duke of York's house to the play, and saw "The Tempest," which he had often seen, "but yet I was pleased again, and shall be again to see it, it is so full of variety, and particularly this day I took pleasure to learn the tune of the seamen's dance, which I have much desired to be perfect in, and have made myself so." Whether the "Jig of the Ship," the seamen's dance of the time of Pepys, and the sailor's hornpipe of a later date were directly connected we are unable to decide. But as they were all associated with the theatre it is permissible to assume that some kind of histrionic exhibition was among the entertainments of the early mariners, however rough and uncouth it may have been.

There is no reason, however, for supposing that because he was rough and boisterous in his amusements, the seaman was more brutal than the landsman in any age. But if he had been, there was in the olden time much excuse for him. In addition to running the ordinary dangers of life he had to take those of the sea in addition, and when he was not fighting human foes he was engaged in combat with the elements. Ill-found ships, bad provisions, harsh usage, and no comfort in the landsman's sense of the word; were his lot, and it was likely that this environment produced a personality whose nature was of a rugged, uncouth, not to say savage type. Necessarily the discipline of the sea was harsh in the extreme. There were but a few officers in the ship, and many men ; brute force and mastery of mind were essential to keep order in such a rude community, yet it was seldom save in the relaxation of law after battle that the evil passions were displayed, when licence came as a comparatively momentary reward for many months of hardship and rough usage.

So far we have found our sailor on the stage, and what is perhaps of more import and significance, we have discovered traits in his character and features in his environment which should distinguish him among his fellows when the dramatic instinct of the nation blossoms and bears fruit.

REAR-ADMIRAL OF THE BLUE,
SIR RICHARD BICKERTON, Bart.

REAR-ADMIRAL OF THE RED,
BARON NELSON OF THE NILE.

(Book Plates, 1779.)

TO COMMEMORATE THE FAVOURITE
OPERETTA, GEORGE III. (1764).

TO CELEBRATE THE ANNOUNCEMENT
OF PEACE, GEORGE III. (1814).

(Watch Plates.)

To face page 160.

tution being to a large extent a speculative description
of an improved state of English life and manners. Thus
the literature of learning and science runs upon parallel
lines with the history of exploration and discovery,
and now that we enter that period which is richest in
dramatic and poetic literature we shall find that just as
the language of the sailor had got into the mouths of the
people, so the social and professional life of the sea
exerted a strong influence upon the Tudor and Stuart
writers, rooting the nautical expressions in the national
literature. The practice of the sea had crystallised.
The seamen had become a distinct class in dress and
manners. The sea terms in use had reached a very full
development, and thus when the writers of the age found
the art, science, and mystery of seamanship at their
service, with the larger experience of the Tudor explorers, they could not fail to reflect more or less such
a prominent feature of the national life.

Meantime a wonderful development had taken place
in regard to the national drama. After the miracle
plays came the moralities, with personified vices and
virtues, the former comic characters to give relief to
the platitudes of the latter. Then a wholesome desire
for livelier plays, with incident and action, caused scenes
from history generally to be selected for representation,
usually with some monitory or didactic purpose. Hence
the human interest in the play grew and developed,
and in the comedies and tragedies sea imagery became
common, so that the business and technicalities, as well
as the dangers and difficulties, of the mariner's calling
were made known to a larger section of the population,
and tended to encourage that restless energy which
sent the more mercurial and impetuous spirits afloat,
where, inured to discipline, hardened by peril, and
tempered by experience, they became magnificent
seamen. Even the commercialism of the adventurers
was reflected in the dramas of the period, and although
Sir William Monson says, " The sea language is not soon
learnt, much less understood, being only proper to him

that has served his apprenticeship," yet we shall find that Shakespeare and his fellow-dramatists were often apt in the use of this language, having a right conception of the meaning of many technical terms in the seaman's vocabulary.

The earliest characterisation of a seaman on the stage is to be found in one of the first of the Tudor plays, which bears his name, " Hicke Scorner." The author of this merry interlude is unknown, but it enjoyed great popularity, probably because of its essentially English nature, and it was printed by Wynkyn de Worde. It has little plot, but, under the guise of a moral dissertation on the temptations of youth, gives a sketch of the characters and manners of the age, and thus is a distinct dramatic advance upon the moralities which preceded it.

The interlude begins with the entrance of Pity, who complains of the poverty which he finds everywhere, the sinful and evil living which abounds. He is joined by Contemplation and Perseverance, the former of whom declares that he is neglected by people of all classes, while Perseverance can give them but scant comfort. There is, however, a very self-satisfied pharisaical air about all three which marks them out for ridicule. While they are lamenting, to them comes Freewill, who is a raffling blade. He has been to sea, and has experienced its dangers. He talks about putting the helm a-lee, striking his sails, and the anchor holding. He says, " I can fight, chide, and be merry," and so long as he has a penny he will bid his friends " fill up the cup, and make good cheer." Freewill has come to the conclusion that the life of a highwayman or a footpad on Shooter's Hill is to be preferred to seafaring, and he chaffs Imagination about his sad looks, eventually beguiling that unfortunate into confessing that he has been in trouble about a girl and has been put in the stocks. Imagination is now waiting for a kinsman, Hicke Scorner, who has been in prison with him, probably for a similar indiscretion.

Then Hicke Scorner enters, with rolling gait, and nautical expressions on his lips. "A lee the helm, a lee, veer shoot off, veer sail, veer-a." The exact bearing of these nautical remarks may not be clear at first glance, and it is quite possible that they have been mangled in transliteration by various editors whose erudition did not include the sea alphabet. It is obvious, however, that they would not be put into the mouth of Hicke Scorner unless it were intended to indicate his knowledge of the sea calling and its terms. The later dramatists, including Shakespeare, were in the habit of indicating their seamen in a similar manner, but they were more precise or correct in their use of phrases. To put the helm to leeward, or to put it down, would throw the ship into the wind, checking her way. The expression " veer shoot off " may have been in the original " veer the sheet off," in which case to " veer," or pay out, or ease off the sheet would be consonant with putting the helm alee, and at the same time " veer sail " would mean to lower away or take in the sail. " Veer-a " would then answer to the more modern order, " Let go of all." The expressions thus explained would then be those used in bringing a vessel to anchor, and this is exactly what a sailor might picture himself as doing on his return from a cruise. Not only does Hicke Scorner use the sailor language, but his remarks and appearance are such that Freewill exclaims, " Hark to him, he is aship on the sea," or, in other words, in a ship, that is to say, he still fancies himself afloat.

Hicke Scorner's first thoughts are to wish his friends " Good cheer "—" What cheer ? " says the Boatswain to the Master in the " Tempest," and the Master replies, " Good "—and then he starts in to spin them a yarn, in quite the customary seaman's manner, and with the seaman's picturesque and vivid imagination. During his voyages, he has visited many parts, from Biscay Bay to an imaginary country which he calls Rumbelow. What Rumbelow meant and where it was is by no means clear. The word came to be used later in many a rousing

chorus, and Marlowe makes Lancaster say in the second
act of " Edward II ":—

> With a heave and a ho,
> What weeneth the King of England,
> So soon to have won Scotland,
> With a rombelow ?

Hicke Scorner has seen many sights, and met with a
number of ships ; but all those which carried people too
good to live were wrecked, and those on board were
drowned.   In his ship it was very different.   In her
there was good company, a very mixture of all kinds
of rogues and vagabonds, pleasant fellows to live amongst,
and people who found England by no means such a bad
place as the prudes would have them believe.   He
relates to his companions such tales as Chaucer's seaman
told the company of pilgrims, and with such vivid
colouring that at last Imagination is excited, and proposes that they should go and make a night of it at some
ale-house.

This is agreed to, but Freewill calling Imagination a
lubber, they quarrel and fight, and Hicke Scorner,
like Mercutio, while trying to part them, is wounded.
Then Pity comes on the scene to try to restore peace
between the revellers, but his lecture to them to avoid
sinful living and be as good and holy as he, excites
their scorn.   At the characteristic suggestion of the
sailor, therefore, they tie him up, and having eased him
of the wherewithal to make themselves merry, they
depart.

That is all the part that Hicke Scorner takes in the
play, and precisely why it should be called after him is
not easy to determine, unless the character of the sailor
was more popular, as it might well be, than those of
the others. He is a jovial rover, a boon companion,
ready with a blow or a blessing. Like Captain Manly,
in the " Plain Dealer," he scorns hypocrisy and cant, but
is not prepared to resist the temptation of carousing
with a set of jolly fellows, even though he knows them
to be sinners.

Not so his companions. The good Samaritan, Pity, is released by Contemplation and Perseverance. Freewill, who has been caught and sent to prison, tardily repents, and his friend, Imagination, is also presently persuaded by Perseverance and Contemplation to follow his example. But Hicke Scorner is seen no more, and we are left to suppose that he may have gone to sea again. The character, though slight, is well drawn and original; it is at least recognisable and not without raciness and spirit. Like Jack Juggler in another interlude, Hicke Scorner's motto is " To be merry when I may and take no thought for the morrow." The popularity of this play was so great that not only was it printed with illustrations which had been obtained from foreign sources, but a good deal of it, particularly the more witty dialogue, was incorporated in later dramatic works.

Hicke Scorner is about the only distinctly seafaring character to be discovered in those interludes which have been saved from destruction, but there are in others many indications of a knowledge of the sea life and sea terms. In the interlude of the " Four Elements," one of the productions of Rastell's Press in the early part of the sixteenth century, in a description of the route to America, we are told that " Westward be found new lands, that we never heard tell of before this, by writing nor other means. . . . For divers mariners had it tried, and sailed straight by the coast side, about five thousand mile. . . . But they that were the adventurers have cause to curse their mariners, false of promise and dissemblers, that falsely them betrayed; which would take no pains to sail further than their own lust and pleasure, wherefore that voyage and divers others such caitiffs have destroyed. O what a thing it had been then, if that they that be Englishmen might have been first of all; that they should have taken possession, and made first building and habitation a memory perpetual; and also what an honourable thing, both to the Realm and to the King, to have had his dominion extending there, into so far a ground, which the noble King of late memory,

the most wise Prince, the VIIth Harry, caused first
to be found." This is supposed to have been written in
scorn of the English mariners who in Sebastian Cabot's
alleged voyage in 1516–17 are said to have relinquished
the enterprise in disgust, and permitted other nations to
discover the new world. After describing the new-found
land, the writer regrets that the French and others have
found the trade, and " yearly of fish there they lade
above an hundred sail." *

In the same interlude is given a description of how
the mariners can tell that the world is round, because
" if a fire be made at night upon the shore, that giveth
great light, and a ship in the sea far, they in the top
the fire see shall, and they on hatch nothing at all. . . .
Yet when they draw the land more near, then the hill
tops begin to appear, still they near more high and high,
as though they were still growing fast, out of the sea till,
at last, when they come the shore to, they see the hill,
top, foot, and all ; which thing so could not befal, but
the sea lay round also."

The term " on hatch " may need some explanation.
Shakespeare uses it in " Richard III ":—

> . . . As we paced along
> Upon the giddy footing of the hatches,
> Methought that Gloster stumbled, and in falling
> Struck me—that thought to stay him—overboard.

And again in " The Tempest " : " We were all dead of
sleep and—how we know not—all clapp'd under hatches."
An aperture in the deck is a hatchway, and the coverings
hatches. To clap on the hatches is an expression frequently used in tales of storm or boarding. " Under
hatches," sings Dibdin, and in the old wooden vessels
the gangways which ran from the quarter-deck to forecastle were composed of hatches, movable gratings,

* Richard Eden appears to be the only authority for this fiasco,
in an epistle dedicatory to the Duke of Northumberland, which he
prefixed to his translation of the fifth part of Sebastian Münster's
" Cosmography." Ramusio has a similar statement in the Preliminary
Discourse to the third volume of his " Collection of Voyages," but
it seems to refer to an earlier enterprise in 1497.

walking on which, when there were no bulwarks, would
be to a landsman giddy work.

In " Everyman " there is a reference to the " reckoning " of the voyagers, and to the coarse and hard fare
of those who go afloat, while in John Heywood's " Four
P's," the 'pothecary recommends one of his ointments as
a sheet-anchor, because no doctor had ever known it to
fail as a last resource. The term is used in a similar
sense in Nicholas Udall's " Ralph Roister Doister "
(1550). Heywood also alludes to the use of a tampion
for plugging the muzzle of a " tewel," a term which the
old seamen used as a synonym for a great gun. That
he knew something about the Navy is also clear because,
speaking of the depth of a river, he says " the *Regent*
could have there ridden," the *Regent* being one of the
largest men-of-war of the time.

In " Ralph Roister Doister " one of the characters
is named Sym Suresby, master of a ship, whose characteristic motto is " Be of good cheer, man, and let the
world pass." Suresby believed that Neptune was angry
with some one in his ship, since they had been afflicted
with such outrageous tempests. He assures Dame
Custance that the merchant, his employer, has returned
home as fast as wind and sail could carry him. His
character is that of an honest, loyal servant, unused
to the ways of the shore, and earnest in his duty. He
is under the impression from something he has seen that
the merchant's sweetheart has treated his employer badly,
but when he is addressed by the latter as " My trusty
man," and exhorted to tell the truth, he replies, " To
reporte that I hearde and sawe, to me is ruth, but both
my duetie and name and propretie (honesty as between
servant and employer), warneth me to you to shewe
fidelitie," and so he tells the story, which is like to part
the two lovers. But no one is more delighted than he
when he finds that he has made a mistake, and he asks
his employer's future wife to bear him no ill will, " for
he did a true man's part." Here there is distinct characterisation, and an evident intention to impress the

audience with the honesty and right-mindedness of the rough and untutored sailor.

In "The World and the Child," printed in 1522, the word "prest" is used in the sense of readiness for action as it was used at sea. In "Gammer Gurton's Needle," a comedy reputed to have been written by John Still about 1566, there are one or two naval phrases, and others may be found in "The Triall of Treasure," printed in 1567, but probably written a good deal earlier.

More interesting still is the sea song to be found in "The Comedy of Common Conditions," which is believed to have been written about the same date. There not only is the equipment of the ship set forth, her victuals, weapons, and flaunting flags, that she is a swift skimmer of the seas, with her mariners tried and worthy, but the titles and qualities of the officers are also described.

Coming to the Elizabethan Drama, of which it has been truly said that it had "its first flush of dawn in Marlowe and its meridian splendour in Shakespeare," the great number of nautical phrases and expressions scattered through the works of the dramatic poets, if not evidence that some of them had had experience of a sea life, at least would lead us to suppose that they were frequently in the company of seamen. Nothing is, indeed, more likely than that this was the case; although the fact that it was an age of exploration and discovery, and that the commercial spirit was growing up in the nation, must also be regarded as potent factors among those intellectual influences which were at work, and which bore fruit in the literature of the period. Then, too, it must be remembered that the atmosphere of the time was one of exultation after victory at sea, and comradeship with the men who had done so much for England would give to those who enjoyed it an insight into the sea life and sea lore which they could not fail to utilise. It is most probable that it was the fashion in a court of which Drake, Raleigh, and Essex, with other sailors, were distinguished stars, to interlard the speech with sea phrases, and as the stage was under court patronage, the more reason that we should find them reflected there. So they would get into the language, and thus into the mouths of the people, and we know that many of their phrases are common in our every-day speech, even now. That not only Shakespeare, but lesser men, used this language of the sea correctly will be shown by quotations from their works, but he is, of course, ahead of all of them even in this respect. Lodge was himself a seaman. Marlowe had been a traveller by land and sea, and gives us many correct descriptions of ships and their equipment. He probably obtained his idea of oriental life and character, at least in part, from the seamen he met. He knew, too, the value of a navy, for in the play of " Edward II " he makes young Mortimer say :—

> The haughty Dane commands the narrow seas
> While in the harbour ride thy ships unrigged,

and Tamburlaine explains, too, how by the strategical distribution of his sea forces and brigantines, etc., " the Persian fleet and men-of-war" were disposed in such a manner from the East to the furthest West, that :—

> They shall meet and join their force in one,
> Keeping in awe the bay of Portingale,
> And all the ocean by the British shore;
> And by this means I'll win the world at last.

In " Dido, Queen of Carthage," where there are de-tailed accounts of ships and their equipment, we find the Navy described as :—

> The very legs whereon the State doth lean as on a staff
> That holds us up, and foils our neighbour foes.

It is not only a general view of the Navy and its material that we get from the pages of the dramatists, but we are able to reconstruct a picture of the seaman and to understand how the character was drawn which became typically representative of him. Taking, too, a selection of quotations from the different writers, we are shown the picturesque side of naval life, its

dangers, its pleasures and its contrasts.   In these dramas,
also, there are exhibited the circumstances of the seamen,
their dress, their victuals, and harsh punishments,
even their views of religion and their superstitious fears.
If we do not find that confirmatory evidence of their
steadfastness of mind and daring resolution which the
stirring and heroic acts described by the historians
warrant, we must remember that it has always been
difficult for the landsmen to appreciate the motives of
those who make their home on the sea.   Certainly we
find the sailor of the stage, if careless to the verge of
foolhardiness, yet impressed with the noble qualities
of patriotism, generosity, and courage, neither indifferent
to the interests of his employers nor unmindful of his
duty to the State.   Indeed, it is clear that so long as
he served under canvas—and it is not proposed to follow
him further—there was no material change in his character for centuries.

Let us turn to Shakespeare for a view of him in his
professional aspect.   In the opening scene in " The
Tempest " there is a very taste of the brine.   We can
picture the deck of the ship, and, as her dangerous position
becomes apparent, the sailors flying to their stations.
The treacherous rocks close at hand are lit up by the
flashes of lightning, the thunder peals terrifying the
passengers.   We hear the directing voice of the commander :—

" *Master.*   Boatswain !
Boatswain.   Here, Master ! what cheer ?
Master.   Good ! speak to the mariners ;   fall to't
yarely, or we run ourselves aground : bestir, bestir."

The Boatswain calls the sailors, who enter, and are
addressed by him.

" *Boatswain.*   Heigh, my Hearts ! Cheerly, cheerly,
my Hearts, yare, yare ! Take in the topsail. Tend
to the Master's whistle. Blow till thou burst, thou wind,
if room enough ! "

The ship is evidently carrying too much sail, and the

officer, encouraging the men by such expressions as
" Cheerly " and " Yarely " to heighten their activity,
instructs them to take in the topsail.

Landsmen may as easily be led amiss in regard to the
meaning of these words as the soldiers were in South
Africa, when the naval officers told them to haul " handsomely," and they hauled the harder. " Handsomely "
in nautical parlance means slowly, steadily, with more
care and less energy. " Yare " may be a seaman's
contraction for " Ye are to take care," or to be, in fact,
ready for anything. Massinger compares a pretty
maiden to " a new-rigg'd ship, both tight and yare."

Many ships at that time carried only one topsail and
this upon the mainmast, although a few of the heavier
men-of-war and merchantmen carried two topsails, and
some even a top-gallant-sail. The boatswain's injunction
to the wind to blow till it bursts has no connection with
the previous remark about the master's whistle, but
indicates that he cares not how hard it blows, so long
as there is sea room for his ship. The effort of the seamen is indeed to get the vessel clawed off the land. When
the boatswain has roughly ordered the passengers below
to their cabins, that they may not be in the way, he addresses the men again with a " Cheerly, good Hearts ! "
and then :—

"*Boatswain.* Down with the topmast ! Yare ! Lower,
lower ! Bring her to try with main-course."

He is now getting down the top hamper, as the upper
and lighter sail was no longer of use, and the spar
would hold the wind and impede the progress of the
ship. He orders the man at the halliards to lower away
handsomely that the mast may come on deck. And then
he explains that he intends if possible to heave to, the
modern equivalent of bringing the vessel " to try." Until
quite recent times, ships still carried try-sails, sails used
to steady the ship when hove to in a storm. Now it is
clear why he hoped for sea room, for, hove to, the ship
would sag to leeward, and unless she had sea room would

go on shore. Almost before the words are out of his
mouth he sees that they are embayed and must try
another expedient, so he cries:—

"*Boatswain.* Lay her a-hold, a-hold ! Set her two
courses ; off to sea again ; lay her off."

They are evidently encircled by reefs, and their only
chance is to make more sail, to set the forecourse (the
sail on the foremast) as well as the mainsail, to endeavour to get to sea again. But their efforts are un-
availing, and the mariners cry, as they strike upon the
rocks—" All lost ! To prayers, to prayers ! All lost ! " and
a little later the stage direction is " A confused noise
within," and then the cry, " We split, we split, we split ! "

There is the true ring of the seaman's art in this opening scene of " The Tempest," and it would be almost
impossible in fewer words to give expression to the various
thoughts and actions of the sailors in such a predicament
as is here portrayed.

The use of the whistle by the sailors is mentioned by
several of the dramatists. Philip Massinger, in " A
Very Woman," act ii. scene 1, makes the captain say,
" Hark, how the boatswain whistles you aboard. Will
nothing move you ? " And in " The City Madam,"
act iii. scene 1, "*Ramble.* I knew you a waistcoateer
in the Garden Alleys, and would come to a sailor's
whistle." Ben Jonson, too, in " The Alchemist," act v.
scene 2, makes one of the players say, " Yes, and the
whistle that the sailor's wife brought you to know an'
her husband were with Ward." These quotations remind us that the whistle as an emblem of office was
worn by the admirals of the period. On the day of
the great fight in Conquet Bay in April, 1513, Sir Edward
Howard, in the *Sovereign*, when he found that he was
overpowered, " took his chain of gold nobles from about
his neck, and his great gold whistle, the ensign of his
office, and threw them into the sea to prevent the enemy
from possessing the spoils of an English admiral."

John Baltharpe, in "The Straights Voyage, or St.

David's Poem," speaks of the whistle as a "call," which
is probably the earliest mention of the term commonly
used by seamen.

> Samuel Hatfield is our Boatswain's name,
> He's man enough, I'll say the same:
> With silver call on deck he stands,
> Winds it, make haste, aloft more hands,
> Come on my lads, look to your gear,
> Be sure that we have all things clear.

The use of the nautical terms for handling a ship on
a lee shore, and the like knowledge of similar terms, are
clear proof that the aptness of the sea language was
fully appreciated by the audience in those days. If this
were not so, these terms would not have been applied to
colloquial use, as where Maria, in "Twelfth Night,"
says to Viola, who is dressed as a man, and who, having
obtained her disguise from the captain of a ship, may
have indicated in her dress an acquaintance with the
sea: "Will you hoist sail, Sir? Here lies your way."
And Viola retorts: "No, good swabber; I am to hull here
a little longer." To hull was to lie to with the sails ar-
ranged so that the ship moved as little as possible. Viola
therefore meant that she was not prepared to make sail
and sheer off as Maria wished. The "swabber" is also
used as a term of reproach in "The Ordinary," a comedy
written by William Cartwright probably in the first
quarter of the seventeenth century, and Massinger, in
"The Parliament of Love," makes one of the characters say, "I am a swabber, doctor, a bloodless swabber,
that have not strength enough to cleanse her poop."
Ben Jonson uses it in the same sense in the play of
"The Silent Woman."

On the other hand, there were some writers who,
attempting the sea language, either misused the terms
or have had them mangled for them by their editors.
There is, for example, a curious description in a play
called "The Return from Parnassus," which was publicly
acted by the students in St. John's College, Cambridge,
and printed in 1606:—

> 'Mongst the tempestuous waves on raging sea
> The wailing merchant can no pity crave.
> What cares the wind and weather for their pain?
> One strikes the sail, another turns the same;
> He shakes the main, another takes the oar,
> Another laboureth and taketh pain
> To pump the sea into the sea again:
> Still they take pains, still the loud winds do blow
> Till the ship's prouder mast be laid below.

Here are two expressions, " turning a sail" and "shaking the main," which as they stand have no sense, and yet the writer evidently wished to depict the movements of the sailors and their occupations when the vessel was making bad weather, for later on are the lines, " Our ship is ruined, all her tackling rent." We are to understand that they had taken in sail and were using the oars instead, but if this had been done there was no apparent reason why the mast should have been struck out of the ship. It is possible that the lines originally ran:—

> One strikes the sail, another folds the same;
> He sounds the main, another takes the oar, etc.

Marlowe says of a sailor in a storm that he " all fearful folds his sails and sounds the main, lifting his prayers to Heaven for aid against the terror of the winds and waves." To fold or furl the sails or to take soundings are, of course, operations understood by everybody. In Shakespeare there are few mistakes of this sort, possibly because he has been better edited. Whether he speaks of the officers, the master, the boatswain, the coxswain or the swabber, they are correctly placed; or of the rigging of the ship, or the nautical language used by the seamen he is always apt and accurate. In " Romeo and Juliet" Romeo says to the Nurse:—

> Within this hour my man shall be with thee,
> And bring thee cords made like a tackled stair,
> Which to the high top-gallant of my joy
> Must be my convoy in the secret night.

The tackled stair is the Jacob's ladder still used in sailing ships to reach the top-gallant masthead.

In " The Merry Wives of Windsor," Pistol declares:—

> This punk is one of Cupid's carriers—
> Clap on more sail: pursue, up with your fights;
> Give fire: she is my prize, or ocean whelm them all.

" Fights " were the cloths hung round the gunwale of
the ship or round the tops to conceal the men in an
engagement. Captain John Smith, in " A Sea Grammar,"
printed in 1627, explaining how to manage a fight at sea,
speaks of putting up the waistcloths and top armings,
a long red cloth about three quarters of a yard broad,
edged on each side with calico or white linen cloth,
that went round about the ship on the outside of her
upperworks and about the tops " as well for the countenance and grace of the ship as to cover the men from
being seen." " Close fights " were temporary screens
or barricades against boarders. In " The Comedy of
Errors," Ægeon, a merchant of Syracuse, makes use
of a number of nautical expressions, and one in particular which is frequently used by the dramatists.
He says, " We discovered two ships from far making
amain to us." To make, to call, or to wave amain was
a challenge to give way, to strike the sails or colours, or
to surrender. When the English ship meets an enemy
in Smith's description of the fight at sea, " he waves
us to leeward with his drawn sword, calls amain for the
king of Spain, and springs his luff." Naturally the
honour of the flag demanded that such a challenge should
be answered with a broadside, but a beaten ship would
signify the same by vailing or lowering her sail, as Marlowe
says in " The Jew of Malta ":—

> Because we vailed not to the Turkish Fleet,
> Their creeping galleys had us in the chase:
> But suddenly the wind began to rise,
> And then we luffed, and tacked, and fought at ease:
> Some have we fired, and many have we sunk;
> But one amongst the rest became our prize:
> The captain's slain, the rest remain our slaves,
> Of whom we would make sale in Malta here.

Or, again, in " Tamburlaine " :—

> And Christian merchants that with Russian stems
> Plough up huge furrows in the Caspian Sea
> Shall vail to us, as lords of all the lake.

To the science of navigation and its terms of art there are also many references. In a comedy entitled "A Merry Knack to Know a Knave," printed in 1594, we read :—

> Thy counsel is to me as North Star light,
> That guides the sailor to his wishèd port;
> For by that star he is so comforted,
> That he sails dangerless on dangerous seas,
> And in his deepest sadness comforts him.

Shakespeare also mentions the use of the Pole Star in navigation ; and in " The Merry Devil of Edmonton," published in 1608, reference is made to the pilot who has lost his compass or card, so that " the more he strives to come to quiet harbour, the farther still he finds himself from land." In " A Midsummer Night's Dream " we read: " Your eyes are lode-stars "—stars which drew the magnet or lodestone—and the pilot is sometimes called the lodes-man. Shakespeare and others make allusions to the charts in use, and in "The Parson's Wedding," written by Thomas Killigrew—a play said by Pepys in 1664 to have been represented at the King's House in Drury Lane wholly by women—one player recommends another to get his friends at court to have their pictures " cut ugly in the corner of a map like the old navigators." Marlowe speaks of the pilot and his use of the Jacob's staff, the instrument now superseded by the sextant. It is significant that the adjective most frequently found with the noun " mariner " is " painful," meaning painstaking, careful, and laborious; while it was the dangers of the deep that made the strongest impression on the landsmen. In Kidd's " Spanish Tragedy " we find :—

> My heart, sweet friend, is like a ship at sea,
> She wisheth port: where, riding all at ease,
> She may repair what stormy times have worn;
> And leaning on the shore, may sing with joy,
> That pleasure follows pain, and bliss annoy.

N

In a comedy called "Wyly Beguiled" (1606), we have
the sentiment, "As when the painful mariner, long tossed
by shipwreck on the foaming waves, at length beholds
the long-wished haven, 'though from far, his heart doth
dance for joy. So love's consent at length my mind
has eased, my troubled thoughts by sweet content are
pleased." There is a good deal of the sea in a comedy
by Jasper Mayne, published in 1639 and entitled "The
City Match." It is full of amusing situations and illustrations of manners. The two principal characters are
London merchants; one is called Seathrift, and it is
part of the plot that they pretend to sail for foreign
parts. Seathrift's son, when it is suggested that he
should go to sea also, objects, since he would have to
trust himself "in wooden sheets," and "within three
inches of becoming a Jonas," referring to the story of
Jonah and to the thinness of the planking of the ship's
side. Later on in the play another character, named
Cipher, enters "disguised like a sailor," in order to deceive the merchant by representing that he has been cast
away in one of his ships. He refers to himself as a poor,
seafaring man, and when he takes off his disguise he
says, "I hired this travelling case of one of the sailors
that lie at Blackwall." From a remark made in another
scene it would appear that a tarred canvas jacket,
dimity breeches, and kersey hose formed the dress
of the sailor at this period. There are, however,
other references to the distinguishing character of the
sailor's dress. In that "right excellent and famous
comedy called The Pleasant and Stately Moral of
the Three Lords and the Three Ladies of London,"
printed in 1590, three of the characters, Fraud, Dissimu-
lation, and Simony, are by the stage direction to be
"dressed in canvas coats like sailors." This favourite
play is supposed to have been written about 1588 by
R. Wilson, who was the leader of a company of players
in Queen Elizabeth's time, and is very valuable for its
illustration of manners. Simplicity, who is the comic
man, the direct descendant of the clown of the morality,

explains, when another player asks, " What mean these canvas suits ? Will ye be sailors ? " that the actors merely use the dress for purposes of disguise.

Nathaniel Field, the author of " A Woman is a Weathercock " and other plays printed in the early part of the seventeenth century, makes Lord Fee Simple, a blustering coward, declare that if his enemies appeared, " I would be upon the jack of one of them instantly." The expression is used by Hawkins and Monson, and refers to the jackets or jerkins of canvas worn by the seamen and soldiers, which were frequently emblazoned with the national or town's colours and arms. Another character in this play says, " I have a great mind to see The Ship at the Fortune." No doubt there was a dramatic piece with this title produced at the Fortune Theatre, which was built in 1599 by Edward Alleyne, the founder of Dulwich College, and burnt down in 1621. The piece does not appear to have been preserved. In another play a sailor's stomach is said to be of tougher stuff than his canvas jerkin. Massinger also refers to the canvas suits worn by the sailors, and to " a sleepy rug-gown'd watch." In 1602 there is a payment in the Navy Accounts for clothing for the Spanish prisoners which includes " rugge " for gowns, and doubtless rug gowns were used by the Tudor sailors when they stood their watch. As, too, seamen are frequently mentioned as appearing in the plays, yet seldom speak, their dress must have shown their occupation.

Nautical similes and the imagery of the sea were indeed freely used by the poet dramatists, and it is possible that the ideas of Oriental life and conduct as displayed on the stage were in part derived from the tales of the seamen and voyagers. Feeling sea-sick after one has landed, the woes of the passengers and their contemptuous treatment by the sailors, the high opportunity of those who sailed the seas, the inner life of the old Navy, its barbaric laws, colour, and character, are all mirrored in the plays of the sixteenth and seventeenth centuries. Chapman says that seafaring men are but sparingly

provided by nature with words in which to clothe their
thoughts, but they are not the less solid and sensible
because of their terseness. Though they may have
had but a small vocabulary, it was rich in terms and
phrases, and these must have been in fairly common
use, or the people who frequented the theatres would
not have understood the many allusions scattered
through the comedies and dramas. Moreover, it is
unlikely that the writers could have picked them up
from books, since the many mistakes made by their
editors and commentators show how little reliance can
be placed upon the dictionaries.

A few further quotations will illustrate this view of
the matter. Hear the regretful aspiration of Nicholas
Trotte, in the introduction to "The Misfortunes of
Arthur," printed in 1587. "O! that before our time
the fleeting ship, ne'er wandered had in watery wilderness, that we might first that venture undertake, in
strange attempt t' prove our loyal hearts." Thomas
Lodge, who sailed with Clark and Cavendish, and mentioned that he wrote at a time when "every line was wet
with the surge and every human passion counterchecked
with the storm," wishes that fortune may lend a pleasant
gale unto the spreading sails of his friend's desire. Henry
Porter must have had experience of sailors, for he says,
in "The Two Angry Women of Abington," a play
which Charles Lamb thought to be not inferior to "The
Comedy of Errors": "Within the heart's blood ocean
still are found jewels of amity and gems of love." And
elsewhere Hodge, a maltster, when told that his man,
Dick Coombs, is mightily drunk, replies, "I bad him
keep under the lee, but he kept down the weather two
bows; thus the wisest of us all may fall." The language
is obscure, but the meaning is clear. To be under the
weather is an expression still current. Coombs had been
warned by his master not to hoist too much sail, but he
carried on until he drove the ship bows under, or as
sailors a short time back had it, was about "three sheets
in the wind," or "half seas over." A common expression,

too, is that used by Barry in "Ram Alley, or Merrie Trickes," published in 1611, in which play one of the characters talks of shooting another " 'twixt wind and water." In one of Beaumont and Fletcher's plays, certain *gobemouches* are described as being absorbed in reading a book of the great Navy :—

> Of fifteen hundred ships, of cannon proof,
> Built upon whales, to keep their keels from sinking ;
> And dragons in 'em that spit fire ten miles.

That was a very respectable fleet as to numbers, and curious as to construction, but when we come to armament it was not stranger than fact, since we read of that ship of Scotland, the *Great Michael*, that she carried " three hundred shot of small artillery, that is to say, myand and batterd falcon, and quarter falcon, slings, pestilent serpetens, and double dogs, with hagtor and culvering, crosbows and handbows." The hagtors and pestilent serpetens are not less appalling than the dragons which spit fire ten miles from the whale's back. Seamarks, lighthouses, and many other adjuncts to navigation are mentioned, but more surprising is it to find reference to modern scientific machines of war. In "The Pastoral, the Shepherd's Holiday," the torpedo is mentioned, and Young Mortimer in " Edward II " explains, " I mean that vile torpedo, Gaveston, that now I hope floats on the Irish Seas." Still stranger is the query propounded by Jasper Fisher about 1630 in " The True Trojans " when he asks, " Or can our watery walls keep dangers out which fly aloft ? " One other phase of sea life must be mentioned. Naval history is as full of pageantry as it is of battles, and the nautical picture would be incomplete without what Shakespeare calls " the pageants of the sea," the glorified and radiant spectacle of a ship dressed out with all her flags and pennants and ensigns fluttering from yardarm and masthead.

So far in this chapter we have observed how the seaman and his language are reflected in the dramatic literature of the time. We have not discovered the man himself, except as a subjective impression of his character is received from the way in which writers regarded him and the things that concerned him. Now we may turn to some features of his own personality as they were revealed on the stage.

The courage and audacity of the sailor, his love of a fight and desire for plunder, find frequent illustration in the dramatists. In " The Unnatural Combat " there is a passage descriptive of one phase of the seaman's character, his eagerness for the fight, his love of fighting for fighting's sake, his coolness, his skill, and his loyalty to those he serves :—

> The miracle's greater when from the maintop
> A sail's descried, all thoughts that do concern
> Himself laid by, no lion, pinched with hunger,
> Rouses himself more fiercely from his den,
> Then he comes on the deck, and there how wisely
> He gives directions and how stout he is
> In his executions we, to admiration,
> Have been eye-witnesses: yet he never minds
> The booty when 'tis made ours; but as if
> The danger, in the purchase of the prey,
> Delighted him much more than the reward.

The improvidence of the sailor is also referred to by Massinger, and along with it a character opposite to that last described, and one probably more common to his temperament, viz. his fearlessness in quest of plunder, his love of spoil, and the recklessness with which he squandered what he gained :—

> Wherefore do we put to sea or stand
> The raging winds, aloft, or spit upon
> The foamy waves, when they rage most ; deride
> The thunder of the enemy's shot, board boldly
> A merchant ship for prize, though we behold
> The desperate gunner ready to give fire,
> And blow the deck up ? Wherefore shake we off
> Those scrupulous rags of charity and conscience,
> Invented only to keep churchmen warm,
> Or feed the hungry mouths of famish'd beggars ;
> But, when we touch the shore, to wallow in
> All sensual pleasures ?

And when it is suggested that it might be as well to save something against a rainy day the seaman exclaims :—

> When this is spent, is not our ship the same,
> Our courage, too, the same, to fetch in more ?
> . . . The sea which is our mother
> Yields every day a crop, if we dare reap it.
> No, no, my mates, let tradesmen think of thrift,
> And usurers hoard up; let our expense
> Be, as our comings in are, without bounds.
> We are the Neptunes of the ocean,
> And such as traffic shall pay sacrifice
> Of their best lading.

This gentleman was little better than a pirate, and a hint as to his future may be gathered from John Cook's play of " The City Gallant," published in 1614, in which the following conversation takes place :—

" *Bubble.* Whither do you mean to go, Master ?

Stains. Why, to sea.

Bubble. To sea ! Lord bless us, methinks I hear of a tempest already. But what will you do at sea ?

Stains. Why, as other gallants do that are spent, turn pirate.

Bubble. Oh ! Master, have the grace of Wapping before your eyes. Remember a high tide ; give not your friends cause to wet their handkerchiefs."

Reference is here made to Wapping and a high tide because pirates were hanged at Execution Dock, Wapping, and it was the custom to turn them off just at the top of the flood tide. Prince Hal says: " Now as low an ebb as the foot of the ladder and by and bye as high a flow as the ridge of the gallows."

The religion of the sailor, as well as his superstition and credulity, are other phases of the seaman's character upon which light is thrown in the old plays. It has been already noticed how, when the ship split upon the rocks in " The Tempest," the sailors went to prayers, and another dramatist declares that those who do business in blue waters have a simple faith in Almighty purpose.

But in a play by Thomas Nash called " Summer's Last Will and Testament " it is mentioned :—

> Witches for gold will sell a man a wind,
> Which in the corner of a napkin wrapped
> Shall blow him safe unto what coast he will.

There were always people to sell the sailors winds, and clergymen as well as witches and wizards were supposed to possess this valuable privilege. There is a story in most of the old collections of voyages of how a certain mariner purchased a selection of winds from a witch on the coast of Finland. The winds were contained in three knots tied in a rag, which rag was to be fastened to the mast, and the knots untied as the winds were required. Those first unloosed suited the sailors exactly and blew the ship homeward at a fine rate, but the third was a hurricane, so furious that the poor sailors thought God had sent it to punish them for their dealings with the Infernal One instead of trusting to His providence. Fortunately, they possessed another charm which presently mitigated the force of the gale, and they arrived home safely. Macbeth's witches were able to give away winds, drawn from all the quarters " that they know i' the shipman's card," that is to say, from all the points marked on the compass.

The dramatic writings of this period undoubtedly represented the larger national experience of the sea, which was no longer full of terrors to those who used it. So far as human foes were concerned, the sailor's dauntless bravery was sufficiently answerable, and, as Digby says, he was always ready to fight. When, on the other hand, it came to supernatural agencies, he either frankly relied on some charm as a child's caul, or else with Gilbert exclaimed, " We are as near to heaven by sea as by land."

BEN BACKSTAY.

T. P. COOKE AS

LONG TOM COFFIN.

MR. DUCROW IN THE "VICISSITUDES OF A TAR" AT ASTLEY'S THEATRE.

SKELT.

To face page 184.

Hard up and weary of waiting, on their beam ends for diversion, the news that a lady with whom they have some acquaintance has arrived in town comes as a blessing of which they immediately determine to take advantage. She is a widow, Lady Lovewright, whose husband, a captain of skill and valour, had been killed at sea.

The characters of the three captains are cleverly differentiated, and in a measure they may be compared with those heroes of Dumas, Athos, Porthos, and Aramis. Captain Seawit is the darling of the court and town, a gentleman with a very high sense of humour and honour. Captain Cable is the eldest and roughest; he speaks of his build being unfit for capering, and he makes furious love to the landlady. Topsail is the youngest, the flightiest, and has a sweetheart in every port. All three interlard their conversation with references to their sea life and the varied experiences they have met with afloat.

In the second act we are ashore at the inn, where the arrival of the lady with an attendant cavalier, a duenna and an uncle, has created quite a stir. The landlady is also a widow; her husband was a sailor who now rests in Neptune's bosom, "for his body fed the haddocks." But he had been lucky in his ventures, and had left his widow well provided for, so well, indeed, that she is now looking out for another husband. She gives her porter strict injunctions to permit no one in the inn dressed in canvas or coarse kersey, or smelling of tar or pitch. Nor any man of war, either, unless a young volunteer with plenty of good clothes such as Topsail wears. The porter asks if a buff jerkin or one made of chamois leather, well embroidered, with a touch of amber may pass, and when the landlady gives permission he mentions in an aside that this is Captain Cable's wear. The captains call in pursuance of their design, and again we get a touch of their character. Seawit is all for an honourable assault, Topsail hopes that the lady may prove amiable and not impervious

to the batteries of his gallantry, while Cable wants
to know the length of her purse. Lady Lovewright
invites them to a dinner and some entertainment, which
causes Cable to say he can no more dance than a lobster.
Mrs. Carrack, the landlady, is much attracted by Cable,
and determines to invite him to a *tête-à-tête* supper.

The plot turns upon the treatment of her various
sweethearts by Lady Lovewright, their number being
increased by a knight who is a passenger on board
Seawit's ship, a bully of whom the boatswain says,
" Your master, purser, gunner and his mate and I
have felt him about the shoulders." Like other bullies
he turns out to be an arrant coward. The jealousy
of the various rivals leads to many comical situations
and more than one challenge to fight. The under-
play also between Cable and the widow Carrack is not
without laughable features. Eventually, however, the
wind shifts and the sailors have to go to sea, but not
before Lady Lovewright has shown her preference for
the cavalier who has followed her into the country,
and Cable and his widow have come to an arrangement
to be married as soon as he brings home a sufficiently
profitable prize. Here and there throughout the play the
captains and their comrades use expressions with which all
seamen will be familiar, and the general atmosphere of a
seaport town largely frequented by sailors is maintained.

In two other plays Davenant introduces seamen—
in " The Siege of Rhodes " (1656), and in the musical
masque " The History of Sir Francis Drake " (1659).
In the latter there is a song, with chorus, wherein the
characters of the master, his mate, the purser, and the
boatswain are described.

In " The Canterbury Guests, or A Bargain Broken,"
a comedy written by Ravenscroft and produced towards the end of the seventeenth century, there is a
character such as was not infrequently introduced by
the dramatists by way of contrast to the land gallant,
with his finicking manners and shallowness. The
blunt sailor, with little knowledge of the fashions, un-

accustomed to the ladies, and bewildered by the ways
of society, makes many a laughable *faux pas*, but his
transparent honesty, his brave and handsome bearing,
his tact and his good looks, bring him success in the end.
Such a one is Jacomo, the leading character in Beaumont and Fletcher's " The Captain," a rough sailor
and a woman-hater, who falls a victim to the wiles of
the girl who loves and marries him. Such another,
as we shall see, is Ben Legend, but even more pronounced
is the characterisation of Captain Durzo in " The Canterbury Guests." He is described as an honest tarpaulin,
who was never ashore beyond a seaport town except to
burn and plunder among the Indians and the Spaniards ;
a stout and brave fellow, now returned to England,
who would employ his valour in the service of his native
country. He is brought by his friend, the hero of the
play, into the society at Canterbury, where among
others is Hillaria, the daughter of a London alderman,
a skittish lass who is not above masquerading in boy's
clothes, and who takes a liking to the blunt sailor.
Captain Durzo admits to her that he is a good deal
at sea when he is on land. He can walk about his frigate
fore and aft, even in his sleep, and finds his way between
decks alow and aloft and yet return to his cabin without
waking. But here in town he is lost and needs a pilot.
So Hillaria and her friends take him in hand. He is
not very curious in his dress, says one lady, and they
recommend him to lay by his sea habit, which smells
of tar, and assume a land attire. This he promises to
do " as fast as we heave dead men overboard in a sea
fight." He speaks of the girls as " three very snug
frigates, well rigged ; 'twas a pity, too, that they were
not as well manned." And when they ask him what he
thinks of them he admits that a woman is a fine thing,
but a ship under full sail is a finer. When invited to
dinner he expresses his willingness to take in ballast in
order that he may sail the stiffer, and requests that he
may be allowed to introduce his boat's crew in order to
entertain the company with a song and dance.

There is an excellent scene in which the captain makes love to Hillaria. In order to show the strength of his affections he is anxious to find some one to fight for her. Then when she asks him about his sea life he describes a battle—

" We, with topsails out, flags and streamers flourishing in the wind, and trumpets sounding, bear down upon the foe, then like thunder fall amongst them. There we are seen in clouds of fire and smoke. The slaughter now begins. We play at tennis with iron balls. Death comes whistling round our ears. Heads take fire in their brain pans and burst like grenadoes, scattering wild fire around. Other heads fly from one ship to another like bullets. Limbs, like langrel shot, mount, scattering in the air, and hands that could not reach their enemies before now fly into distant vessels to give their foes a box on the ear ; while other hands, grasping their swords, clear a whole deck in their flight. We are now in confusion. The fireships flame, and their half-moon is divided into blazing stars. Some burn, the men leap overboard and drown themselves to save their lives. Other ships reel, drunk with the salt brine, and at last sink to the bottom to follow these brave men in 'em with as much courage as they drank. The flags and pennants that hung wantonly playing in the air now on the decks lie stained with blood, and the taut masts of the ships lie on the hulls as in coffins."

There is much more of this description, punctuated by the lady's cries of alarm and dismay. Evidently it is intended to travesty the seamen's conventional stories of battle. In the end the boisterous love-making of the gallant seaman prevails, and Hillaria exclaims—

" Captain, I strike to you. You now with triumph in love's ocean steer. Calm is the sea and from all pirates clear. Here is my hand, my trusty tarpaulin, and we will sail together out of the haven of love into the tempestuous sea of matrimony."

In an adaptation from Molière by Otway, called " The Cheats of Scapin," Scapin, who is a rogue, tries to cheat the usurer by telling him that his son has been pressed on board ship, and that the captain will not release him unless he pays a large sum of money. Scapin, who is said to have served on board a privateer, counterfeits several sailors in order to carry out his schemes, and it is not clear how the disguise is effected unless the sailors were distinguishable by their dress. In the same manner the principal character in a play by Marston, called "Antonio and Melida," disguises himself as a sailor, but there is little in his language to indicate that he was accustomed to use the sea.

Several of the early plays deal with pirates, such as that written by Daborne and entitled "Christian Turned Turk, or The Tragical Lives and Deaths of the Two Famous Pirates Ward and Dansiker." The lives of these pirates were published in two pamphlets in 1609, and the play in 1612. Ward was a fisherman of Kent, who, after having served in the Navy, became a pirate, changed his religion, and settled down in Tunis. Dansiker, a Dutchman, was his partner. There were many ballads written about the legendary exploits of these pirates, but, as in the play, there is a very slight foundation of fact. In Daborne's tragedy there is a good deal of killing, Dansiker being put to death and Ward committing suicide, but if history is to be believed Ward died of old age in his marble palace at Tunis, where he lived "more like a prince than a pirate," while Dansiker was pardoned by the King of France, and eventually entered the service of the Duke of Guise. In the play there is a French lady disguised as a ship-boy, and other female characters fall in love with the supposed youth, thereby creating comic incidents and business. "Fortune by Land and Sea," a comedy printed in 1655, also deals with the pirates Purser and Clinton and their achievements. Here, again, there is a substratum of fact, inasmuch as two rovers so named did flourish in the reign of Queen Elizabeth, and their misdeeds and punishment are set forth in several ballads and poems published about 1587. They declared that they had only followed the example of Robin Hood, robbing the rich for the benefit of the poor, and that, moreover, they had never attacked the ships of their countrymen. The rovers in the play, however, fall victims to the superior skill of the captain of a merchant ship, and are hanged at Wapping. The dialogue of the two pirates with the hangman throws a curious light upon the methods of the time. The gallant merchantman is suitably rewarded before the fall of the curtain with a rich man's widow.

There is a spirited description of a sea battle in this play, beginning from the time when the boy at the masthead hails the deck, " Ho, there ! "; to which the master replies, " Ha, boy ? "; and then the boy explains, " A sail ho ! " Then there is the challenge to the stranger to show his colours, the retort quarrel-some, and the fight, which, beginning off the stage with " alarums and excursions," is continued in front of the audience, the prompt copy directing " the pirates with their mariners, furnished with all sea devices for a fight, enter." In the same way the captain of the merchant ship and his mariners are to be similarly attired, and the fight goes on until all the pirates are prisoners. The hangman, by the way, turns off his victims with the tag :—

> The world reports, two valiant pirates fell
> Shot betwixt wind and water, so farewell.

There are not a few plays the titles of which might lead one to suppose that their subject was the sea life of the time, but when looked into they are disappointing, and the action is found to have but little connection with naval or nautical matters. Shirley's " Young Admiral," printed in 1637, a tragi-comedy, and " Chabot, Admiral of France," by Shirley and Chapman, printed in 1639, are plays of this character without sea flavour. " The Sea Voyage, or The Commonwealth of Women," originally written by Fletcher but adapted by D'Urfey, and produced at the Theatre Royal in 1685, is another play of this description. The plot sets forth how some Portuguese voyagers, fleeing from pirates, were wrecked, the men on a desert island and the women on a more pleasant and fruitful one. The play opens on board a ship, but the characters can hardly be described as seamen. The arrival of a man on the island of the women leads to romantic incidents, and eventually those who have been parted are reunited and several weddings take place.

In a still earlier play by D'Urfey, called " Sir Barnaby Whigg," there is a character very much like that of Captain Durzo in " The Canterbury Guests." He is called Captain Porpuss, and is described as a blunt tarpaulin. He objects to the kind of songs they sing ashore, preferring those such as he was accustomed to when he commanded the *Success* at Solebay. He describes how he and his officers used to meet at nights in the great cabin, and over a bowl of punch his lieutenant used to give them the best sea songs. One of these Captain Porpuss sings, beginning :—

> Blow, boreas, blow, and let thy surly winds
> Make the billows foam and roar !
> Thou canst no terror breed in valiant minds ;
> But, spite of thee, we'll sail and find the shore.
> Then cheer, my hearts, and be not awed,
> But keep the gun room clear ;
> Tho' hell's broke loose, and devils roar abroad
> Whilst we have sea room here, boys, never fear.

Another notable instance is " The Rover, or The Banished Cavaliers," by " the ingenious Mrs. Aphra Behn," but although this lady had actually been to sea herself, and, as we learn from the story of her life, had seen and heard strange things there, the experience does not appear to have touched her lively imagination. Possibly the mysterious and strange floating fabric, adorned with figures and festoons, with rows of fluted and twisted pillars with cupids atop, circled with vines and flowers, which she is reported to have seen, was of too fairylike a nature to lend itself to the kind of play which she wrote.

" The Rover" was played at the Dorset Garden
Theatre for the first time in 1667, and the principal
character is said to have been taken from a play by Killigrew. A second part was produced in 1681, probably
because of the success of the original play. This was
also largely an adaptation from earlier comedies. The
first part of " The Rover" was afterwards produced,
with some necessary alterations, as " Love in Many
Masks." It is noteworthy, perhaps, that Nell Gwyn
played the principal female character in " The Rover "
at its first production. The scene in the first part is
laid in Italy and in the second in Spain, and the rover
is the only character that can lay claim to any sort of
nautical flavour. Mrs. Behn, however, introduces a
few expressions which have interest, and may be detached from the context. Her hero is thus described
by his friend: " He is a rover of fortune, yet a prince
aboard his little wooden world. He swears by the blind
ones, but he cares not to let his ship lie within a league
of the Mole, lest they play him a tramontana's trick."
We know of the Tramontana wind blowing over the
mountains, but the phrasing reads as if seamen here
were meant.

Upon the tricks of the tramontana seamen we have
no light to throw, but they were apparently a light-
fingered gentry whose predatory habits it were better not
to tempt by bringing the vessel alongside their wharves
or, in fact, too near their shores. Congreve uses the
expression, and in a somewhat similar sense, in " The
Old Batchelor." As will be shown elsewhere, the term
" wooden world " as a synonym for a ship was a favourite
one with literary men about this time, and Ned Ward,
the author of " The London Spy " and other scurrilous
works, calls his tract on the character of a ship of war
" The Wooden World Dissected." That Mrs. Behn
wants us to believe the rover to be a thorough seaman is
clear, and it may be supposed, therefore, that in depicting him as swearing by the blind ones, Love and Fortune,
she indicated two of the most conspicuous elements of

o

his character. Moreover, she makes him say that there is " no friend to love like a long voyage at sea."

We must not, however, complain of the paucity of naval character in the pieces which were produced at the theatres from about the middle of the seventeenth century to the middle of the eighteenth, because the exceptions to this rule are most valuable as affording illustrations of naval life and manners. Wycherley, in " The Plain Dealer," although his Captain Manly and Lieutenant Freeman have but little in their speech that would denote them as seamen, incidentally, by giving his comedy a naval setting, sheds not a little light upon the sea manners of his time. And then, too, he had been to sea and had been under fire, and knew wherein the sailor differed from the landsman. Next, almost at the end of that century, Congreve produced " Love for Love," and in Ben Legend manifestly intended us to recognise a sailor who may have seen service at Bantry Bay, at Beachy Head or Barfleur ; who might, indeed, have served under stout Benbow before he relinquished the Merchant Service for that of the King. And, in 1714 or thereabout, Charles Shadwell wrote the " Fair Quaker of Deal ; or, The Humours of the Fleet," a virile, breathing picture of the Navy in its social aspect which is invaluable. It is not only so because the characters are unmistakably officers and seamen of the Navy, drawn with their environment from life, but after an interval of nearly sixty years the play was rewritten by a captain in the Navy, " Poet " Thompson, whom we have met already, and who, in altering it and bringing it up to date, sheds not a little light upon the changes, such as they were, that had taken place during the interval. Shadwell, like Wycherley, had seen service as a volunteer, and had certainly rubbed shoulders with the naval men of his time. His characters have unquestionably been drawn from personal experience or observation, and although Thompson spoke of them as exaggerated, he recognised them as sketches from life, and acknowledged that their representatives still existed in his day, although their language had altered and their manners were modified if not much improved. Like the characters of Smollett, their prototypes were familiar, and it was not, indeed, difficult apparently to name actual naval officers who might have served for their originals. Caricatures they may have been, but legitimate caricatures, typical figures in the sea world, with their idiosyncrasies merely heightened and exaggerated to suit the necessities of fiction or the stage.

Wycherley's hero in "The Plain Dealer" is Captain Manly, of the Royal Navy, and it should be remembered that at the period at which this play was written regulations for the maintenance of a permanent force of commissioned officers had only recently been issued. Prior to the reign of Charles II, flag officers, captains, and lieutenants were discharged to the shore as soon as their ships were paid off, and it was not until 1667 that half-pay was instituted for certain captains, and not until nearly ten years later that the privilege was extended, and not even then to all the captains unemployed. Manly had made money in his profession, some "ten or twelve thousand pounds," presumably prize money, although another lucrative business practised by captains of men-of-war was the carriage of freight and merchandise—a privilege which had been so grossly abused that it was abolished in 1686, or just ten years after the first edition of "The Plain Dealer" was licensed for printing. Manly, we are told, had made an early choice of a sea life, to quit which, however, he had determined, as he had fallen in love. He had proposed to marry and take his wife with him to the Indies, a step to which her relations objected. Then came an offer to command a convoy, which his patriotism would not permit him to refuse, and before he went afloat he deposited his cash with his sweetheart, whom he left in charge of his bosom friend, until he should return and make her his wife. From the conversation of the sailors we learn that the convoy had been attacked by the Dutch men-of-war, and that in

the action which ensued he had lost his ship, but had
saved the convoy. Although he had had such ill luck,
he was evidently popular with the men, who speak of
him as a bully tar and a brave fellow, never pleased but
in a fight, " and then he looked like one of us coming
from the pay table, with a new lining to our hats under
our arms." This custom of the men sweeping the money
off the pay table into their hats or caps has continued
ever since, and appears to have first come into vogue
in the days of the Commonwealth, when a sailor who
commanded a Parliament ship says, " I cannot express
the satisfaction I have had to see with what cheerful
and lively countenances our men would come to the pay
table, and as they swept the money into their hats, they
would pray for the prosperity of the Government, and
for the health of their captains and other officers."
Manly is, as his name denotes, a plain dealer, a straightforward, honest seaman, contemptuous of the conventional manners of society, but credulous to an extreme where his heart is concerned, as is shown by the
trust he has placed in his sweetheart and his friend.

His trust is ill-placed, for no sooner has he gone to
sea than the treacherous pair get married, intending to
cheat him out of his fortune. For certain reasons,
however, in furtherance of their plans, the wedding
is a secret. The play opens upon Manly's return,
accompanied by his brother officers, Lieutenant Freeman
and a young volunteer. The lieutenant, we are told,
is a gentleman of good education, but of broken
fortune, a complier with the age. The volunteer is
an heiress, the daughter of a gentleman from the north,
who, having seen Manly, has fallen in love with him and
followed him to sea in man's clothes. She was among
the first of the stage heroines, but not the last, to take
this course, and doubtless Wycherley was here drawing
upon his own experience of naval life.

Certainly, the idea was not altogether novel, since
we read in a ballad entitled " The Maidens' Frolic ;
or, A Brief Relation of how six lusty lasses have pressed

full fourteen taylors on the back side of St. Clement's, and other adjacent places ":—

> Of late near the Strand, we well understand,
> Six lasses that took a brisk frolic in hand ;
> 'Twas thus, I profess, they in seaman's dress,
> Not far from the Maypole, resolved to press
> Fourteen taylors.

There are, too, many instances in naval history which are well authenticated of females who went to sea as sailors, and some of them not only made excellent seamen—if the expression may be permitted—but exhibited courage and gallantry in battle with their country's enemies. Two well-known instances are those of Hannah Snell, who enlisted as a marine and saw active service, and Mary Ann Talbot, otherwise John Taylor, who was wounded in the action of the Glorious First of June. Both these women received pensions from the Government when they were no longer able to follow a sea life. How these and other women (two of whom turned pirates, Anne Bonney and Mary Read) were able to remain on board ship, doing the sailor's work and to live with the men without being discovered, is amazing, but that such was the case, and that there have been similar cases in quite modern times, is unquestionable.

Fidelia Grey was a volunteer, or, as we should say, a naval cadet, and Manly, believing her story that she was the son of an old naval officer, had compassionately taken her to sea with him according to the custom of the day. It was actually in the year that the play was licensed that Charles II issued orders for regulating the entry of volunteers, in order, as he said, by way of " giving encouragement to the families of better quality among our subjects to breed up their younger sons to the art and practice of navigation, in order to the fitting them for further employment in our service." In these regulations, which were founded on existing institutions and practice, the principles are laid down which have governed the entry and qualification of naval officers from that time. But alongside these " volunteers by

order " the older system still flourished, and until quite
the end of the eighteenth century youngsters continued
to go to sea with a friend, and so served their apprenticeship to the quarter-deck.   It is interesting in this connection to notice how this character of the volunteer
was treated by the illustrators of the edition of the play
which appeared in 1735 (which was an exact copy of
the first edition published by Bentley in 1677, even
to the names of the players), and the edition which appeared in 1796 of the play as it was altered and adapted
for Garrick by Isaac Bickerstaffe in 1766 (Bickerstaffe
was the dramatist who supplied the libretto to " Thomas
and Sally," an early naval operetta of importance and
the prototype of " H.M.S. Pinafore " and " Billee
Taylor ").   In the first of the illustrations the volunteer
is dressed in the costume of the period, whereas in the
second she is dressed in the uniform of a midshipman
as prescribed by the orders of 1748.   The same incident
is chosen for both illustrations, the moment at which
her sex was discovered by Vernish, Manly's false friend
and the husband of Olivia, his sweetheart.   The plot
deals with Manly's discovery of the ingratitude and
baseness of the perfidious couple, and the revenge he
takes, which is characteristic of the period and involves
a loss of honour and disgrace to both parties.   Incidentally the sex of Fidelia is revealed, and her generosity
and devotion rewarded.   Her love for Manly is recipro-
cated, and the curtain falls with a promise of renewed
happiness to the Plain Dealer.   Mrs. Jordan played the
part of Fidelia in a later edition, and her portrait was
painted in the character.   The picture was engraved as
a frontispiece to the play.

A comparison of the two versions, that of Wycherley
with that revised by Bickerstaffe ninety years afterwards,
indicates a number of changes in the way in which sea
life was regarded by the authors.   Throughout the
original play Manly is accompanied by several seamen
belonging to his boat's crew, and his attachment to
these men, and the esteem in which they hold him,

although his manners are rough, is exhibited in many ways. To them he gives the last money he has left in the world rather, he says, than that the poor, honest, brave fellows shall want. The seamen are armed with drawn cutlasses, and they are adjured to stand at the captain's door and prevent any one passing with as great care as if they were guarding the scuttle to the powder-room. Although he calls them rogues, rascals, dogs, and brandy-casks, they are jealous of his reputation and most keen in his interest. It is somewhat curious nowadays to find the last-named of these epithets used to a sailor, but Captain Fireball, another naval officer, whom George Farquhar introduces in " Sir Harry Wildair," when one of the other characters shows a preference for claret to brandy, shouts, " Brandy, you dog ! Abuse brandy ! Flat treason against the Navy Royal !—Sirrah, I'll teach you to abuse the fleet—Here, Shark ! Get three or four of the boat's crew, and press this fellow aboard of the *Belzebub.*" Fireball, by the way, is not a very typical sea officer, though when he does lose his money at the gambling table he cries, " Allons for the Thatched House and the Mediterranean." The Thatched House was always a sea officers' club, and there presumably the captain thought he might meet those who could assist him to a ship and active service. Manly, when he finds himself ruined, says, " If they won't give me a ship again, I can go starve anywhere with a musket on my shoulder." And when Freeman exclaims, " Give you a ship ! Why, you will not solicit it ? " he replies, " If I have not solicited it by my services, I know no other way." Obviously to ask the authorities for a ship was not deemed the right thing by the best seamen. On the other hand, in the prologue to a play produced at Oxford about 1791, which was spoken by a woman " dressed like a sea officer," she satirically refers to the need for solicitation thus :—

> With Monmouth cap, and cutlash by my side,
> Striding at least a yard at every stride,
> I'm come to tell you, after much petition,
> The Admiralty has given me a commission.

Before leaving Farquhar it may be said that, since he also had had experience of sea life, it is significant he should make the naval man say, " We seamen speak plain, brother." And the soldier replies, " You seamen are like your element, always tempestuous, too ruffling to handle a fine lady."

To return to the sailors in " The Plain Dealer," these are replaced by Manly's servant in the later edition, and a paraphrase of their speeches is sometimes put into the mouth of this man, who is called Oakum, but whereas the sailors in the reign of Charles II speak of having left the river and of being engaged in action with the Dutch, Oakum says he sailed out of Portsmouth Harbour and sank the ship rather than let her fall into the hands of " the rascally French." Similarly, the former speak of Manly as being " dogged as an old Tarpaulin, when hindered of a voyage by a young Pantaloon captain," but for this is substituted in the reign of George III, " Though he's as crusty as any one sometimes, and will be obeyed, there's never a captain in the Navy that's a truer friend to a seaman." And, again, the earlier seamen explain their inattention to duty by the circumstance that they " were at Hob in the Hall, and whilst my brother and I were quarrelling about a Cast, he slunk by us." But Oakum says : " I had just stepped into the back parlour to play a game at All-Fours with our landlady's daughter ; and, while we were wrangling about the cards, the little boy let the gentleman up unknown to us." Manly, accusing the volunteer of cowardice, says, " Did I not see thee more afraid in the fight, than the Chaplain of the ship, or the Purser that bought his place ? " But the implied charges against these two classes of officers are omitted in the new version. On the other hand, the trouble a seaman's relatives had in drawing his pay or pension had not apparently diminshed, for in both editions we find a scolding, importunate woman compared to a sailor's widow at the Navy Office. In regard to the dress, the change to which reference has already been made receives emphasis by the stage direction in the new version that Manly is to enter "in his uniform," whereas in 1676 it is intimated that a sea captain is known by his red breeches, tucked-up hair or peruke, a great broad belt and a short sword; while Manly is accused by Olivia of the carelessness displayed in his dress, "especially your scarf, 'twas just such another, only a little higher ty'd, made me in love with my tailor as he passed by my window the last training day." What, says a lady when her son wants to read "St. George for Christendom," you will next be studying military discipline "and wearing red breeches!" But the same lady ninety years later exclaims, "I shall have him teasing me to-morrow or next day to buy him an ensign's commission." Enough, however, has been said to indicate the value of "The Plain Dealer" and the light which it throws upon our subject.

Ben Legend, in Congreve's "Love for Love," is a real seaman, possibly not a very definite portrait, but doubtless true to average life, and certainly a credible human being. It is evident that although his author wished to use him as a foil to the other characters, he intends us to see in him the more prominent features of one who, a gentleman by birth, had been rough-hewn by the training of the sea. He is naturally a brave man; all seamen must be that, but knowing what it is like he does not prefer fighting for its own sake. Thus when Miss Prue threatens him with a thrashing by Tattle he says:—

"Will he thrash my jacket? Let'n, let'n. But an he comes near me, mayhap I may give'n a salt eel for's supper, for all that."

Doubtless he wants polishing, and his humour is of a boisterous kind. "A little rough," says his father, "but a very wag." Absorbed in his own profession he is without care, thoughtless, and forgetful of what has happened ashore, so when told that his brother Dick has been dead these two years, he exclaims:—

"Mess, that's true; marry! I had forgot. Dick's dead, as you say. Well, and how?"

He has a very proper idea of what is due to him, as

when the young lady addresses him as a sea-calf and a
stinking tar barrel, he replies that if she should give
him such language at sea she'd have a cat-o'-nine-tails
laid across her shoulders. Nautical metaphors he uses
freely. A girl is a tight vessel, well rigged. He heaves
off, when told to sit further away, and he is all for carrying
things above board and keeping nothing under hatches
when it comes to speaking the truth. Straightforward
he is, too, unused to the guile of the shore, and given to
speak his mind. " I'm not false-hearted like a landsman,"
he says; " a sailor will be honest though mayhap he has
never a penny of money in his pocket." Like Captain
Durzo, he has his boat's crew in to dance, and declares :—
" We are merry folks, we sailors : we ain't much to
care for. Thus we live at sea ; eat biscuit and drink
flip, put on a clean shirt once a quarter ; come home
once a year, get rid of a little money, and then put off
with the next fair wind. How do you like us ? "

He exhibits an acquaintance with the sea super-
stitions, for he tells Miss Prue that he would as soon
marry a Lapland witch " and live upon selling contrary
winds and wrecked vessels." Courageous, careless,
honest, helpful, roving in disposition, merry and easily
satisfied, contemptuous of the fripperies and make-
believes of shore life, Ben Legend must have been a
character easily recognisable at the period, and although
the play was frequently revived for stage purposes throughout the century, but little difference was made in his part.

Doggett, who was the original Ben Legend, and who
is best remembered in connection with the Coat and
Badge he gave to be rowed for by the watermen of
London, was acknowledged to be a strict observer of
nature, and particularly skilful in dressing a character
with exactness. It is quite possible that as he had seen
something of the sea, and was familiar with water-side
life and the seamen who frequented the Pool, he may
have helped Congreve to fashion the part. He was a
good singer and dancer, and the song which Congreve
gave him, but for which another was afterwards sub-

stituted, formed the basis of a burletta in one act called " Buxom Joan." The scene is laid at Deptford, and the characters are a tinker, a tailor, a soldier, and a sailor, Joan and her mother. The motive is " of all sorts of tradesmen, a sailor for me." It appears to have been a favourite with the audiences which flocked to the theatrical booth at which Doggett acted at Bartholomew Fair when the theatres were closed.

Although we have no record that Doggett played in a nautical sketch at the Fair, this class of entertainment was most popular there, for the free-handed sailors were an important feature among the frequenters of the booths, and the performances seldom concluded without some tribute to their presence. As a rule, " drolls " or selected parts of plays, digested into humorous scenes, with interpolated songs and dances, formed the stock pieces at the fairs, and one of the earliest was known as " John Swabber." Another called " The Constant Quaker, or the Humours of Wapping," has a title reminiscent of " The Fair Quaker of Deal, or the Humours of the Navy." And similar pieces and titles were common. The political feeling of the nation also was reflected in such plays as " The Royal Voyage, or the Irish Expedition," in the last scene of which the royal fleet was seen in the Bay of Bangor, with the *Mary*, yacht, flying the standard; indeed, nearly every naval action and incident found its counterpart at the shows at the Fair. Nor were there wanting allusions to the complaints of the sailors and their victualling grievances. The comedians and proprietors of the booths were quite alive to the two phases of a seaman's life, which Baltharpe happily expressed in rhyme in 1671: —

> What meat before the King for four
> Allow'd, now six men it devour ;
> A dollar to each man is due,
> Each twenty and eight days 'tis true ;
> When we can get it, we drink wine,
> Healths to their friends then we combine.
> A seaman when he gets ashoar,
> In one day's time he spendeth more
> Than three months' short allowance money.

CHAPTER X

"THE FAIR QUAKER OF DEAL"

THERE is a distinct quality about Charles Shadwell's comedy, "The Fair Quaker of Deal,"
which makes it worthy of a longer notice than we have
given to other plays. It is obviously intended as a
picture of real life, and although there is little delicacy
in the treatment and an entire lack of self-restraint,
it must be remembered that the standard of conduct
and manners at the time was not what one can call
high. All writers were outspoken to a degree, punishments ashore and afloat were cruel in the extreme,
and life, especially among the lower orders, was regarded lightly. The Navy was not yet a thoroughly
organised machine. Officers and men fluctuated between the Merchant and the Royal Service, merchantman and pirate were commonly convertible terms,
and each captain was an absolute monarch in his own
little wooden world. The pamphlet literature of the
time is full of the complaints of the seamen, presented
for the most part by interested parties, for the seamen
themselves, with sentiments, prejudices, and a language
of their own, were almost incapable of expressing their
feelings. It is not necessary to accept Ned Ward as
an authority in order to believe that all who adopted
by inclination or force the sea calling were subjected
to great hardship in circumstances always rough and
often brutal. It is altogether satisfactory, then, as
certainly it is instructive, to find a writer placing a
picture of naval life upon the stage in which there is

little indication of that malign influence which some modern naval essayists would have us believe blackened the whole of the sea canvas. For the most part, the officers are gentlemen and men of honour, as well as seamen, while the men are loyal and brave, and after their kind enjoy themselves. It would be entirely unfair to judge them by present-day standards.

When Captain Thompson came to take Shadwell's play in hand and alter it so that the comedy might be produced by Garrick, it is remarkable how little he changed its essence. He imparted a new local colour, he introduced topical allusions, but the types of the sea worthies remain very much the same, and this although more than half a century had passed. We had a new set of foes at sea, and he substituted Frenchmen for Dutchmen. A uniform for the senior officers had been adopted, and the Service had been more systematised, but there were still captains who thought little on shore of carousing with their old messmates who were still serving before the mast, however different might be the treatment they accorded them when afloat. The views of the seamen had undergone little change; their tastes, their manners, and their pastimes were unaltered, while their courage and their loyalty shone as brightly as ever. We may be shocked now both by their language and their manners, but Thompson meets the reproach in a passage from his preface quoted later. It is characteristic of the time that the most popular character Garrick could assume in speaking the prologue to several of his plays was that of a drunken sailor.

"The Fair Quaker of Deal" was first produced at Drury Lane on 25th February, 1710. Miss Santlow was the original Dorcas, and on 2nd June of the same year it was produced for the second time for the benefit of "Commodore" Leigh and "Coxswain" Birkhead, these being the names of the two actors who played the parts of Commodore Flip and his coxswain. Charles Shadwell, who wrote the play, seems to have served

as a volunteer in Portugal, for he says in his preface:
" It may be expected I should give some reasons for
my scribbling, and make excuses for the irregularities
of the play, find fault with those things the town are
good enough to overlook, most arrogantly stand up
for time and place, brag of the newness of the characters, etc. But I must beg pardon for not showing
the conceited part of me. I am called in haste to my
duty in Portugal, but, at my return, it's probable I
may be as insolent as the rest of the scribblers of the
town." The play was a success from the first, the
principal characters being well performed, particularly
that of Dorcas Zeal by Miss Santlow. She had pre-
viously been admired as a dancer, but she now met
with a favourable reception as an actress. " The gentle
softness of her voice, the composed innocence of her
aspect, the modesty of her dress, and the reserved
decency of her gesture, made her seem the fair Quaker
she represented." The comedy was frequently played
up to about 1730, and then was not revived again until
7th October, 1755, when it again achieved some little
success. In 1773 Captain Edward Thompson altered
the play, at the suggestion of Garrick, and on 9th November in that year it was produced at Drury Lane.

The characters in the two plays are the same with
few exceptions. Justice Scruple, a hypocritical match-
maker, a very small part, is omitted in the second edition,
and in his place we have Mr. Derrick, a midshipman,
who is in charge of Captain Worthy's boat (this boat
having in the previous edition been in charge of the
coxswain), with Jack Hatchway and Dick Binnacle,
two sailors whose names are not mentioned in the first
edition, and whose parts, as will be seen, are altered
considerably.

The scene was laid by Shadwell at Deal. A squadron
of ships from the Virginia plantation has just put into
the Downs, and some of the officers have landed. Captain
Worthy, of the Navy, a gentleman of honour, sense,
and reputation, commanding one of the vessels, and

Dorcas Zeal, known as "the Fair Quaker of Deal,"
are mutually in love. Arabella Zeal, the sister of Dorcas,
who has been educated as a Churchwoman, wishes to
prevent the match. She first writes a letter to Dorcas by
which the latter is informed that Worthy has already
a wife and two children. She afterwards dresses as a
man and makes love to Dorcas, but her disguise being
penetrated, she owns her fault, and accepts the advances of Sir Charles Pleasant, a young naval lieutenant
in Worthy's ship, who has been for some time her suitor.
Captain Worthy marries Dorcas, and Mr. Rovewell,
a gentleman of fortune and a friend of the naval officers,
marries her ally and school-fellow, Belinda. Commodore
Flip, who is described as an obstinate, positive, ignorant
Wappineer tar, and Captain Mizen, a finical sea fop
and a naval reformer, are trapped into going through
the ceremony of marriage with Misses Jiltup and Jenny,
each man believing himself to have been married to
Dorcas Zeal, but after they have been well roasted by
their brother officers they are let into the secret that the
weddings were performed by Cribidge, another lieutenant, disguised as a clergyman, and they are released
from their hard bargains by settling pensions on the
women. From this description it will be understood
that the action of the play is not directly nautical,
and it is in the characterisation of the seamen, their
remarks, and the changes made by Thompson, that
light is thrown on the naval life.

It is noteworthy, in the first place, that Shadwell
only makes one of the group of officers a boor, and this
one the oldest among them, who says of himself: " I
have served in every office belonging to a ship, from
cook's boy to a commodore ; and have all the sea jests
by heart, from the forecastle to the great cabin ; and
I love a sailor." This speech, and the following, are
omitted by Thompson :—

"Worthy. Ay, so well as to get drunk with every
mess in the ship once a week.

Flip. Why, that makes the rogues love me ; my

joculousness with them makes them fight for me, they
keep me out of a French gaol. I'll follow my old method
till I'm superannuated, which I believe I shan't petition
for this twenty years.

Worthy. Since you love your common sailors so well,
what reason can you have for using your lieutenant so
like a dog ?

Flip. Because he sets up for a fine gentleman, and
lies in gloves to make his hands white, and tho' 'tis his
watch, when I ring my bell, the rogue is above coming
to my cabin. I sent him ashore yesterday to the post
house with a letter to the Admiralty, and I ordered him
to buy me a quarter of mutton and threescore cabbages
for my own use ; the landlubber (for he is no sailor)
had the impudence to tell me he would not be my boy.
I told him I would bring him to a court-martial, and he
threatened to throw up his commission and cut my
throat.

Rovewell. Ha, ha, I am glad thou hast met with a
young fellow of life and vigour, that knows how to use
you according to your deserts."

As a contrast to this picture of the old commodore
(who, by the way, may be compared with Smollett's
Trunnion), we have those of Captain Worthy and the
lieutenants Sir Charles Pleasant and Cribidge, whom
we are obviously to regard as representatives of the
majority of the officers and gentlemen of the period,
both when Shadwell wrote and Thompson revised the
play. On the other hand, Captain Mizen (who has
his counterpart in Smollett's time in Captain Whiffle),
if a caricature, must certainly have been representative
of a class, probably small and exceptional, but not less
well known in the reign of George II than in that of
Queen Anne. In the earlier edition Flip thus describes
him :—

" I value myself for not being a coxcomb, that is
what you call a gentleman captain ; which is a new
name for our sea fops, who, forsooth, must wear white

linen, have fixed beds, lie in holland sheets, and load
their noddles with thirty ounces of horse hair, which
makes them hate the sight of an enemy for fear bullets
and gunpowder should spoil the beau wig and lac'd
jacket. They are indeed pretty fellows at single rapier,
and can, with a little drink in their heads, cut the throats
of their best friends; but catch them yardarm and
yardarm with a Frenchman, and down goes the colours.
Oh! it was not so in the Dutch wars, then we valued
ourselves upon wooden legs, and stumps of arms, and
fought as if heaven and earth was coming together.

Rovewell. Yes, yes, you fought very gloriously when
you let the Dutch burn the fleet at Chatham.

Flip. That act was owing to the treachery of some
rogues at land, and not to us seafaring folks."

Thompson altered this speech considerably, making
the new name for a sea fop that of macaroni captain,
and, omitting nearly all the remainder, puts the following
words into Flip's mouth :—

" It is such fellows as these, who fire into an enemy's
ship that has struck ; who have their cabins lined with
green baize, who carry cows to sea for milk to wash their
hands with, who banish pea soup and beef from their
tables, and treat with amulet, blancmange, fricandeaux,
ragoutes, fricassee, and sylabubs ; but catch them
yardarm and yardarm with a Frenchman, and down
goes the colours. It was not so the last war, when
Ned Boscawen would not permit De Clue to go on shore
with both his legs. He was the boy that spoilt their
dancing."

Both Shadwell and Thompson describe Mizen's ship
and his cabin, and the descriptions are given in such
detail that we must assume that in each case we have
here actual pictures of what the writers had seen. In
Shadwell's edition we read :—

"*Mizen.* My great cabin : I dare affirm it, no town
lady's withdrawing-room, nor country gentlewoman's

P

closet, is nicer furnished than my cabin ; 'tis wainscoted
with most charming India, Japan, and looking-glass.
I have a very noble scrutore, and the most celebrated
screen in Europe. I have an invention which makes
the great guns in my cabin appear to be elbow chairs
covered with cloth of tissue. I have six-and-thirty silver
sconces, and every vacancy is crammed with china.

Rovewell. These rarities are worth seeing indeed.

Worthy. Oh ! he keeps a visiting day ; you and I
will wait upon him.

Mizen. I shall think myself prodigiously obliged
to you. Maybe you will see as great a concourse of
people as there is at a general's when he returns victorious ; barges, pinnaces, Deal yawls, and longboats
innumerable.

Rovewell. Pray, who visits you in the longboats ?

Mizen. Why, Dutch admirals. You must know
I range them into the following order ; my barges
I call coaches and six, my pinnaces are chariots with
two horses, my Deal yawls are sedans, and my longboats hackney coaches. All my sconces are loaded
with wax tapers. My lieutenant and warrant officers,
nicely dressed and perfumed, place themselves on each
side of my steerage. My midshipmen and quarteers are
ranged from the bulkhead to the gangway in my own
white shirts. The ship's side is manned by my boat's
crew in spruce apparel and clean gloves, and the rest of
the ship's company are ready upon all occasions to give
cheers and hussas according to the quality of my visitors.

Rovewell. Well, and what entertainment are we to
meet with ?

Mizen. Why, I generally treat with tea, but the most
modern way is to give nothing.

Rovewell. Pshaw, methinks a bowl of punch would
be most proper.

Worthy (with sarcasm). Oh, beastly, we at sea always
smoke when we drink, and that would spoil all his gay
furniture.

Rovewell. What is your conversation ?

Mizen. We imitate the ladies as near as we can, and therefore scandalise everybody. We laugh at the ridiculous management of the Navy Board, pry into the rogueries of the Victualling Office, and tell the names of those clerks who were ten years ago barefoot and are now twenty thousand pound men. Sometimes we quarrel about whose ship sails best, who makes the finest punch, and who has the greatest hardships by having great men's favourites put over their heads, but I keep them within the bounds of good manners and moderation.

Worthy. That is a very great point gained.

Mizen. May I be keel-hauled, if any man in the universe has more reformed the Navy than myself. I am now compiling a book wherein I mend the language wonderfully. I leave out your larboard and starboard, hawsers and swabs. I have no such thing as haul-cat-haul nor belay ; silly words, only fit for Dutchmen to pronounce. I put fine sentences into the mouths of our sailors, derived from the manliness of the Italian and the softness of the French, and by the time I am made an admiral I doubt not of bringing every sailor in the Navy to be more polite than most of our country gentlemen, and the next generation of them may pass very well for gentlemen of the first quality."

Thompson makes Mizen describe his cabin as furnished as elegantly as anything Cornelly's has produced, lined with green cloth and covered with a Turkey carpet, with girandole glasses, pictures of Venus and Adonis, a piano, and a guitar. He is also described as working his ship by music. " I weigh my anchor to *Nancy Dawson's Hornpipe,* hoist my topsails to the *Belleisle March,* exercise my great guns to *Voi Amanti,* haul the cat to *Oh, the Cruel Tyrant Love,* veer away to *Shelen-a-gigg,* and give chase to *Say Little Foolish Fluttering Thing."* Thompson also preserves the story about the boats and the book for refining the sea language, with very little change.

Shadwell introduces three other officers, but these characters are either not referred to by Thompson or their parts are considerably cut down. Easy, a lieutenant of marines, is given two short sentences by Thompson, but Shadwell has the following dialogue :—

"*Pleasant.* Why, by your report, old Flip makes your life a very uneasy one. Thank Heaven my captain has another way of management ; with his affable, easy, and genteel air he gains applause from all.

Easy. I know he is a gentleman by his being civil to our corps ; 'tis only the brutes of the Navy that we marine officers disagree with.

Cribidge. Why I believe I shall frighten the old bear into some civility, for that day we came to anchor he had some friends aboard, and in the height of their mirth I was called into the cabin ; the negro fills a glass and hands it over his shoulder with a ' Here, lieutenant, will you drink ? ' I made as if I would take it, but overset it into his collar, laid the fault upon him, and pretending to have been wet myself, went out of the cabin in a passion.

Easy. Pshaw ! These are small faults, and natural to you subs of the Navy. But the old dog had the impudence to confine me three months to my cabin, only for knocking down a boatswain's mate that had struck one of my marines ; nay, if it had not been for Captain Worthy he would have broke me at a court-martial. If the colonels of our corps don't hinder this rascally imposition upon us, nobody will buy commissions of them.

Pleasant. That is a new trick put upon you gentlemen, and I fear will breed ill blood amongst us.

Easy. Hang it, Pleasant, we agree well enough with all you young fellows, 'tis the old sots that hate we should come aboard them.

Cribidge. True, we agree well enough, but most of you stay ashore till all the money's gone, and then you come aboard and expect to mess with us, who must find fresh provisions for you."

A little later Easy remarks that he will go and draw a bill upon the Government agent, get some necessaries for his men, cheat his captain a little in the sum total, and thus have money in his pocket for a carousal. Why Thompson should have omitted these speeches, and made the lieutenant of marines an entirely colourless part is not clear, unless he felt that to refer to any disagreement between the marine and the naval officers would have been inappropriate and out of place. Shadwell, in this scene, makes Indent, the purser, cross the stage, when the following conversation takes place :—

"*Cribidge.* See, yonder's Indent, our purser, gone to Daniel's. He'll be glad to be of our company.

Pleasant. A very honest fellow, and keeps a much better character in the Navy than people of his employ generally do.

Cribidge. Why, the fellow has lived well; he was bred a mercer in Covent Garden, was ruined, but managed his matters so well, he cleared himself of a gaol by a commission of bankrupt without forswearing himself, which is the only precedent of that nature since the Act was made."

Throughout the earlier edition " Daniel's " is mentioned as the house of call frequented by the junior officers at Deal, which Thompson altered to the " Blue Posts " at Portsmouth. Flip preferred " The Three Mariners," because the landlord, " Tom Cragg, and I were boatswain's mates together," while the more fashionable house at Deal is styled the " India Arms." Thompson changed the names of these inns to the " Spotted Dog," and " The Fountain," respectively, while he omitted the commodore's reason for going to the former place.

Afterwards, when the officers are drinking together at the inn, Indent asks for leave to pay for a bowl of punch, suggesting that the time may come when he will sail with Worthy. Of the following dialogue, only Worthy's first speech is retained by Thompson :—

"*Worthy.* Why, if you should, it won't be much to

your advantage, for I never allow my purser to oppress the men, nor will I keep a whole ship's crew miserable to make one man rich.

Indent. Oh, Sir, I don't desire that, Sir, but as a gentleman you won't hinder me from those common perquisites allowed to all pursers.

Pleasant. The word perquisite comprehends a good deal of roguery, and under that notion the Government is sufficiently cheated.

Indent. Ay, but all people have regard for the methods of the Navy.

Worthy. Why, yes, purser, I own you may plead custom for abundance of villanies committed in the Navy, but we have now got men of honour at the helm who will not suffer rogues to go unpunished.

Cribidge. It has been the method to let a stinking butt of beer stand six days abroach, and when complaint is made the captain (who should do the sailors justice) punishes the complaining rascal for mutiny.

Pleasant. It has been the method for cooks with pitchforks sharp to squeeze the fat from out the meat, for fear the grease should rise in poor Jack Sailor's stomach.

Easy. It has been the method to waste a pound to ounces ten, which makes the bread, the butter, and the cheese a poor allowance for those hard-working men.

Worthy. In short, what with chest money, hospitals, slops, twopences, groats and mulcts they are mere galley slaves.

Pleasant. The captain uses them like dogs, which forces them to run away, the chequering clerk puts on the R, and then the purser loads their pay with slops they never had, and so cheats the Queen and her subjects too.

Indent. Why, you may rail at these proceedings, but when you stand the captain and the purser too you will often wish to be indenting; half money and half stores have tempted most of you.

Worthy. Come, no more, Indent, since we have discovered you, I hope you will let us pay our clubs.

Indent. No, faith, gentlemen, I'll treat you all."

The third officer to whom reference is made by Shadwell is the surgeon, and this is also omitted by Thompson. A sailor says : " Our rogue of a loblolly doctor, being not satisfied with his twopences, must have a note for two months' pay for every cure, and the last time the ship was paid, what between the officers and the sailors, he swept about half the ship's company's money into his own hat." It is not to be supposed that because Thompson struck out these references to the complaints which the seamen of Shadwell's time preferred against the pursers and surgeons, similar grievances did not exist in the Navy in his day, but the particular reason for reviving the play appears to have been the fact that in 1773 the King reviewed the fleet under Vice-Admiral Pye at Spithead, and this event is referred to frequently in the new edition, the play, indeed, ending with a tableau in which the scene opens and discovers the fleet reviewed at Spithead. In a scene, too, at the beginning of the second act which is substituted for one at the end of the first act in Shadwell's edition, a sailor who in the latter represents himself as having been sent by the commodore to his coxswain to order him to come to the inn for a jollification, in the former is made to exclaim : " Oh, Jack Hatchway, have I found you ? Yonder's the commodore, captain, and first lieutenant swearing and storming as if the ship was on shore. His Majesty is to be down to-day, and the ship is to be turned keel out to receive him. Every man is to have a double allowance. The fleet is mooring in line, the guns are loading, man ropes are clapping on the yards and all will be flip and fun."

The few sentences relating to naval chaplains which are introduced by Shadwell are retained by Thompson. They occur when Lieutenant Cribidge, disguised as a clergyman, is about to perform the ceremony of marriage for the commodore, who suggests that if the reverend gentleman will come on board his ship he shall be as drunk in half an hour as he was at the wetting of his warrant, the last word being changed by Thompson to commission :—

"*Cribidge.* Sir, people of my cloth never launch out beyond the rules of modesty [decency, Thompson].

Flip. I can't say anything to you shore folks, but I am certain our sea chaplains, generally speaking, are drunk as often as our sea captains.

Cribidge. The more's the pity that religion should be abused by such profligates.

Indent. Why, indeed, the sailors are apt enough to be wicked of themselves, and such examples from their guides may be one great reason of so much immorality in the Navy."

We have already referred to the scene which is supposed to take place in a room behind the bar at " Daniel's " at Deal, or in the second edition at the " Blue Posts " at Portsmouth, where Rovewell, Worthy, Mizen, Pleasant, Cribidge, Easy, and Indent are all drinking punch together. The omission of the conversation turning on the iniquities of the purser has already been described, and to make up for this Mizen is given in the later edition a song, which is introduced immediately after the loyal toast has been drunk, with a sentiment, " Her (His) Majesty's health, and may she (he) live for ever. May all her (his) subjects be as true friends as we are." This is Mizen's song :—

> Hear me, gentle sailors, hear me,
>   When my duty calls away ;
> Nothing then, my boys, shall steer me,
>   But the fashions and my pay.
>
> Vulgar terms, and vulgar sayings,
>   Shall be plung'd into the main ;
> No haul cat, and no belayings,
>   Shall my gentle manners stain.
>
> All shall then be puff and powder,
>   Smart lappels, and well-dress'd hair ;
> Nothing than a whisper louder,
>   Shall denote to tack and wear.
>
> Would our chiefs attend the nation,
>   And correct the vicious great ;
> We might hope a reformation,
>   In the Navy, and the State.

The remainder of the conversation, which is the same in both cases, is mainly chaffing Mizen about his foibles and the advantages that would result to the younger men if all the old tar captains were removed from the list, and the younger ones thereby had advancement.

The other scene, which takes place at the inn favoured by the commodore, discovers Flip and the sailors drinking together, but Thompson, while cutting out very little from Shadwell's scene, prefaces it by an introduction which admits of a song by Hatchway in honour of grog :—

> 'Tis grog is the soul of the sailor,
> 'Tis that makes him squeeze the French frog,
> Was the boat full, by Neptune, I'd bale her,
> Or drown in an ocean of grog.

It is almost unnecessary to state that in the original play there was no mention of grog, brandy, flip and some mixture which went by the name of " Sir Cloudesley " being used instead. It has been conjectured that an old song entitled " The Sailor's Resolution " which Beard sang in Thompson's editions at Drury Lane, was the original song sung in this scene, but if so it must have been altered, since it refers to a war with the French, and the last verse, which begins

> While here at Deal we're lying,
> With our noble commodore,

has for its last two lines the following, which put it into a later reign :—

> Here's a health to George the King, boys,
> And the Royal Family.

In this scene, too, the new characters, Dick Binnacle and Jack Hatchway, have their opportunity to develop what is evidently intended for maritime humour. That the commodore should get drunk in company with his seamen would be almost incredible had not such an incident actual foundation in historical fact, as may be seen from a story told in the life of Sir John Balchen in the " Dictionary of National Biography," while Thompson would hardly have retained it without cause.

At the same time it may be pointed out that in January, 1807, there was produced a comedy at Drury Lane called the "Assignation," in which an admiral gets drunk with some sailors. The play was damned the first night, and mainly, as it appears, in consequence of this scene. The tars' carousal, which both Shadwell and Thompson accept, is as follows :—

"*Flip* (*to the sailors*). Don't flinch your ladle; he that will do that will run down into the hold in an engagement, and say his prayers in a storm.

Sailor. Why, I am married, Sir, and must see my wife to-night, which I have not done this eighteen months.

Flip. You rogue, can't you get drunk first and see her afterwards ?

Sailor. Ay, Sir, but my ill quality is, when I get drunk I beat my wife immoderately and kick her out of doors, which I would not willingly do the first night.

Flip. Oh, I'll save you the trouble of that, you shall go on board to-night and shan't see your wife these two months.

Sailor. Oh, then, Sir, I'll be drunk with all my heart.

Flip. Come, confusion to all fops and coxcombs of the Navy. When I'm at the helm I'll rout the knaves from thence. As for you, coxswain, I'll make you captain, and all the boat's crew shall be lieutenants.

Sailor. Look'e, I'll be no lieutenant, I'll be a captain the first stroke.

Flip. Why, what pretentiveness have you to it, lubber ?

Sailor. My pretentiveness to it is, Sir, that I was rated Able when your worship was Ordinary, and I thank my stars I've always continued Able and your worship Ordinary.

Flip. That's no rule, for at that rate I should be king of the seas now, for I was a midshipman when some that shall be nameless were swabbers of the upper gun deck.

Sailor. And I could say my compass, reef, hand, and splice, when ne'er a commissioned officer in our ship could tell starboard from larboard [port, Thompson]. I wonder your honourable worship, being so notorious a man with the Ambralty, don't get made captain of the Royal Sufferans.

2nd Sailor. And I likewise wonder your worshipful honour don't get to be knighted.

3rd Sailor. 'Tis a wonderful thing that, Jack, to have the Majesty's honour clap a cutlass on to a man's skull and bid him rise up, Sir anything.

Flip. Look'e, rogues, the design is very good, and 'tis a gracious piece of preferment, but it has puffed up so many of our sea coxcombs that their pride and vanity will ruin the credit of the Navy. But here's to ye, Coxswain, fill it up.

Coxswain. I am almost drunk already, and like your honour; another cup will make me clap the ship on board to windward.

Flip. Why, then, I'll clap you in the bilboes to leeward.

Sailor. To be free with your right reverend worship's honour and glory, I must tell you, being you and I were afore the mast together, it would look, as it were, something clever of your honourableness to throw three things overboard.

Flip. Why, what are those things, Sirrah?

Sailor. The boatswain, the purser, and the bilboes.

All the sailors. Ay, overboard with them, I faith.

Flip. What, do ye mutiny, ye dogs? Don't you know there's a court-martial and that I am presidentum?

Coxswain. I was sure these rogues would bring themselves into a prime-in-iron.

Sailor. Why, most worthy captain and my messmate that was, look'e, we have no design of mutinying, but only by the way of telling our grievances to your grace's honour, and so my humbleness to you (*drinks*).

Flip. Well, well, to show my natural goodness to you all, give me good reasons for throwing overboard

the bilboes. I begin at the latter end of your propo-
sitions, and because I intend to ask them all gradually.
And so, sirrah, here's to you (*drinks*).

Sailor. Thanks, your monsterousness, the bilboes
an't like your wonderfulness, is a great stumbling block
in the way of a sailor's agility, to have our heels land-
locked when we have sea room enough is worse than to
run ashore where there's no land.

All the sailors. Oh, worse by half.

Flip. Come, no more of your nonsensicalness, but
get drunk as fast as you can."

The commodore is then called out by Indent in order
that he may be taken to meet Jiltup, and as in the next
scene it is expressly stated that Flip enters drunk, we
are apparently to believe that he was already in this
state, or near to it, when he left his companions. These
two scenes are evidently intended to expose the failings
of officers who, like Mizen in the one case and Flip in
the other, were objects of ridicule and contempt both
to their brother officers and the seamen. As to the
seamen themselves, no very great change appears in
their character. When Worthy lands with his boat's
crew on Deal beach he gives the coxswain money and
tells the crew to go and refresh themselves. When
Thompson's captain lands on the Hard at Portsmouth
he treats his men in the same manner, but in addition
says to the midshipman, " They may have half an hour
aback of the Point, but no more, and mind you do not
load the boat too deep with ladies ; they are a heavy
commodity ! " The suggestion here is that after the
men have wet their whistles they are to be permitted
to carry their sweethearts on board in the captain's
boat. That such things actually happened, and that in
order to lessen the temptation of the men to come on
shore women were permitted to go on board the ships
in large numbers, receives ample testimony from the
records of this and a much later date.

It is unnecessary to mention many of the minor

differences which occur throughout the two editions
of the play. Some of these are brought about by the
changed locale, as in the case of the names of the inns,
and where Gosport is substituted for Dover and the like.
Others are necessary owing to the lapse of time. The
commodore is no longer a Wappineer tar, for the connection of Wapping with the Navy had considerably
diminished. Rovewell, when asked how his love affairs
succeed, replies in 1710: "Much after the manner of
the French King's affairs, they have a dismal aspect.
We quarrel like man and wife or High Church and Low,
and she treats me as tyrannically as the French King
does the Protestants." But in 1773 he says they are
much like the affairs of the East India Company, and
she keeps him alarmed as the King of Prussia does the
Dutch, or uses him with more tyranny than the Pope
does the Jesuits. Then, too, the commodore no longer
proposes to toss off a can of "Sir Cloudesley" before sailing, but is content to crack a bottle instead. Mizen no
longer says that every man on board his ship shall
have a clean white shirt at his charge, but it still holds
true, as Rovewell remarks, that because some brutes are
sailors it would be an entire mistake to suppose that
none can be sailors but brutes. Thompson introduces
a curious speech which is not in the older edition, in
which he says, "Nowadays there is no such thing as a
real English tar. Every midshipman is above his duty,
and if his superior officer gives him a difficult piece of
business or speaks to him for not keeping the deck he
cries out, 'Damn ye, Sir, I'm a gentleman, and I wear
a sword!'" Where Shadwell calls a seaman a rogue,
Thompson calls him a tarpaulin, but in general the sea
language is little changed, and although Thompson has
toned down the expletives somewhat and eliminated
the grosser remarks, he has scarcely done so to the extent
indicated in his preface, where he writes :—

    "'The Fair Quaker of Deal' has long been an acting
comedy, and at the time it was written it stood high
in dramatic reputation; the characters being well

drawn, and not more heightened than the natural pictures allowed of. Although the seasoning may be too high for the palates of the present age, yet, in times of less luxury and more chastity, the drama was always more loose and unguarded. It is an uncontrovertible truth that the more vicious we grow in conduct and disposition, the more chaste and refined we become in sentiment and conversation ; for when we have really lost our chastity and reputation, we artfully assume a foreign character, and endeavour, by a prudish behaviour, to hide the very vices we practise. "

He also says in his preface that he believes Shadwell must have served afloat, since the sea phrases are admirably adapted and the characters so well delineated that he must have had naval experience to paint so well life in a nautical academy. So far as the alteration of the play is concerned, he says the first idea came from Mr. Garrick; the maritime characters are made more modern, and though many may think that those of Flip and Mizen are too extravagant, yet he vouches for it that the Navy still produces such as finical and as boisterous. " If in this mirror some naval gentlemen should see their likeness I wish they may not be ashamed to alter their peculiarities for the sake of that service they belong to ; and if the cap is not found to fit any sailor's head, we hope so pure a set of people will smile at the tars in Mr. Shadwell's time."

It has become a fashion among some modern writers on the Navy, whose reading, perhaps, has been of a limited nature, to picture the naval officers of the eighteenth century as ruffianly boors, capable enough as seamen, but absolutely unfit to associate with even moderately decent people on shore. These writers assume that because Shadwell and Ward, Thompson and Smollett, agree in describing such characters as Flip and Bowling, Mizen and Whiffle, therefore sailors such as these were typical of the general run of officers, and that gentlemen were uncommon. The facts are directly opposed to such reasoning, or why, for example, should Thompson go out of his way to apologise for the extravagance of any of his characters? It is probable that the Navy has every now and again produced such a brute as Smollett pictured in Captain Oakum, but the school alluded to would have us believe that because Smollett was a keen observer and an accomplished student of manners and motives, therefore naval officers of this description were neither exaggerations nor caricatures, but generally reflected the character of the whole Service on the quarter-deck. That the sea officers were brave has never been in dispute, that they were rough, when they had, as the saying is, come in at the hawse holes, may be admitted, but these were the exceptions. That some of them were spoilt by the rude training they received in their younger days is also likely, but the majority were of gentle birth, and if we take them as mirrored on the stage and judged by the standard of manners ashore, they will compare very favourably for honesty, straightforwardness, candour, and good comradeship. It is unfair to draw inferences from exceptions such as those picked out by Smollett and others, and heightened for the purpose of giving piquancy to their pictures of naval life.

Captain Thompson was by all accounts a popular and efficient officer, although he seems to have owed his later appointments to the influence of Garrick. When he was appointed to the *Grampus* the men who had served with him in his last ship volunteered without exception to join the new one. The story goes that they had just been paid off, and that they asked for a week in which to spend their money, which he granted, whereupon they gave him three cheers and went ashore. The captain was told he had done a foolish thing, and that he would not see the men again for a month, whereupon he replied that he was ready to answer for every man rejoining the new ship to time and was ready to stand the consequence if they did not. This speech was reported to the men, and at the same time they were told that " The Fair Quaker of Deal," the piece that was in the bill that night at the Plymouth theatre, had been written by the captain. Accordingly, the greater part of them, with their sweethearts, appeared at the doors of the theatre and requested to be admitted without payment, seeing that it was their captain's play, and they knew he would not want to take the sailors' money. Some little disturbance occurred, and Captain Thompson happening to be in the theatre, the manager appealed to him to settle the matter. " Let them all come," said the captain, " and I'll pay for them." Of course, as soon as they were seated and understood what had happened, they cheered the captain to the echo, and when the play was finished they would not permit the audience to separate until they had sung one of the songs which Thompson had written himself. Having thoroughly enjoyed themselves and spent their money, the sailors all turned up to the day, as they said they would, and the *Grampus*, we are told, was reckoned a very happy ship. Thompson died as commodore on the West Coast of Africa in 1786.

CHAPTER XI

THE EVOLUTION OF THE NAUTICAL PLAY

IT was promised, in the introduction to this section of the work, that dramatic literature should not only be examined for characteristics of the seaman, but that an attempt should be made to trace the evolution and development of the nautical play. So far, in what has been called our voyage of discovery, if the navigation has been at times difficult, this has been due rather to the novelty of our object than to the opportunities afforded by the area explored. There was very much to look at ; very little to bring away, although we trust that that little will be found to be worth the time and labour expended in bringing it into a broader light. Something, doubtless, has been overlooked, something left for other gleaners in the field ; all that is claimed for what has here been set down is that it should be found useful to those students of dramatic literature who follow a similar quest. There are many other plays of Shakespeare and his contemporaries and successors which would doubtless repay search, and it is not disputed that but a tithe of the more tedious productions of the dramatists from the Restoration to the end of the seventeenth century have been reconnoitred. In the comedies of the period we have unquestionably a faithful mirror of the time, and since many of the writers had experience of the sea and sailors, further exploration may elicit something of value. But these plays, if they are not deficient in wit and quiet humour, are at the same time so vulgar and coarse that to read them is very weary work.

in the hippodrome—for at Astley's the sailor performed on horseback—were, in many instances, only grotesque caricatures of the men-of-war's men of the time, their language, behaviour, and appearance.

It would not be expedient, even if it were possible, to deal with the drama as with history in a previous section, if for no other reason than the circumstance of the sameness, or at least the similarity, of much of the material under examination. It is extraordinary how one writer after another annexed the work of his predecessors, plots, character, business, and dialogue. It will be enough for our purpose to take a few specimens and use where needful others of a like character for illustration or exposition. One of the earliest farcical plays with a nautical setting is entitled " A Bickerstaff's Burying," by Mrs. Centlivre, and was produced at Drury Lane in 1710. The plot is apparently taken from one of Sinbad's stories in " The Arabian Nights," and turns upon a custom of the country which obliged the living husband or wife to be buried with his or her dead spouse. In the first scene we are told there is to be a working sea, with a ship on a rock, and mermaids. Then as this spectacle is closed in we have the beach, and the sailors who have been saved from the wreck meet with the inhabitants of the country. At first the new-comers are delighted with their fresh quarters. They fall in love, and several weddings seem likely to follow. A lady, however, who is already married, but dislikes her husband, reveals to the captain of the ship this custom of the country, whereupon the sailor expresses his preference for ship's biscuit, the cat-o'-nine-tails, and the sound of the boatswain's whistle. Another ship happening on the coast affords them an opportunity of leaving the country, which they do, with their sweethearts and such booty as they are able to lay their hands upon. This farcical play has two points of interest, the first of them connected with the scenery. The spectacle with which the piece opens, a working sea with the wreck, appears to have been the

first attempt of the machinist at anything quite so realistic.
It is regrettable that we have no description of the
machinery used for the representation of this scene.
There must have been something of a similar nature in
" Fortune by Sea and Land," which we have already
described, and in which there was a sea fight apparently
illustrated at first on the scenery, and then continued
on the stage, as if one vessel had been boarded by the
sailors of the other.

It is interesting to note that in the first play sold in
England with illustrations, one of these shows a fleet
at anchor, and is apparently a reproduction of the scene
shown at the back of the stage.

The stage directions for this act are : " The scene
opens with the prospect of a large river with a glorious
fleet of ships." The title of the play is " The Empress
of Morocco," and the writer was Elkanah Settle, the last
of the city laureates, whose duty it was to write the
official poem in honour of Lord Mayor's Day and other
city pageants. The tragedy of " The Empress of
Morocco " was produced in 1673, and the illustrated
copy is to be found in the British Museum Library.
While on the subject of scenery, it should be mentioned
that at the theatre of Lincoln's Inn Fields in 1731 a
scene in a play called " Orestes " showed a ship under
full sail which is said to have been made to move away
as if sailing. There was an actor at this theatre named
Boheme, who had been a sailor, and of whom it is told
that, although a very good comedian, he could never
divest himself entirely of the rolling gait which he had
acquired on shipboard at sea. He does not appear to
have played sailor parts, but it is conceivable that he
had some responsibility in the production of this moving
ship. About 150 years later great excitement and
enthusiasm were aroused at one of the Surrey side theatres
by a ship under full sail on the stage which was made
to move towards the audience until the bowsprit and
head sails were well over the orchestra, then she was
put about and appeared to be sailing away, when the

curtain came down. This was a veritable triumph of stage machinery.

Of a very different character from Mrs. Susanna Centlivre's play was a tragedy called " Fatal Curiosity ; or, The Cornish Shipwreck," which appears to have been originally produced in 1736 and founded on an occurrence which actually happened in the early part of the seventeenth century. A man and his wife living near the sea coast at Penryn are in great want. A ship is wrecked, and amongst those saved is their own son, to whom they offer hospitality without discovering his identity. It is not, indeed, until they have killed him for the sake of the treasure they find he has brought ashore that they recognise they have murdered their own offspring. Then the man kills his wife and commits suicide. It must be acknowledged that since the days of Plautus a shipwreck has always been regarded as a very proper and popular feature in nautical drama.

Chronologically, " The Reprisal ; or, The Tars of Old England," by Smollett, should be mentioned here, as Garrick produced it for the first time in January, 1757. In a printed copy illustrated, which we have before us, it is called a farce, but it has also been described as a comedy, and was in two acts. Musical plays of a patriotic tendency had already appeared, and will be referred to later on. Smollett seems to have intended his play to revive the interest of the country in the Navy, which had been deeply humiliated at the loss of Minorca by Byng's failure in the previous year. Although we are at peace with France, Heartlie, a gentleman of Dorsetshire, and his sweetheart Harriet, while sailing in a pleasure boat, have been captured and robbed by a privateer, commanded by a French naval officer called Champignion, " an instance of rapaciousness I did not expect to meet with in a gentleman and an officer," says Mr. Heartlie. Two Jacobites in the French service, Occlabber and Maclaymore, who have between them many of the characteristics of the more famous Lieutenant Lismahago in " Hum-

phrey Clinker," disapprove of the action of their commander. But although they exercise certain restraint
upon his libertine propensities they draw their swords
on the side of their paymaster when, as presently happens, an English man-of-war comes to the rescue. The
English seamen, Tom Lyon, a lieutenant, Tom Haulyard, a midshipman, and Ben Block, are as good pictures
in their way as any Smollett ever drew. The English
public were, no doubt, delighted by the contrasted
pusillanimity and cowardice of the French captain and
the gallantry and thoroughness of their countrymen.
Lyon, however, says that he has been taken prisoner,
and can vouch for the valour and politeness of the French
nation. "There are Champignions in every service."
Naturally also at this time Block gets tipsy and is allowed
freedom in conversation with his superior officer which
is to some extent explained by his remark that "Ben
Block was the man that taught you, Tom Lyon, to hand,
reef, and steer." Haulyard, the midshipman, was
played by Beard, the celebrated English tenor and the
best singer of his day. He was afterwards manager
of Covent Garden, and he wound up "The Reprisal"
with "Come, cheer up, my lads, 'tis to glory we steer,"
apparently the earliest version of this song. Two
years later it was again sung in a satirical piece called
"Harlequin's Invasion," produced in celebration of
Hawke's victory. It is said to have been written by
Garrick.

Another comedy in two acts, written by Pilon and
produced in 1779, contains a tribute to Keppel, whose
trial had not long before taken place. A merchant
named Debenture and an old sea captain named Teneriffe,
who is addicted to using nautical terms and similes,
fit out together a privateer, and send her to sea under
command of a seaman named Russell Cloudesley Wilmot,
whose very name, it is remarked, was enough to make
prizes of a whole fleet. The hero, George Belford, and
his sweetheart, Harriet, Debenture's daughter, wish to
marry, but the avaricious old merchant is anxious to

have a richer son-in-law. Harriet intends to elope, and appears in the disguise of a naval officer's uniform, whereupon her sweetheart remarks, "You look as bewitchingly terrible and as formidable a beauty as a cockade can make you." Old Teneriffe is deceived by her appearance, exclaiming, "Choke my chain pumps, by his uniform he should belong to the Navy"; and when Harriet draws her sword and cheeks him he cries, "Why, unbend my topsails, do you mean to board me, you young lubber?" Presently Wilmot, who has captured a rich ship and made prisoners of a French general and a supposed Dutchman, affords an opportunity to the avarice of Debenture, who has stopped the elopement, and who in turn offers his daughter to each of the characters whom he thinks to be wealthy. Finally the Dutchman turns out to be Belford's father, and the young pair are allowed to follow their inclinations. Midships, Teneriffe's servant, is an old sea dog who has been in the Navy and is a very good character. The play ends with a parade of the prisoners and a patriotic song, of which the chorus is "And a-cruising we will go."

From a large number of other comedies, dramas, or farces, in almost all of which songs are introduced, the following may be mentioned. "The Purse; or, The Benevolent Tar," by Cross, produced in 1794, is of that class in which the action takes place on shore and the nautical flavour is given by the introduction of seamen. In this play the two principal male characters have just returned from an eight years' cruise at sea. There is nothing inherently improbable in this, since Lord Dundonald states that in his time some of the vessels had been on the East India station without the men receiving their pay, the *Centurion*, eleven years; the *Albatross*, twelve years; the *Rattlesnake*, fourteen; and the *Fox*, fifteen years. Coming ashore, then, with plenty of back pay, Will Steady puts his purse into the pocket of a page-boy, who, asleep on a doorstep, excites his sympathy. The boy, who turns out to be Steady's son, is accused of theft by the villain of the piece, and upon this incident turns the plot of the play.

John Bannister, who played Steady, was the principal low comedian on the stage at this time, and Leigh Hunt said of him : " Let an author present him with a humorous idea, whether it be of jollity, of ludicrous distress, or of grave indifference, whether it be mock heroic, burlesque, or mimicry, and he embodies it with an instantaneous felicity." He played many sailor parts, including Ben in " Love for Love." One can imagine him rolling out to the delight of his audience such a speech as this : " Yo, ho ! your honour. Here we are within pistol shot of port. Let me alone for a pilot. I'll steer you into the harbour of happiness." Or, in an attitude of defiance, declaring that " an English tar never strikes his colours while he is able to strike another stroke." Or, in a sententious mood, to the discomfited villain : " Take a tar's advice, lad. Use the rudder of honesty instead of deceit, and then you'll steer clear of the shoals of punishment and the quicksands of disgrace." " British Fortitude," by the same author, dealing with the recovery of a naval officer from a French prison, and " The Turnpike Gate," by Knight, are of a similar character. In the latter an old sailor, Joe Standfast, gives a thrilling description of a sea fight, revealing the fact that Lieutenant Travers, the hero, who is supposed to have been killed, is alive and promoted for his gallantry. This character was played by Incledon, a vocalist for whom many sailor parts were written. Similarly, in " The Smugglers," the sailor's part of Trim was written for Bannister, who assists Captain Pendant and his daughter to foil the machinations of the villains, who are in reality wreckers and not smugglers. " Delays and Blunders," a comedy by Reynolds, deals with the troubles that beset the unsuspicious naval officer fresh from the sea, who says that money is such a load that to sail pleasantly he must chuck some of it overboard. " I know but little of the world, and seeing no joy in guilt myself I cannot conceive how others should pursue it." When he first arrives on shore he thanks Heaven he is not married, for the word " wife " spells to him " slavery, chains, leaks, short allowance, sea-sickness, and the press-gang." But in good time he falls in love, and before the curtain comes down he has discovered that a wife to him is a ship well manned, a prosperous pilot, a successful voyage, victory, prize money, and a First Lord of the Admiralty.

Cumberland's " Sailor's Daughter " has a land set-ting, and though there are several sailors in it their sea life seems to have made little impression on their language, and they are merely distinguished from the landsmen by the patriotic sentiments they utter, their open-handedness, and courage. " Bannian Day," a farce in two acts by George Brewer, with songs, has more nautical colour, since the scene is laid in Plymouth. The plot deals with a gentleman whose son, a lieutenant in the Navy, having married a lady without fortune, has been disclaimed by his father. The young officer is in low water, distressed for want of funds, or, as Jack Hawser calls his condition, suffering from " Bannian Day." Jack brings about a meeting between the lieutenant's wife and her father-in-law, when his pre-judices are overcome and he makes atonement. Then, as Jack Hawser says, " All that I hope is—that the Bannian Day of every messmate in distress may end as happily as ours, and with the approbation of our best friends."

The earliest reference to Banyan or Bannian Day we have found is in " The Straights Voyage," the rhymed narrative written by an officer of the *St. David*, the flagship in the Mediterranean of Sir John Harman in 1669–71, quoted from in an earlier chapter. The ex-pression is frequently used as a synonym for a famishing time, as in another play by Pocock with the title of " For England, Ho ! " The seamen only appear in the under-plot, but Tom Tough, an old sailor, was played by John Emery, an actor and vocalist who was at his best in rustic parts. Meeting a beggar he addresses him : " What Bannian Day mayhap. You shall mess with me. See, here's a victualling office. I'll line your planks with some English beef and a can of grog." Tom is sent with a love letter, which he delivers to the aunt instead of the niece, and this mistake is the cause of complications and much amusement.

That the title of a comedy or drama may be no guide to its subject will be understood from the following, all of which are more or less concerned with the proceedings of sailors on shore. "The Widow Bewitched," produced in 1730; "The Maiden's Whim," 1756; "The Brothers," 1769; "£30,000; or, Who is the Richest?" 1804; "The Times: A Tell Tale," 1808; and "The Boarding House; or, Five Hours at Brighton," 1812.

We may now turn to the more spectacular pieces. Of this class of play, one of the earliest is Phillips's "Britons, Strike Home; or, The Sailor's Rehearsal," produced at Drury Lane in December, 1739, and evidently inspired by the capture of a Spanish ship, the *St. Joseph*, by the British men-of-war *Chester* and *Canterbury* in the same year. The title of this piece is taken from the song written or set to music by Purcell for the operetta ("Bonduca") produced in 1695. The form of the play shows that it was intended to give the characters opportunities for songs, dances, and patriotic speeches. The scene is laid on the deck of the *St. Joseph*, where the British officers are visited by Sir John Freehold, a hearty John Bull, with his daughter, the only lady in the piece, a merchant (Export), and a critic (Dapperwit). They have come on board to see a musical trifle, written by the lieutenant of the ship, rehearsed by the sailors, and all the scenes in this piece have reference to the taking of the Spanish ship. Miss Kitty Freehold has a part in the performance called Donna Americana, and she is made to say, "There is a great deal in having politics set to a proper tune, and thank our stars they have lately been set to the tune of ' Britons, Strike Home,' and there is not an Englishman in the kingdom but thinks this is the best tune that has been played these

several years." This is the only nautical piece of its
kind we have been able to discover, but the introduction
of tableaux representing contemporary or historical
naval incidents became common later on. In "Eliza,"
a musical piece produced at Drury Lane in 1756–7,
the last act presented a remarkable contrast to the condition of affairs in Sheridan's "Critic," where the governor of the fort at Tilbury remarks :—

> The Spanish Fleet thou canst not see—because
> It is not yet in sight.

In the last act of "Eliza" there was a representation
of the destruction of the Spanish Armada by the English
fleet. Nor was it always or often that the battling of
the seamen afloat was cut out like the gallant behaviour
of Don Whiskerandos in the sea fight, which Tilburina
assured Mr. Puff no one would miss. In "The Veteran
Tar" an engagement between an English merchant ship
and a French privateer took place in sight of the audience
in all its varying phases, and eventually the hero, who
was assisted by Tom Clueline, Ben Bowline, Jack Bobstay,
Dick Traverse, and Bob Steerwell, his companions in the
action, brought the captured flag ashore and placed it
at the feet of old Sturdy, the veteran tar. This character
described himself as "cradled on shipboard, as rough and
uncivil as the rude elements that rocked my youthful
slumbers, yet within this tempest-beaten hulk I have still
a sound heart of oak, and may that heart be shivered
into splinters if ever I insult a woman. Women, bless
'em, they're the sailor's sheet anchor, his joy ashore, his
hope at sea, they're the treasures that reward the toils
of life and the sweets that enable us to taste its sours
without making wry faces."

The masque was a spectacular exhibition of great
antiquity, in which pageantry was combined with
recitation, poetry, music, and dancing. In the olden
days this kind of performance was in great favour with
the Court, and Ben Jonson collaborated with Inigo
Jones in the production of masques of great beauty

and artistic merit. With the restoration of Charles II
there was a renewed demand for masques, and Sir
William Davenant among others produced them. It
was the prologue to " Britannia," a masque by David
Mallet, and the music of which was supplied by Dr.
Arne, that Garrick spoke in the character of a drunken
tar reading a playbill. And in another masque entitled
" Alfred," by James Thomson and Mallet, the first
edition of " Rule, Britannia" occurs. These masques
were produced between 1740 and 1755. Still earlier
was " Albion ; or, The Court of Neptune," produced in
1724, in which the scene was laid on the British seas.
Captain Edward Thompson wrote a masque, in which
the characters were naval, called " The Syrens." In
his preface Thompson says that " having studied at sea
and taken his degrees at the Admiralty, it did not become
the wits of the period to attack a Nautic Bard whose
dank seaweed could not abate the lustre of their classic
and more verdant bays." He apologises for introducing
sea characters on the plea that they are at least original.
Along with his sailors there are nymphs and dryads,
syrens and a Druid, who give the unfortunate mariners
much trouble. Among the other seamen there is a
marine officer who is a rather loose fish, a " tawny "
sailor who talks about the masts going by the board
before we could cry " Peccavi "; and another, who
calls himself a poor bluejacket, opines that the island
makes a fine site for exploration. Altogether, " The
Syrens" is a very whimsical piece, but the poetry,
which includes a capital song beginning " The topsails
shiver in the wind," is much better than the prose.

Another masque, or, as it was also called, a musical
extravaganza, " The Seraglio," has often been attributed
to Thompson, and is so in the British Museum, but
Dibdin, in his autobiography (" Life," 1803, Vol. I, p. 168),
claims its authorship, including the favourite song :—

> The signal to engage shall be
> A whistle and a hollow,
> Be one and all but firm, like me,
> And conquest soon will follow ;

and another, better known, which Dibdin says he wrote
in a gale of wind on a thirteen hours' passage from Calais,
where he had been with some friends on a party of
pleasure. " It arose out of the reflection that I was on
my return to her, who has since lent inspiration to so
many similar sentiments, of which this is a specimen :—

> Blow high, blow low, let tempests tear
>   The mainmast by the board ;
> My heart with thoughts of thee, my dear,
>   And love, well stored,
> Shall brave all danger, scorn all fear."

It is among the most charming of sea songs.

We have already alluded to the many plays inspired
by contemporary naval incidents, including " Britons,
Strike Home ! " which appeared in the year that Vernon
took Portobello, and Smollett's " Reprisal," which had
an indirect connection with Byng's disaster. During
the Seven Years' War a farce called " The French Flogged ;
or, British Sailors in America," introduced scenes evidently suggested by the struggle for Canada. In 1773
George III visited Spithead and reviewed the Fleet,
and a piece was produced at the Haymarket in August
of that year called " A Trip to Portsmouth," in which
scenes illustrative of the event were shown. In 1779
an amusing little play called " Illumination ; or, The
Glazier's Conspiracy," was suggested by the rejoicings
on the acquittal of Admiral Keppel. The glazier and
his apprentices go out to break the windows in order
to create business. An attorney's clerk, who is in love
with the glazier's daughter, engages some of his legal
friends to pretend to be a press-gang. They seize the
glazier, and are apparently about to take him on board
ship when the budding lawyer turns up and effects his
release, for which kindness he is rewarded by the hand
of the young lady. In the same year the alarm in
England, and especially in the south, owing to the
enemy's fleet being in the Channel, found reflection in a
musical piece called " Plymouth in an Uproar." The
plot is similar to that of the " Maid of Kent," 1773, and

many other musical pieces, Lord Heartless endeavouring
to carry off a sailor's sweetheart. Unfortunately for
him, this particular sailor happens to be in command of
the press-gang, and his lordship finds himself in the
bilboes. " Cheerily, my hearts," says the lieutenant,
" now's the time, lads, to show what you're made of.
We shall have laurels as plenty as nettles, for here they
come, Frenchman and Spaniard, my hearts of oak ! "
And further on he remarks that " I am a gentleman by
descent as well as by profession. The sincere love of a
true British tar can be despised by none." There is an
underplot in which William, the coxswain, and Susan,
the lady's maid, who are in love with one another,
play at cross purposes. This is not the first time that
these names were brought into conjunction for a similar
purpose, a musical piece called " William and Susan ;
or, The Sailor's Sheet Anchor," having been produced
in 1765. In this case Susan, disguised in men's clothes,
is pressed by the gang in which is her own sweetheart.
Alluding to the love of her mistress for the young lieutenant, she says, " Ay, these cockades, these cockades.
I used to think it was the redcoats that did all the mischief, but I find the young rogue never shoots so true as
from behind a cockade." In the last scene a number of
patriotic miners arrive from Cornwall to man the fleet,
and are subjected to much chaff by the sailors.

In 1780 the relief of Gibraltar was the subject of a farce
in which there was a comic sailor, who in the concluding
verse of his song referred to Prince William Henry, who
as a midshipman in the *Prince George* had taken part
in the battle. After reciting the deeds of Rodney, and
other naval worthies, he sang of

> England's young, but future pride ;
> William's a name which fate ordains
> To spread his country's glory wide.

In that year, too, in an operetta called " Fire and
Water," we seem to have an echo of Jack the Painter's
attempt to burn Portsmouth Dockyard in 1776. French
spies make friends with the storekeeper, whose daughter

is in love with a middy. The young folk flirting on the ramparts, which Besant made famous in " Celia's Arbour," overhear the plots of the foreigners. They are caught red-handed in the dockyard by the midshipman, who then naturally gets the reward he desires. In 1794 the Glorious First of June was commemorated by a musical entertainment at Drury Lane, the dialogue of which is said to have been supplied by Sheridan and the songs written by a number of celebrities. At Covent Garden an entertainment in connection with the victory was given under the title of " Arrived at Portsmouth." And in the same year four other naval pieces commemorative of naval incidents were produced: " The Fall of Martinique " ; " Naples Bay ; or, The British Sailors at Anchor " ; " Netley Abbey ; or, Yardarm to Yardarm " ; and " A Trip to Plymouth Dock ; or, The Launch of the *Cæsar.*" It was this *Cæsar*, commanded by Captain Brenton, that flew the flag of Sir James Saumarez in the battle of Algeciras Bay. The engagement occurred on a Sunday, and before going into action Divine Service was celebrated. The *Cæsar* was terribly mauled in the engagement with the forts, and it was thought impossible to repair her in time to go to sea with the rest of the squadron. The crew petitioned not to be left behind, and worked with such ardour that six days after she had entered in a most shattered state she was warping out of Gibraltar, the band playing " Britons, Strike Home ! " ready for any service ; and on the afternoon of the same day she was again in action.

The capture of the French frigate *Pique* by the British frigate *Blanche* in January, 1795, after a bloody and desperate action, in which the English captain was shot just before his prize was secured, was commemorated by a musical piece produced at Covent Garden, " The Death of Captain Faulkner ; or, British Heroism." In this piece, the scene of which is laid in the West Indies, the first act opens with the men discovered drinking outside a public-house, where they are addressed by the captain. There is then some comic business, and

the English and French frigates appear at
the stage, when the engagement takes place,
...ner is killed, a tableau representing the actual
...urrence. Another character is Lieutenant David
Milne, who swam to the captured vessel, as neither ship
had a sound boat, and afterwards commanded her; his
son, Sir Alexander, and grandson, Sir Berkeley, have
both attained eminence in the Royal Navy. "The
Point at Herqui; or, British Bravery Triumphant,"
an operetta, was produced at Covent Garden in the
following year to celebrate a brilliant feat of arms by
Sir Sidney Smith, on whose escape from France in
1798 a pantomime, produced in that year at Drury
Lane, was founded. Two pieces in 1797 celebrated
the surrender of Trinidad; another the attempt at landing
of the French at Bantry Bay; a fourth, "Britain's
Brave Tars; or, All for St. Paul's," the battle of St.
Vincent; and still two others, "Battered Batavians;
or, Down with the Dutch!" and "England's Glory,"
the defeat of the Dutch Fleet by Admiral Duncan at
Camperdown. In this year and the next there were
benefits at Covent Garden and Drury Lane for the widows
and orphans of the seamen who fell in these two battles.
"The Naval Pillar; or, Britannia Triumphant" commemorated the Nile, and "A Breeze in the Baltic; or,
The Danes in the Dumps," the battle of Copenhagen:
while Trafalgar was the occasion of three if not more
pieces, "The Victory, and Death of Lord Nelson,"
a drama by Cumberland, in which Braham sang his
celebrated aria; "Nelson's Glory," an interlude by
Dibdin; and "National Gratitude," a medley of song
and spectacle, produced at Covent Garden.

We have left to the last the mention of two characteristic pieces, a nautical operetta called "Thomas
and Sally; or, The Sailor's Return," with music, by
Dr. Arne, and Douglas Jerrold's naval melodrama of
"Black-Eyed Susan; or, All in the Downs," each of
these pieces being representative of a large number
of others of a similar character. In the former music,

vocal and instrumental, was almost everything, while to the latter it was merely an adventitious adjunct. " The Press Gang ; or, True Blue," by Henry Carey ; " The Cobblers' Opera," by Ryan ; " The Sailors' Opera ; or, A Trip to Jamaica " ; and " William and Susan ; or, The Sailor's Sheet Anchor," were all produced between 1740 and 1760. The theme of " Thomas and Sally," produced in 1760, and that of " Black-Eyed Susan," which made its first appearance at the Surrey Theatre in 1829, were practically the same, and were that of a good many other pieces. An absent sailor returns just in time to save his sweetheart or his wife from the evil intentions of the wicked squire or the dissolute captain. There were only four characters in " Thomas and Sally" : a sailor played by Beard, his sweetheart, by Miss Brent, the wicked squire, and Mother Dorcas, a bad old woman. The squire is about to abduct Sally, with the help of Dorcas, when Thomas returns from sea just in time to assert his rights. This operetta was an immense success ; the four performers were at the top of their profession, and so much was the singing of the two principals appreciated that a writer of the time declared : " Shakespeare and Garrick were obliged to quit the field to Beard and Brent."

The plot of Jerrold's play may be compared with that of the operetta. William and Susan are married, and the former has gone to sea on board a man-of-war. He has made no remittances, and Doggras, Susan's uncle, has refused to assist her. She is, in fact, to be " sold up." William's ship returns to port, and her captain, Crosstree, sees Susan and falls in love with her. Later, when in liquor, he tries to kiss her. Her cries of alarm reach the ears of William, carousing with his shipmates. He enters with a drawn cutlass and cuts the captain down. William is brought to trial by a court martial for striking his superior officer and condemned to die. The court, in passing sentence, admit that his case is a hard one, but the maintenance of discipline obliges them to inflict the penalty of death.

R

There is a very touching scene of farewell, and then the tableau, on the forecastle of the ship, where William is about to be hanged. Enter Crosstree, who has already before the court acknowledged that he was in fault, and he now produces William's discharge dated the day before the occurrence, so that when he struck the captain he was no longer amenable to the laws of the Service, and is, therefore, set free. There is an amusing underplot dealing with the love affairs of Gnatbrain and Dolly, two friends of Susan.

It will be seen that Jerrold, by the substitution of the tar's senior officer for his social superior, introduced an element entirely novel, affording great development and topical colour. The way out of the tangle was also a stroke of genius, but everything else, including the court martial, has its complement in other and earlier plays. There can be no doubt that Jerrold's experience in the Service gave him the cue for the interesting evolution which he carried out with such success. He was also very fortunate in having the principal part played by T. P. Cooke, who had also served in the Navy, was present at the battle of St. Vincent, and is said to have got his taste for the theatrical profession by taking part in the amateur performances which formed a feature of the entertainments provided in the ships to relieve the monotony during the blockading operations off Brest. A question has been raised as to the exact date of the first production of " Black-Eyed Susan." The advertisements in the " Times," and a notice in that paper, seem to settle the matter. On 1st June, 1829, there was an advertisement "under the clock," to the effect that there would be produced on that night at the Royal Coburg Theatre, under the management of Mr. Davidge, " Black-Eyed Susan ; or, The Lovers' Perils." On 8th June there was another advertisement stating that on that evening there would be produced at the Royal Surrey Theatre, under the management of R. W. Elliston, " Black - Eyed Susan ; or, All in the Downs." On 15th June a notice of the piece appeared, stating :—

" We were prevented from noticing last week a new and extremely interesting melodrama which was brought out at this theatre [the Surrey] on Monday [Whit-Monday, 8th June]. It is called ' Black-Eyed Susan ; or, All in the Downs ' ; but it has no other connection with the subject of that popular ballad than that the names of its hero and heroine are William and Susan."

It was further remarked by the critic that the piece was supported by Cooke's best style of acting, that Miss Scott was the Susan, and did every justice to the part, and that Buxton (from the Adelphi) had a character in the piece (Gnatbrain) which he sustained with his usual buoyancy of spirit.   Further it may be mentioned that the advertisement of the piece, " Black-Eyed Susan ; or, The Lovers' Perils," at the Coburg Theatre, ceased after Saturday, 13th June, and a new piece, entitled " The Post Captain ; or, A Sailor's Honour," was advertised at that house until 29th June.   The explanation appears to be that Jerrold had been writing for Davidge up to 1828, and had written a number of farces, dramas, and other dramatic pieces for production at the Coburg.   It is quite likely that he may have mentioned the plot of this nautical drama to the manager ; however, in 1829 he engaged himself to Elliston to write for the Surrey, and " Black-Eyed Susan " was put in rehearsal.   When this was announced Davidge, possibly feeling himself aggrieved, had hastily put together and produced a play with a very similar name and character.   That this was a failure seems also to have been indisputable, although from the title of the piece that followed it the play may have had a short run.   The success of Jerrold's melodrama constituted a record, for it was played for 300 nights, a unique occurrence in those days.   It was transferred to Covent Garden, and then to Drury Lane, to Bath, and to many other places in the provinces, while it has been frequently revived, and was a success even so recently as 1896, when the town rang with the praises of poor William Terriss in the part of the hero.   Miss Milward made a

sweet and tender Susan, and Harry Nicholls gave an
excellent character interpretation of Gnatbrain.

How far " Black-Eyed Susan " is representative of
the Navy of its time is a moot question. While all the
characters are simple and distinct, the sailors act naturally
in the situations created for them, and exhibit those
characteristics which we should expect, the phraseology is bombastic and incongruous. We cannot believe
that any seaman talked as William does, for his use of
sea terms and his aptitude for nautical similes are
tremendous. The officers, too, from Captain Crosstree
downwards, are hardly convincing, and the procedure
of the court martial is farcical at times. At the same
time, with due allowance for necessary exaggeration and
other requirements for adaptation to stage purposes,
it is possible to believe that taking the play as a whole,
and remembering that Jerrold and Cooke had both been
in the Navy, while the audience, too, must have been
largely composed of sailors, we have here a veritable
picture of naval occurrences such as appeared perfectly
natural and appropriate to the time when it was produced.
That it is an excellent drama, buoyant, bright, and
breezy, appealing strongly to the sympathetic chords of
the human heart, is indisputable.

Much more might be written about the many nautical
melodramas of the early nineteenth century, plays in
which T. P. Cooke, O. Smith, J. Gal ot, and other
exponents of nautical character fascinated the public
of their time, and with the assistance of Dibdin's songs
helped to increase the popularity of the Navy. T. P.
Cooke was celebrated for his bold, vigorous, and romantic picture of the British Tar, but it was said of him also
that as " Long Tom Coffin " in " The Pilot " he gave a
new feature to the seaman's character—that of thoughtfulness and mystery, of deep-toned passion and pathos.
O. Smith, who had also served in the Navy, played parts
in which the seaman was invested with a semi-super-
natural character—pirates, smugglers, and the like. He
was noted for a mysterious, abstracted, half-crazed look

and manner, an ominous hollow voice, a stealthy step, with similar indications of subtle deviltry. He was great as the dare-devil "Vanderdecken" in "The Flying Dutchman." John Gallot as "Jack Junk" in "The Floating Beacon," we are told, "rolled, looked, and roared like a true son of Neptune." Apropos of the nautical melodramas and musical sea plays of this period, a contemporary writer says :—

Gratitude to the three Dibdins for doing justice to the British sailor! Congreve has made him a sea calf—a tarpaulin; and the elder Colman, a crimp and a bully;—but the Dibdins have raised him to the rank of a rational being, with feelings and affections, without any abatement of his eccentricity and humour. Old Charles has written sea songs that cut the heart in twain with their pathos, and his two sons, Tom the First and Charles the Second, have produced nautical lyrics that shall live till Neptune retires from the white cliffs of Albion and leaves no longer an ocean of difference between Dover and Calais.

This section would be incomplete without some mention of the amateur theatricals of the Navy. Adequate treatment of this subject, however, would require another chapter. We have found notices of amateur performances on board men-of-war as far back as the time of the Restoration. Many of our great commanders, Nelson among them, approved of this form of entertainment as a means of keeping the devil out of the minds of the sailors, and they fostered the aptitude for acting among officers and men, even, it is said, to the extent of forwarding the interests of the one or raising the rate in the case of the other, as an incentive to the efforts of those who laid themselves out to amuse their shipmates. It was by this means that in the long dreary blockades of the enemy's ports, and in the dull gloom of the Arctic Seas, the monotony of life on shipboard was broken, and the good humour, well-being, and needful discipline of the Service were maintained.

It is in some ways more difficult to present a picture of the seaman's individuality from dramatic literature than from the pages of history or fiction, because the world behind the footlights is an unreal world, subject to the convention of the drama, and, while holding up the mirror to nature, its reflections are tinged with the hue of phantasy or imagination, more especially when the nature it presents to us is found in a world little known, as a rule, to those who have written for the stage. Nevertheless, there is no mistaking the characteristic personality of the man. Stripping away from him the romance and the absurdities with which he has been clothed, we see him, as in the character of Manly, singularly downright in his nature, above all things plain spoken in his large honesty—honesty in the best and truest sense, covering and excusing all lapses of detail—faithful to his charge and strong in his brotherhood. A man of whimsical mood, also, is brought before us, for the humours of the stage demanded oddity and strangeness, and, indeed, on the stage as elsewhere in actual life, the sailor lent himself to representations of that character. In most ships there were men who had a talent for impersonation in the grotesque or burlesque manner, and it was often men of this class that the playwright seized upon for his characters. They were true in the sense that they represented, with exaggerations, the real men of the sea, but it must not be supposed that every seaman was an oddity or a buffoon such as was seen on the melodramatic or farcical stage. It was the unusual that the dramatist took as the subject of his representations, calling forth, in untoward mishaps, strange adventures, or dire misfortunes, both laughter and tears. But those who reflect upon the meaning and significance of what has been said will recognise the essential truth of the figure of the seaman on the stage, and will see what is his relation to the seaman of history and historical literature, and to the seaman of fiction, whose personality is to be drawn in the succeeding section of this book.

PART III

SEA STORIES, NOVELS, MAGAZINES, AND CHAP-BOOKS

CHAPTER XII

DEFOE AND HIS PREDECESSORS

NO recognisable portrait of the seaman is to be found in the early vestiges of English fiction. If we sought him in the dim pages of Beowulf, the wonder-worker, or attempted to discover him in the romances of Roland, or Arthur, or Lancelot, which the Normans, Bretons and laughter-loving Gascons brought with them to England, we could figure him to ourselves only by giving a free rein to the imagination. William of Malmesbury, Gerald of Wales, Geoffrey of Monmouth, and Walter Map, do not body forth the seaman, but give him by record or reference, and never present him in strong type or character. Chaucer, the one writer who gave us a real seaman, exercised little influence upon the progress of English fiction. It was the age of discovery that brought the mariner into the beginnings of the English novel.

Sir Thomas More, one of the greatest, best, and most beautiful-minded of Englishmen, found in the distant land of Utopia, wherein he revealed the heart of the new learning, the seat of a better government than England had produced. He describes how he heard of this kingdom imagined beyond the sea. " On a certain day, when I had heard Mass in Our Lady's Church, which is the fairest, the most gorgeous and curious church building in all the city of Antwerp, and also most frequented of people, and service being done, I was ready to go home to my lodging. I chanced to espy my friend, Peter Gilles, talking with a certain stranger, a man well stricken in age, with a tanned, sun-burned face, a long beard, and a cloak cast trimly about his shoulders, whom, by his favour and apparel, forthwith I judged to be a mariner." There was something, then, in the stranger's appearance that bespoke his personality—the weather-beaten face, the alert and earnest eyes, the stalwart pose of the figure, wearing the cloak in a manner that revealed the man of the sea. This was in 1516, and the sailor turned out to have been a companion of Amerigo Vespucci, in those voyages to the New World, " that be now in print and abroad in every man's hand." More invited the old seafarer —who, it appeared, was not a seaman by profession, but had by long familiarity assumed the aspect of one —to accompany him to his house, and " there in my garden, upon a bench covered with green turves, we sate down, talking together" of marvellous adventures, of how Vespucci had abandoned him, and how he had wandered under the equinoctial line, and at last of his sojourn in the kingdom of Utopia, or " Nowhere."

Here it may be observed that it is not always possible to draw a definite line between fact and fiction in some early narratives. In the collections of Hakluyt and Purchas there are records of adventure which partake of both characters. Perhaps we may say that Peter Carder, whose narrative was preserved by Purchas, was one of the first of sea romancers. He describes himself as a comrade of Drake, who drifted in an open boat, passed through the Strait of Magellan, and being cast ashore in Brazil, had many adventures with the natives. In this style of narrative Carder seems to have anticipated Defoe.

John Lyly, the " Euphuist," was to come a little nearer to the modern novel than any earlier writer. His style was based fantastically upon that of the Italian decadents, and it influenced a whole literature, represented by Shakespeare's Armado, " that hath a mint of phrases in his brain." But in Lyly's " Galathea," one of the comedies which he wrote in the latter part of the six-

teenth century, played before the Queen on New Year's
Day in 1592, we meet with a recognisable mariner—
a man who had sailed with Drake. Says Robin: "Sea!
nay, I will never sail more, I brook not their diet; their
bread is so hard that one must carry a whetstone in
his mouth to grind his teeth; the meat is so salt that
one would think after dinner his tongue had been powdered ten days." Raffe joins in laughing at the seaman.
"Oh, thou hast a sweet life, Mariner, to be pinned in
a few boards, and to be within an inch of a thing bottomless. I pray thee how often hast thou been drowned?"
To which the mariner replies, "Fool, thou seest I am
alive," and after more conversation he gives the seaman's reproof to the coxcomb. "Thou art wise from
the crown of thy head upwards; seek your new fortunes
now; I will follow my old. I can shift the moon and
the sun, and know by one card what all you cannot do
by a whole pack. The lodestone that always holdeth
his nose to the North, the two and thirty points of the
wind, the wonders I see would make you all blind;
you be but boys. I fear the sea no more than a dish
of water. Why, fools, it is but a liquid element. Farewell!"

Lyly had many followers and imitators. In Barnaby
Rich's "Travels and Adventures of Don Simonides"
we are hurried from port to port, with little or no description, and discover no real seaman. Nor does
Greene—who, in the introduction to "The Royal Exchange," 1590, told the citizens of London that their
ships harboured in the Thames were a match for all the
argosies, galleys, galleons, and pataches of Venice or of
any city in the world—ever bring us in his stories face
to face with the mariners who manned them, even when,
as in his "Alcida," he describes a shipwreck.

Lodge is a greater figure in this inquiry than Greene.
Born in 1557, he had himself turned from the university
and the Inns of Court to become a seafarer and adventurer. His romances are not, indeed, of the sea,
though he penned them in the rage of Atlantic storms

and in the rigours of the Strait of Magellan. They are pastoral stories, cast in woodlands or vineyards, or of romantic happenings pictured in the play of fancy and grace of style, showing how the mind of the storm-tossed seaman turned to the arcadian graces of the shore. His " Rosalynde ; Euphues' Golden Legacies found in his cell at Selixedra," published in 1590—the same year that saw the production of the uncompleted text of Sidney's " Arcadia "—gave to Shakespeare the original idea and some of the characters of " As You Like It," the pastoral play transferred to the forest of Arden from the vineyards of Gascony, where Lodge had located his banished Duke as a forester, and whither returned his daughter, the fair Rosalynde. Now we think, or are pleased to imagine that we know, why the melancholy Jaques uses a sea simile of the brain of the " motley fool "—" as dry as the remainder biscuit after a voyage." But, in Lodge's " Rosalynde " the seaman is found not in the romance but in the author, who, in his dedication to Lord Hunsdon, says: " Having with Captain Clark made a voyage to the island of Terceras and the Canaries, to beguile the time I wrote this book ; rough, as hatched in the storms of the ocean, and feathered in the surge of many perilous seas." And he addresses the " Gentlemen Readers " with a rousing voice. " To be brief, gentlemen, room for a soldier and a sailor, that gives you the fruits of his labours that he wrote in the ocean, where every line was wet with a surge, and every human passion counterchecked with a storm. If you like it, so ; and yet I will be yours in duty, if you be mine in favour. But if Momus or any squint-eyed ass, that hath mighty ears to conceive with Midas, and yet little reason to judge, if he come aboard our barque to find fault with the tackling, when he knows not the shrouds, I'll down into the hold, and fetch out a rusty pole-axe, that saw no sun this seven year, and either baste him with it, or heave the coxcomb overboard to feed cods. But, courteous gentlemen, that favour most, backbite none, and pardon what is overslipped, let such come and welcome ; I'll into the steward's room, and fetch them a can of our best beverage. Well, gentlemen, you have Euphues' Legacy. I fetched it as far as the island of Terceras, and therefore read it, censure with favour, and Farewell." The seaman here steps out straight from the page, with all his heartiness, his detestation of false pretenders, his genial hospitality shining in his face ; and in the book itself is a figure drawn from the sea experience of the writer. " Oh, how the life of men may be compared to the state of the ocean seas, that for a day's calm hath a thousand storms, resembling the rose tree, that with a few fair flowers hath a multitude of sharp prickles."

In the introduction to " A Margarite of America," a romance printed in 1596, Lodge tells us that it was written " in those Straits christened by Magellan, in which place to the southward, many wondrous isles, many strange fishes, many wondrous Patagones withdrew my senses ; briefly, many bitter and extreme frosts at midsummer continually clothe and clad the discomfortable mountains, so that there was great wonder in the place wherein I writ this, so likewise might it be marvelled that in such scanty fare, such causes of fear, so mighty discouragements, and many crosses I should deserve or eternise anything." Lodge tells the Gentlemen Readers that four years before he had been at sea with Cavendish, " whose memory, if I repent not, I lament not," and that he chanced to find in a Jesuit library this history in the Spanish tongue which delighted him, won him, and made him write it. " The place where I began my work was a ship, where many soldiers of good reckoning finding disturbed stomachs, it cannot but stand in your discretions to pardon me an undiscreet and unstayed pen, for hands may vary where stomachs miscarry. The time I wrote this was when I had rather will to get my dinner than to win my fame."

And now we shall find the seaman in the " picaresque " novel and description—the novel of the picaro, the rogue, knave, thief, and vagabond, the novel of the new and incisive realism which anticipated Defoe. Thomas Nash was one of the group of young writers who despised convention revelled in delineating the ridiculous side of human nature, and showed small respect for authority. Himself born in a seaport town of East Anglia in 1567, he knew and loved the salt sea, held in contempt the mock and pretending seaman, and had no great liking for the swaggering adventurer. Most of all he loved the hard-lived fisherman. Always ready for a literary brawl, he rushed into a hot dispute in a quarrel in which Gabriel Harvey, a pedant, had attacked Greene, and in a witty and caustic pamphlet, entitled " Have with you to Saffron Walden," 1596, he denounced certain calumnies against himself as "a lie befitting a base, swabberly, lousy sailor, who, having been never but a month at sea in his life, and ducked at the main yard twice or thrice for pilfery, when he comes home swears he hath been seventeen years in the Turks' galleys." In a pamphlet entitled " Nash's Lenten Stuffe," 1599, in praise of the town of Great Yarmouth, he brings before us with a masterly touch the sea adventurers returned from " our English discoveries," in all their gallantry and flaunting pride, contrasting them with the sober habit, speech, and gesture of the fishermen of Yarmouth. " Nor, walking in her streets so many weeks together, could I meet with any of these swaggering captains (captains that wore a whole ancient [i.e. a flag] in a scarf, which made them go heavy-shouldered it was so boisterous) or hufti-tuftie youthful ruffling comrades, wearing every one three yards of feather in his cap, for his mistriss' favour, such as we stumble on at each second step at Plymouth, Southampton and Portsmouth."

It is worth while to quote Nash's fine word-picture of the fishing smacks at Yarmouth. "That which especiallest nourisht the most prime pleasure in me was, after a storm when they had been driven in swarms, and lay close pestered together as thick as they could pack ; the next day following, if it was fair, they would cloud the whole sky with canvas, by spreading their

drabbled sails in full clue aboard a-drying, and make
a braver show with them than so many banners and
streamers displayed against the sun on a mountain top."

In the historical section of this volume a sketch of
a sailor is taken from the "Whimzies" of Braithwaite,
1631. It was the age of character sketches, in which,
before the modern novel had begun, clever and sarcastic
writers sought to picture types of men and women in
their habit as they lived. Braithwaite's sailor is of that
character. He does not pretend to describe him with
fidelity, and gains his effect by exaggeration. Perhaps
that picture may be regarded as fiction. Another sarcastic picture of the mariner of the time may be ascribed
to Sir Thomas Overbury, whose "Characters" went
through a great many editions, partly owing to their
brilliance, and partly to the circumstances that attended and followed his tragic end. They received
augmentations from many hands. Overbury, born in
1581, was, it will be remembered, that friend and coun-
sellor of Somerset who became fatally entangled in the
toils of that intrigue which made the youthful Lady
Essex, divorced from her husband, the wife of Somerset,
and who is said to have been poisoned at her instigation
as he lay in the Tower.

The sketch of the sailor, which is found in " Sir Thomas
Overbury, his Wife, with Addition of new Characters,"
does not appear in the earlier editions, and seems almost
as if it bears the mark of Braithwaite's hand. "A sailor
is a pitched piece of reason, caulked and tackled, and
only studied to dispute with tempests. He is part of
his own provision, for he lives ever pickled. A fair wind
is the substance of his creed, and fresh water the burden
of his prayers. He is naturally ambitious, for he is
ever climbing, out of which as naturally he fears ; for
he is ever flying. Time and he are everywhere contending who shall arrive first ; he is well winded, for
he tires the day and outruns darkness. His life is like
a hawk's, the best part mewed ; and if he live till three
coats is a master. He sees God's wonders in the deep,

but so as rather they appear his play-fellow than stirrers
of his zeal.   Nothing but hunger and rocks can convert
him, and then but his upper deck neither ; for his hold
neither fears nor hopes.   His sleeps are but reprievals
of his dangers, and when he wakes, 'tis but next stage
to dying.   His wisdom is the coldest part about him,
for it ever points to the North ; and it lies lowest, which
makes his valour every tide o'erflow it.   In a storm 'tis
disputable whether the noise be more his or the elements',
and which will first leave scolding.   On which side of
the ship he may be saved best, whether his faith be starboard faith or larboard, or the helm at that time not
all his hope of heaven, his keel is the emblem of his
conscience ; till he be split he never repents ; then no
farther than the land allows him, and his language is
a new confusion, and all his thoughts new nations.
His body and his ship are both one burthen, nor is it
known who stows most wine, or rolls most, only the
ship is guided ; he has no stern ; a barnacle and he are
bred together, both of one nature, and 'tis feared, one
reason.   Upon any but a wooden horse he cannot ride,
and if the wind blow against him, he dare not ; he
swarves up to his seat as to a sail-yard, and cannot sit
unless he bear a flagstaff ; if ever he be broken to the
saddle 'tis but a voyage still, for he mistakes the bridle
for the bowline, and is ever turning his horse-tail.   He
can pray, but 'tis by rote, not faith, and when he would
he dares not, for his brackish belief hath made that
ominous.   A rock or a quicksand plucks him before
he be ripe, else he is gathered to his friends at Wapping."

A writer of character sketches after the manner of
Overbury and Braithwaite was Wye Saltonstall, whose
" Picturæ Loquentes " was first printed in 1632.   His
gallery includes no seaman, but he describes a waterman
as " like a piece of Hebrew spel'd backward, or the emblem of deceit, for he rows one way and looks another."

Nicholas Bretton was another writer of the time who
followed in the footsteps of Greene in his descriptions
of low life.   He has some reference to existence on sea

and land in his "A Mad World, my Masters, Mistake
me not; or, A Merry Dialogue between Two Travellers,
the Taker and the Mistaker," 1635. Lorenzo tells how,
when first he left his country and went aboard the *Bona-
venture*, no sooner had they weighed anchor, made sail,
and put to sea, with a fresh wind and fair weather,
than they became so merry above hatches that he thought
there was none so merry as the sailor. But within a
short space of time the sky became overcast, the wind
went about, and grew high, fog came on, with drizzling
rain, and so they were glad to seek shelter under hatches,
while the tempest became more furious, and the ship
laboured so much that they were glad to secure safety
by throwing their possessions overboard. Thus Lorenzo
came ashore with a very slender purse, and then he
began to reflect that he had been mistaken in thinking
one fair day and a little fair weather made up the sailor's
life—"which every minute is subject to danger of one
harm or other, and betwixt a board and the water hath
a walk but in a short and unsteady room." He did not
know how this life could be compared with the comforts
of life on shore, with pleasure in the fair weather and
shelter against the foul. This, he said, was his first mistaking. But his friend Dorindo remarked that they
might have fallen in with a prize, and then he might
not have thought himself mistaken in the merry life of
the mariner. "Whereupon they fell to talking of taking
helping mistaking, and the thief, overtaken, taking the
gallows for his inn, and the joyful taking in the beginning bringing a sorrowful mistaking in the end."
The only importance of this extract is its illustration of
the manner in which the landsman regarded the sea life,
after some experience of its hardships.

The great moral and intellectual change which was
manifested in England in the spirit of Puritanism did
nothing to give us any fiction in which the seaman of
that time could be perpetuated. Tracts, poems, medi-
tations, and controversial treatises were the staple of
the writers, and the progress of Christian from the City

s

of Destruction to the Heavenly City was the allegory
of a land journey, in the images of prophet and evangelist,
of the pilgrimage of the soul. Bunyan was lying in
Bedford Gaol when the Dutch War began, which was
waged by those seamen of serious mould whose character
and temperament have been suggested in the first part
of this volume. " English sailors may be killed," said
De Witt, "but they cannot be conquered." The seaman of the Restoration likewise is revealed more in the
pages of history than of fiction. He is not met with in
the licentious novels of Mrs. Aphra Behn or Mrs. Manley,
although, as we have shown, he made his appearance
upon the Restoration stage.

In the days of Anne and the first George, the wits,
satirists, and politicians who sat in a circle round the
table at Will's, the divines who smoked their pipes at
Child's, the men of fashion who played cards and talked
politics at the St. James's and the Cocoa Tree, and the
lawyers who discussed cases at the Grecian, knew but
little of the mariner and cared less for him. Addison
and Steele have given us no seaman in the famous gallery
of portraits which includes Sir Roger de Coverley, Sir
Andrew Freeport, Captain Sentry, and Mr. Will Honey-
comb. But the "Spectator" is not without some reflection
of sea affairs or of the character of the seaman. A visit
to Westminster Abbey aroused reflections both general
and particular. When the Spectator had " surveyed
this great magazine of mortality as it were in the lump,"
he turned again to the monument which had recently
been erected to the memory of Sir Cloudesley Shovell,
and made some very just remarks upon the subject.
" Sir Cloudesley Shovell's monument has very often
given me great offence. Instead of the brave, rough
English admiral, which was the distinguishing character
of that plain gallant man, he is represented on his tomb
by the figure of a beau, dress'd in a long periwig, and
reposing himself upon velvet cushions under a canopy
of state. The inscription is answerable to the monument, for instead of celebrating the many remarkable

actions he had performed in the service of his country, it acquaints us only with the manner of his death, in which it was impossible for him to reap any honour."

Richardson and Fielding concerned themselves very little with the seaman. The author of " Tom Jones " did, indeed, as we have seen, come to recognise at the end of his life the essential difference between the mariner and the man who lived on shore—that all flesh was not the same flesh, but that there was one kind of flesh of seamen, and another of landsmen. But in his novels the seaman has no place. Fielding knew little or nothing of the sea until he made his last voyage to Lisbon. The sea adventures of Mr. Jonathan Wild, the prince of swindlers and flash-men, and his action when cast adrift in a boat, betray no acquaintance with ships or the men who sailed the seas in them. They have no relation to sea life, and present no impression of maritime fact or character.

We arrive now at the novels of Daniel Defoe, in which transactions at sea play the leading part. Defoe had talked with many seafaring people, and with men who had fought in the great rebellion and in the old German wars. He had himself been a campaigner, and had been out with Monmouth at Sedgemoor. His insatiable appetite for tales of adventure and knowledge of strange happenings by sea and land, in wide ocean travel and the solitude of desert islands, caused him to listen eagerly to the narratives of many voyagers returned from distant navigations. In inns and coffee-houses he heard the experiences of sea rovers and pirates, and his impetuous imagination was stirred by the dramatic recital. But Defoe was a journalist and politician long before he became a novelist, and his unsparing satires and biting gibes levelled at authority made him the popular hero of the pillory. In his " Review of the Affairs of France, with Observations and Transactions at Home," in which he anticipated the " Tatler " and " Spectator," he dealt frequently with naval affairs from the political point of view. In 1705 he advocated the abolition of the

press, which he represented as a standing grievance of
the lower-class population. He had no countenance
for illegal acts of impressment, and said the man, press-
master or other, who refused to go before a magistrate,
and who by violence took a man that was not a seaman,
and carried him to sea against his will, " without doubt
he is a thief, a robber, a murderer in the eye of the law,
and may be treated accordingly." A few days later he
pursued the same subject, and asked, " Why should a
brute, a mere tar, a drunken sailor, judge by the force
of his cudgel, who is, or who is not, fit for the public
service at sea ? " In the " Review," in October, 1707,
he wrote a sardonic panegyric upon money, with this
reference to naval affairs. " Thou makest bullies admirals, libertines captains of men-of-war, cowards com-
modores, and brutes leaders of men."

The sympathies of Defoe were evidently not with
the officers of the Navy, nor, in a certain sense, with the
Navy itself. His interest was more in piracy, slaving,
and sea pillage, in the profits and not the glories of the
seaman's calling. The victories of Russell and Rooke
had left him unmoved ; the treacherous captains of
Benbow were perhaps in his mind. His pirate is something of an honest pirate—a robber who has his eye on
the main chance, and looks forward to a prosperous
retirement on shore. In one of the " Characters "
attributed to Sir Thomas Overbury, a pirate is described
as " a plague the devil hath added to make the sea more
terrible than a storm. . . . He is the merchant's book
that serves only to reckon up his losses ; a perpetual
plague to noble traffic, the hurricane of the sea, and the
earthquake of the Exchange. Yet for all this, give him
but his pardon, and forgive him restitution, he may live
to know the inside of a church, and die on this side
Wapping." Defoe's pirate is of that character. His
robberies and slave cruises are conducted by rule and
order, with a nice calculation of means to ends, and in
a thoroughly businesslike spirit.

But it is, nevertheless, disappointing to find that

the writer, who of all others in those days could have delineated the men who walked the quarter-deck and worked on the forecastles of ships of war, was content with the description of unimaginative piratical trans-actions. No man had ever a greater power of apparent fidelity of description than Defoe. He realised things to himself as permanent conceptions, to be examined, estimated, and measured, as with the logical consistency of fact and the accuracy of existent things. His "Journal of the Plague Year" and "Memoirs of a Cavalier" were written with such intimate verisimilitude that they imposed upon men who knew the circumstances, and recognised the truth of local description, as representing actual narratives of fact. Defoe separates himself, as it were, from the ostensible author, even to the literary artifice of throwing a little doubt at times upon that author's accuracy. Such a writer might well have given us the real seaman, officer and lower-deck mariner, of his day, but Defoe's mind was commonly turned away from the influences of authority. His stories never move us to any emotion. He never makes us either laugh or cry. His force and conviction, the matter-of-fact character of his descriptions, which make little appeal to imagination or credulity, and not much to sympathy, are the secret of his power.

"Robinson Crusoe," which first appeared in April, 1717, made such a great impression that other editions rapidly followed, and Defoe, who was then in ill health and nearly sixty years of age, was encouraged to add the "Farther Strange Adventures," and finally the little-read "Serious Reflections." The youthful Crusoe had in him an original perversity which drove him to evil courses, although it did not carry him so far along the path of wickedness as such perversity did his less-known successor, Captain Singleton. Despising paternal in-junctions, Crusoe was beguiled by the enticements of seafaring men, and when he had run away from home, and had been tossed about by a capful of wind, which he thought a terrible storm, he soon forgot his regrets.

" To make short this sad part of my story, we went the way of all sailors ; the punch was made, and I was made half-drunk with it ; and in that one night's wickedness I drowned all my repentance, all my reflections upon my past conduct, all my resolutions for the future." He might have returned homeward to York, being cast upon the Norfolk shore, but, possessed with " an obstinacy that nothing could resist," he pursued the course he had adopted. Crusoe was not himself a mariner, and he remarks that it was his misfortune that in his adventures he did not ship himself as a sailor. The work might have been harder, but he would have learned the duty and office of a foremast man, and in time might have qualified for a mate or lieutenant, if not for a master. " But as it was always my fate to choose for the worse, so I did here ; for, having money in my pocket and good clothes upon my back, I would always go on board in the habit of a gentleman ; and so I neither had any business in the ship nor learned to do any." In the famous voyage, in which he was cast ashore on the desert island, he was merely super-cargo in a slaving vessel, with right to an equal share of the negroes.

In the island his life is known to every one who has read the narrative in youthful days. He tells us with minute attention to detail how he secured his supplies, how he built his house, and with careful accuracy measures and estimates everything. He even makes a list of the savages he kills. His account of his boatbuilding is most methodical, and in all his work he is anxious that things shall be done decently and in order. Sometimes he consults his Bible ; at other times he encounters the devil. In the later adventures he gives an impression of the ferocity of pirate and slaving crews. One of the company was killed on the shore of Madagascar, and the seamen went off for pillage and revenge. " Bolder fellows, and better provided, never went about any wicked work in the world. When they went out, their chief design was to plunder, and they were in mighty hopes of finding gold there ; but a circumstance which none of them was aware of set them on fire with revenge, and made devils of them all." They discovered the mangled body of their comrade, and wholesale burning and slaughter followed, while Robinson Crusoe had leisure to think "of Oliver Cromwell taking Drogheda, in Ireland, and killing man, woman, and child," and also of "Count Tilly sacking the city of Magdeburg, and cutting the throats of twenty-two thousand of all sexes." It is impossible to doubt that in this massacre Defoe described such events as did actually occur. A certain decline had become noticeable in the Navy itself at the period. Men were attracted to sea by the prospect of prize money, and not a few of them learned that the profits of privateering and piracy, which could not always be clearly distinguished from one another, were often greater than the pecuniary rewards which service in the Navy allowed.

Charles Lamb remarks upon the singularity of the fact that while all ages and descriptions of people have hung delighted over the "Adventures of Robinson Crusoe," few, comparatively, would bear to be told that there exist other fictitious narratives by the same writer, four of them at least of no inferior interest, except what results from a less felicitous choice of situation.

The volume entitled "The King of Pirates, being an Account of the Famous Enterprises of Captain Avery, the Mock King of Madagascar," which is attributed to Defoe and bears all the marks of his authorship, is a narrative of rank piracy, told in matter-of-fact fashion, without any scruple or compunction, and with no personality that can be said to represent the seaman of the period, apart from the sea rover, who made of piracy a business of profit and nothing more. "Captain Singleton," whose "life" was published in 1720, is a longer narrative, but also a tale of genuine buccaneering of the pirate type, possessing a certain strange resemblance to the conduct of ordinary business at sea. Like Crusoe, Singleton is perverse from the beginning. He is bad, wicked, and ripe for any villainy, and having thrown in

his lot with mutineers and vagabonds, he remarks,
" as the English proverb runs," " he that is shipped with
the devil must sail with the devil." Captures of merchantmen, dealings with cargoes of slaves, shipwrecks,
and shipbuilding, as in " Robinson Crusoe," are the staple
of the narrative. The character of Singleton seems to
have been based upon that of Captain Kidd, who is
mentioned in the story as being gunner in the ship in
which Singleton served. " I that was an original thief,
and a pirate, even by inclination before, was in my
element, and never undertook anything in my life
with more particular satisfaction." As an illustration
of the method, it may be noted that Captain Wilmot,
the skipper of this pirate vessel, was " more particularly
cruel, when he took an English vessel, that they might
not too soon have advice of him in England, and so the
men-of-war have orders to look out for him; but this
point I bury in silence." The only aspect of humour
in this company of scoundrels is the presence of the
Quaker surgeon in the second voyage, who, while in
principle averse to fighting, has always some good reason
for engaging the enemy with the prospect of plunder,
and without the responsibility.

It is necessary to realise that Defoe, in all this vivid
and yet unemotional description of events, is depicting
only one side of maritime life. He never shows us its
lightness or its gaiety ; we have no part, in his stories,
in the occupations or social life of officers or men ; we
never see them inspired by any high ideals of duty. We
are not made to realise their brotherhood, spirit of comradeship, good humour, or readiness to assist others
while forgetting themselves. This is, no doubt, partly
because Defoe was constitutionally unable to see the
brighter side of things, and partly because his scenes
were cast in places where greed of gain was the sole incentive to endeavour. It is impossible not to record the
conviction that his writings, from the point of view from
which this book is penned, must be a lasting disappointment to the inquirer.

In concluding this chapter, reference may be made
to Swift and to the adventures of Lemuel Gulliver,
who, it may be remembered, in his voyages to Lilliput,
Brobdingnag, Laputa, and other places, was a surgeon,
and afterwards captain of merchantmen. He had been
apprenticed to a surgeon in London, and had studied
at Leyden, being afterwards appointed surgeon to the
Swallow, in which he made a voyage or two to the Levant.
The conditions in which naval surgeons acted have been
referred to in the first part of this book. Swift's purpose
was not to describe nautical character or events at sea,
though he gives us a shipwreck, but to satirise political
parties at home. Accordingly, "Gulliver's Travels" do
not help us far on the way in our search for the character
of the seaman in the pages of fiction. It will not be
until we reach, in the next chapter, the vigorous descriptions of Smollett that we shall find ourselves breathing the real salt air of the sea in the company of men
who were characteristic seamen of the eighteenth
century.

CHAPTER XIII

SMOLLETT AND THE NAVAL NOVEL

IT has been said of Tobias George Smollett that his
mission in life was " to take portraiture of English
seamanhood with due grimness, due fidelity, and convey the same to remote generations, before it vanished."
That he gave us the portraiture of seamanhood is true,
but it was not on the point of vanishing when he knew
it in 1740. Indeed, he saw it at a rather low ebb, in the
age of Mathews and Byng, and its full tide came later,
when he had laid down his pen. It is certain that the
author of " The Adventures of Roderick Random,"
which appeared in 1748, would have earned fame as a
novelist and prince of humorists if he had never gone
to sea at all, but it was his experience of life in the Navy
that gave him the types of men with whom he will for
ever be associated, and whom he has made immortal.
They stand alone as great originals in the literature of the
eighteenth century. That they are caricatures, almost
every one of them, must be admitted; but that, with all
their exaggeration, they are real men none can doubt,
men with human hearts and human passions whose
actions touch us to the quick, exciting us to indignation
at cruelty and vice, and arousing in us compassion in
suffering and misfortune. All of them are delineated
with profound understanding of personality and the
sympathy of genius, and the foibles, extravagancies,
and oddities of some of them are the subject of an infinitely humorous comedy of the sea. Smollett tells us
that he modelled his " Roderick Random " on the plan

of Le Sage, but with this difference, that whereas in " Gil Blas " we are made to laugh at vice or disgrace, we are, in the moving story of the sea surgeon's mate, excited to generous indignation "against the sordid and vicious disposition of the world." As Thackeray points out, Smollett did not create a character from a general observation of mankind ; he took an individual, and yet so placed him on the stage of his fancy that he stands as a real personality, though not to be identified with any single original. Smollett has himself explained his method in his preface to " Roderick Random." " Every intelligent reader," he says, " will, at first sight, perceive that I have not deviated from nature in the facts, which are all true in the main, although the circumstances are altered and disguised to avoid personal satire."

It is desirable that we should begin by realising Smollett's point of view. He was born in 1721, and was the son of Alexander Smollett, whose father was Sir James Smollett, of Bonhill, a Scottish laird of Lennox in Dumbartonshire. As the youngest son of a youngest son, Tobias enjoyed no great advantage from his birth, save perhaps a little influence that may have helped him later on. The youth of Roderick Random cannot be regarded as strictly autobiographical, because Smollett's relatives were his supporters and protectors, and not his persecutors, though possibly he may have conceived that he had some cause of resentment against them. He was brought up, as many young Scotchmen were in those days, in a hard school, and when apprenticed to an apothecary and surgeon in Glasgow, he attended courses at the university there, probably at the time " licking a lean thible." He cherished literary ambitions, but when he came to London his tragedy failed, and its failure gave him the great opportunity of his life. Sir Chaloner Ogle's fleet was fitting out for the punishment of the Spaniards in their American possessions, but it was to suffer a great misfortune before Cartagena, and through influence or favour Smollett procured a warrant as surgeon's mate in one of the big ships, of which the name is unknown, though she may have been the *Cumberland.*

In " Roderick Random " the episodes of Cartagena are described with some exaggeration. The unsuccessful expedition profoundly impressed Smollett, and he wrote also a serious account of it, to which reference has been made elsewhere in this book. For courage and capacity he had real admiration, but he had little patience with such incompetence as was displayed, or with men who quarrelled as Vernon and Wentworth did. Of Sir Chaloner Ogle he says nothing, but it may be remarked that a particularly unfriendly picture of that officer appears in the malicious and often libellous volume entitled " The Naval Atlantis " (1788), by " Nauticus Junior," who is said to have been Joseph Harris, secretary to Vice-Admiral Milbanke. It is a volume which defames the professional or personal character of some of our most eminent flag officers, including Howe, Rodney, and Alexander Hood.

The surgeon's mates in 1740 were a very inferior class of warrant officers, but might, nevertheless, be gentlemen of some education, as Roderick Random and the irascible, kindly Welshman Morgan were. They entered irregularly, the system being lax, by recommendation from the Navy Commissioners to Surgeons' Hall and by examination, but also by bribes to the Secretary at the Navy Office, or others. In the case of Roderick Random he was seized by the press, made a " loblolly " boy, or sick-berth attendant, on board the *Thunder*, 80, and then by favour received a warrant.

Pepys describes a seaman returned from the Dutch War with a plug of oakum stuck into the socket of his lost eye, but naval surgery had made much progress. A superannuated " sea chirurgeon " named John Moyle had written " Chirurgus Marinus ; or, The Sea Surgeon," in 1693, and John Atkins, a surgeon, who was also the author of a volume of travels, wrote before 1737 " The Navy Surgeon ; or, A Practical System of Surgery."

Therefore we may safely assume that there were some men of education and consideration amongst the mates of the sea surgeon. Indeed, scarcely had Roderick descended to the gloomy abode of his mess in the cockpit, a malodorous place about six feet square, enclosed with canvas and chests, when Morgan became inquisitive about his birth, and " no sooner understood that I was descended of a good family, than he discovered a particular goodwill to me on that account, deducing his own pedigree in a direct line from the famous Caractacus, king of the Britons, who was first the prisoner, and afterwards the friend of Claudius Cæsar."

It has sometimes been questioned whether Smollett, as a mere surgeon's mate, with a comparatively short experience, could ever have had the means of knowing intimately the persons and conditions he describes so vividly, and it might be thought that he himself throws some doubt upon the matter where he says, " the lieutenants I have no concern with ; and, as for the captain, he is too much of a gentleman to know a surgeon's mate, even by sight." But here, obviously, Smollett was speaking with bitter sarcasm of such captains as Oakum and Whiffle, and explaining the attitude of some of the lieutenants towards the inferior warrant officers. No one was better able than he to penetrate and describe the personalities of seamen. Their characters are strongly individualised in his stories, and they are plainly men of the sea and not of the shore, men who may have been round the world, but have never been in it. In the " Critical Review " of February, 1757, which Smollett edited, is a comment upon his own play, " The Reprisal, or the Tars of Old England," wherein we read concerning sailors, " that they have a dialect and manner peculiar to themselves, and that they are a species of men abstracted as it were from every other race of mortals." They are men of this species that we meet in " Roderick Random." The picture given of sea life in the first part of this present book will assure us of the veracity of Smollett's descriptions. It is impossible to doubt that he speaks of his own experience, where he tells of the meal in the cockpit, with a piece of old sail for table-cloth, the unclean metal platters and spoons, and the mess of boiled peas seasoned with a lump of salt butter, scooped from an old gallipot, and a relish of onions and pepper, which formed the meal on " banyan days," being Mondays, Wednesdays, and Fridays, when there was no allowance of meat. The salt and pungent salmagundi, the potent and spicy bumbo are both known to us. Nor can we question the accuracy of Smollett's account of the privations at Cartagena. If he tells us, too, of hardness, cruelty, and brutality in the *Thunder*, we have but to remember that James Anthony Gardner, who retired as a commander in 1830, speaking of the *Salisbury*, 50, in which he served as late as 1783, said that she should properly have been called the " Hell Afloat." Smollett knew the sea at first hand. He gives us what Defoe as a landsman, with all his power, never could have given us.

The first naval figure he places before us is his uncle, Lieutenant Tom Bowling, one of the finest characters in all fiction, who will live, we think, in story and song as long as the language is spoken—a man in whose speech is the salt savour of the sea, in whose personality is the breezy, open disposition of the seaman, all the seaman's courage, all his simplicity, his generous prodigality, his spirit of comradeship, his simple philosophy, his practical sense, and yet his ignorance of the world as the men knew it on shore.

The character is expressed by the name, which seems to speak of the elements of such a personality, a cheery brother of the sea, thoughtless in manner, but direct and downright in purpose, going straight to his object, and keeping a course as near to the wind as might be. It was not a new name in naval fiction, and we find one who might well have been a kinsman of Tom Bowling revealed in a fictitious letter supposed to have been written by one Paul Crape and published in the " London Magazine " of December, 1737. " When I was in Jamaica, as we were going off one evening, Jack Bowline, who was then a midshipman with us, starts up all at once, and falls foul of one of his fellows who resisted, and in the scuffle we were fairly overset; but very luckily for us another boat was putting off at the same time, and saved us. Who can guess the cause of Jack's wrath? They had left his keg of rum ashore! What do you think he replied when we expostulated with him? He replied with an oath, that 'he had rather we were all drowned than want punch.' "

In " Roderick Random " the indignation of the honest tar boiled within him to find that his nephew Roderick had been neglected by the boy's grandfather. He declared his confidence in the youth, and exclaimed, " Neither is he predicted to vice, as you affirm, but rather left like a wreck, d'ye see, at the mercy of the wind and weather, by your neglect, old gentleman. Come along, Rory, I perceive how the land lies, my boy—let's tack about i'faith—while I have a shilling you shan't want a tester." " B'we, old gentleman," he said to the hard grandfather, " you're bound for the other world, but I believe damnably ill-provided for the voyage." Bowling had been in the *Thunder* with Captain Oakum, and thought he had killed that tyrant in a duel, but took small blame to himself for so doing. " His majesty, (God bless him) will not suffer an honest tar to be wronged." His reputation lived behind him in the *Thunder*, and when Roderick Random was pressed and carried on board that ship, he asked Rattlin if he knew Lieutenant Bowling. " ' Know Lieutenant Bowling!' said he, ' odds my life! and that I do; and a good seaman he is as ever stepped upon forecastle, and a brave fellow as ever cracked biscuit—none of your Guinea pigs, nor your fresh water, wish-washy, fair-weather fowls. Many a taut gale of wind have honest Tom Bowling and I weathered together. Here's his health, with all my heart; wherever he is, a-loft, or a-low, the lieutenant needs not be ashamed to show himself.' "

Bowling is afterwards found in an extremity of distress at Boulogne, at a time when Roderick is himself the victim of misfortunes, suffered at the hands of his enemy Crampley, and his uncle consoles him with sea philosophy, " observing that life was a voyage in which we must expect to meet with all weathers; sometimes it was calm, sometimes rough; that a fair gale often succeeded a storm; that the wind did not always sit one way, and that despair signified nothing; but that resolution and skill were better than a stout vessel: for why? because they require no carpenter, and grow stronger the more labour they undergo." Never was the trustful, simple, generous character of the seaman better disclosed than in this chapter of "Roderick Random." Oakum is alive, instead of having gone to feed the fishes, and a petition to the Admiralty shall bring the pay that is due to Lieutenant Bowling, and all shall be well with him and his nephew. " Perhaps I may have interest enough to procure a warrant appointing you surgeon's mate of the ship to which I shall belong—for the beadle of the Admiralty is my good friend: and he and one of the under clerks are sworn brothers, and that under clerk has a good deal to say with one of the upper clerks, who is very well known to the under secretary, who, upon his recommendation, I hope, will recommend my affair to the first secretary; and he again will speak to one of the lords in my behalf; so that you see I do not want friends to assist me on occasion." Roderick could not help smiling at the strange ladder by means of which his seaman uncle hoped to climb to favour with their lordships, but if he had known as much as his uncle knew, he would not have despised the aid in those times even of beadles, clerks, and under secretaries, especially if he had had that small present ready which might possibly despatch the business the sooner. The lieutenant found a want in that matter. " Why, yes, I believe Daniel Whipcord, the ship-chandler in Wapping, would not refuse me such a small matter. I know I can have what credit I want for lodging, liquor, and clothes; but as to money, I won't be positive. Had honest Block been living I should not have been at a loss."

The lieutenant was a true seaman in his downright understanding of sea matters. " As for the fellow Crampley, thof I know him not, I am sure he is neither seaman nor officer by what you have told me, or else he could never be so much mistaken in his reckoning, as to run the ship on shore on the coast of Sussex before he believed himself in soundings ; neither, when that accident happened, would he have left the ship until she had been stove to pieces, especially when the tide was making ; wherefore, by this time, I do suppose, he has been tried by court-martial, and executed for his cowardice and misconduct." Honest courage is dominant in this fine sea character. Failing to get his own from the Admiralty, he goes as mate in a trader, and when a big stranger bears down, he makes a stirring appeal to his men, concluding, " So now you that are lazy, lubberly, cowardly dogs, get away and skulk in the hold and bread-room ; and you that are jolly-boys, stand by me, and let us give one broadside for the honour of Old England."

Before we leave Tom Bowling it is interesting to note that a character so named appeared in the nautical sketch called " A Trip to Portsmouth," already mentioned as being produced at the Haymarket in August, 1773. This later Bowling was played very happily, said the " Town and Country Magazine," by Mr. Charles Bannister, " hitting off the genuine humour of a tar in the character of a boatswain."

But to return to " Roderick Random." Flip and Mizen, of Shadwell's play, " The Fair Quaker of Deal," anticipated the captains of the *Thunder*. Probably no captain was ever quite so brutal as Oakum in his inhuman treatment of the sick, nor any surgeon ever quite so mean and malicious a sycophant as Mackshane, who incited him to his cruelty. The report ran on board the *Thunder* that Oakum, to use Rattlin's description, was " lord, or baron knight's brother, whereby (d'ye see me,) he carries a straight arm, and keeps aloof from his officers, thof mayhap they may be as good men in the

T

main as he." Whatever may have been Oakum's origin, he was in some ways a ruffian of the worst type of his age, but there was the saving virtue in him that he could despise cowardice, as he stood leaning wounded against the mizen-mast of his ship. Brutality such as Oakum's was rare in the Navy, but there was a good deal of harshness and cruelty at the time.

A writer in the " Connoisseur " of 4th September, 1755, some years after " Roderick Random " was published, remarked that the conversation of sea officers was turbulent and boisterous. " This roughness, which clings to the seaman's behaviour like tar to his trowsers, makes him unfit for all civil and polite society. That our ordinary seamen, who are, many of them, draughted from the very lowest of the populace, should be thus uncivilised is no wonder ; but surely there ought to be as much difference in the behaviour of the commander and his crew as there is in their situation, and it is beneath the dignity of the British flag to have an admiral behave as rudely as a swabber, or a commander be as foul-mouthed as a boatswain." But the writer who makes this remark is fain to admit that, after all, there were many officers who deserved to bear the character of gentlemen and scholars.

Whiffle, Captain Oakum's successor in the *Thunder*, was neither a brute nor a scholar, and would have been described by Commodore Flip as a " macaroni captain." He was a scented dandy, having a white hat, with a red feather, on his head, and his flowing ringlets tied behind, and he wore a pink silk coat, lined with white, a white satin waistcoat, a fine cambric shirt, edged with Mechlin lace, fastened with a garnet brooch, crimson velvet breeches, and blue Meroquin shoes studded with diamond buckles, a sword with gold-inlaid hilt and tassel, and an amber-headed cane hung at his wrist. Morgan, upon whom he had put a dire affront, said of him, " I will proclaim it before the world that he is disguised, and transfigured, and transmogrified with affectation and whimseys ; and that he is more like a papoon than one of the human race." Whiffle is a foil to Oakum, and a manifest caricature, though no doubt Smollett was casting satire upon the class of dandies who had made their way incongruously into the fleet, and who had already been caricatured by Shadwell.

Of the rest of the admirable gallery of personalities found on board the *Thunder*, none holds so large a place as the genial, proud, and humorous Welshman, and it is worthy of note, as illustrating a naval custom, that when he and Roderick parted company, on the latter going to the *Lizard*, they exchanged sleeve buttons in remembrance of one another. Smollett has little to tell us directly in "Roderick Random" of the tars who lived on the lower deck, but Jack Rattlin is there as the best and finest type, the first friend Roderick found when he was pressed and carried out to the ship. In the fury of the bombardment at Cartagena, Rattlin had his hand shattered with a grape-shot. "I lamented with unfeigned sorrow his misfortune, which he bore with heroic courage, observing that every shot had its commission : ' it was well it did not take him in the head ! or if it had, what then ? he should have died bravely, fighting for his king and country. Death was a debt which every man owed and must pay ; and that now was as well as another time.' I was much pleased and edified with the maxims of this sea-philosopher, who endured the amputation of his left hand without shrinking." Another class of seamen is exhibited to us in the story, where the incompetent Crampley runs the *Lizard* aground, and the sloop is in peril of breaking up. The mast was cut away to lighten the vessel, but without success, and " the sailors, seeing things in a desperate situation, according to custom in ill-disciplined ships, broke up the chests belonging to the officers, dressed themselves in their clothes, drank their liquors without ceremony, and drunkenness, tumult, and confusion ensued."

In " The Adventures of Peregrine Pickle," which appeared in 1751, there is presented what is more clearly a grotesque exaggeration of the character of the sea officer

than we find in "Roderick Random." Commodore
Hawser Trunnion is more salt than the sea in his lingo,
but he is an honest, generous man, and a seaman all
through. The host of the inn describes him well. "He
has a power of money, and spends it like a prince—that
is, in his own way—for to be sure he is a little humour-
some, as the saying is, and swears woundily; though I'll
be sworn he means no more harm than a sucking babe.
Lord help us! it will do your honour's heart good to
hear him tell a story, as how he lay alongside the French,
yard-arm and yard-arm, board and board, and of heaving
grapplings, and stink-pots, and grapes, and round and
double-headed partridges, crows, and carters." There is
Trunnion's friend and critic, Hatchway, the lieutenant,
who had lost a leg on board the Commodore's ship, and
is now his companion—a brave man, and a great joker,
a philosopher, also, who firmly believes that everything
which happens is for the best, and a man who, like
Corporal Trim, "loves to advise, or rather to hear himself talk." And there is the faithful Pipes, Trunnion's
old boatswain's mate, who now keeps his servants in
order, a man of few words, "but an excellent hand at a
song, concerning the boatswain's whistle, hustle-cap and
chuck-farthing." "The fellow has sailed with me in
many a hard gale, and I'll warrant him as stout a seaman as ever set face to the weather." Trunnion himself
is one of those sea officers who came in through the
hawse-hole, as his name implies. How true, if exaggerated, is his outburst of indignant professional pride,
when he hears that Will Bower, "a fellow of yesterday,
who scarce knows a mast from a mangle," is made a
peer, while Hawser Trunnion, who commanded a ship
before Bower could keep a reckoning, is laid aside and
forgotten. "If so be as this be the case, there is a rotten
plank in our constitution, which ought to be hove down,
and repaired, d—— my eyes! For my own part, d'ye
see, I was none of your Guinea pigs; I did not rise in
the service by parliamenteering interest, or a handsome
wife. I was not hoisted over the bellies of better men,

nor strutted athwart the quarter-deck in a laced doublet, and thingumbobs at the wrists. D—— my limbs! I have been a hard-working man, and served all offices on board from cook's shifter to the command of a vessel."

Smollett does not take us afloat in this story. Some of the scenes are enacted in the Commodore's strange dwelling, where " he does not live like any other Christian land-man, but keeps garrison in his house, as if he were in the midst of his enemies, and makes his servants turn out in the night, watch and watch, as he calls it, all the year round." Nor was there ever anything but a hammock to sleep in, until the Commodore took to himself a wife. As Tristram Shandy says : " De Gustibus non est disputandum—there is no disputing about hobby-horses." The garrison of Commodore Trunnion was like the famous ravelins, bastions, curtains, and horn-works of Namur, to be formed by Uncle Toby and Corporal Trim on the bowling-green near Shandy Hall, but in Trunnion's hobby-horse Smollett anticipated Sterne.

The inimitable humour of the Commodore's progress towards the church on the day appointed for his wedding —he and his cavalcade, in line ahead, making very short trips in tacking in the country lane, keeping, if they could, within six points of the wind, and firing a pistol whenever they stood over on the other tack—presents one of the most amusing pictures in all fiction. We see his attendants rigged with the white shirts and black caps formerly belonging to his barge's crew. It is de lightful human comedy, full of rollicking fun.

Then, as a contrast, there is the picture of the old sea-man's end, which perhaps few people can read unmoved. His nephew, whose benefactor he has been, stands at the foot of his bed. " Swab the spray from your bow-sprit, my good lad, and coil up your spirits. You must not let the toplifts of your heart give way, because you see me ready to go down at these years : many a better man has foundered before he has made half my way : thof I trust by the mercy of God, I shall be sure in port in a very few glasses, and fast moored in a most blessed riding." Then he goes on. "Here has been a doctor that wanted to stow me chock-full of physic; but when a man's hour is come, what signifies his taking his departure with a 'pothecary's shop in his hold? Those fellows come alongside of dying men like the messengers of the Admiralty with sailing orders; but I told him as how I could slip my cable without his direction or assistance, and so he hauled off in dudgeon." After this the Commodore commends his dependents to those who are his beneficiaries, and gives orders for his burial. "I would also be buried in the red jacket I had on when I boarded and took the *Renummy*. Let my pistols, cutlass, and pocket-compass be laid in the coffin along with me. Let me be carried to the grave by my own men, rigged in the black caps and white shirts which my barge's crew were wont to wear." Nor would he have the inscription upon his tombstone in Greek, Latin, or French, but in plain English, "that when the angel comes to pipe all hands at the great day, he may know that I am a British man, and speak to me in my mother tongue." And we must not omit to quote the tribute of the faithful Pipes to his dead master's virtues. "Well fare thy soul! old Hawser Trunnion; man and boy I have known thee these five-and-thirty years, and sure a truer heart never broke biscuit. Many a hard gale hast thou weathered; but now thy spells are all over, and thy hull fairly laid up. A better commander I'd never desire to serve; and who knows but I may help to set up thy standing rigging in another world?"

It has been remarked above that in "Roderick Random" Smollett tells us little concerning the seamen who actually worked the ship, but in the "British Magazine" for March, 1763, which Smollett edited, is a clever sketch of a tar's visit to London which seems to bear the unmistakable mark of his hand. "Bob Binnacle's Epistle to the Landsmen who cleared Decks on board the Playhouse, Covent Garden," is as fresh in the salt spray of its language as is the discourse of Commodore Trunnion,

and the honest tar uses some of the very phrases that
are put into the mouth of Tom Bowling. Bob's communication, which reveals him in his character as a champion
of beauty in distress, is in the nature of an apology for
his own conduct at the opera-house, and he says, " if ever
I would board any of my own countrymen, in the way
of damage designedly, keel haul me."   He had shipped
on board the Portsmouth machine, to make a trip to' the
metropolis, and was sea-sick because they clapped him
under hatches. But he got up on the poop, where he
was in right trim until one wheel came athwart a stone,
and he would have been canted overboard, if he had
not caught hold of the weather-braces. When he arrived
in London, he shaped his course to the playhouse, in
order that he might " see the English hoppera." He paid
three shillings for a seat, and was piloted into the hold.
" But avast there, thought I, I a'n't going to be clapp'd
to windward in that manner neither."   Accordingly he
paid for a five-shilling seat, in one of the quarter galleries,
where he sat " as snug as a maggot in the bread-room."
But scarcely was the fore-sheet clewed up when trouble
occurred. There was noise—" roaring like so many
watermen at a plying-place "—and then " there was a
chace shot Chany orange fired," but whether from the
round-tops or the lower deckers he could not tell. It
" wounded the handsome young gentlewoman in the
starboard eye," and Bob wanted to know who fired the
shot. " I only wish I was alongside of him, that's all."
The simple tar knew it was no business of his, but he
could not bear to see anybody used ill. " No, when I do
may I be cut into four-pound pieces, and put into the
devil's pickling tub. So I got down and stept upon deck,
and said I would fight the best man among 'em." Bob
says he may have loved the fun of fighting, but all in a
friendly way. A tremendous disturbance ensued, and
apparently a free fight in which much damage was done.
His account of what occurred is obscure, but he speaks
of the staving out of dead-lights, scuttling between decks,
heaving the benches overboard, and making a wreck of

the state-rooms. The French ambassador was present, for which he was sorry. " It is a pity he saw us fight among ourselves. Pray tell a body," he says helplessly, " what was all this about ? " " I shan't say who's right or who's wrong no more, not I. I can say my compass, and, as to anything else—why I'll keep a stopper upon my tongue, while the wind's in this quarter. But I wish you were all friends—quarrelling's a bad trade, if you can't get prize-money out of it. Forget and forgive, I say—peace and good neighbourhood—and let us fight that have served our times to it."

Smollett had imitators and followers, who in sketches, stories, and comments described the seaman in the latter half of the eighteenth century, and his striking pictures of sailors influenced the stage. Captain Edward Thompson, himself a naval officer, whose " Sailor's Letters " and plays have been already quoted, was a voluminous author. He published certain poetical effusions, which would not bear reprinting in these more refined days —" The Demirep," 1756 ; " The Meretriciad," 1765 ; " The Court of Cupid," 1770 ; and " Bell Montè," 1784. He is presumed, though without direct evidence, to have been the author of a novel entitled " Edward and Maria," which appeared in the " London Magazine " in 1774-5. It presents many resemblances to " Roderick Random," by which it may have been inspired, and throws additional light upon the life of warships and the character of men at that time.

Maria, the heroine, was a country wench of Kent, " the darling of every swain, and the admiration of the gentry round." The hero became infatuated with her, and his father thereupon decided to send him to sea. At this point the author contests the received and established maxim that, when a youth is so obstreperous and abandoned as to be fit for no situation in civil society, the Navy or the gallows must have him. On the contrary, " a moral good character, a genius, and an education is more necessary to form a complete naval officer than any other profession whatever." Edward embarked in a

ship commanded by Captain Cormorant, but lived in the
hope of seeing the fair one again. He met in the ship
some "riff-raff scum," "the bra' lads of Edinburgh."
Like Roderick Random, he found a friend who conducted him to the dark regions of his mess on the orlop
deck, where they ate together a piece of roast mutton,
which lay upon the lid of a chest, without any platter,
and with a candle stuck alongside. His hammock was
slung near the well—a sad berth, for every time the ship
rolled the bilge stank enough to poison him. His messmates were John Tibb, a petulant Scot of many virtues,
and an able seaman. The father of the mess was Benjamin Buntline, "a veteran tar, very religious, very
upright, but very nasty." His third comrade was a
youth of eighteen, new to the sea, but blest with amazing
spirits. Tom Oakham had also been wounded in love,
but was cheery all the same. "He ate with everybody
that had a pudding to dinner, thrashed every fellow that
was impertinent to him, and was in every mess that had
a can of flip to give." Thus did Tom bid defiance to the
elements, and when he found the love-lorn Edward pen-
sive he would slap him on the back, merrily singing:—

> "For women are changeable things,
> And seldom a moment the same."

The ship was employed in the Channel, and between
Dover and Calais, when invasion was threatened, in
order to abate the fears of the citizens of London, "for
there was not an old Cheapside draper but what believed
these tremendous boats could sail at any time or season
down his very chimney into his very frying pan." A
humorous description is given of some of the officers,
among whom Edward became popular, as everywhere in
the ship, because he could sing. He used to delight his
comrades with "To all you Ladies now at Land," the
Earl of Dorset's famous sea song, written in 1665, and
with "Early in the morn, the Ides of May," and of the
latter he remarks that the poetry is excellent and the
description of the fight minute, natural, and picturesque.

With these two songs he made his way to every mess in the ship "where a pandoodle, a bowl of burgoo, or a dish of scratch-platter was to be given." There is an amusing account of the inhabitants of his mess and of the realm in which they lived. But the sailor, we are told—and it was the same verse with which Tom Bowling cheered his nephew—despised trouble, singing "A light heart and a thin pair of breeches goes thro' the world, brave boys." The sailor's return to port is described, where he had the reward for his hardships, and thought the dowdies goddesses, and "the viands and vegetables of earth nectar and ambrosia."

The ship went round to Portsmouth, where her company were very sick, owing to infected men having been impressed, and Edward also fell ill, was carried ashore, had hard experiences, was rescued from misfortune by a widow, and finally arrived in London, in order to procure a nostrum which should cure him, from one Doctor Ward of Hampstead, a practitioner not recognised by the faculty—from which we are led to infer that the author anticipated some methods of advertisement not unknown in later times. "I took his red pills every night, and soon found an amazing change in my constitution." He rejoined his ship as she was preparing for sea, was enthusiastically welcomed, and describes episodes that preceded her departure. Seamen were giving their pay to their sweethearts, "for the sailor always winds up his argument with this easy philosophy after he has spent his cash, 'Well, never mind, Moll—here's to sea for more,'" and spirits were being smuggled on board in bladders hidden in the bodies of geese. Edward was sent with a message to Boscawen's flagship, and talked to that famous admiral rather freely, making whimsical sallies at him, thinking him all the time a junior officer. Captain Cormorant was an old man of small education, but generous and passionate. Bobadil Bounce, the captain of marines, was boisterous and satirical, and a plague to the chaplain and his comrades, and therefore he messed alone. The lieutenants were a motley crew—one a brave old Scotsman, another a swab who had beaten out the teeth of his black servant with a boot-jack, another " an empty, drunken fungus, all puff-paste, ignorance and impertinence," and another an agreeable coxcomb. Faddle was an officer who dressed his hair, wore clean linen, played the flute and strummed on the guitar. The parson was a tame, ignorant, naval man, the surgeon was wholly ignorant of his business, and the lieutenant of marines was a scholar and a " veteran soldier." Such are the ingredients of a diverting narrative, and Edward, after all his adventures, returns home and marries the heroine.

There was a great vogue at the time for stories and plays illustrating the life of the sea. Smollett, in the rollicking, humorous, and somewhat cynical pages of " Roderick Random," had set the fashion. With what many consider his most attractive novel, " Humphrey Clinker," his literary career closed with his life in 1771. Through all the pages of the periodical literature of the time we seem to find the echo of his manner whenever things of the sea are described. His characters were the great originals. Not until the time of Marryat had he any worthy successor.

CHAPTER XIV

SOME EIGHTEENTH-CENTURY SEA STORIES

A GREAT period in the history of English fiction
may be said to have ended with Smollett and
Fielding. They had created the school of fierce realism,
developed from the incisive manner of Defoe, and of
keen humour in sustained narrative, one of them in a
description of the life of the sea, just as Richardson had
created the novel of sentiment. None of the books that
became famous subsequently touch the subject of this
volume. " Rasselas," " The Vicar of Wakefield," and
" Tristram Shandy," philosophical, pathetic, and mordant in humour, in their several moods, yield nothing to
this inquiry. Among the imitators of Smollett, including
the author of " Edward and Maria," there were none
who rivalled his genius. Occasionally, in those moral
narratives of the time, in which Virtue, battered and be-
smirched through many a chapter of unedifying experiences, eagerly described, emerges in the last chapter
triumphant over Vice for the salving of conscience, there
is some reflection of sea life or sea character. Such a
book is " The Life and Adventures of Joe Thompson,"
by Edward Kimber, which appeared in 1750, and went
through several editions up to 1783, besides being translated into French. Thompson, the son of a Yorkshire
clergyman, is a youth whose dissolute life in London
fills a volume. He has a friend who enters the Navy
with a King's letter, and of whom we hear as a midshipman and lieutenant. The second volume takes the hero
afloat on a voyage in an East Indiaman, and episodes

occur which give the opportunity of speaking in praise of
seamen. Describing a storm, Thompson says that, if he
ever had advantageous notions of British seamen, he
now more than ever found them just, " and their dili-
gence and bravery, on such occasions, surely dignifies
them before those of any country I ever knew." Again,
when he relates how the crew of a ship destroyed by fire
are rescued, he remarks that he never " received more
pleasure than in seeing how eager the generous seaman
is in relieving his fellow in distress ; every man strove
who should be foremost in giving them or procuring them
refreshment." On the other hand, the captain of the
same Indiaman is pictured as " a mere brute," who
wanted common humanity—a compeer, therefore, of
Smollett's Oakum.

The violent torrent of unrestrained political and personal satire that filled the press and pamphlet and
narrative literature also at times touches the Navy.
Charles Johnstone, the author of certain novels de-
servedly forgotten, attained notoriety by the publication
in 1760 of his " Chrysal, or the Adventures of a Guinea."
Being a merciless political satire and attack upon the
character of public men, it became an instant popular
success, and was augmented by two additional volumes
in 1765. " Chrysal " is a sprite used by Johnstone as
Le Sage uses Asmodeus, as the means of prying into
the sins and weaknesses of society, and of giving a satirical
picture of various classes of people, including seamen.
The picture is, at least in one case, slanderous, but there
is the redeeming feature that Johnstone's attacks are
upon those in high places, that he gives praise to real
merit, and that his sympathies are with the suffering
and oppressed. For a key to his characters we are indebted to a scarce volume published in 1814, William
Davis's " Olio of Bibliographical and Literary Anecdotes." Johnstone knew something of the disappointments of naval life in those times, when no influence
was found to strengthen the claims of merit. In the
hands of one of his masters, " Chrysal " hears the story

of a lieutenant, who, like Tom Bowling, is a man of middle age. He is the son of a poor military officer, who had lived nursing his remaining leg and supported a large family on slender means in the country. A neighbouring clergyman had urged him to put his son into the Navy, where he thought he could exercise some influence. " That is the service in which merit is never disregarded," he had assured the boy's father. The clergyman educated the boy, and " if ever a man of merit in the sea service," would he often say, " fails of rising, it is for the want of having a good education to found his hopes upon." " A mere seaman may work a ship, but an admiral should be a scholar."

At the age of sixteen the boy had gone to sea, provided with a chest of books and mathematical instruments and a good suit of clothes, recommended to an admiral, who is recognised as Mathews of the inglorious action off Toulon—a choleric old man of the John Bull type. At first Mathews did not remember the country parson's name, but on circumstances being recalled, exclaimed, " Very true, I remember him now ; he made the best bowl of punch of any man in the Navy." This is all the notice the great man took of the youth, except that, on the captain observing he would make a good figure on the quarter-deck, he was immediately rated a midshipman. It had been noticed that he was well clothed. Disappointment followed, but the midshipman resolved to devote himself to the work of his profession, and, not liking the conversation of his messmates, he retired to his books, whereby he was brought into general ridicule, and was nicknamed the " Parson " and avoided. He remained a midshipman for fifteen years, but being sent on shore with a press-gang, he saw it announced that those qualified for lieutenants were to attend for examination, which he did with success, and having no influence was a lieutenant still after serving twenty-five years in that rank.

Besides Mathews, " Chrysal " met another admiral, identified as Sir George Pocock, in the action at Havana in 1762. Johnstone had heard of the heartburning over the division of the enormous prize-money, and the huge sums shared by the admiral and the military commander, the Earl of Albemarle, who had £122,607 10s. 6d. each out of a total of about £736,000. Pocock was both an active and a capable officer, but Johnstone gives a malicious picture of him. When the admiral is " Chrysal's " master we find him, like Captain Whiffle in " Roderick Random," " lolling in a listless manner on a sofa in his state-room, where every art was exerted to counteract nature, and elude the midday heat in one of the fiercest climates of the torrid zone. A gown of thinnest silk hung loosely over his large limbs, the radiance of the sun was softened by shades of linen drawn before the open windows, and kept constantly wet, to cool the air as it entered through them, and every disagreeable savour was drowned in the most delicate perfumes." The awkwardness with which the admiral bore this state showed that it was not natural to him, and therefore " Chrysal " looked back to his past life to see what illustrious actions had brought him to such an exalted state, " but to my surprise discovered no more than a phlegmatic indolence and servility of soul which induced his superiors to entrust power to his hand without apprehension of its raising him to a consequence that might clash with their designs on any future occasion."

The officer next in command enters, being Commodore the Hon. Augustus Keppel, to say land has been sighted from the mast-head, being the place they are to attack. Keppel, in the story, is a man of very different character from Pocock, and the moment he returns to his own ship, the *Valiant*, he signals to all the captains to come on board and the General with them. Meantime the men are called aft, and he addresses them : " Come, my lads, the day is ours. The admiral has given us leave to take yonder town, with all the treasure in it, so that we have nothing to do now but to make our fortunes as fast as we can, for the place can never hold out against us. The purser will give every brave fellow a can of

punch to drink prosperity to Old England, and then
we'll go about our business with spirit. We shall all be
as rich as Jews. The place is paved with gold, which
the lubberly Dons have gathered for us. Old England
for ever is the word, and the day is ours." Soon the
captains are on board with the military commander, and
he greets them in the great cabin. " ' Good news, gentlemen,' said my master in an ecstasy, shaking every one
of them by the hand as they entered, ' I bring you good
news ; yonder is the object of our hopes, the place that
is to make our fortunes, and to crown us with glory, if
it is not our own faults, for the admiral has given us
general orders to proceed in the best manner we can,
and without losing time or opportunity in waiting to
consult him on every occasion.' "

All this is good, but there is a malicious touch of
satire, which does not surprise us in this author, in his
picture of daring gallantry, fighting for England, in the
eager pursuit of Spanish doubloons. But Johnstone has
also left us the picture of a generous seaman from the
lower deck. With the object of denouncing the corrupt
administration of the law, he introduces this prodigal,
kindly sailor into a court of justice in his true character
of a champion of the distressed. A poor woman has been
hauled up on a charge of shop-lifting, and the justice is
enraged both at the heinousness of her crime and at
being kept from his supper of chicken and asparagus,
which is cooling on the table. The poor creature, almost
dead with wretchedness, protests that her husband is a
sailor who had been pressed on board a man-of-war six
years before, and after being all the time in the West
Indies, when his ship is ordered home to be paid off at
Portsmouth, he is turned over to another ship, without
getting a shilling of his six years' wages or prize-money,
and is sent to America. His wife has spent every penny
in the world to come from Ireland with her children to
meet him. " Ay, I thought so ! I thought you were one
of those Irish thieves that come to rob us and cut our
throats ! " The poor creature is ordered to Newgate,

with the remark from the justice that it is better for her brats to die of hunger now than to be hanged like their mother later on. But the honest tar, who has paid his sixpence to see the fun, cannot stand such barbarity, and making up to the clerk, he pays him two guineas to let the woman free. " Cheer away, sister, sister," says he. " Cheer away, we'll bring up all this leeway next trip. D—n my eyes and limbs if I'll see a brother seaman's family at short allowance while I have a shilling. Come, heave ahead ; I'll rig and victual you and your children against your husband comes home. I'll swing my hammock in the next berth, and you shall cook the kettle while I stay ashore." Saying which the honest seaman leads her off in triumph.

Prodigal, generous, and unselfish persons like this honest tar of Johnstone's, were dear to the Englishmen who knew them. Some, acquainted with their hard lives, their poor reward, and the way in which ashore they were cheated out of their rights, endeavoured to protect them, sometimes by practical advice, and sometimes by religious exhortation. There is a volume entitled " The Way to be Wise and Wealthy, Recommended to All," which a merchant published in the middle of the century, and of which a second edition appeared in 1755. The advice is applied to various conditions of life, and a chapter is addressed to the seaman. It is remarked that sailors will come under a twofold consideration, because they not only sail, but on occasion fight for their country. They are described as marine defenders as well as navigators, and it is said of them that they deserve a double portion of respect and honour, being gentlemen of such complicated merit in respect of their laborious, skilful, and hazardous profession, so that they are " their country's glory and renown." " And if anything that shall be here offer'd to them shall persuade them to be as much their own friends as they are their country's, it will complete their character, by adding great wisdom and prudence to their other heroic good qualities, which will attract affection as well as admira-

U

tion." The exhortation concludes as follows: " Were it to be hoped that the generality of British mariners could be made to add to their skill and courage, wisdom and wealth by becoming industrious in the improvement of their time and money so as to make the most of it, according to the opportunity they have for so doing, and frugal in the sparing and saving what they get, and not part with it as they have been wont, much in vanity and folly, and not a little in vice and immorality, Great Britain might then boast of such a set of sailors, not to be equall'd by any nation upon earth."

A veritable curiosity of nautical literature which appeared in the year 1770 seems to have originated in part in the same care for the seaman's life and salvation. Certainly it may be considered a remarkable thing that some ten years after the victories of Boscawen and Hawke, and in the year before Smollett published his last work, " The Expedition of Humphrey Clinker," the voyage of a ship and the character of her company should have been used as an allegory to explain, in a vague fashion, a particular theory of Christianity. In " A Voyage through Hell, by the Invincible Man-of-War, Capt. Single-eye, Commander ; dedicated to your Grand Father," sold by Richardson and Urquhart at the Royal Exchange, the writer, " Toby Meanwell," sets forth, like Milton, to " vindicate the ways of God to man," as appears by his title-page. His volume may have some distant kinship, perhaps, to the " Shyp of Folys," printed by Pynson in 1509, but it has a nearer relationship to " The Pilgrim's Progress." The voyage is by sea instead of by land, and is dedicated, with what might be regarded as profanity, to " the God of Wisdom," Who is besought to patronise the treatise. There is some evidence of humour in Toby Meanwell, but his book itself is serious enough. He says, in his preface, that some readers may find his pages amusing. " Methinks I see one class of them merry upon the occasion, at the humour of the thing ; another class saying, it is a queer, confused messmedly of things, I do not know what to make

of it ; another sort, screwing up their faces and eyes
into a proper form, in order to condemn it, as a very
profligate, ignorant performance ; another sort, though
with the same phiz, he never could be a gracious good
man, that is but too plain, by the undue liberties he has
taken ; another sort, oh ! I see plain enough what he is,
he is an old apostate, and a rank deist." There is more
of the same sort, which need not be quoted in this place.
The names of the ship's officers are given. The lieutenants are Pureviews, Strong, Hopewell, and Standfast ;
and the midshipmen, Timourous, Purblind, Squint, and
Faint ; while the parson is the Rev. Mr. Truth-and-
Daylight. The master is named Neverdie, and his mates
are Cheerful, Neverdoubt, Allsafe, and Lookforward.
The gunner is Conquerall, and his mates are Hit-the-
Mark, Nevermiss, Chargewell, and Thoughtful. The
ship's cook is Messmedley, and his mate Alldirt !

The captain and officers go aboard the ship at a place
named Blackmouth Port, on 9th May, 1767, and the
captain addresses them all, not upon the working of the
ship, but upon matters of conduct and religion, promising
them the enjoyment of a land of milk and honey, with all
good and acceptable things, if they will sail with him.
They are eager to do so, and the boatswain's mate calls
out, " Come, my lads, jump about, bend the sails ;
hallow, between decks there ; you, fore-castle men, jump
up here, the captain says we sail to-morrow ; captain of
the main-top, how are you aloft ? All hands here ; we
have no time to lose." They set sail, and articles of
faith are fixed to the mainmast, while a part of the company tack up another sort of creed near the gunroom
door. There are addresses and sermons, conversations
amongst the men, such as we may be sure never were
heard in any ship that ever sailed the seas, with some
descriptions. The following may illustrate the style of
the latter. " So Charlie parted with him for a time, and
Dick Holyprattle run about preaching to his old companions hell and damnation if they continued as they
were. Nick Longprayer was so exasperated at this

sudden change in him, that he sent a whole can of grog in his face. Dick got off as fast as he could, with this piece of unexpected treatment, unexpected it was sure enough ; for Dick thought that he could convert the whole tote of them ; however it happened otherwise, and Dick had a dry shirt, stockings, &c., to seek after ; so when he was got repaired again, he thought he would not leave 'em so, and straight begins preaching to them again."

The *Invincible* at length arrives at the Gate of Hell and passes through, being hailed by Prince Apollyon, who demands seizure both of ship and cargo with all hands on board. The captain defends himself and the ship's company, but ninety-three of them, who appear to have clung to earthly things, in the shape of medicines, ornaments, etc., are carried into the bottomless pit, while the *Invincible* sails away, and the remainder of her company sight the Delectable Mountain on 21st June, 1770, and are enrapt into the beatific vision.

We must now pass over an interval of time in order to reach the next century and the novelists who dealt with the period of the great war, many of them as men who had fought in it, and were strong, vigorous, and humorous writers. Moreover, an age which delighted in " The Mysteries of Udolpho " and " The Castle of Otranto," which drew satisfaction from the " Evelina " of Miss Burney, could hardly give us a real seaman in the pages of its novelists. But the period of the great war, if it produced no remarkable work of sustained naval fiction, provided an abundance of material for much fiction that followed. In periodical literature many nautical sketches, descriptions, and humorous sallies are to be found, as in the " Naval Magazine," the " Naval Chronicle," and the " Britannic Magazine." Thus in the volume of the first named of these for the year 1800 are satirical accounts of the duties of officers. The captain is told that if he takes a French prize it is no more than reasonable that he should have some claret for his own table. " You may therefore venture to take a few pipes, but as this would be an abuse if carried to too great a length, do not permit any to be brought on board for the inferior officers or seamen." A satirical instruction for the lieutenant is that, when he has a watch from eight till twelve at night, as soon as he is sure the captain is in bed, he is to go below, and if he does not find anybody up, he is to shake the cot of one of the officers and oblige him to turn out, and take a glass of grog with him. They are to play a game of backgammon, and probably the noise of the tables will keep alert and ready to rise the lieutenant who is to relieve his comrade upon watch. The midshipman is to make it an invariable rule always to be friendly with the purser while the latter continues sociable, that is, as long as he visits the midshipmen's berth every Saturday night and they partake of a bottle of his liquor ; but when he discontinues this compliment, he is to be branded with appellations of "Nipcheese," "Skinflint," and other polite phrases, "which these gentlemen of the lower regions are said commonly to retain at their fingers' ends." By following this and other advice the inhabitant of the midshipmen's berth is told that he will become " a complete Cockpitarian."

In a series of papers entitled " The Jester " in the " Britannic Magazine " many smart allusions occur, as in the volume for 1804, where it is observed that a sailor who got on horseback at Mile-end, not being accustomed to equestrian feats, seized the horse by the neck, to the great diversion of the jockeys who beheld him. " But a wag remarked that nothing could be more natural for a *tar* than to ride on the *mane*." Then we are told that there is no reason for wonder " at the *gallantry* of our seamen whenever an enemy's ship comes in their way, since they know her almost always to be the *weaker vessel*." Again, the French journals are bidden to remember that, though they discourse about the costumes of various officers, " their marine officers receive their best *lacing* and *trimming* from the English, and very frequently a complete *dressing*." Such witty observations are amusing enough, but they are not much to our

purpose, and we pass on to a novelist who rose to fame
in her day.

It cannot but be a subject of great regret that Jane
Austen, who lived in circumstances which must have
given her the means of obtaining an insight into the life
of the Navy, and who occupies a considerable place in
the history of English fiction, should have left us no
living, breathing, vital picture of the seamen of her time,
which was that which preceded and followed Trafalgar.
She could not have been a naval novelist in the sense
of Smollett or Marryat, but some personalities of convincing force might have been found in her pages. Two
of her brothers who entered the Navy were employed in
the great war. Francis was in command of the *Peterel*
sloop in the Mediterranean in 1800, where he captured
the brig *Ligurienne*, being thereafter raised to post rank,
and he lived to hold many important commands, and
died a G.C.B. and admiral of the fleet in 1855. Charles
had also an active career, and died from fever when
commanding as rear-admiral on the East Indies station
during the second Burmese war in 1852. Jane Austen
died long before, in 1817, but though thus brought into
relations with naval society she was not constituted by
temperament to reproduce it in fiction. She was devoid
of poetry and lofty imagination, and rarely displayed
deep sentiment, her great powers of observation and
quiet satirical humour being devoted, in deliberate narrative, to a careful portrayal, lacking spontaneity, of the
aspects of country society. The influence of her naval
brothers is found chiefly in " Mansfield Park " and " Persuasion," both of them written in the years shortly before
her death.

She had a very great appreciation of the naval profession, which is described in " Persuasion " as, " if
possible, more distinguished for its domestic virtues than
for its national importance," though there is nothing in
her pages of its breezy humour, its hearty sympathy, or
its practical spirit of comradeship. Once she tells of a seaman's leave-taking and returning, but the language is

cold and artificial. Captain Harville, in " Persuasion," is speaking to Anne Elliot. " If I could but make you comprehend what a man suffers when he takes a last look at his wife and children, and watches the boat he has sent them off in, as long as it is in sight, and then turns away and says, ' God knows whether we ever meet again.' And then if I could convey to you the glow of his soul when he does see them again ; when coming back after a twelvemonth's absence, perhaps, he calculates how soon it be possible to get them there, pretending to deceive himself and saying, ' They cannot be here till such a day,' but all the while hoping for them twelve hours sooner, and seeing them arrive at last, as if heaven had given them wings, by many hours sooner still." In the same story some rather foolish remarks are made to Captain Wentworth concerning his appointment to the *Asp* sloop, which was scarcely fit for sea. " ' Phoo ! phoo ! ' cries Admiral Croft. ' What stuff these young fellows talk ! Never was there a better sloop than the *Asp* in her day. For an old built sloop you would not see her equal. Lucky fellow to get her ! He knows there must have been twenty better men than himself applying for her at the same time. Lucky fellow to get anything so soon, with no more interest than his.' " All this Captain Wentworth admits, and proceeds to explain how great had been his luck in her. " She did all I wanted. I knew she would. I knew we should either go to the bottom together, or that she would be the making of me."

The dry, sub-sarcastic manner in which Jane Austen casts contempt upon certain ways of viewing life is illustrated in the same story. Anne Elliot has been speaking of the indebtedness of the country to the Navy, and of the hard lives of sailors. Thereupon Sir Walter Elliot, who represents quite another section of the community, remarks, " The profession has its utility, but I should be sorry to see any friend of mine belonging to it." It offends him as being the means of bringing persons of obscure birth into undue distinction, and raising men to honours which their fathers and grandfathers never dreamt of. "A man is in greater danger in the Navy of being insulted by the rise of one whose father his father might have disdained to speak to, and of becoming prematurely an object of disgust to himself, than in any other line." Thus is expressed the extreme of snobbishness and complete ignorance of the subject spoken of. With all her admiration of the Navy, Jane Austen saw the faults of some of its officers. There is a slur upon some flag officers in "Persuasion," where Admiral Croft says, "If you look across the street you will see Admiral Brand coming down, and his brother. Shabby fellows, both of them ! I am glad they are not on this side of the way." Again, in "Mansfield Park," the open scandal of Admiral Crawford's life has driven his niece from the shelter of his roof, and his character is only redeemed by his kindness to the young midshipman William Price. Mary Crawford speaks of some of her uncle's comrades with the characteristic sarcasm of Jane Austen. "'You have a large acquaintance in the Navy,' says Edmund Bertram. 'Among admirals, large enough ; but we know very little of the inferior ranks. Postcaptains may be very good sort of men, but they do not belong to *us*. Of various admirals I could tell you a great deal ; of them and their flags, and the gradation of their pay, and their bickerings and jealousies. But, in general, I can assure you that they are all passed over, and all very ill used. Certainly, my home at my uncle's brought me acquainted with a circle of admirals. Of *Rears*, and *Vices*, I saw enough. Now do not be suspecting me of a pun, I entreat.'"

All this, it will be admitted, is very unconvincing. It shows, perhaps, that Jane Austen had heard of some admirals whom her young brothers did not like. But it has no suggestion of Nelson's "band of brothers." It does not give us the ceaseless care of the great admiral for the welfare of his officers and men ; we have in it nothing of the sturdy, honest qualities of Hood or Jervis ; it does not speak of the geniality of Cornwallis, the

A MAN-OF-WAR TOWING A FRIGATE INTO HARBOUR.
Published by Carington Bowles, 1781.

To face page 296.

CHAPTER XV

FICTION OF THE GREAT WAR

THE latter half of the eighteenth century and the beginning of its successor are a rather disappointing period in the history of fiction. The full volume of the literature of the war came later. There is nothing here to compare with the famous figures found in the novels of Smollett. Scattered through the magazines of the period are abundant sketches and anecdotes, and the chap-books and broadsheets of the time are rich in history in the guise of fiction. They tell many a gallant tale of the seamen whose names were in every mouth. There are romances of the girl impressed as a sailor and sent to sea. They extol the brave tar who lost leg, his arm, or his eye at Trafalgar or Camperdown, or in some other less-known action. There are bold romances of privateering, piracy, and shipwreck, and tales of hardship and adventure, often illustrated with copper plates or wood-cuts of incidents or heroes. Many of these issues have to do with the perennial complaints of the seamen—their revolt against dirty burgoo, rotten meat, mouldy biscuit, often ascribed to the transgressions of the purser, but more often now to the nepotism, venality, and meanness of the higher authorities. There are tales also of the cruelties of officers and the hardships inflicted by the press-gang, often cast in the form of verse, and to be read in the " Roxburghe Ballads " and other collections, with which we shall deal later. Nothing was added to permanent literature by such publications, and not much to our knowledge of nautical character.

Books which will repay the perusal of the curious are
Mark Moor's "Original Anecdotes of a Naval Officer,"
1795; "The Naval Trident," 1804; John Thelwall's
"Trident of Albion," 1805 ; Charles Loftus's "By Sea
and Land "; Urquhart's "Naval Sketches," 1814; R.
Warneford's "The Jolly Boat," 1815 ; and Llewelyn
Penrose's "Old Sailor's Tales," 1815.

Such amatory narratives as "The Voyages and
Adventures of Capt. Robert Boyle," 1805, are neither
of naval nor of literary value.   Something may be gained
from an ephemeral volume entitled "Professional Characteristics : Consisting of Naval Squalls, Military Broils,
etc.," 1808, in which Admiral Crosstree explains, in the
Pump Room at Bath, the misfortunes and discomforts
of the seaman's life.   "Walking the deck of a cold wet
night, in the North Sea," he says, "under the lee of
the mizen-stay sail, with the agreeable episode of wetting
your fingers every hour with the log line, till the snow and
sleet get frozen in your hair, and your teeth chatter in
your head like a Chinese mandarine."   This is one of the
"delights" of a naval life, in the recital of which the
Admiral rivals his military friend Spitfire, who recounts
the ups and down of soldiering.   Here is another experience.   "In the height of the yellow fever in the West
Indies, turning into your hammock on the tier, alongside a sick messmate, until by the rolling of the ship you
happen to touch him, and find him cold dead."

A novel little known, but in many ways humorous
and interesting, is "The Post-Captain ; or, The Wooden
Walls Well Manned," of which a new edition appeared in
1815.   It is announced as comprehending a view of
naval society and manners, and is the work of one writing
in exaggerated language, who had some knowledge of sea
life.*   It opens with a scene in the cabin of a frigate in
the British Channel, whose captain is longing to get
home in order that he may lay siege to the heart of the
daughter of Admiral Roughknot.   He is found looking

* Dr. J. J. Moore, also the author of "The British Mariner's
Vocabulary," illustrated with copper plates, 1801.

at her picture. "Blow, my good breeze! Fill all my
sails! Driver and ring-tail, sprit-sail, and sprit-top-
sail! Royals and sky-scrapers! Flying jib and jib
of jibs! Waft me, oh, waft me to the arms of Cassandra!" Mr. Hurricane, lieutenant of the watch, is
summoned, and to him the captain gives orders. "I
hope all the reefs are out!" "The top-men, sir, are
aloft shaking them out." "Is there any land in sight?"
"The master says he can see land broad upon the bow;
but I, sir, am of opinion it is only cape fly-away." The
lieutenant hastens on deck to make all sail. "Boatswain's mate! boatswain's mate! I say, you boatswain's mate! send the after-guard aft here to the main-
topsail halliards. Corporal of Marines! send the marines
aft on the quarter-deck to clap on the main-topsail
halliards. Master-at-arms! go down below, and send
all the idlers up! Send all the idlers up! Do you hear
there, master-at-arms? Send all the idlers up! Stewards
and servants, barbers and sweepers, cook's mates and
cook's-mate's ministers, doctor's mates and loblolly-boys!
After-guard! I don't see the after-guard coming aft!
Where's the captain of the after-guard? Pass the word
there in the waist for the captain of the after-guard!"

There is a good deal of chaff amongst the officers on
the quarter-deck, throwing light upon the practices
and humours of the times. The purser is getting the
better of his sea-sickness. "Yes," says the lieutenant of
Marines; "and now you will be occupied in making dead
men chew tobacco." The allusion is, of course, to the
practice of some pursers of drawing victuals and stores
for men who were dead or who had run. The purser
and lieutenant have their gibe at the doctor. "Does the
doctor eat his allowance?" asks Captain Brilliant of
Mr. Nipcheese. "Yes, sir," answers the purser; "he
picked the plums for the gun-room pudding last banyan
day, and ate more than half what I had served out."
"When our pudding, sir," added the lieutenant, "was
put upon the table, the plums, I will vouch, were not
within hail of each other." An English West Indiaman

taken by the French is recaptured, and an ancient gentleman and his youthful wife are brought on board the
frigate, and the lady is subsequently found as the wife
of Lieutenant Hurricane, while Captain Brilliant espouses
Cassandra Roughknot. This is how the lovelorn lieutenant has laid siege to the affections of his *innamorata*:
" Yes ! goddess of goddesses ! a shot from either one or
both of those heavenly bow-chasers has raked my heart
fore and aft, and knocked it into splinters—splinters
that no carpenter can repair, but the magic of your smiles.
. . . Lowering my top-gallant sails to you, I am your
dying lieutenant, Henry Hurricane." " Belay, there ! "
exclaims Captain Brilliant, with something more of the
quarter-deck in his manner, to the lieutenant, who
declares he has wept like a child; " you may tell that to
the Marines, but I'll be d—d if the sailors will believe it."
Both ladies are subsequently with their husbands on
board the *Desdemona* when she discovers a French frigate
lying at anchor " all a-taunto," that is ready for sea, in
Hampton Roads, and a desperate fight and boarding
action takes place, in which the *Desdemona* is victorious,
and the heroes are thereby enabled to live in affluence.

Sir Walter Scott, one of the greatest figures in the
history of English fiction, throws no real light upon
naval character in his novels. But he must have a
place in this volume, because one of his stories, " The
Pirate," is based upon a side of seafaring life which had
already attracted Defoe. This romance of the Orkney
Islands, which the " Author of Waverley " wrote, is
dated 1821, but is founded upon episodes which are
said to have occurred nearly a hundred years before.
Captain Cleveland, who is cast ashore in his wrecked
vessel at Sumburgh Head, is recognised as a seaman by
his bronzed, weather-beaten countenance, and " the
frank and open manner of a sailor," and Mordaunt
Mertoun, born " to hold man-of-war's men in great
respect," is flattered by the invitation of " a thorough-
bred seaman " to accompany him afloat in quest of
Spanish pistoles. The stranger enters into the life of

the household of the old Udaller of Burgh-Westra, and
lays siege to the heart of one of his fair daughters. To
her he confesses himself " a sailor of fortune, an adventurer, a buccaneer, or, if you will have the broad word,
a pirate." What part he plays in the story is not to be
related here. He is a kind of " gentleman captain,"
at least in apparel, wearing what seemed "a sort of
uniform," richly laced, and exhibiting no small quantity
of embroidery. He is contrasted with another pirate
captain, who mixes "his words and oaths in nearly
equal proportion," and some of the latter's men scoff at
him. " It is a shame for men of spirit to have such a
Jack-a-dandy scare-crow on board." But Cleveland
has stronger qualities in him, and at the end of the story
we hear of his having fallen, " leading the way in a
gallant and honourable enterprise, which was successfully
accomplished by those companions to whom his determined bravery had opened the road." Here Scott
grasped an essential of naval character. As to Cleveland's fantastic follower in good and evil, Bunce, Dr.
Dryasdust believed he might be identified " with an old
gentleman who, in the beginning of the reign of George I,
attended the Rose Coffee-house regularly, went to the
theatre every night, told mercilessly long stories about
the Spanish Main, controlled reckonings, and bullied
waiters, and was generally known by the name of Captain
Bounce."

As we approach the conclusion of this quest for the
living figure of the seaman in fiction, we find the stream
of nautical literature broadening, making it incumbent
upon us to sketch more slightly the burden of naval
narrative and characterisation which it bears. But
before we go onward, we are swept, as it were, into a
retrospective backwater, in order to glance at a really
remarkable novel published in three volumes in 1831—
" Sir Edward Seaward's Narrative of his Shipwreck, and
Consequent Discovery of Certain Islands in the Caribbean
Sea." The story is by Miss Jane Porter, and purports
to give " a detail of highly interesting events in his life

from the year 1733 to 1749, as written in his own diary."
There is something of the apparent fidelity of Defoe in
the leisurely narrative of shipwreck on the shore of a
desert island, and many subsequent adventures, though
no such striking episode as that of the footprint in the
sand arrests attention.

Seaward, like Robinson Crusoe, enters upon his
adventures as a supercargo, but, unlike his prototype,
he has his young wife with him, and he ends his career
as an officer of the Navy, his vessel being taken over
by the Admiralty, while he receives a commission, after
amassing a large fortune. The narrative is cast in the
period of Vernon's operations at Portobello and Cartagena, and the Seaward Islands, to the great chagrin of
their discoverer and planter, are handed over to the
Spaniards at the Peace of Aix-la-Chapelle. Miss Porter
could not give us the personalities of the seamen of that
time, and her story is chiefly interesting as an attempt
at realistic description. In describing the blue uniform
coats, lined with white, of the officers of the *Solebay*
frigate, she anticipates by a few years the actual institution of the uniform by George II, who, it may be remembered, having seen the Duchess of Bedford riding
in the Park in a blue habit faced with white, was so
pleased with her costume that he adopted it for the new
naval uniform. Miss Porter also describes the uniform
with a little more particularity than actual knowledge
of the details would warrant.

Marryat, it will be remembered, went back to this same
period in " Snarleyyow," but, with all his merits and,
it may be added, all his defects, he is a naval novelist of
such note and real importance that a chapter shall be
devoted to him. Before turning to his stories and to
those of some of his contemporaries, it will be well, however, in this place to deal with a good deal of naval fiction
and other literature belonging more or less to his time, but
based upon the incidents and circumstances of the earlier
part of the century.

It was the lighter side of sea life that mostly attracted

and occupied the pens of lively nautical writers, and
Cruikshank, " Phiz," and other artists of the time
gave visible form to their creations with the etching
needle. Thus we have brought before us a whole world
of quaint and curious, but always lovable characters—
often in the hurly-burly of wild, care-for-nought, harum-
scarum, good or bad, and occasionally indifferent materials to be found in the cockpits of men-of-war. In
this world apart the good predominates, because the
vicious scamp or incorrigible blackguard would not have
been tolerated in the sea society. The eager youth is
contrasted with the veteran of the Billy Culmer school,
whose hair, by hope and promotion long deferred, had
been turned white, without spoiling the trusty heart
of the gallant seaman. Captain James Scott gives, in
his " Recollections of a Naval Life," 1834, many a glimpse
of the life in the wooden world in his early days—the
thoughtless character of Jack, his hand as open as his
heart, so long as he had a shot in the locker, his often
ludicrous folly in money matters, and his care for any
one's welfare but his own. He tells of one fine thorough-
bred seaman who was not content until he had made his
chère amie eat a sandwich between whose slices of bread
and butter he had placed a five-pound note. Another
of his figures is of a seaman who, having come into a
little fortune, entertained his messmates, and having
paid for a six-guinea seat in the London coach, exclaimed,
" No, no, I am for the upper deck," and straightway he
climbed up to the roof. " Tip us your daddles, my
hearties ; God bless you, my boys ! "

Similar pictures are given by Lieut. W. Bowers, R.N.,
in his " Naval Adventures during Thirty-Five Years'
Service," 1833. He casts back his mind to the days
when the race of Trunnions and Hatchways was not
extinct, and when the quarter-deck, cockpit, and gunroom presented a different picture from that of his own
day. On foreign stations, more especially, he says,
a simple primitive style of costume, of little uniformity,
characterised the officers of the various grades. " Sus-

penders for the trowser being by many considered an
article supererogatory, the nether garment, not over-
remarkable for its snowy whiteness, might be seen peeping
from the waistband and unmentionables of many a hero.
Straw hats, many of them real sombreros, with rims like
an umbrella, or covered with nankin, blackballed, tarred,
or painted, manufactured by the seamen, were for the
most part the order of the day ; while checked shirts
among the mids and warrants, and blue, yellow, and
white nankin, dungaree, duck, or fine canvas, the former
in jackets, the latter in trowsers, principally prevailed.
Stockings were by no means considered an essential,
and happy, thrice happy, was he who could achieve the
purification of his duds in *aqua pura*."

From the " Naval and Military Library of Entertainment," published by Henry Colburn, much light is
thrown upon these vigorous times. These volumes are
ascribed to distinguished officers. One of them entitled
" The Night Watch," 1834, abounds in descriptions of
sea life. We are introduced into the wardroom of a 74,
with its canvas bulkheads, forming the officers' sleeping
cabins, in each of which is a gun, and into the cockpit
to witness the miseries and diversions of the midshipmen.
One is playing the violin, another the flute ; two are
occupied at the chessboard ; one is working out a tide
from John Hamilton Moore ; another is drawing a pipe
and glass of grog in the hands of the rudely engraved
figure on the frontispiece of that old seamanship book.
We are given a specimen of the humours of the sportive
" Cockpit Chronicle," and witness the midshipmen's farce,
which is humorously interrupted by the hoarse bawling
of voices on deck, giving portentous evidences of the
approach of a coming storm. There is much of reckless
enjoyment in all these pictures of life afloat, with which all
the qualities of good seamanhood are conjoined.

There was a large reading public both afloat and ashore
for nautical sketches and tales, and the supply did not
lag behind the demand. " The Sailor's Log Book ; or,
Nautical Miscellany," brought together a most entertain-

x

ing series of sketches, stories, and anecdotes, and the
" Old Sailor " who made the collection had a most lively
appreciation of the services and merits of the " jolly
tars," than whom, he says, no class of men were more
susceptible to kind treatment, and still they were actuated
by the same thoughtless indifference to self and the same
generous feelings for others. The " Old Sailor," H. M.
Barker, a naval officer, was the author of the first collection of facts and anecdotes relating to Nelson, and of a
whole series of nautical sketches—" Jem Bunt," " Naval
Sketches," " Tough Yarns," " The Naval Club," and
others. Each one of them is informed with a real love
of the seaman and a wholesome zest for the life and
occupations of the sea. Episodes of battle, galley yarns,
tales of love and heroism, scenes of humour and pathos,
fill these excellent volumes, and the seaman is the same
simple, generous, thoughtless being throughout—tender-
hearted and susceptible to the charms of the other sex—
often too easily captured by those unworthy of him.
" Sweet creatures ! " exclaims one of them in " Tough
Yarns"; " I loves 'em all a little, d'ye see; for what's a
sailor without a sweetheart ? Why, he's like a ship
without a rib, like a mast without stays, like a binnacle
without a compass, or a block without a sheave. Pretty
dears ! they're the very ach-me of a sailor's hopes, the
maintop of his heart. . . . All the Wenuses of Italy, all the
beauties of Buss-aloney, all the brilliant black eyes of
Spanish America, can't box the compass with the dear
little lasses of our native land."

A writer of the same period, who was the author of
several naval novels, but who added nothing to literature
and not much to our knowledge or conception of the
seaman's personality, was William Johnson Neale.
His first book was " Cavendish ; or, The Patrician at
Sea," being a tale of the Navarino period, published in
1831. Marryat thought the work crude, but saw some
promise of future merit in it, and did a little to improve
it. A second edition appeared in 1832. " The Port
Admiral," 1833, was Neale's next novel, and Marryat

spoke harshly of it in the "Metropolitan Magazine,"
being disgusted, as he subsequently said, because it
contained " a villainous libel upon one of our very best
officers, the gallant Troubridge," and he described the
book as devoid of " talent as it was malignant and base
in its feelings." A very embittered correspondence
passed between Marryat and the author concerning
this book. Neale wrote other stories of naval life—
" Will Watch," 1834, and " Gentleman Jack," 1841.
He had some idea of scourging and correcting naval
abuses, and he thought that midshipmen entered the
Navy too young, but his books would not repay examination here, though they should not escape the notice of
those who are studying the naval character of the time.
" Paul Periwinkle ; or, The Press Gang," may perhaps
be accounted the best of Neale's books.

A writer who loved the sea and seamen was the author
of " The Greenwich Pensioners," describing himself as
" Lieut. Hatchway, R.N." His naval yarns, published
in 1838 by Colburn, are cut into lengths to form the
chapters of what looks like a three-volume novel, and
are not without interest. It was the author's object
to preserve, though it might be in the guise of fiction,
the character of the race who in the long and eventful
war had fought their country's battles, and shed their
best blood in its defence, before they disappeared. To
this end he collected some old veterans round the fire in
a ward of Greenwich Hospital, and with a glass of grog
cast loose their tongues. They tell of fighting at the Nile,
at Trafalgar, in the encounter between the *Shannon* and
the *Chesapeake*, and in other less-known actions. As a
series of sketches, there is a good deal of entertainment
in the volumes, and the reader will understand a little
better than he otherwise would the quality and temperament of the men who fought in the long war—their
reckless indifference to danger, the readiness of their
resource, their artless simplicity, the generosity of their
sympathy, their fond recollection of their services, their
sense of the essentials of discipline, and their quickness

to resent the cruelties that drove them to mutiny. It is
more from the spirit of the book than from its incidents
that this impression is derived, and its narratives will
not detain us here. From the same point of view we
shall regard an amusing volume entitled " Jack Tench ;
or, The Midshipman turned Idler," by " Blowhard,"
published in 1842. Once more we are introduced to
the humours of the midshipmen's berth, and the hero,
discovering the chief secret for a youngster's guidance
on entering for the first time the cockpit of a man-of-war,
determines not to be outdone by the oldest " mid "
amongst them in fun and good humour. He had been
appointed to his uncle's ship, but—and this is a point
deserving of notice—he was soon informed that such
persons as uncles were unknown on board, and were un-
acknowledged in ships of war. He was likewise instructed that the words " I can't," " I won't," and " I am
afraid " were not admitted ; that to all orders there was
but one answer, and that always accompanied by touching
or lifting the hat, namely, "Aye, aye, sir "; that all " sky-
larking " was limited to the cockpit and cable-tier ; and
that on coming upon the quarter-deck, by day or night,
whether from " in board " or out, the hat must be touched
or lifted in compliment to the " flag " or " pendant " and
" King's parade." Another volume that takes us afloat
on the quarter-deck — this time of a merchantman—
is by the surgeon of the ship in question, C. J. R. Cook,
M.R.C.S., and is entitled " The Quarter-Deck," 1844. All
that we need say about it is that it also is inspired by the
spirit of comradeship, and shows us the ship getting
into what was termed " ship-shape and Bristol fashion,"
an expression that carries back the mind to the times
when the navigators of Bristol were amongst the pattern
seamen of the British Isles, and it is an expression not
quite disused in these days.

CHAPTER XVI

THE AUTHOR OF "PETER SIMPLE"

NOW we turn to the vigorous pages of Captain Marryat and of some of his contemporaries, all of whom were seamen, and therefore knew well the things of which they wrote. Marryat may have fallen a little out of fashion nowadays, but we have all laughed with him as boys. Some of us have known that his purpose was not laughter and entertainment only, and there are those who regard it as a defect of his novels that he endeavours too much to enforce his personal views. Sometimes he thereby deprives his incidents of reality. There are some characters also whom he created in retaliation for wrongs and disappointments he had suffered. Nevertheless, his descriptions of the sea life and of society in the wooden world will endure as long as the literature lasts of our sea-girt isles. He had lived in the atmosphere and acted in the life he writes of, and his personalities, though they may be types and not individuals, are generally real men, as true in their forceful character as any that Smollett ever drew.

It was a piece of good fortune for English fiction that Frederick Marryat went to sea in the *Imperieuse* frigate with that great seaman Lord Cochrane, afterwards Earl of Dundonald. He would probably have made a name in literature if he had never joined the Navy at all, but it was his dramatic experience in the *Imperieuse*, which he joined in 1806, that gave direction to his genius. If he had entered the Service in a ship of the line at the date when he joined the frigate, he would have

seen less of fights and adventures, and he has himself left
us an account of the experience that may be described
as the mainspring of his writing power. The *Imperieuse*
was continuously employed on the French coasts, crowning her fame in the celebrated affair of the Basque
Roads in 1809, when Marryat was in one of the fire-ships.
In 1807 he had been in the Mediterranean, and had visited
Malta, seeing some hard fighting in circumstances associated with the adventures of Frank Mildmay and Peter
Simple. Before the end of the war in 1815, when he had
reached the rank of commander, Marryat had been the
witness and actor in a whole world of adventures, many
a time in hair-breadth escapes, in saving life, and in
fighting with enemies and tempests. All was treasured
in the storehouse of his memory, and he garnered fresh
experience on the coasts of North and South America,
and in the West Indies. For fifteen years subsequently
he was constantly employed with very great credit,
but a feeling of disappointment grew upon him. He had
aspirations toward literary life, and " Frank Mildmay "
was published and " The King's Own " written before
he relinquished the command of the *Ariadne*, and be-
took himself to shore life, in 1830, as a hard-working
and successful man of letters.

Marryat as a man must not be judged by Marryat
as an author, in the pages of " The Naval Officer ; or,
Scenes and Adventures in the Life of Frank Mildmay."
He had witnessed mutiny and was aware of its forms ; he
knew there were tyrannical captains and weak captains,
and he held them up as examples in his dark pictures of
cruelty and failure. He forgot that he might misinterpret
to the uninstructed reader the Navy that had among its
captains many gallant and honourable gentlemen, like
Cochrane himself, and the men who were Nelson's
" band of brothers." In his later books he was in a
happier mood, and on his behalf it must be remembered
that he had himself suffered in his younger days. It
was unfortunate, nevertheless, that he made fiction a
vehicle for his revenge upon those who had persecuted

him. As a narrative, "Frank Mildmay" is visibly autobiographical, and Marryat did himself a wrong, because, protest as he might that he was not the rather unpleasant person whom he had made his hero, it was impossible for his contemporaries to distinguish him from that character. He had chosen deliberately to perpetuate the darker side of naval life, making it more brutal than it was, instead of describing, as he did later on, its honest gaiety and cleanly virtue.

In many respects Marryat was under the influence of Smollett, and the midshipmen's berth in "Frank Mildmay" is a reproduction of that in which Roderick Random had his experience, though we miss the genial Welshman and some others who suffered with him under the hard rule of Captain Oakum. The gloomy retreat into which Mildmay descended was redolent with the stench of bilge, the reek of foul tobacco, the effluvium of gin and beer, and the pungent odour of frying steak, onions, and red herrings. A dirty cloth was on the table, a sack of potatoes in the corner, " and the shelves all round and close over our heads were stuffed with plates, glasses, quadrants, knives and forks, loaves of sugar, dirty stockings and shirts, and still fouler tablecloths, small toothcombs, and ditto large, clothes brushes, etc." Of his messmates he says : " Their pursuits when on shore were intoxication and worse debauchery, to be gloried in, and boasted of, when they returned on board. My captain said that everything found its level in a man-of-war ; true, but in the midshipmen's berth it was the level of a savage."

Marryat's commiseration for the hard lives of seamen is seen in most of his stories, and not less his desire to expose the character of some officers who were guilty of aggravating the hardness of their lot. In " The King's Own," where the cruelties and sufferings are described which led to the mutinies at Spithead and the Nore, the character of Captain A—— is painted in the darkest colours. But Marryat had a most ardent love for the Service, combined with deep admiration of most

of his officers and men, and in the same book the
qualities of Captain M——, commanding the *Aspasia*,
a man of undaunted bravery, and a fine character,
are sharply contrasted with the cowardice and tactless-
ness of Captain A——. " As an officer he was a perfect
master of his profession, both in theory and practice,
and was what is termed afloat ' all for the Service.'
Indeed, this feeling was so powerful in him that, like
Aaron's rod, it swallowed up all the rest. If there was
any blemish in his character, it was in this point. Correct
himself, he made no allowance for indiscretion. Inflex-
ibly severe, but always just, he in no instance ever spared
himself, nor would he ever be persuaded to spare others."
He knew that he was liable to error, and therefore made
a compact with himself never to punish until twenty-
four hours after the offence had been committed. Marryat
afterwards, in " Mr. Midshipman Easy," claimed that
his plea in " The King's Own " for delaying punishment,
had caused the Admiralty to order the procedure of
Captain M—— to be adopted in the fleet.

The officers of the *Aspasia* are excellent types of seamen. Mr. Bully, the first lieutenant, was an officer who
understood his duty, and had the merit of implicitly
obeying orders, and " considering the well-known fact
that a first lieutenant has always sufficient cause to be
put out of temper at least twenty times during the twelve
hours, he was as good-tempered as a first lieutenant
could possibly be." The second lieutenant was a good-
looking young man, who kept his watch and read Shakespeare, whom he constantly tried to quote, but forgot
the quotations. The third lieutenant was a little bilious-
looking personage, of serio-comic humour. The master
had a rough and unpromising exterior, but every re-
quisite for his office. His nerves were like a chain cable ;
he was correct and zealous in his duties, and was a great
favourite of the captain's. The surgeon, Macallan,
was a naturalist, a man of profound research, and of an
amiable and gentle disposition. He was accustomed
to discourse upon the wonders of Nature, and on one

AN ENGAGEMENT BETWEEN THE HEART OF OAK AND
CHARMING SALLY.
PUBLISHED BY CARINGTON BOWLES, 1781.

To face page 312.

Master Henry's trousers, Miss Ellen's petticoat, and other domestic requirements to look to.

From this humorous parody of things that did actually take place in the Service, we pass on to " Peter Simple." It is more pleasant to enjoy the spirit, jollity, and real humanity of this story. Marryat's reputation was not built up by " Frank Mildmay," nor by " The King's Own," though their appearance marked the advent of a new force in literature. In " Peter Simple " he displayed qualities that were all his own. Never were better nautical descriptions written, and incidents and character are all presented with the true grasp of essentials and the soundest hold of personalities. Humour and geniality bubble over in the pages, and many of the characters are loved as if they were real men. Goodness of heart and whimsical fun, carried sometimes to the point of absurdity, but real joyous humour all the same, are there, and with all the exaggeration there is essential truth. We cannot deal with all Marryat's novels in these pages. " Newton Forster," a tale of the merchant service, " Jacob Faithful," " Snarleyyow," that vigorous and vivid story of scoundrelly Vanslyperken and his vile cur, " Poor Jack," " Masterman Ready," and several more are all lively pictures of sea life and of things concerning the sea. But perhaps " Peter Simple " is the best of all the stories, delineating the society of the wooden world with a charm, geniality, and true humour that are irresistible.

At the very beginning we find Peter Simple the victim of the frolicsome practices of his laughter-loving future messmates, who play, with good-natured lightness of heart, upon the greenness of the newly arrived " fool of the family." Escaping from the fraudulent hands of Trotter, the master's mate, and his unctuous wife, Simple finds himself in the midshipmen's berth of the *Diomede*, and there is " another cub " for the first lieutenant " to lick into shape." In Marryat's private log he has left an account of his experiences in the *Impérieuse*, upon which much of " Peter Simple " is based. He

speaks of the continued excitement, the day passing
without a shot being fired in anger being reckoned as
a blank day. He notices the expedition with which
parties were formed for service ; " the rapidity of the
frigate's movement, night and day ; the hasty sleep
snatched at all hours ; the waking up at the report of
guns, which seem the very keynote to the hearts of those
on board, the beautiful precision of our fire, obtained
by constant practice ; the coolness and courage of our
captain, inoculating the whole of the ship's company."
He delighted to remember the proved character of every
man and officer on board, the implicit trust and adoration
they felt for their commander, the ludicrous situations
which would occur in extreme danger, the hair-breadth
escapes and indifference to life shown by all. " When
memory sweeps along these years of excitement even
now," he wrote, " my pulse beats more quickly with the
reminiscence."

" Peter Simple " is the reflection of this experience,
and the characters are probably drawn mostly from
Marryat's comrades at that time. Cochrane was the
prototype of Captain Savage—the brave, generous,
courteous, kindly, firm, and resolute officer of the story,
whose frigate is the school and nursery of the true spirit
of seamanship in officers and men. Falcon, the first
lieutenant, is another admirable type of the zealous and
efficient officers of the time. He was one of the most
amusing men Peter Simple had ever known, yet he never
relaxed the discipline of the Service, nor took the least
liberty with his superiors or inferiors. He was very
particular about the whiteness of his decks, and punishment awaited those who were careless in this matter,
humour of not the most refined type being displayed in
the form of the penalties. In such a world Peter Simple
could not but soon feel himself at home. " Now that
I have been on board about a month, I find my life is
not disagreeable. I don't smell the pitch and tar, and
I can get into my hammock without tumbling out on
the other side. My messmates are good-tempered, al-

though they laugh at me very much ; but I must say
that they are not very nice in their ideas of honour.
They appear to consider that to take you in is a capital
joke ; and that because they laugh at the time that they
are cheating you, it then becomes no cheating at all."
When Peter Simple wrote this he was still a bit of a
greenhorn, and something of a prig to boot. But he soon
learned to know his companions better, and to value the
strength and trustiness of their comradeship.

A striking picture of fine seamanship is that of the
Diomede in the direst peril, beating off a lee shore, in
a gale of wind. Marryat remembered his own experience in the *Imperieuse*, when she was sent to sea un-
fitted and unready, and was only saved by the seaman-
like skill of Cochrane and his officers. " By the powers,
it was as nate a thing as ever I saw done," observes
O'Brien in the story ; " the slightest mistake as 'to time
or management, and at this moment the flatfish would
have been dubbing at our ugly carcases." But still
they were driven down towards that rocky point on
the lee bow which, if they failed to weather it, would
break up the frigate on its cruel reefs. "The captain eyed
it for some minutes in silence, as if in calculation. ' Mr.
Falcon,' said he at last, ' we must put the mainsail on
her.' ' She never can bear it, sir.' ' She must bear it,'
was the reply. ' Send the men aft to the mainsheet.
See that careful men attend to the buntlines.' . . . ' If
anything starts, we are lost, sir,' observed the first lieutenant again. ' I am perfectly aware of it,' replied the
captain, in a calm tone. ' But, as I said before, and you
must now be aware, it is our only chance. The consequence of any carelessness or neglect in the fitting and
securing of the rigging will be felt now ; and this danger,
if we escape it, ought to remind us how much we have
to answer for if we neglect our duty. The lives of the
whole ship's company may be sacrificed by the neglect
or incompetence of an officer when in harbour. I will
pay you the compliment, Falcon, to say, that I feel convinced that the masts of the ship are as secure as know-

ledge and attention can make them.'" We may be quite sure that no captain ever spoke in such circumstances as Captain Savage speaks in the novel. Good sense was put into his mouth, but it was the reflection of Marryat in his study and not the language of the quarter-deck.

Two officers of warrant rank stand out prominently in "Peter Simple"—Muddle, the carpenter, who went by the name of "Philosopher Chipps," and his friend and rival, the inimitable boatswain "Gentleman" Chucks —the "tautest (that is the most active and severe) boatswain of the service." The philosophy of Muddle, which sometimes sorely tried the patience of the skipper and the first lieutenant, did not embody the doctrine of any particular school. He was not to be dissuaded from a theory of his own that the universe had a cycle of events which turned round, so that in a certain period of time everything would happen over again—"that in 27,672 years everything that was going on now would be going on again, with the same people as were existing at the present time." Mr. Muddle would expound this idea to Mr. Falcon, who, on one occasion, replied, "I dare say that it is all very true, but the repairs must be finished this night, and 27,672 years hence you will have the order just as positive as you have it now, so let it be done." The theory had the disadvantage of making Muddle not only indifferent to danger, but to everything else, because nothing was of consequence, merely taking its station in the course of time.

Mr. Muddle's philosophy made him the butt of the wags, and brought him under the contempt of Mr. Chucks. The latter gentleman was a philosopher also in his way. "Mr. Simple," he observed, "there is a moral in that knot. You observe that when the parts are drawn the right way, and together, the more you pull, the faster they hold, and the more impossible to untie them; but see, by hauling them apart, how a little difference, a pull the other way, immediately disunites them, and then how easy they cast off in a moment.

That points out the necessity of pulling together in this world, Mr. Simple, when we wish to hold on, and that's a piece of philosophy worth all the twenty-six thousand and odd years of my friend the carpenter, which leads to nothing but a brown study, when he ought to be attending to his duties." Mr. Chucks acknowledged to " a slight flaw " in his early history, when unkindly Fate had prompted him to impersonate or represent officers superior to himself in station, whereby he was afterwards much humiliated on the discovery of his presumption. It was his way to be very polite and gracious in addressing ordinary seamen, in order to prove his gentility, but with a *crescendo* of increasing denunciation, out of zeal for the Service, and to show that he was in earnest. Here is a specimen of his style: " Allow me to observe, my dear man, in the most delicate way in the world, that you are spilling that tar upon the deck—a deck, sir, if I may venture to make the observation, I had the duty of seeing holystoned this morning. You understand me, sir, you have defiled his Majesty's forecastle. I must do my duty, sir, if you neglect yours ; so take that—and that—and that—" (thrashing the man with his rattan), " you d—d hay-making son of a sea-cook. Do it again, d—n your eyes, and I'll cut your liver out."

The boatswain had a very handsome person, inclined to be stout, keen eyes, and hair curling in ringlets. He held up his head, and strutted as he walked. He declared " that an officer should look like an officer, and comport himself accordingly." In his person he was very clean, wore rings on his great fingers, and a large frill to his bosom, which stuck out like the back fin of a perch, and the collar of his shirt was always pulled up to a level with his cheekbones. He never appeared on deck without his " persuader," which was three rattans twisted into one, like a cable, and sometimes he called it his " Order of the Bath " or his " Trio juncto in Uno " ; and this persuader was seldom idle. With regard to his cursory remarks, he observed to Peter

Simple that " the life of a boatswain is a life of 'mergency, and therefore I swear." Thus the genteel Chucks is filled with the consequence of his office. After the storm, he said he considered it not fair play that the elements had drowned the sound of his pipe. " How is it possible for a ship's company to do their best when they cannot hear the boatswain's pipe ? " Chucks is the best character in the book, and is Marryat's masterpiece, but there are others scarcely less worthy to be mentioned. There is fat and easiful, pork-loving Captain John To with his lady, and there is good-tempered, boastful Captain Kearney, and there are many other excellent figures of note in that wonderful gallery of sea characters.

" Mr. Midshipman Easy " is the last book of Marryat's from which we can attempt to gather impressions of naval character in his writings. The same genial spirit that distinguishes " Peter Simple " is found in this story also. The hero is introduced to us in pages that seem to have a far-off resemblance to those at the opening of " Tristram Shandy." It is a humorous idea to send Jack Easy to sea to find equality and the rights of man, which his father had failed to discover on shore. The midshipman's desire to " argue the point " is the source of many of the most amusing passages in the book, as where Jack is ordered to the masthead by Sawbridge, the first lieutenant, and fills that officer with amazement by wishing to discuss the propriety of his action, and asks him where the masthead is mentioned in the Articles of War, which Captain Wilson had told him were the guides of the Service, that all officers and men were bound to obey. The captain's kindly tolerance of Jack's vagaries and odd social ideas is the keynote of the story.

His comrades in the midshipmen's berth are like the gay youths in " Peter Simple." There was a pudding-faced boy as the butt of the mess, whose intellect might have been respectable, if he had not lost confidence through the jeers and mockeries of his comrades. Other midshipmen " were like midshipmen in general, with little appetite for learning, but good appetites for dinner, hating everything like work, fond of everything like fun, fighting *à outrance* one minute and sworn friends the next—with general principles of honour and justice, but which were occasionally warped according to circumstances; with all the virtues and vices so heterogeneously jumbled and heaped together, that it was almost impossible to ascribe any action to its true motive, and to ascertain to what point their vice was softened down into almost a virtue, and their virtues from mere excess degenerated into vice." The rude shocks sustained by Jack's political philosophy, after some experience of discipline in the Service, tempt him to leave it, but Mr. Jolliffe, the discreet master's mate, persuades him to remain. "What do you imagine made me come to sea, Jolliffe?" To which the mate dryly replies, "Because you did not know when you were well off." He continues: "No, my dear Easy, the best thing that you can do is to stay in the service, for it will soon put an end to all such nonsensical ideas; and it will make you a clever, sensible fellow. The service is a rough, but a good school, where everybody finds his level—not the level of equality, but the level which his natural talent and acquirements will rise or sink him to, in proportion as they are plus or minus. It is a noble service, but has its imperfections, as everything in this world must have. I have little reason to speak in its favour, as far as I am concerned, for it has been hard bread to me, but there must be exceptions in every rule. Do not think of quitting the service until you have given it a fair trial."

Many other amusing characters are in "Midshipman Easy." The new gunner of the *Harpy*, who had once been a captain's clerk, and having done good service, had received a warrant as a gunner, had conceived a very high idea of the importance of his office, considering it absolutely necessary that he should be a navigator also. "Now, sir, if the gunner is no navigator, he is not fit to take charge of his Majesty's ships.

The boatswain and carpenter are merely practical men ; but the gunner, sir, is, or ought to be, scientific. Gunnery, sir, is a science—we have our own disparts and our lines of sight—our windage, and our parabolas and projectile forces—and our point blank, and our reduction of powder upon a graduated scale. Now, sir, there's no excuse for a gunner not being a navigator ; for knowing his duty as a gunner, he has the same mathematical tools to work with." Another character delineated is that of the first lieutenant of the *Aurora*, Mr. Pottyfar, who had a special fancy for a certain quack medicine, taking it when he was ill, and often when he was well, lest he should fall ill. Notwithstanding this he was a very good officer, though he had contracted a habit of putting his hands in his pockets, and could never keep them out, even when the ship was in a gale of wind. He had once broken his leg through this habit by falling down a hatchway, and had a large scar on his forehead received from being thrown to leeward against one of the guns.

In this nautical school Jack Easy's notions of equality rapidly disappeared, and he continued to defend them more from habit than conviction, the discipline of the Service having gained its influence over him. That he was a typical sea officer no one can believe. When he left the Service there was regret that one had departed who had a positive talent for adventure, but, said his friend the Governor, " if I understand right from Captain Wilson, you were brought into the profession because he thought that the service might be of use in eradicating false notions, rather than from any intention or necessity of your following it up as a profession." " I suspect that was the case, sir," replied Jack. " As for my own part, I hardly know why I entered it." " To find a mare's nest, my lad !" the Governor responded.

There is one dark character in the story, in the person of Captain Tartar, who is a brute and a braggart. Marryat has explained his theory of the didactic purpose of fiction. He had not written merely to amuse. It had always

Y .

been his view to instruct, and he would not have it
supposed that he had no other end in view than to make
the reader laugh. If he wished to point out an error he
drew a character, and although that character appeared
to be woven naturally into the tale, it became as much
a beacon as it was a vehicle of amusement. He considered this the true art of novel-writing, and thought
that vice and folly and error could be as severely lashed
as virtue and morality could be upheld by the personalities and incidents presented in entertaining guise in
fiction. No doubt there were many abuses to be scourged,
and many errors to be corrected, and in the wooden world
were displayed the perverse moods of many men, the
methods of discipline being necessarily severe for some
of them. In the generally easily recognisable genus of
the seaman, great varieties of personality and temperament were displayed. Marryat, while glorying in the
naval career, and full of admiration for good officers and
men, has thought it well to describe, with the purpose
of chastising, certain abuses which he deplored but did
not always regard impartially. Partly they had reference to the hardships of the seaman's career and the
severity of his punishments. His greater object was to
censure the brutality which characterised but a few
officers, and the follies and weaknesses which were not
found in many, and some of his views were such as
officers of his time found it difficult to agree with.

In that amusing series of sketches of naval society,
" The Discipline, Customs, and Usages of the Royal
Navy, about 1815," by Captain Archibald Sinclair, R.N.,
printed at Edinburgh in 1858, we learn how ships varied
in character and condition, and Sinclair's remarks illustrate some things that Marryat said. He remarks that
if you heard an officer excusing himself for the bad and
inefficient state of his ship on the plea that she was
badly officered and worse manned, you would not be far
wrong in quoting the old Scotch proverb, " A bad shearer
never has a good hook." What in one ship would be
considered as serious crime, and punished with great

severity, would in another be considered as a slight breach
of discipline, corrected by reprimand and caution.   Some
captains were all for seamanship, working the fingers of
both officers and men to the bone—reefing, working ship,
with an occasional pull at the rigging by way of keeping
their hands in.   Another would be all for navigation,
sacrificing every other object to the observation of the
sun, moon, and stars.   A third would be all for gunnery,
and considered reefing topsails or shifting a yard in a
certain number of seconds beneath his notice.   A fourth
officer would flatter himself that his system was a model
of perfection, combining a proportion of all the requisites
of a perfect man-of-war, and if he were a bit of a seaman,
endowed with common sense, would have his ship in
working order with a united ship's company, and at the
end of his three years would receive the compliments of
the inspecting admiral.

The ships of those captains who had written theoretical
treatises on discipline were known, says Captain Sinclair,
to be in the worst possible order.   It might be said of
a captain, "First-rate disciplinarian; never gives less
than three dozen, and seldom without at least a couple
of midshipmen at the masthead."   Captain Sinclair
had himself known when the mastheads had their complements, and a beginning was made upon the yards.
As to punishments, there had been much exaggeration,
and punishments were the instruments of discipline.
Abhorrent as flogging might be to the modern mind, it
was part of the corrective system which gave us the
splendid fighting complements of our ships, manned
largely by impressment, and including all sorts and
qualities of men, even the sweepings of gaols—the
K.H.B.'s, or King's "hard bargains."   Collingwood,
whom the seamen loved—" old Cuddy " they affection-
ately called him—described these men as miscreants,
amenable only to hard punishment, and the influence
of better men.   The stern discipline which Jervis introduced into the Mediterranean is famous in our naval
history, and five years later, when it was rumoured

that he was to have the Channel command, the toast was drunk by those who liked the slacker system—" May the discipline of the Mediterranean never be introduced into the Channel." The great admiral met with antagonism almost amounting to disloyalty, but he suppressed it with sternness, and in course of a few months won the firm adhesion of the best of admirals and captains. Captain Sinclair says that no element of discord seemed wanting from the ships, thus expressing a partial and unjustifiable view; and he regarded as absurd the popular idea prevailing in his time that men sank under shame and degradation after being flogged. He says that he never knew a case of the kind, that flogging was a necessary evil, that the sailors got used to it, and that when the punishment was over the debt was paid, and no blot remained unless the man had been a thief or had skulked in his duty. This was the view of many contemporaries of Captain Marryat.

A NAUTICAL DISPUTE.
PHILLIPS, 1827.

THE SAILOR'S DESCRIPTION OF A CHASE AND CAPTURE.
GEORGE CRUIKSHANK AFTER LIEUT. JOHN SHERINGHAM, R.N., 1815.

To face page 324.

rective of this evil that Glascock set out Jack's character
in his original " galley stories." He tells us that an idea
had begun to gain ground that the material of the common sailor had of late years undergone a great alteration—that he was no longer the same gay, unsuspecting,
artless being, whose garrulity, rambling episodes, and
figurative phraseology, every cadence of which was
marked by the oscillation of a long queue of hair reaching
to his waist, never failed to detain a landsman's ear, and
render him the hero of every group with which he mingled
—" in a word, they presume very generally that the
spirit of the tar is fled with the tail." Therefore, to
give consolation to these lovers of the fast-fading glories
of the tar, he said he had picked out a few relics of the
genuine antique, yclept eccentricities.

Sailors, says Glascock, in introducing a galley yarn
about the famous retreat of Cornwallis—" Billy-Blue,
as brave a fellow as ever wore a flag "—" sailors are a
remarkably plain, downright race, as no man acquainted
with their character would deny. Devoid of all guile,
the seaman never thought to disguise his object, though
he might sometimes be found ' veering and hauling '
to get rid of some difficulty which he imagined lay in his
way." His narrative resembled a ship's course in working
to windward, " which is fain to yield obliquely to the
blast in order to weather her object indirectly and fetch
her port in the end." The sailor also had his super-
stitions. He implicitly believed in omens, mermaids,
the flying Dutchman, evil spirits, the appearance of the
ghosts of the departed, and the pranks of malicious
spirits and goblins. He familiarly talked of frightful
sounds and preternatural noises coming up from the
deep, all having an import of fearful warning, and occasionally portending accident or the death of a messmate.
Elsewhere Glascock remarks that the materials of which
our Navy was formed were, like granite, principally
valuable for their hard, rough, and lasting wear and tear
quality. If they had been of less stern stuff, he says,
the empire of the ocean would no longer have been ours.

In many of his yarns he presents the superior advantages of the Navy as compared with the merchant service. There is a seaman who tells his messmates to remember that what they lose on one tack they gain on another. "Overhaul both sides o' the business—turn it just 'end for end,' and in spite o' your shore-going, know-nothing growlers, you'll find a man-o'-war's berth's not so bad after all." And this same seaman had run from his ship, had been captured, and had been sentenced to one hundred lashes on board his own ship. He had begged not to be punished by being whipped round the fleet. "No, no; none o' your court martials for Jack! If so be as I'd a'gammoned the skipper to a' settled the score at once and sarved me out himself, I'd a' napped no more nor four dozen at the outside!"

A second series of the "Naval Sketch Book" contained other galley yarns, anecdotes, and dialogues, throwing light upon the character and temperament of seamen, their honesty, loyalty, good temper, and objection to change—sometimes their resistance to new ideas, and their questioning of so-called progress. In the first volume of this series is an inimitable sketch of a group of seamen collected round the galley of a frigate discussing the "march-o'-mind" afloat—the growth of "larnin'," and the lore of the sea-lawyer. "But come, come," interposes one seaman, "come, I say—I say. What's the meanin' on it?—I axes afore for that—I wants no more nor the real, reg'lar-built meanin' o' the matter—*March-o'-Mind!—March-o'-Mind*—I'm blest if it isn't a thoro-bred pauler [puzzler], isn't it, Joe?" His messmate interprets the phrase to mean that if a man has a mind to march, march he may. Then comes the simple honest utterance of the good old-fashioned seaman. "Oh! that's it, is't?—Well, in course, Tom, in course you ought to know best;—but *I* knows this—*I've* no mind to *march*. I knows when I've a good berth—a good barkey [favourite ship], and meets with good usage. I knows more too—I knows my sarvitude time will tell at a *time* when I neither can sarve myself or

Sal.—Talk o' the marchan'-sarvus—what d'ye get in it, now ?—Small wages and worse wittels, for precious hard wearin' out work.—Get hurt in the hold, fall from aloft, fractur your pate, or catch a West-Ingy fever, who *then's* to cure you ?—a groggy skipper or a greasy cook ?— No, no, a good man as knows well his work, and knows how to respect himself—mind ; I says *himself*—for if a man won't respect *himself*, where's the fellow as will ? Yes, yes, let a man but respect himself, obey his officers, and keep from *lip* and lickor, and he need never, no, never, shy at a King's ship, or, in any way, dread a man'-o-war. The man as desarves the *name* o' man is sure, *sure* to be treated *like* a man, and sure, in the end, to meet wi' reward."

Then says another : " And, moreover, Jim, you knows *well*, the very chaps as sneer an' snarl 'bout the cruelty o' the *cat*, and the likes o' that 'ere shore-goin' lubberly trash, are only your pieabald parlimin'-praters—chaps as are sore an' savage at seein' seamen *contented*—'stid of growlin' and dissatisfied like their sulky selves. And yet, yet, these very same hipper-crocodile varmins as pretend to pity, and feel, so much, as they tarm it, ' for their *fellor-creturs*,' are always the first, the very *first*, to cut down an' dock a poor fellor-cretur's hard-earn'd pay, or to try an' knock off the harder-earn'd pension his king and country allows him to keep the little life that's left from leakage."

But times were changing in the Navy, and the " march-o'-mind " was tending to introduce a new spirit upon the lower deck. Here is a lament in the galley of the frigate by one who had served in a " March-o'-Mind man-o'-war." " No, Ned, you doesn't *now* often hear the staves as we used to sing it in the war. You never now hears— ' *Will-ye-go-to-Cawsin-Bay-Billy-Bo-Billy-Bo ?* '—nor the ' *Saucy Arethusa* '—nor the ' *Bold Brittanny* '—' *Black-colours under her mizen did fly* '—' *From Ushant to Scilly is thirty-five Leagues* '—an' many more o' the sim'lar sort." " No, no, Sam, you're right enough—your *March-o'-Mind-men* must now come your simmy-dimmy quiv'ring quivers—tip ye soft sentimental touches—sigh-away-like ladies in love, an' never sing nothin' but your silly sicknin' stuff, as often used to frighten the geese an' make 'em cackle in the coop, for all the world like the comin' of a heavy hurricane. Moreover, your *March-o'-Mind-men* never *will* sing a single stave as admits of the *main* thing—for what's a song as won't allow all hands to jine in reg'lar coal-box [chorus]? No, no, your March-o'-Mind-men hav'n't, you may depend on it, the mind o' men—they think far more like people as rig in petticoats nor them as tog in trowsers. Now what looks more young-ladyish nor to see a fellor with a fist like a shoulder o' mutton flingin' his flipper about, an' suitin' his antics to his song, as he snivels out—'Strike—strike the light guitar.' . . . Well, look here, men—if I was a man as had weight in the world, I'd make a reg'lar built law as no lubberly songs should be sing'd in the Sarvus, I'd make it, by Joe! one o' the Articles o' War.''

Captain Glascock wrote two other books—" Tales of a Tar," 1836, and " Land Sharks and Sea Gulls," 1838. Much might be drawn from both of these, but we must be content to say that they are volumes full of the honest qualities of good seamanhood, and that the spirit of comradeship and sound discipline is the keynote of the lessons they convey. In one of the sketches in " Tales of a Tar," a group of pensioners are seated on the grass in Greenwich Park, discussing the " Breeze at Spithead." One of them says that he never knew a clandestine disturbance begin with a thorough-bred tar. They were always set a-going by " your King's benchers, your galley growlers, your jail birds, and them there jaw-breaking chaps as are reg'larly brought up to the law." It was the sea-lawyer that was at the root of the evil, playing upon the weakness of the men, and exaggerating and misinterpreting the real hardships of which they had to complain. " Why, bless your heart, Parker was never no seaman. He was a long-headed chap, to be sure, and had a hatful o' brains afore they was reg'larly turned, for at times

th' unfortnet fellow was as mad as poor psalm-singing
Dick as died t'other day in th' infarmiry—but Parker was
never, never, reg'larly bred to the sea. No, no, when you
wants to weather a grievance, there's nothing like going
quietly aft under easy sail, axin' permission to pass
within hail, and then once granted, you know, speaking
out like men as knows their duty, and wants no more
nor is their due. What says the Articles of War?—Isn't
it better to steer by they, nor to let your head run riot
round the compass, trusting to an under-hand paper
palaver? D—n your round-robins, says I. I never
clapt my scratch to one on 'em yet, and, what's more,
I'm d—d if ever I would." Another seaman remarked,
in regard to their grievances, that they only told the
truth, and that they were not like a parcel of children
singing out before they were hurt. " We never said a
word, no, not as much as the sign of a syllable, against
the use of the cat, for we knew, aye, better, by George,
nor the officers themselves, there was a precious sight
too many chaps in the sarvis, as couldn't be managed
without it." The delegates at the Nore, says Glascock,
in another sketch, unhappily for themselves, invariably
rejected the salutary counsels of their brethren at Spithead. He tells a story of how these political tars were
accustomed to pull round the fleet in their barge, and
visit those ships whose crews were suspected to be cool
in the " cause." The rebellious men on board would
" pipe the side " for them. When they visited the *Vestal*
frigate, the boatswain's mate was ordered to pay this
compliment, but he declined to do it, and loosing the call
from his neck threw it, chain and all, at the heads of the
consequential delegates in the boat, exclaiming, " There,
d—n your eyes ! Take it, and wind it yourselves, for
it never shall be said as Bill Stikey piped the side for
a parcel o' tarry delicates." But when the " delicates "
in question came on board, they dispensed with the
usual preliminary of reading the Articles of War, and
the boatswain's mate was seized and received thirty-six
lashes for " mutinous conduct."

A ship was a little world governed by its own peculiar laws and customs, as is remarked by the author of " The Quid," a small volume of naval sketches published in 1832. It contains tales of the writer's messmates—a collection " of yarns, ditties, quid-ditties, and odd-ditties." Like Glascock, the humorous author gives the lighter side of sea life—" its pleasing varieties and diversified vicissitudes, its moonlight tales, its cheerful carouse, and above all, its Saturday night, when the grog is pushed about so fully to make amends that few have been known to regret a voyage or complain of a sailor's life." He likewise remarks that in a ship vice seemed not to exist ; there were humours and dispositions, but no plotting and contrivance—all plain sailing. " It might certainly be fancy, prejudice, or the like, but I have never been able to bring myself to think that man ashore possessed the same good nature, frank, open-hearted, liberal, genuine, unadulterated, off-hand friend-ship I ever experienced on board." So he describes his shipmates, and amongst them one who was as jolly and jovial-hearted a fellow as ever breathed, fond of every-thing good—singing, smoking, dancing, joking, his glass and his lass—yet preserving amid all the decorum neces-sary to his situation, that of father of the mess.

The spirit of gaiety that inspired Glascock and the author of " The Quid " was the inspiration also of Captain Frederick Chamier, another naval novelist, who followed in Marryat's footsteps. Chamier, who was born in 1796 and died in 1870, served in the Mediterranean as a mid-shipman, and in 1811–14 was with Sir Peter Parker in the *Menelaus*, and was on shore with Parker when that officer was killed at Bellair n 1814. Paying off the *Britomart* sloop in 1827 Chamier was not further employed, and retired in 1833. His first book was " The Life of a Sailor," published in 1832, and none who wish to know the social side of the naval career at the time will omit to read it. " It is the life to some of in-credible misery. How often have I seen a midshipman of forty-five years of age and a lieutenant of sixty !

From these poor fellows, destitute of worldly interest, and existing entirely on their humble pay and ship's allowance, the lighter hours of life are not entirely withheld ; they find recreation in the merited abuse of their seniors, and fight the battles of the Nile and Trafalgar on the oak table, designating ships by drops of water and the admirals by pieces of biscuit." Chamier was more fortunate, and he says that to the fortunate there was no life like that of a sailor. " We roam the world at no expence ; our libraries travel with us ; and if we are not men of some research and some acquirements it is through our own negligent idleness. We ought to be the best judges of human nature ; we see the riches and gaiety of all tribes and all countries." He describes the midshipmen's berth in 1809 in the days of hard service, before the Navy had " approximated to civilisation," as well as life on board in fair weather and foul, fighting, and all the ups and downs of a sailor's life, much in the manner of Captain Basil Hall's autobiography.

" Ben Brace," Chamier's first essay in sustained fiction, appeared in 1836, and is a tale of the " last of the Agamemnons "—a rousing story of the life of a seaman, who first saw service on board the *Raisonnable*, joining her just before Nelson joined her, and living to be a Greenwich pensioner, the " jolliest dog " in the establishment, with shot holes in his right side, which gave him a slight list to port, and sometimes, when his larboard bow " look-out " got a little dim with draining a glass or two in Nelson's memory, he would make a wrong tack and land in a ditch, but, as the last of the Agamemnons, every waterman in the place became his guide and supporter. He had heard Nelson say, " Aft the more honour, forward the better man." We follow him with Nelson in the *Carcass*, the *Seahorse*, and the *Hinchinbroke*, and as coxswain in the *Albemarle* and the *Boreas*. Of the latter he says that she was a happy ship. " We had all manner of amusements on board, from play-acting amongst the officers to single-stick between the men,

and when the hurricane months came on, we used to
shelter in English Harbour, Antigua, and took to music
and dancing as if we had been French skipjacks." We
do not hear of anything but good seamanship, good comradeship, and honest service. " The lass that loved a
sailor " brings romance into the story, and we see the
hero in smart attire, with his tail down to his stern-post,
ducks tight round the waist, " with enough canvas in
the legs of them to dress an Irish family," and a pair
of sailor's shoes, with about a yard of ribbon in each.
Chamier puts into the mouth of Ben Brace his own opinion
in favour of corporal punishment. Those who disap-
proved of it were a kind of sea-lawyers or devil's attor-
neys, trying to make the men believe that they were
whipped and kicked like dogs by every man with a pair
of epaulettes who happened to walk a quarter-deck. " Let
them be educated, say some. I say no, you'll make them
worse. Instead of talking of the good old times, spinning
a yarn about the Nile, rubbing up one's memory about
Nelson, and such like, they would all be squatting about
the decks like a set of Turks, with newspapers before them,
settling the affairs of the nation, and talking about that
which none of them understand. Let them alone;
they are used to it, they think less of the disgrace than
the pain ; and whilst we have officers who are as humane
as they are brave, we have little to fear from tyranny,
and that tyranny can always be stopped." In the same
old-fashioned, conservative way, very characteristic
of the seaman, Ben Brace is all in favour of impressment.
The story is more of a narrative than a novel. Its value
is that it gives us a picture of life on board warships in
Nelson's time, with much of the atmosphere which was
created by the high-minded character of Nelson and his
" band of brothers."

Chamier was the author of some other books. " The
Saucy Arethusa," 1837, is a tale of naval life, adventure
and fighting, the honourable spirit of the seaman shining
through it all, and gaiety and good humour preside over
a pleasant and instructive narrative. Here, again, we

have Chamier's view of the question of impressment. There is a captain who regards the press with disfavour, while admitting that the constant employment, the continued exertion, the hope of prize-money, and the delight with which they welcomed the land after a long cruise, used to compensate the seamen for their wrongs and hardships. On the other hand it is pointed out that impressment was the only way of manning the Navy, and that it was as easy as it was represented to be. Another of Chamier's books, " Tom Bowling," 1841, is the tale of the life of the hero immortalised in song by Dibdin—a story showing how poverty was no bar to advancement, and how Bowling, after good service in the fever-stricken *Hinchinbroke*, commanded by Captain Collingwood, is rated by Nelson a volunteer, first-class, afterwards being promoted to midshipman, rising to high rank, and dying as governor of Greenwich Hospital. Chamier also wrote " Jack Adams the Mutineer," being a tale of the mutiny of the *Bounty*, 1787.

Michael Scott, described by Christopher North as " the best sketcher of sea-scenery that ever held a pen," was not, like Marryat, Glascock, and Chamier, a seaman, but he drew the staple of his narratives from life and experience, with an uncommon power of interpreting character, and a sympathetic and understanding mind that placed him in the forefront of novelists of the sea. Born in 1789, he was the son of a Glasgow merchant, and went out as a young man to Jamaica to manage some estates for Mr. George William Hamilton, who appears in " Tom Cringle's Log " as Aaron Bang. He travelled much by sea and land, and finally settled in Glasgow in 1822. In 1829 " Tom Cringle's Log " began to appear at intervals in " Blackwood " as a series of sketches, and was completed in 1833 ; and in the two years next following " The Cruise of the *Midge* " appeared in the same way. Michael Scott at once took the public fancy by the vigour and force of his narratives, the reality they possessed, their variety of character, their rapid changes of incident, and their picturesque descriptions of pirates and shipwreck and

strange happenings on shore. Scott displays little
restraint in his writings, and he painted his pictures of
men and things with a fuller brush than was commonly
used even in those days. He always depicts seamen
with a loving hand, never with bitterness or satire, but
always finding the sterling nature of the men, and not
excluding from his sympathy and admiration the bold
pirates who were scourges of West Indian waters.

A fine picture of an old sea captain is given in " Tom
Cringle " in the person of Captain John Deadeye, commanding the sloop *Torch*, in the wreck of which vessel
that gallant seaman was afterwards lost. " Captain
Deadeye was a staid, stiff-rumped, wall-eyed, old, first-
lieutenantish looking veteran, with his coat of a regular
Rodney cut, broad skirts, long waist, and stand-up collar,
over which dangled either a queue or a marlinspike with
a tuft of oakum at the end of it—it would have puzzled
Old Nick to say which. His lower spars were cased in
tight unmentionables of what had once been white
kerseymere, and long boots, the coal-scuttle tops of
which served as scuppers to carry off the drainings from
his coat-flaps in bad weather. He was, in fact, the ' last
of the sea-monsters,' but, like all his tribe, as brave as
steel, and, when put to it, as alert as a cat." When
poor Johnstone was mortally wounded in the fight the
skipper went down and prayed at his side. " The tears
trickled down the old man's cheeks and filled the furrows
worn in them by the washing of many a salt spray."
There is Treenail the lieutenant, " one of the nattiest
fellows in the Service," who went to deliver despatches
to the Spanish authorities at Cartagena, " cased in
tight blue pantaloons that fitted him like his skin, over
which were drawn long, well-polished, Hessian boots,
each with a formidable tassel at the top, and his coat was
buttoned up to the chin, with a blazing swab on his right
shoulder, while a laced cocked hat and dress sword completed his equipment."

As to the seamen, their fine qualities fill the book.
Even when kidnapped on board the pirate Tom Cringle

was quick to seize the character of the men. " What queer animals sailors are ! . . . I cast my eye down the hatchway into the men's berth, and there were the whole crew at breakfast, laughing and joking, and enjoying themselves as heartily, apparently, nay, I verily believe in reality, as if they had been in a yacht or on a cruise of pleasure, in place of having one enemy nearly within gunshot astern and another trying to cut them off ahead." The men of the *Firebrand* corvette, to which Tom Cringle was appointed after the loss of the *Torch*, are described as a good set—square-shouldered, narrow-flanked, tall, strapping fellows, full of fun and frolic, and hard fighting men. Scott's humorous liking for seamen is shown in his picture of honest Joe Rumbletithump giving evidence in the public court at Kingston against the pirates, by whom he had been seared with a hot iron, until he disclosed the place where the gold was hidden, and he " twisted and lolloped about in his quaint efforts to describe the part of his anatomy which had suffered, without giving offence."

It has been said of Michael Scott's other story of sea life, " The Cruise of the *Midge*," that it is spoiled by a certain laboured jocosity. However that may be, the exciting yarn has all his qualities as a vivid picture of sea life and seamen. Benjamin Brail, the hero, is a harum-scarum youngster, with the love of the sea in his blood, wherefore he is sent out to his father's old friend Sir Oliver Oakplank, senior officer on the coast of Africa, whose broad pennant flies in the *Gazelle* frigate. Like Captain Deadeye, Sir Oliver is the father of his crew, and is ever looking after their health and welfare. " The Commodore was a red-faced, little man, with a very irritable cast of countenance, which, however, was by no means a true index to his warm heart, for I verily believe that no commander was ever more loved by officers and men than he was. He had seen a great deal of service, and had been several times wounded, once, in particular, very badly by a grape-shot that had shattered his left thigh, and considerably shortened it, thereby giving him a kick in his gallop, as he himself used to phrase it, until the day of his death. He was a wag in his way. . . . The gallant old fellow was dressed in faded nankeen trowsers, discoloured cotton stockings, shoes with corn-holes cut in the toe, an ill-washed and rumpled white Marseilles waistcoat, an old blue uniform coat worn absolutely threadbare, and white and soapy at the seams and elbows ; each shoulder being garnished with a faded gold lace cap to confine the epaulettes when mounted, and that was only on a Sunday. His silk neckcloth had been most probably black once, but now it was a dingy brown ; and he wore a most shocking bad hat—an old white beaver, with very broad brim, the snout of it fastened back to the crown with a lanyard of common spunyarn ; buttoned up, as it were, like the chapeaux in Charles the Second's time, to prevent it flapping down over his ears. He walked backwards and forwards, taking two steps for Sprawl's one, and whenever he turned he gave a loud stamp, and swung briskly about on the good leg, as if it had been a pivot, giving a most curious, indescribable flourish in the air with the wounded limb, like the last quiver of Noblet's leg in an expiring pirouette." Sprawl was the first lieutenant, and so strange a figure that every one naturally exclaimed, " Bless me, what an oddity ! " But he was a most excellent warm-hearted officer, straightforward and kind to the men, never blazoning or amplifying their faults, but generally softening them, and often astonishing the poor fellows by his out-of-the-way and unexpected kindness and civility.

Within our period, but on the borderland of it, is one other naval novelist of importance. James Hannay is best known for his excellent stories, " Singleton Fontenoy," 1850, and " Eustace Conyers," 1855— both of them valuable for an understanding of the Navy of his time—less known for his satirical and humorous narrative " King Dobbs: Sketches in Ultramarine," published in 1849 and dedicated to Thackeray. Hannay entered the Navy in 1840, on board the *Cambridge,* 78,

z

and was employed in the blockade of Alexandria in the Syrian War. He was a born journalist and satirist at heart, and shortly after entering the Service he started a comic manuscript journal, in which he ridiculed the admirals and captains in the Mediterranean. He left the Service in 1845. For our purpose we are more interested in his minor books than in his better-known works, but they must be regarded rather as satires than as representations of actual facts. " Biscuits and Grog " is described as " Personal Reminiscences and Sketches," by Percival Plug, R.N., late Midshipman of H.M.S. *Preposterous*, edited by James Hannay." When the book appeared it was recognised to be the product of the mordant wit of a writer of uncommon ability. Baggles, captain of the *Caliban*, is an officer of the " Benbow school," and the old " port and prejudice school—a man of narrow intellect and large personal dimensions, a plethoric antithesis, who thought little and ate much, a Justice Shallow on the quarter-deck, and a Hercules at the dinner table." Commander Peppercorn is one of those men of whom every one says that he is " a good fellow at the bottom," but you have to go rather deep into his character before you come to the good. The interest of the humorous satire is that it pictures the Navy prior to the Russian War, and shows how the strong feeling of Whigs and Tories divided the Service into factions, sometimes leading to an actual separation of a mess, and frequently to much discord and contention.

" A Claret Cup—Further Reminiscences and Sketches of Percival Plug, R.N.," published in the same year, drops the artifice of editorship. It describes the same Baggles as a relic of the good old times, when vessels were fifteen months at sea, and the very admiral in command had not a teapot ; and after dinner (he himself being provided with the best port and claret) told how Collingwood had nothing but Tenedos wine to drink, and how the bluejackets had often seen the gallant old fellow hang his old coat and waistcoat out of the cabin ports to air

—" which fact, no doubt, was the real cause why these gallant old boys always beat the French." In this book we see the rise of the engineer in the Service, able to report a " screw loose," and not allow the *Roarer* steamer to go to sea until he has been propitiated with cold pie and a bottle of porter. At the end of the volume are " Portraits from the Painted Hall, Greenwich." The boatswain is preferred to the other " monsters of the deep " ; he is generally a good fellow, Ajax in the field and an alderman at the banquet. " Weather has no effect upon him ; his skin is tanned hard and dry. Eastern suns have dried it hard—north-eastern seas soaked it again ; hail has peppered it, and fire scorched it. Still, there it is with a rough good humour warming it. On Sundays he appears in a huge white waistcoat, and on Christmas days is generally invited to dinner by the captain, when he feels terribly awkward, and does not know what to do when asked to take wine. ' No, thank ye, Sir, I'll take a potato,' is, we believe, the traditional orthodox reply, as laid down in the boatswain's code of etiquette for these occasions. When superannuated he retires to some neat little cottage at a seaport town, a nautical oracle on weather and war among his neigh- bours. You may see him toddling along with his pipe, on a summer evening, devoutly raising his hat to every naval man he meets." There is a sketch also of the carpenter, who deems himself superior to the boatswain as a scientific man, and hints darkly at his mathematical acquirements. Another figure in the gallery is the gun- ner, who rules supreme over the weapons of war, and we learn that gunners of the " Benbow school " were very much plagued by having a crew under them from the *Excellent*, who had heard a smattering of science there, and gave themselves " all those airs which make a person who is beginning to be educated the most disagreeable object in the world." Hannay also describes the master- at-arms as the beadle of the Navy, and he gives other nautical sketches. Officers educated under the old system were at that time, he says, dragged from the obscurity of a cottage or a farm, after having been on shore for a quarter of a century, to command, and found themselves as much out of their element as Rip van Winkle when he descended from the mountains. " The ships they command are the ones where flogging goes on —men run away before they sail . . . when they are paid off the men riot in all the brutality of unrestrained debauchery."

We have reached the end of our search for the seaman in the pages of fiction. Further, indeed, we might go through many a glowing chapter of enticing adventures in the romances of modern times, but our object has been achieved. There were writers after the Russian War who told the tale of the seaman's buoyant gaiety, humorous simplicity, original temperament, and courage in privation and hardship in the early days of steam. Amongst them was Admiral Hercules Robinson, who was a midshipman at Trafalgar, and who garnered many a yarn in his " Sea Drift," 1858, and told a tale of love, adventure, and treasure-finding in his " Harry Evelyn ; or, Romance of the Atlantic," 1859. Nor should we forget Charles Dickens, whose inimitable Captain Cuttle gives us the living picture of an old-time seaman, with his glazed hat, his proverbial philosophy, and his right arm terminating in a hook. Brave men and true were the old seamen—those alike who walked the quarterdeck and those who were the " undistinguished crew," as Falconer calls them, the " jolly lads " of the ballads, who lived on the lower deck, and worked the ship in conflict with the elements and with the enemies of king and queen.

PART IV

POEMS, BALLADS, SONGS, AND DOGGEREL

CHAPTER XVIII

SEA POETRY: ITS ORIGIN AND USES

I sing the British seamen's praise,
  A theme renowned in story ;
It well deserves more polished lays,
  For 'tis your boast and glory.
When mad-brained war spreads death around,
  By seamen you're protected ;
But when in peace the nation's found,
  These bulwarks are neglected.

NEVER since the vessels of Englishmen first ploughed the seas have the stirring adventures, heroic deeds, and jovial character of our seamen failed to inspire the poet, the balladist, and the song writer. There has been so much of the mysterious and unknown in the seaman's life, so much of tragedy, joy, and humour in his picturesque existence, so many have been his partings and home-comings, so often has he fired the imagination, so often stirred the depths of pathos, so many have listened breathless to his wondrous tales, so many have shared his joys and sorrows, so near has he ever stood to the pulse of national and home life, that pen and pencil could not but find a fruitful theme in his deeds and personality. So it is that the life and occupations of the sea service have had their eloquent story told in a whole cycle of songs and ballads. Thus, too, do we find the pathos and humour of the seaman's existence providing unnumbered subjects for the brush and the pen of the artist. The perils and tribulations by sea and land of Captain Whiffle, Lieutenant Bowling, Mr. Midshipman Easy, Jack Spritsail, and their shipmates, their pleasures and pastimes, their love affairs, with their carousals and merry-makings, have inspired the satirists and caricaturists, and have formed the subject matter of an infinite number of chap-books, song-books, jest-books, garlands, broadsheets, song-slips, and the like.

The seaman's life in the days of oak and hemp and canvas was in a measure a thing apart from, and only partially known to, the landsman. When, therefore, its incidents were chronicled in heroic, humorous, sentimental or pathetic verse, more or less accompanied, too, by pictures, like the poetry itself, very rough at times, but of a high standard of artistic excellence at others, these were assured at once of a wide and popular circulation. To this very circumstance it is doubtless due that the bulk of the class of literature above referred to is now but rarely seen, except in the portfolios of collectors, the libraries of the Universities, or public archives like those of the British Museum.

Only those who have attempted to make a study of nautical life as it is revealed in this particular class of publications can be aware of its deeply interesting, always amusing, and often historically valuable character. It mirrors, as it were, a national development, and throws a vivid sidelight upon that little-known aspect, the social side of the seaman's individuality. His thoughts, his sentiments, his hopes and fears are here pictured in a manner which one may search for in vain in the serious histories, log-books, journals, and biographies of the Navy. Many entertaining anecdotes, it is true, may be found scattered here and there in such volumes, as we have endeavoured to show, but for humour and light-hearted jollity these cannot compare in any way to the song-books, broadsheets, and collections of ballads which were issued for the delectation of Jack and those who admired him over a period of more than two centuries. From this source we get a real insight into the way in which the people of his own class regarded the seaman of their time, and participated in his enjoyments and pleasures, or sympathised with him in his troubles and woes.

Nor was it merely the balladist and writers of lyrics that sang of the sea and the sailor; the poets have written much of a higher quality on the same interesting subjects. Thus the rough life of the sea was not foreign to the soft note of the trouvère, for singing of love and battle, he could not overlook the sailor who has always been conspicuous in both. In the "Roman de la Rose," written about the thirteenth century, one poet, a professional minstrel, had doubtless had his experience of sea life, perhaps during a pilgrimage to the Holy Land, and among other matters relating to the art of the sea he describes the magnet, its attraction to the Pole Star and its use in navigation as he might have seen it on board ship. The song of the Compass, as this portion of the "Roman" is sometimes called, was very possibly used as a chanty by the Mediterranean sailors. Auguste Jal, who made a study of this subject, suggests in his "Archéologie Navale" that the sea language is essentially poetic in its origin, as proved by the easy way in which, however technical, it lends itself to rhythmical treatment. Falconer's poem of "The Shipwreck" certainly lends support to this theory. An Italian poet, Francesco da Barberino, also in the thirteenth century, wrote the "Documenti d'Amore," in which the life and character of the sailors are so aptly and lucidly described that it has been conjectured that Barberino must have been a seaman himself, while Jal enthusiastically declares that no better lesson in the seaman's art of the period can be found than in these verses. So a reflection of the lives of the sailors is found in the pages of the French and Italian poets, and the light of medieval learning cast a beam upon the occupations and character of the men who were concerned in the business of the sea.

It would, indeed, have been strange also, if with a sea-loving nation like ours, the national literature had been poor in this respect; it is not so, but according to the age in which the poet lived and to which the poetry belonged, so the latter is found to reflect what was doubtless the popular view from the landsman's standpoint.

Thus in the Middle Ages it is the incomprehensible nature
of the haunted vastness of the ocean, with its alluring
syrens and other uncanny denizens of its depths, mostly
marvels bred of ignorance and wonder, that determined the poet's outlook and ¦made him shudder at
its unknown terrors.   Nor could he but transfer some
of this suspicion to the mariners who frequented these
waters, and who by their rough and boisterous manners,
even if seeming good fellows, were better kept at arm's
length.   A little later, and while the violence and in-
humanity of the sea, with its variableness, shocked the
poet, the manifestation of its mysteries appealed to his
imagination, and he endowed it with magical islands,
mischievous sprites, and enchanting fairies.   Then, too,
he began to recognise the valour, the hardihood, and the
usefulness of those who dared its perils.   Then there came
a further awakening to the variety of its aspects, to its
utility as a pathway, and to its priceless advantage as
a defensive moat, and the appreciation of the poets is
manifested in many striking passages.   At the same
time, the character of the seamen and their achievements
were celebrated in verse, and the higher literature of
the period exhibited the influence of the sea, while the
nation's pride in its Navy found expression in many
elaborate poems.   But we will not dwell upon this phase
of the subject, which is somewhat outside our scope;
nor need we point out those examples of poetry and
the labour of the poet, even of our own day, which are
coloured by a loathing which suggests that the sea life had
been tried to the derangement of the writer's stomach, and
by a grim recollection of its more discomfiting character.

> Tier above tier, the squalid spectres mourn,
> Heave up their soul, and hug the constant urn !
> Ye streaming flags, dread omens to the foe,
> Ye brazen tubes, dire ministers of woe,
> Ye casks, ye puncheons, stow'd with gen'rous cheer,
> Blocks, cables, cordage, catheads, capstan, hear,
> Blithe cans of flip, and jest-promoting grog,
> And thou, great naval way-wiser, the log,
> While scoff'd, unnerv'd, and spiritless we moan,
> Witness our torments, and attest each groan !

There have been many selections made of naval songs and ballads, many anthologies of nautical poetry and verse, and it is not our purpose to add to the number of such publications. In these pages no attempt has been made to compete with the many excellent collections of naval songs and ballads which have been brought together at various times. From these and many other more recondite sources we have drawn in the endeavour to give a faithful reflection of the character of the seaman in his professional and social aspects, the environment in which he lived, and the conditions of sea life as these are delineated in the national poetry. We have thought it unnecessary to establish a distinction between the two great branches of the sea service, because it is our belief that, certainly up to the end of the great war, there could not have been any broad line of demarcation. Officers and men alike fluctuated between the two services, and must assuredly have taken with them from one to the other whatever they cherished or had a liking for.

That the songs which in more recent times have been called " fore-bitters " and " chanties " were common in the eighteenth century to both the messrooms and forecastles of men-of-war and merchant ships must be manifest to any one who has delved in the byways of our naval literature, and among the work of the chapbook writers and others who catered for all seafaring folk and their well-wishers alike. The verb to chanty is frequently met with in the dramatic and ballad literature of the eighteenth century. A well-known example of its use is found in "The Boatswain's Whistle," that favourite song of Commodore Trunnion's which Pipes sang on a memorable occasion. This ballad is of the same period as that in which John Gay wrote "Black-Eyed Susan," but it does not look like the work of a genuine sailor. It was set to music by Greene and various versions are to be found in the garlands and song-books about the time that Smollett wrote "Peregrine Pickle."

Life is chequer'd—toil and pleasure
Fill up all the various measure :
Hark ! the crew with sun-burnt faces
Chanting Black-eyed Susan's graces.

Chorus : Then hark to the Boatswain's whistle, whistle !
Then hark to the Boatswain's whistle, whistle !
Bustle, bustle, brave boys.
Let us sing, let us toil,
Let us drink all the while,
For labour's the price of our joys,
For labour's the price of our joys.

It would not be wise either that any hard and fast line
should be drawn between the songs written by sailors
and those written by landsmen for them. The former
are comparatively few in number, and the latter were
as a rule the work of poetry and ballad writers who endeavoured to express the sentiments or describe the
exploits of the seamen in language which those they
addressed would understand and appreciate. The greater
proportion of naval ballads begin with an invitation,
" Come, all ye gallant sailormen, give heed unto my tale,"
or something of the kind, thus indicating that they
were intended to be sung by the seaman to his messmates. Such songs were generally descriptive of action
or incident, the woes of lovers, the perils of the seamen
or their heroic exploits. Sentimental or patriotic,
it was much the same to Jack, and a happy conclusion
or a lugubrious ending to one or both of the lovers
seems always to have equally pleased him, although,
perhaps, he had a preference for safety after shipwreck
and victory after battle.

It has been stated, and repeated recently, that the
popularity afloat of the songs of Charles Dibdin was
neither wide nor deep. This charge appears to have
been originally laid in the pages of " Blackwood's
Magazine " some time in the thirties of the last century.
It was sneeringly asserted that such a " tissue of trash "
was never " popular in the galley." These criticisms
at once called forth a stinging reply from a naval officer
in " Colburn's United Service Journal," who, after

pointing out that Christopher North was no sailor,
and therefore no judge from a nautical point of view,
wrote: "We have personally witnessed the hilarity,
contentment, and good feeling disseminated by those
vilified verses, in the merchant service, in the East India
ships and in men-of-war; in ship's galleys and 'tween
decks, in store-rooms and in cockpits; in guard-boats
and in gun vessels; and from habitually hearing, we,
as well as thousands of our Neptunian brethren, have
got most of them 'by heart.' We have heard many
of the best officers in the Service express their conviction
that a spirit of loyal bravery, resignation, and humanity
had been thereby fostered; and that they have been thus
considered by the Naval Administration also is evident
from the boys in the Greenwich Asylum being taught
to sing them."

It is true that Charles Dibdin himself admitted that
for years he never received any public acknowledgment
of his work in the Navy, but he could not have wished
for a more popular appreciation of the merits of his songs
and the worth of the doctrines he endeavoured to
inculcate than is to be found in the following quotation
from the same article in the "United Service Journal":
"Without lauding the whole mass of songs, written by
a man whose bread depended on their daily production,
we think that two or three dozen might be selected,
printed, and distributed by Government with much
better effect than many of the 'tracts' or even the
pamphlet of 'Gazette Letters,' which we remember to
have seen circulated in our fleets. 'Ben Backstay,'
though so flippantly condemned, is in the spirit of
Falconer's beautiful episode of Palemon, which no
bungling Zoilus has yet had the temerity to carp at—
and we have frequently heard seamen singing it with
regard and animation. 'Tom Bowling' is in so fine
a strain of piety, pathos, and melody that it may be
safely recommended as a naval anthem. We cannot
reasonably imagine that Dick Dock's misfortunes which
'ever claim the pity of the brave,' or Bill Bobstay's

never keeping a shot in his locker, when ' by handing it out he can succour a friend,' are repeated by all classes of sailors without producing associations of kindly feelings and a corresponding impression of principles. The ' Venturous Die-hards,' the ' Sailor's Journal,' ' Come all hands ahoy to the anchor,' ' True Courage,' ' Tom Tough,' and the charming strain of ' Lovely Nan,' have saluted our ears on many a Saturday night in Europe and in Africa, in the Atlantic and the Pacific, and, indeed, in various parts of the world, from the Channel to the most remote stations."

There are also many scattered references in naval diaries and letters to the songs which were sung by the men of the ships blockading the French ports, as a relief to the monotony of their life, which lend support to the boast of Dibdin that his songs had been " the solace of sailors in long voyages, in storm, and in battle ; and they have been quoted in mutinies to the restoration of order and discipline."

Another mistake sometimes made is to assume that the seaman objects to his songs having a shore origin ; certainly for more than two hundred years we have evidence that it was from the shore that they came, and that as he gradually discarded those which had pleased his predecessors he accepted the later productions of the landsmen verse writers, which in the eighteenth century generally had a vogue at Covent Garden, Rane-lagh, and places of a like nature before they reached him. It is true also that this circumstance has often been deplored by seamen of finer literary taste and wider culture. Nevertheless, the seaman continues to fashion his choice in this manner upon the popular standard of the moment, and to draw, as his forbears did before him, his songs from the repertoire of the theatre, the concert-room, and the music-hall.

Comprehensive as several of the more recent collections of sea songs have been, whether they cover some special line or range over the whole field of this class of literature, yet from each there are notable omissions, which is not surprising and quite excusable when the enormous mass of lyrics of this character is taken into consideration. Only the collector knows how continually something new is turning up, or some variant of an old friend ; how nearly every sea fight of any importance brought forth its contemporary poem, satire, or ballad, while most of the great naval commanders had their achievements commemorated in classic line or ruder verse. How, too, while the battles and the commanders were thus celebrated, all kinds of sea experiences and nautical misadventures received similar treatment, the stanzas depicting shipwrecks or other catastrophes being of a particularly harrowing kind. The exploits of Jack in Merryland or on Fiddler's Green, his meetings and partings with his sweethearts, Susan, Poll, and Betty, his thoughtfulness for his kindred, his love of home, his woes when pressed or joys when paid off, his faithfulness or inconstancy, his reckless courage and tolerant philosophy, his truth, his affection, and his loyalty, all have been depicted with candid fidelity.

Many of the incidents described in the ballad poetry of the sea were founded on fact, and some of them have been woven into dramas which have touched the hearts and opened the floodgates of emotion in successive generations to whom the original stories were unknown. The later songs, it may be said, were almost invariably illustrated, and sometimes, it must also be admitted, the less polished the verse, the more charming the picture, while conversely the exquisite thoughts of a highly cultured mind may be found accompanied by a crude or even a coarse woodcut. The ballads, printed on slips or loosely stitched together, were sold at the street corners by itinerant hawkers who were not infrequently old or disabled seamen, or who represented themselves to be such.

It has been truly remarked that education and training have as much for their object the formation of character as the imparting of knowledge, and it would be odd if we did not find this fact illustrated in the case of the

sailor. His character, so simple and trustful, yet so full
of audacity and fearlessness, is the direct result of his
training in a school free from the guile of the shore,
tempered by the constant need for preparation against
danger and full of stimulus to action and endeavour.
The conditions of sea life are such that they call for the
qualities of cheerfulness, obedience, comradeship, and
devotion to duty. The sailor's temperament of gaiety
and breezy open disposition was due to the salt savour
of the sea, and his philosophy and tolerance of mind
were bred in a knowledge of the common dangers and
responsibilities inherent in his calling and occupation.
The hardships and privations he underwent aroused
sympathy which found a ready response in his warm
heart; and his simple trustfulness, his hatred of shams
and false colours, the joy of living for a few days in unrestrained liberty leading to that element of boisterousness
in his humour, his generous prodigality, his credulous
folly, and his belief that every woman was an angel.
Over-indulgence he could easily forgive, because he
knew by sad experience what it was to be tempted.
His weaknesses were inebriety, fickleness, and a love of
change, but he could not forgive the man who took
advantage of woman's weakness or another's distress.
His loyalty, his candour, his valour, his physical fitness,
and his readiness of resource were unquestioned, and
the work he did for his country and its cause entitled
him, he thought, to claim a different measure of valuation
from the landsmen, for whom he had a contempt when
they appeared to lack the clear insight which the sailor
had himself for all that concerned his profession. Do
unto others as you expect that they will do unto you,
was his maxim, and he had a short, sharp way of dealing
with his foes. But his prompt response to the call of
patriotism and loyalty or the demands of the unfortunate
were coloured by the spirit of seriousness, the sentiment
of romance—the result of his life's business and the claims
of a brotherhood of peril. We should expect to find
these traits animating the seaman of the old ballads if

they present a faithful reflection of his character, and we shall not be disappointed.

It was the love of adventure inbred in their island nature which called the seamen with irresistible force to a life necessarily of discomfort and deprivation. To these disadvantages were added others, which in olden times, when the wind was the motive power and the ship herself was frequently of uncouth shape and flimsy construction, besides being ill-found in many respects, increased the peril and the chances of disaster. Generally, too, there were disabilities which arose from careless-ness, penury, or other shortcomings on the part of the owner or those responsible for the finding and freighting of the ship, while the mariners themselves contributed not a little by their want of foresight and shiftlessness to a similar result. Moreover, the food was bad, the emolument small, and the punishment for breaches of discipline severe in the extreme. Truth to tell, the sailor's life from many causes was one of danger at all times. The circumstance that it was spent mainly upon an unstable element, subject to changes and chances of many kinds, and beset with liabilities from which those who live ashore are free, made it one of extraordinary hazard and danger. It is small wonder that the feeling of the sailors should have crystallised into a proverb, "Those who would go to sea for pleasure would go to hell for pastime."

Yet in spite of these adverse conditions the attractions of the sea life, especially to the young, invariably out-weighed its dangers and disadvantages. Once a sea-man, also, always a seaman. The adventurous spirit, a thirst for discovery, and even greed of gain, were among the motives which have contributed in the past to supply our marine, both mercantile and military, with suitable material for the making of sailors. And whatever may have been the motives which attracted the youth of the nation and its more daring spirits to a naval life, to these we owe the development, the ex-pansion, and the vastness of the Empire.

2 A

We get an indication of the adventurous spirit which
inspired the seamen of the Elizabethan period in " A
ballad in Praise of Seafaring Men " (Sloane MSS., 2497,
folio 47), where we read :—

> To pass the seas some think a toil,
> Some think it strange abroad to roam ;
> Some think it grief to leave their soil,
> Their parents, kinfolk, and their home,
> Think so who list, I like it not ;
> I must abroad to try my lot.

From a note to this ballad it seems probable that it
was written about 1585, but the same spirit is found in
a song which, according to Smollett, was popular in
the Navy 150 years later. When Lieutenant Thomas
Bowling wanted to persuade his nephew, Roderick
Random, to become a seafarer he quoted from this
verse from an old English opera entitled " Perseus and
Andromeda " :—

> How pleasant a sailor's life passes,
>   Who roams o'er the watery main :
> No treasure he ever amasses,
>   But cheerfully spends all his gain.
> We're strangers to party and faction,
>   To honour and honesty true,
> And would not commit a base action
>   For power or profit in view.
> Then why should we quarrel for riches,
>   Or any such glittering toys?
> A light heart and a thin pair of breeches
>   Goes through the world, my brave boys.

At a much later date two anonymous writers illustrate
in a somewhat similar manner the pleasures of a seafaring life.   One sings :—

> How blest are we seamen ! how jovial and gay !
> Together we fight, or together we play ;
> Our hearts are true sterling—-their worth shall be seen ;
> We'll fight for our country, and die for our Queen !

While the other tells how :—

> On burning coasts, or frozen seas,
>   Alike in each extreme,
> The gallant sailor's e'er at ease,
>   And floats with fortune's stream.

There was a further inducement offered to the sailor in the plunder or prize-money which might fall to his lot. Falconer writes :—

> Can sons of Neptune, generous, brave, and bold,
> In pain and hazard toil for sordid gold?
> They can ! for gold too oft, with magic art,
> Subdues each nobler impulse of the heart.

One picture to be found in this volume shows the true British tar gloating over the money he has made in his voyages, and this aspect finds expression in several of the ballads. In another slip song in a private collection, entitled "The Bold Blades of Old England," we find :—

> Come, rouse up, my lads, let us haste to the main,
> And load home our chests with the dollars of Spain,
> For as we have beat them we'll do so again,
>   And it's, Oh ; the Bold Blades of Old England !

It is noteworthy that at all times in our naval history there were plenty of men ready to ship with a captain who they believed would give them a chance of meeting the enemy. A smart frigate would get her crew when the line-of-battle ship preparing for the blockade service might take months in finding a sufficient company. Even at the time of the Russian War in 1854 no difficulty was experienced in manning the ships to go up the Baltic under Sir Charles Napier, whose gallantry and daring made him popular with the seamen ; whereas the authorities were at their wits' ends to man those for the Black Sea, where service did not hold out the promise of similar excitement. In the old days, too, there were the spirit of revenge, religious animosity, and hate and fear, in addition to patriotic ardour as incentives. In "The Boatswain's Call" (Roxburghe Ballads, III, p. 463), published in the reign of William III, the writer strikes a popular chord by appealing to the natural detestation of Louis, the French King, who desired to "lay a heavy yoke on the free nation," so he invites his brother sailors to forsake friends and relatives in order to fight in the defence of their king and country.

Therefore with courage bold, boys, let us venture ;
Like noble hearts of gold now freely enter
Your names on board the fleet, all friends forsaking,
That we may soon complete this undertaking.

Although, too, impressment was regarded as a hardship by some, there were at all times many others who
regarded it as necessary and essential to the maintenance
of an effective fleet. In "The Sailor's Resolution to
fight the Spaniards " (a slip song), the first verse reads :—

What ship, honest brother Sailor ? You must stop and let us know,
If you're entered or protected, you must tell before you go.
Here's our warrants to impress you. Ne'er repine, my noble blood ;
We don't mean for to oppress you ; it's for your King and Country's
    good.

Then also the feeling of the feminine portion of the
public in the matter about the date of the battles of
Beachy Head and Barfleur is possibly shown by the
ballad entitled "The Maidens' Frolic" (Roxburghe
Ballads, III, p. 402). The first verse has already been
quoted (page 197) ; this is the second :—

Young Nancy she ty'd a sword by her side,
And she was resolved for to be their guide :
This young female crew, Kate, Bridget, and Prue,
And she that went formost was Lieutenant Sue,
    Pressing taylors.

It may be noted that the rhythm requires the rank
of the young lady to be pronounced "Lootenant."
The maidens, we are told, to the cry of " You must serve
King and Queen," eventually pressed fourteen nimble
young fellows, " And all taylors." But the songs about
impressment more often deal with its hardships. It is
easy to understand how from a dramatic point of view
the forcing of a lover away from his sweetheart on the
point of marriage, or the cruelty of taking a man who
had just come back from a long voyage, expecting to
visit home and his friends, and pressing him to sea again,
possibly with the loss of his hard-earned pay, would
appeal to the public sympathy. Thus we find an anonymous writer singing :—

> Sam Sailyard loved Sally, the girl of his heart,
>   And Sall dearly loved him again;
> How hard that a couple so faithful should part,
>   Or either experience a pain!
> But Sam to misfortune was truly allied,
>   A pressgang beset him on shore,
> As coming from church, where he'd made her his bride,
>   And Sam saw his Sally no more.

Not only in England, but in Scotland and Ireland, we have similar incidents. Thus in a Scotch song we are told that :—

> Young Sandy was pressed from his Alice's side,
>   As they strayed to converse in the dale,
> And Sandy was wooing the maid as his bride,
>   When the gang stopped his amorous tale.

The pathetic Irish ballad, also, entitled "On Shannon's Flowery Banks" has been quoted with the plate on page 350. It seems a little inconsistent on the part of the writer of the following doleful verses that he should have added the chorus: "Sing too rol lo," etc. :—

> Oh! cruel were my parents to tear my love from me,
> And cruel were the press-gang that took him off to sea,
> And cruel was the little boat that row'd him from the strand,
> And cruel was the great big ship that sailed from the land.
>
> Oh! cruel was the water that bore her love from Mary,
> And cruel was the fair wind that would not blow contrary;
> And cruel was the captain, the boatswain and the men,
> Who didn't care a farthing if we ever met again.

In another song the writer treats the matter in a still more jocular vein, alluding to the tender to which all the pressed men were taken before being transhipped to vessels on active service :—

> Says he, they're only taking him
>   To the tender ship, you see,
> The tender ship, cried Sally Brown,
>   What a hardship that must be.

But the humorous or burlesque treatment of the subject belongs probably to a much later date than those songs which were written when the action of the

press was a very real grievance, and was a terror to the
seamen returning home from a long voyage.

> For oft, when they have gained their coast,
>   Expecting every peril o'er,
> All hands are pressed, again they're forced
>   To sea, and leave their native shore.

" Horrid work ! " says one who both saw and experienced the action of the press-gang. " People may
talk of negro slavery and the whip, but let them look
nearer home, and see a poor sailor arrived from a long
voyage, exulting in the pleasure of soon being amongst
his dearest friends and relations. Behold him just
entering the door, when a press-gang seizes him like
a felon, drags him away and puts him into the tender's
hold, and from thence he is sent on board a man-of-war,
perhaps ready to sail to some foreign station, without
seeing either his wife, friends, or relations ; if he complains he is likely to be seized up and flogged with a cat,
much more severe than the negro driver's whip, and if
he deserts he is flogged round the fleet nearly to death. . . .
It may be said that England cannot do without pressing.
Be it so ; but then let it be done in a more equitable
manner, and let sailors arriving from long voyages have
liberty a month or more to spend their money and enjoy
themselves with their friends ; then I will be bound to
say they will endure pressing with more patience, be
better satisfied, and not so ready to desert."

That the press was utilised for private purposes by
wives who wanted to get rid of their husbands, lovers
of their rivals, and masters of their apprentices, also
finds proof in the ballads. In " The Lighterman's
Prentice Prest and Sent to Sea " we have an example.
It begins :—

> A prentice I was at Wapping-new-stairs,
> And a smart young lad was I ;
> But that old blackguard old W——d,
> He inform'd, and had forty shillings for me,
> It was on the last day of February,
> In the year of fifty-five :
> He had me taken out of bed ;

When my friends heard it, lord ! how they cry'd.
My mother and my cousin both
They on board of the tender came with speed,
And thro' the grates to them I talk'd,
It was enough to make any heart to bleed.

   *   *   *   *

And now, my lads, we're come to an harbour,
We can go to rest with great content.
So all young men that row in the lighters,
Keep yourselves free from a press-gang.
And whenever you come athwart old W——d
For my sake give him a hearty damn.

It is not surprising, then, that we should find the lady lamenting in another slip song called " The Sailor Laddie " :—

Oh ! I wish the press was over,
And all the wars was at an end ;
Then every bonnie sailor laddie
Would be merry with his friend.

It is doubtful if many or even if any of these songs about impressment were ever sung on board ships of war. Some of them may have been, as a doleful ditty seems to have been far from unpopular on the forecastle. But they have an interest apart from this in so far as they enable the reader to realise what life in the seaports was like in past times, and the influences that helped to form the seaman's character. In spite of this unpopular method of raising men, we yet find the lower deck ringing with the chorus to Harry Hawser's song :—

A sailor I've been, and have ploughed the salt sea, sir,
And, of all sorts of lives, still a sailor's for me, sir.

It was not on the whole the action of the press that made volunteers scarce so much as the severe discipline, the badness of the provisions, and the trouble the seaman experienced in getting his hard-earned wages owing to the villainies of the pursers and the rogueries of the pay clerks. But this is another story, too long to be dealt with at the end of a chapter.

CHAPTER XIX

BALLADS AND POETRY OF SEA SERVICE

Would you know, pretty Nan, how we pass our time
While we sailors are tossed on the sea?

AN attractive section of nautical poetry is that which presents the seaman engaged in his occupation and handling his ship, or exhibits a vivid picture of the vicissitudes of his calling. We get in both the ballads and the more important poems sketches of the sea service showing the ever-varying nature of the sailor's duty, how in the enjoyment of fine weather or battling with the elements he employed his time, how he caroused when the wind was fair or when it was foul, rose to the occasion and ofttimes performed the most stirring or heroic acts. Apart from the discipline of the Service, the discipline of the sea was always upon him. In the execution of his work it was often necessary to leave something to his own initiative, and he was frequently called upon for the exercise of his own wit and discretion, since not only his own life, but that of his shipmates might depend upon his efforts. So he was perforce resourceful, and became possessed of both mental and physical nimbleness, self-reliant, and skilled in the essentials of his art and craft. We shall here observe him exhibiting his frank and breezy personality engaged in duties afloat, accompany him during the incidents of a voyage at sea, learn about his grievances and troubles, and discover the characteristic traits of the typical tar.

All the balladists and song writers are particularly strong upon the subject of the preparation for departure, "hoisting the Blue Peter," and "all hands ahoy to the anchor." As in one of his well-known songs, Charles Dibdin writes :—

> The boatswain calls, the wind is fair ;
>   The anchor heaving,
>   Our sweethearts' leaving,
> We to our duty must repair.

It was ever the care of Dibdin to inculcate the hearty performance of duty in all circumstances. But a reason why there should be no reluctance at leaving, and the general delight which is supposed to inspire the crew, appear in another song. They expect to do some fighting.

> Huzza ! a gun—the signal's made,
> All hands on board, the anchor's weighed.
>   *   *   *   *
> So off again we scud, to lick the saucy foe.

Still more pronounced is the enthusiasm produced by the sailing orders in a song, said to have been written by Mr. Sheridan for a pantomime produced at Drury Lane in 1781, a song which, though the work of a landsman, became a great favourite afloat, and may even now be heard when the seamen give a musical entertainment or " sing-song " on board a man-of-war.

> Come, come, my jolly lads !
>   The wind's abaft :
> Brisk gales our sails shall crowd ;
> Come, bustle, bustle, bustle, boys,
>   Hoist the boat ;
> The boatswain pipes aloud ;
>   The ship's unmoor'd ;
>   All hands on board ;
>   The rising gale
>   Fills every sail
> The ship's well mann'd and stor'd.

> Chorus : Then sling the flowing bowl—
>   Fond hopes arise—
>   The girls we prize
> Shall bless each jovial soul :
>   The can, boys, bring—
>   We'll drink and sing,
> While foaming billows roll.

Songs of this character, it may be recalled, were not infrequent in the musical sketches played at the theatres during the last half of the eighteenth century. One by Cumberland begins :—

> Hark ! the whistle is heard,
> "All hands" is the word,
> Bustle, bustle, boys ! up and away !
> Lo, the anchor is free,
> The ship swings to the sea,
> Huzzah ! for Old England, huzzah !

And another, by Pearce, a little later in date, is even fuller in detail. One and all depict the sailor as rather relieved at leaving the shore again, seeing that he is likely to have some excitement in meeting the enemy, and that his pleasure finds vent in singing when the grog is served out.

> Blue Peter at the masthead flew,
> And to the girls we bade adieu,
>   Weighed anchor and made sail ;
> The boatswain blew his whistle shrill,
> The reefs, shook out, began to fill,—
> We caught a fav'ring gale.
>   And, with a can of flip,
>   To cheer the honest tar,
>   Thus, gaily, may he trip,
>   Tra, la, la, la !

In all these songs the boatswain is referred to as the officer directing the execution of an order given by the captain or lieutenant, the part played by this functionary being not only important, but essentially striking and picturesque. The boatswain with his pipe or call would give the first summoning whistle which drew the attention of his mates in the various parts of the ship, and brought the crew, as it were, to attention. Then the call for " All hands " filled the ship with echoing whistles and the hoarse shouts of the boatswain's mates. And finally came the explanatory order, " Hands shorten in cable." It was not desirable to lift the anchor at once, because sail had first to be put upon the ship, and only when the topsails were loosed and sheeted home, and all was prepared by the trimming of the yards for " casting," was the anchor weighed from its bed and run up to the bows as quickly as possible ; there to be " catted," " fished," and secured for sea. In a much older ballad than those just quoted, " The Jolly Sailor's True Description of a Man-of-War," which from an illustrated copy in a private collection we should date early in the eighteenth century, some detailed description of the operations of weighing the anchor and making sail is given :—

> " All hands, unmoor," the boatswain calls,
> And he pipes at every hatchway ;
> If you Tom Coxswain's traverse tip him
> Take care he don't catch ye ;
> For without a doubt, if he finds you out,
> You may be sure within ye,
> Over face and eyes, to your surprise
> He'll warm you without mercy.
>
> The capstan is already mann'd.
> Shall we hear the boatswain hollow ?
> Sometimes he is listening at a stand
> To hear the answers follow.
> We have now "brought to," there's much ado,
> While some are calling swabbers.
> Now "heave away" without delay,
> And boys, hold on the nippers.
>
> *   *   *   *
>
> " Heave and in sight, men ; heave away !"
> From for'ard the boatswain's calling ;
> " Heave a turn or two without delay ;
> Stand by the capstan for pawling."
> Then one and all to the catt do fall :
> We haul both strong and able,
> Till presently for'ard they cry,
> " Below, stick out the cable."
>
> We "catt" our anchor then with speed,
> And nimbly pass the stopper,
> Then next to "fish" it, we proceed :
> With shank-painter so proper,
> Which we do pass securely fast,
> And lap well on a seizing.
> Our anchors, be sure, can't be too secure ;
> It stands to sense and reason.

When once our ship she is unmoor'd
Our swelling sails set neatly,
The fore-tack's down, the main-tack too,
The sheets haul'd aft completely,
Then away we sail with a nimble gale,
On a voyage or to a station.
Like English hearts, we'll play our parts
In defence of the English nation.

There are one or two expressions here that may need explanation. The " nippers " were pieces of soft rope by which the cable was secured to the " messenger," an endless hawser, which passed round and revolved with the capstan, and to which the cable was " nippered " and thus dragged in. The " pawls " were the iron tongues at the foot of the capstan which, dropped into shoes, prevented it from running back. The " cat " was the tackle which, hooked on to the ring of the anchor, would bring it up to the cat-head. Here it hung up and down, so the fish tackle was then hooked on to the crown in order to pull it into a horizontal position and admit of the " shank-painter " as well as the " cat stopper " being secured. It would be interesting to learn the origin of the expression " Tom Coxswain's traverse," but we can throw no light on this point, although its meaning is clear enough. It is noticeable that in the earlier ballad no reference is made to the " Blue Peter," and, indeed, it was not until Rodney and Howe commanded fleets that the blue flag with a white square in it, which about that time was known as the Blue Peter, became the signal for a general recall of all officers and men to their ships. The hoisting of this flag first at the main, and afterwards at the fore, was usually accompanied by loosing the fore-topsail and firing a gun, the three signals together being a notification that all communication with the shore was to cease and that the fleet would put to sea. We have never yet seen it explained how the flag came by its appellation, but possibly some officer called or nicknamed Peter was in the habit of using it very frequently, so that in the minds of the sailors it became associated with his name.

The beautiful picture which the ship presented when under all sail, with her flying royals sweeping the skies, has been an inspiration to many poetical writers; but it is doubtful if any landsman could have the same appreciation of the delightful feeling to the sailor of his vessel when with all her canvas spread, and gliding through the water, she became almost a sentient being obedient to the slightest touch of the helm. In D'Urfey's "Wit and Drollery" there is a song by a sailor in praise of his ship and her appearance when under sail, when all the canvas is rap full, and the vessel lies over to the breeze. Nothing, indeed, was more characteristic of the capable seaman than the pride he took in his ship. He rated her even higher than his sweetheart, for whose charms he had ever apt similes drawn from the elements and qualities of his favourite craft. Says this old sailor :—

'Tis brave to see a ship to sail
    With all her trim gear on-a,
As though the Devil were at her tail
    She with the wind will run-a.

Lord Byron too :—

She walks the waters like a thing of life,
And seems to dare the elements to strife.
Who would not brave the battle fire, the wreck,
To move the monarch of her peopled deck?

A later writer, not a sailor, but similarly inspired, exclaims :—

Is she not beautiful! her graceful bow
    Triumphant rising o'er the enamoured tides,
That, glittering in the noon-day sunbeam, now
    Just leap and die along her polished sides.
        *   *   *
A thousand eyes are on her; for she floats
    Confess'd a queen upon the subject main.

The ship under way, all that was needed was a fair wind in order that she might lay her course and that those on board might shake down in their places. Nowadays, when steam has made the seaman independent of the wind, it is perhaps difficult for him to realise the delight it must have been to his wind-bound predecessor

when a change took place, and the ship could put to
sea, or when, homeward bound, a favouring gale succeeded the headwinds and calms that kept the sailor
from the port of his desire. It was not strange that in
these circumstances a fair wind was greeted with three
cheers, or that intense pleasure was excited when they
could sing :—

> But see the wind draws kindly aft,
>   All hands are up the yards to square,
> And now the swelling stu'n-sails waft
>   Our steady ship through waves and air.

In still another ballad we get an inkling of the attitude
of the seaman towards the landsman afloat, and his but
half-concealed amusement and contempt at the discomfort of the latter. Here is a verse in which the contrast is vividly presented :—

> When we sail with a fresh'ning breeze,
>   And landmen all grow sick, sir ;
> The sailor lolls with his mind at ease,
>   And the song and the can go quick, sir.
>   Laughing here,
>   Quaffing there,
>   Steadily, readily,
>   Cheerily, merrily,
> Still from care and thinking free,
> Is a sailor's life at sea.

In what is perhaps the oldest sea song extant, a song
manifestly written by a sailor, we have a picture of life
at sea and the sea customs on board a vessel in the
reign of Henry VI, engaged to carry pilgrims to Compo-
stella. This vessel and her crew might have been among
those whose action was commemorated in Hardyng's
chronicle and recorded in the Libel of English Policy,
quoted by Hakluyt. It was a time of naval decay, and
English commerce suffered from the neglect to guard
the narrow seas, but such a vessel would in any case
be armed so as to be able to defend herself against
pirates, and was frequently hired or taken up by the
King for service against the country's enemies. Although
quite half a century later than Chaucer's date, there had
not been any great change in the seamanship during the

interval, and we are justified in assuming that the
master of this pilgrim ship was not unlike in character
the poet's Shipman. The miseries of the pilgrims were
made the subject of rude jokes, but the seamen were
sufficiently good fellows to see that their passengers
were provided with victuals, and that such accommodation for them was found as the ship could supply.

It is, however, the apt description of the handling of
the ship by the sailors, and the portrayal of sea life,
that makes the song of " The Voyage of the Pilgrims "
particularly interesting. Here is a somewhat modernised
version of four of the verses :—

> Anon the mastyr commandeth fast
> To his shyp-men, in all haste,
> To dresse hem sone about the mast
>   Theyr takeling to make.
> With "howe, hissa!" then they cry :
> "What howe, mate, thou stondyst to ny ;
> Thy fellow may not hale thereby !"
>   Thus they begyn to crake.
>
> A boy or tweyn anone up styen,
> And overt-whart the sayle-yerde lyen :
> "Y how talya!" the remenaunt cryen,
>   And pull with all theyr myght.
> " Bestowe the bote, bote-swayne, anon,
> That our pylgryms may pley thereon,
> For some ar lyke to cowgh and grone
>   Or hit be ful mydnyght.
>
> "Hale the bowelyne! Now, vere the shete !
> Coke, make redy anon our mete.
> Our pylgryms have no lust to ete :
>   I pray God give hem rest.
> Go to the helm ! What howe ! No nere?
> Steward, felow, a pot of bere !"
> "Ye shall have, ser, with good chere
>   Anon, all of the best."
>
> "Y howe ! Trussa ! Hale in the brayles !
> Thow halyst not ! Be God ! Thow fayles !
> O ! se howe well owre good shyp sayles !"
>   And thus they say among.
> " Hale in the vare take !" " Hit shall be done !"
> "Steward, cover the borde anon,
> And set bred and salt thereon,
>   And tary not to long."

The whole song will be found in most modern collections, and it was printed by Halliwell in his " Early Naval Ballads " from a MS. in the Library of Trinity College, Cambridge. The master commands the men to bustle and get clear the ropes and tackling for making sail. Then he tells them to hoist the yard, and as the men on the halliards are too closely packed, standing too near one another, he instructs them to take more room in order that they may get their full weight upon the rope. A couple of boys are sent aloft to lay over the yard and to overhaul the brails so that the sail falls clear while the remainder of the men haul aft the sheet. Then the big boat is got on board, stowed amidships, and secured so that some of the pilgrims may get into it before they become too sick to move and encumber the decks. In later times the big boat was frequently used for the stowage of live stock. Next, as the ship is on a wind, the bowline is hauled to taughten the weather leech of the sail, but in order to steady the ship, as it is time for dinner, the sheet is eased off a little. The master cautions the man at the wheel to keep the sails full, " No higher," he says (" No nere "), do not bring the ship any nearer the wind. After trimming the yard he sees to the trusses, the ropes which secured the yard to the mast, and orders another pull of the " vare take," or the preventer fore tack on the weather clew of the sail. Now all is secure. He is pleased with the way in which the good ship sails, and can devote himself to making the pilgrims as comfortable as possible in the circumstances. These are already feeling unwell, and one complains of his head splitting. The owner, or supercargo, of the ship orders straw for their beds, and temporary cabins to be prepared. But unfortunately for them they cannot escape the smell of the bilge water, a testimony to the staunchness of the vessel.

But sailors cannot always expect to have a fair wind, and in another garland of song we find a description of the occurrences on board when it becomes necessary to meet the new circumstances. The writer of this ballad, who tells us that he was born on 14th June, 1705, suggests, like the author of " A True Description of a Man-of-War," that he was beguiled into choosing a sea life in the belief that it would be altogether delightful. Admitting that he has been to some extent disenchanted, he still holds that it has its pleasures, and although he will not allow that these outweigh the disadvantages, yet he acknowledges that the delights of the shore after a long voyage are appreciated by seamen in a manner which no landsman can hope to participate.

When I grew up they asked me,
"What trade must we prepare for thee?"
My answer was to them again,
"I mean to range the roaring sea;"
My whimsic brain did falsely show
The pleasures men enjoy at sea,
But oh, the sorrow, grief, and woe,
They suffer in extremity.

＊　　＊　　＊　　＊

When we are on the roaring main,
The wind right aft, a pleasant gale,
We have our wish and heart's desire,
'Tis then we spread a crowd of sail;
Our mainsail hauled up in the brails,
Our foresail drives us cleanly through,
Then topsails and top-gallant sails
We hoist and make a gallant show.

＊　　＊　　＊　　＊

The wind won't stand, I am afraid,
It beareth forward still, I see,
Get the fore tack to the cat head
And ride it down with a passaree;＊
Down studding sails, from up aloft,
And lay them in the tops awhile,
Then hoist your staysails fore and aft,
And trim your sails all to the gale.

Oh, now she'll hardly lie her course,
'Tis better get our tacks aboard,
Our sheets close aft and bowlines hauled,
And all things handily prepared;

＊　　＊　　＊　　＊

＊ The " passaree" of the eighteenth century was the " vare take" of the twelfth century; a tackle for taughtening the weather leech of the foresail.

2 B

Three single reefs in each topsail
And then we'll furl them, 'tis agreed,
So bear a hand, my hearts of gold,
And make haste down with nimble speed ;
So see the geers cleared fore and aft,
The down-haul tackles hook'd also,
And all things readily prepared
Both up aloft and here below.

*　　*　　*　　*

A good hand stand to the main sheet,
And see all clear to let her fly ;
It looks as thick as buttermilk,
And will be with us by and by ;
So hard-a-weather goes the helm,
Let fly your main sheet now with speed,
The furious squall will soon be o'er,
It breaks apace you may perceive.

*　　*　　*　　*

The down haul tackles must be manned,
Clew garnets, bowlines, leech-lines too,
Loose off the sheet, let rise the tack ;
Come now, my boys, and lift her clew ;
Belay of all, secure the yards,
And up aloft and furl him snug,
Coil up your ropes and then lay aft ;
All hands to tipple the nut-brown jug.

*　　*　　*　　*

We're near to port, the sailors cry,
I see the spire beyond the rocks.
At anchor very soon we'll lie,
Delivered from the ocean's shocks.
With good rum punch we'll play our part,
With pretty girls we'll love to be.
We're never rightly satisfied
But when in their sweet company.

This ballad is very long, and contains twenty-five verses full of life and movement. It is obviously based on the personal experiences of the writer, one who has himself seen and can describe vividly the incidents of a sea-faring life and the occupations of the seamen. For professional detail it deserves in some respects to be compared with Falconer's poem, " The Shipwreck." Almost every occurrence described by Falconer finds its parallel in the ballad, although the former ends with a catastrophe, while in the latter the ship, after losing her main and mizen masts, is brought safely into port. In order that the reader may compare the two descriptions, we now give an extract from Falconer's poem.

It may be mentioned that Falconer served his apprenticeship at sea in a merchant vessel, and had actually suffered shipwreck in the Mediterranean. It was this event, no doubt, and the impression created on his mind, which led him to write the poem, the main subject of which is the loss of a ship called the *Britannia*, a merchantman bound from Alexandria to Venice, which met with a violent storm that drove her on the coast of Greece, where she was wrecked, three only of the crew being saved. After a third edition of the poem had been published in 1769, Falconer sailed as the purser of the *Aurora* for India, but after touching at the Cape the ship was never heard of again.

It is at the time when the *Britannia* is driven out of her course by a furious squall, and the wind still increases in strength, that the following description occurs:—

Fierce and more fierce the gathering tempest grew,
South, and by West, the threatening demon blew ;
Auster's resistless force all air invades,
And every rolling wave more ample spreads :
The ship no longer can her top-sails bear ;
No hopes of milder weather now appear.
Bowlines and halliards are cast off again,
Clue-lines hauled down, and sheets let fly amain :
Embrailed each top-sail, and by braces squar'd,
The seamen climb aloft, and man each yard ;
They furled the sails, and pointed to the wind
The yards, by rolling tackles then confin'd,
While o'er the ship the gallant boatswain flies ;
Like a hoarse mastiff through the storm he cries,
Prompt to direct th' unskilful still appears,
Th' expert he praises, and the timid cheers.
Now some, to strike top-gallant yards attend,
Some, trav'llers up the weather back-stays send,
At each mast-head the top ropes others bend :
The parrels, lifts, and clue-lines soon are gone,
Topped and unrigged, they down the backstays run ;
The yards secure along the booms were laid,
And all the flying ropes aloft belay'd :

Their sails reduced, and all the rigging clear,
Awhile the crew relax from toils severe.

*   *   *   *

The ship no longer can whole courses bear,
To reef them now becomes the master's care ;
The sailors, summoned aft, all ready stand,
And man th' enfolding brails at his command :
And here the doubtful officers dispute,
Till skill, and judgment, prejudice confute :
For Rodmond, to new methods still a foe,
Would first, at all events, the sheet let go ;
To long-tried practice obstinately warm,
He doubts conviction, and relies on form.
This Albert and Arion disapprove,
And first to brail the tack up firmly move :
"The watchful seaman, whose sagacious eye
On sure experience may with truth rely,
Who from the reigning cause foretells th' effect,
This barbarous practice ever will reject ;
For, fluttering loose in air, the rigid sail
Soon flits to ruins in the furious gale ;
And he, who strives the tempest to disarm,
Will never first embrail the lee yard-arm."
So Albert spoke ; to windward, at his call,
Some seamen the clue-garnet stand to haul—
The tack's eased off, while the involving clue
Between the pendent blocks ascending flew ;
The sheet and weather-brace they now stand by,
The lee clue-garnet, and the bunt-lines ply ;
Then, all prepared, " Let go the sheet ! " he cries—
Loud rattling, jarring, through the blocks it flies !
Shivering at first, till by the blast impelled ;
High o'er the lee yard-arm the canvas swell'd ;
By spilling lines embraced, with brails confin'd,
It lies at length unshaken by the wind.
The foresail then secured with equal care,
Again to reef the mainsail they repair ;
While some above the yard o'er-haul the tye,
Below, the down-haul tackles others ply ;
Jears, lifts and brails, a seaman each attends,
And down the masts, its mighty yard descends ;
When lower'd sufficient, they securely brace,
And fix the rolling tackle in its place ;
The reef-lines and their earings now prepared,
Mounting on pliant shrouds, they man the yard :
Far on the extremes appear two able hands,
For no inferior skill this task demands,—
To windward, foremost, young Arion strides,
The lee yard-arm, the gallant boatswain rides :

Each earing to its cringle first they bend,
The reef band then along the yard extend ;
The circling earings round th' extremes entwin'd,
By outer and by inner turns they bind ;
The reef-lines next from hand to hand received,
Through eyelet-holes and roban-legs were reeved ;
The folding reefs in plaits inrolled they lay,
Extend the worming lines, and ends belay.

There can be no doubt that Falconer, in the verse where he speaks of the officers disputing, does not wish us to understand that this discussion could actually take place at such a moment, but he desires to exhibit the obstinacy of the older officer, who, by adhering to rule of thumb, had already split the mainsail, and to contrast with this the more scientific method of the mate, who took the new sail off the ship without injuring it. The relative wisdom and expediency of the two methods remained a matter of dispute, it may be said, quite up to the time when sails disappeared from our men-of-war. It may be noted that in the ballad the sailor let fly his mainsheet, but apparently more by luck than good management the sail, in the instance he describes, was not blown away. The gradual rising of the gale, the appearance of the sea and sky, at such a time, the efforts of the mariners, the gradual closing in of the night, are all finely described by Falconer. But we will take from a very different kind of poem, " The Adventures of Johnny Newcome in the Navy," by Alfred Burton, published in 1818, a work that will be mentioned again—another description, because it gives the view of the lately-joined midshipman. This hero, having kept the second dog-watch from six to eight, has turned in, and in spite of a leak which perpetually dripped over his head, and the noise of the pumps, has fallen asleep. All too soon he is called by the quartermaster to turn out for the morning watch.

He crawled up to the Quarter-deck,
There, by the life-lines held on fast,
And stared astonished and aghast ;
The foaming seas, the roaring wind,
The hail and lightning, all combined ;

The ship that sometimes seemed to rise
As if she'd pierce the sable skies,
Now down the black abyss to glide,
Now hang suspended on its side,
Amazed him !—Every lurch she gave
The gangways rolled beneath the wave,
And large blue seas each other chased,
Cascading over down the waist.—
At every pitch he held his breath
As if he saw the face of death ;—
Amidst the roar there came a crash,—
"She's pitched away a Top-mast, smash !"
All hands to clear away the wreck,
Were in an instant turned on deck ;
From hammock starting out alert,
Up flew each seaman in his shirt !
John said it really did him good
To see their reckless hardihood ;
—And up the straining shrouds they swarm,
Growling and swearing at the storm—
The wreck secured, or cut away,
She snug beneath a trysail lay.—

In another part of this poem it is told how Johnny was fishing out of the jolly-boat hanging at the stern when his lead swung into the cabin windows.

The Captain's bell that instant rung,
John overboard his tackle flung ;
And off, to 'scape the masthead, slunk
Down the lee ladder in a funk !
The Captain twigged him as he traced
"Tom Coxe's traverse" through the waist,
And gave him only a jobation,
His greenness proving his salvation.—

Burton's note to this is : " Tom Coxe was certainly either some great lawyer, or great navigator, for his traverse has become proverbial," so he had probably never seen "The Jolly Sailor's True Description of a Man-of-war."

A storm at sea influenced the imagination of a poet of a far different calibre from Burton. Dr. John Donne, sometime Dean of St. Paul's, in his early life made the Island Voyage with the Earl of Essex, the expedition to the Azores in 1597. This expedition was unsuccessful, and, moreover, it appears to have been uniformly attended by bad weather. It had no sooner left Plymouth than it was forced to put back by adverse gales; on the second attempt it was again in trouble in the Bay of Biscay, and after leaving the Azores the fleet was once more dispersed by a violent gale. It is not surprising, therefore, that Donne found this aspect of the sea life "desolate and horrible," and in "The Storm" he writes of his own experiences :—

> Thousands our voices were, yet we 'mongst all
> Could none by his right name, but thunder, call.
> Light'ning was all our light, and it rained more
> Than if the sun had drunk the sea before.
>
>   *   *   *   *
>
> Then note they the ship's sicknesses, the mast
> Shaked with an ague, and the hold and waist
> With a salt dropsy clogged, and all our tacklings
> Snapping, like too-too-high-stretched treble strings.
> And from out tattered sails rags drop down so,
> As from one hanged in chains a year ago.
> Even our ordnance, placed for our defence,
> Strives to break loose, and 'scape away from thence.
> Pumping hath tired our men, and what's the gain?
> Seas into seas thrown, we suck in again;
> Hearing hath deaf'd our sailors, and if they
> Knew how to hear, there's none knows what to say.

Donne's poems, however, contain reference to the sea in other moods, and in the companion poem, "The Calm," he presents a somewhat different picture. It is to be remarked also that he used the imagery of the sea and the experiences of a sailor in a voyage of discovery to describe his exploration of the charms of his mistress, from which it is to be inferred that he found the "fair Atlantic" not altogether so disagreeable, or such "a scourge" as other passages from his works might seem to indicate. In "The Progress of the Soul," he compares a goodly white swan gliding through the water with stately motion, to a ship in her full trim; nor has he missed "the careful eye of the lusty seaman."

Before leaving this phase of sea life, which shows us the mariner as a prime seaman, master of his craft, another ballad of the sixteenth century may be quoted

which might very well have been written by one of the
many volunteers who adventured in the voyages and
expeditions of the period. The writer was certainly a
seaman, and as certainly from his use of the classical
mythology a scholar, but the combination was not at all
uncommon, as we have shown in previous sections of this
volume.

> I rue to see the raging of the seas,
> When nothing may king Eolus' wrath appease.
> Boreas' blastes asunder rendes our sayles :
> Our tacklings breake, our ankers likewise fayles.
> The surging seas, they battred have my shippe,
> And eke mine oares avayle me not a chippe.
> The ropes are slackte, the mast standes nothing strong .
> Thus am I tost the surging seas along.

He goes on to explain that if he should fall overboard
and be unable to swim he would first sink to the bottom
and then rise thrice, the last time remaining to be borne
aloft " amid the fomyng froth." If, on the other hand,
he should have the cunning or ability to swim, " with
streaking arms, and eke with playing feete," he might
be able to keep afloat till a ship came sailing by, unless
perchance the cramp numbed his feet, in which case he
would be sure to lose his life.

> Wherefore I wishe, who well may live by lande,
> And him forbid the sea to take in hande.

An accident, not uncommon when reefing or shorten-
ing sail, finds illustration in more than one song written
at widely different periods. "The *Benjamin's* Lamentation" belongs to that class of ballad in which a sailor
describes his own adventures, and it was possibly written
by or for an unfortunate mariner who, landed from his
ship, trudged the highways from Plymouth back to his
home and sang it to excite sympathy. The ballad is
in the Roxburghe Collection, and belongs to the later
Stuart period. We have not been able to trace a man-of-
war called the *Benjamin*, but the ballad is a fair specimen
of that kind which in later days was called a " fore-
bitter." The *Benjamin* seems to have been a most

unfortunate vessel, meeting with one disaster after
another, until we read :—

> The next harm that we had,
>   I, boys, O boys !
> We had cause to be sad : I !
> The next harm that we had
> We lost four men from the yard
> In the poor Benjamin. O !

A similar mishap is thus described by Dibdin, who
characteristically winds up his verse with a comforting
reflection which would not have suited the older writer
if his purpose was to excite sympathy from the landsman rather than to inspirit his brother seamen.

> One night as we drove with two reefs in the mainsail,
>   And the scud came on lowering upon a lee shore,
> Jack went up aloft to hand the top-gall'nt sail,
>   A spray washed him off, and we ne'er saw him more !
> But grieving's a folly, come let us be jolly,
>   If we've troubles at sea, boys, we've pleasures ashore.

That all the seamen of the time were not like the
lugubrious songster of the *Benjamin* is demonstrated by
the concluding verse of the ballad in which " a constant
young seaman " tells the story of how he was captured
by the Algerines and forced to work in the galleys, yet
was constantly cheered by the thoughts of his dear
Betty, to whom he sent these words of advice :—

> But be of good cheer, for every one knows
> 'Tis an ill wind indeed that no comfort blows ;
> And again I do hope thee in England to see,
> Then who'l be so happy as Betty and me?

The sailor was, indeed, of a light-hearted, careless
temperament, painstaking in his work and prepared to
meet discomfort and danger, but looking forward rather
to the pleasures of to-morrow than grumbling about the
hardships of to-day. It was well that he should have
been so, for his life, always strenuous, was essentially a
rough one, in which the moments of enjoyment were
few and far between. When he did make a moan there
was always good and substantial cause for it, but the

mood did not last long, for if the victuals were seldom satisfactory, meal hours afloat were regular, and there was generally the wherewithal for a carouse. It was not a lofty aspiration, but it was probably true when the sailor sang :—

> The best cry we like to hear
> On board, as I'm a sinner,
> Is when from the quarter-deck they call
> To the boatswain to pipe to dinner.

Of the pains of the poor mariners, their troubles and dangers, there are several descriptive ballads which belong to the reign of Queen Elizabeth. That which begins " I rue to see the raging of the seas " is one, and another is that of " the Seafardingers describing Evill Fortune " :—

> What pen can well reporte the plighte
> Of those that travell on the sea?
> To pas the werie wynter's nighte
> With stormie cloudes wisshinge for daie,
> With waves that toss them to and fro—
> Thair pore estate is hard to show.
>
> When boistering windes begin to blowe
> On cruel costes, from haven wee,
> The foggie mysts soe dimes the shore,
> The rocks and sandes we maie not see,
> Nor have no rome on seas to trie,
> But praie to God, and yeld to die.
>
> *   *   *   *
>
> O pinchinge, werie, loathsome lyfe,
> That travell still in far exsylle,
> The dangers great on seas be ryfe,
> Whose recompense doth yeld but toylle !
> O Fortune, graunte me mie desire—
> A happie end I doe require.
>
> *   *   *   *
>
> And leave the seas with thair annoy,
> At home at ease to live in joy.

The same writer, however, knew that all men are not of one mind, and he wrote another ballad, which he called " In Praise of Seafaring Men, in Hope of Good Fortune," in which one verse reads :—

> To pas the seas som thinkes a toylle,
> Som thinkes it strange abrod to rome,
> Some thinkes it grefe to leave their soylle
> Thair parents, cynfolke, and thair whome.
> Thinke soe, who list, I like it nott ;
> I must abrod to try my lott.
>
> *   *   *   *
>
> To purchus fame I will go rome.

Of a similar character is the more famous ballad of
Martin Parker. This worthy flourished in the reign of
Charles I, and is supposed to have died in 1656. He
produced a great number of broadsides, ballads, and
chap-books, and was the author of the celebrated song,
" When the King Enjoys His Own Again," a great
favourite at the time of the Restoration. In spite of
his alleged practice of " bathing his beak " in nut-brown
ale, he was the best ballad-maker of his day. His
" Saylors for My Money," was the original of Campbell's
" Ye Mariners of England," or perhaps it would be more
correct to say, the ballad upon which, as it was sung in
his time, Campbell founded his famous poem. Martin
Parker's ballad has for its second title, " A New Ditty.
Composed in the praise of Sailors and Sea Affairs, briefly
showing the nature of so worthy a calling, and the effects
of their industry." There are fifteen verses, of which
we give the first, the third, and the twelfth :—

> Countrie men of England, who live at home with ease,
> And little thinke what dangers are incident o th' seas,
> Give eare unto the saylor who unto you will shew
>   His case, his case : how e're the winde doth blow.
>
> *   *   *   *
>
> Our calling is laborious, and subject to much care ;
> But we must still contented be with what falls to our share.
> We must not be faint-hearted, come tempest, raine or snow,
>   Nor shrinke : nor shrinke : how e're the winde doth blow.
>
> *   *   *   *
>
> Into our native country with wealth we doe returne,
> And cheere our wives and children, who for our absence mourne,
> Then doe we bravely flourish, and where soe e're we goe
>   We roare : we roare : how e're the wind doth blow.

Of a similar kind is " The Jovial Marriner ; or, The Seaman's Renown," by Laurence Price, who was a con-

temporary of Martin Parker, but changed sides at the
time of the Commonwealth. He also dealt in pamphlets,
broadsides, and political squibs, and to this ballad he
attaches a legend, which reads :—

> Sail forth, bold seamen, plough the liquid main ;
> Fear neither storms nor pirats, strive for gain ;
> While others sleep at home in a whole skin
> Your brave adventures shall great honours win.

The period assigned to both these ballads is the reign
of Charles I, and the King's name is mentioned in one
of the verses written by Laurence Price. At the same
time, looking at the state of affairs from a naval point
of view, the latter, at all events, would seem to fit the
Commonwealth period much better than that which saw
Cecil's expedition to Cadiz and Buckingham's to the
Isle of Rhé. Possibly the professional song writers found
it to their interest to describe what ought to have been
the case rather than what it was. We quote four verses
from " The Jovial Marriner " :—

I am a jovial marriner : our calling is well known ;
We trade with many a foreigner to purchase high renown ;
We serve our country faithfully, and bring home store of gold ;
We do our business manfully, for we are free and bold.
  A seaman hath a valiant heart, and bears a noble minde ;
  He scorneth once to shrink or start for any stormy wind.

*   *   *   *   *

Brave England hath been much inricht by art of navigation ;
Great store of wealth we home have fetched for to adorn our nation :
Our merchants still we do supply with traffick that is rare.
Then, seamen, cast your caps on high, we are without compare.

*   *   *   *   *

Our land it would invaded be if sea-men were not stout ;
We let our friends come in on sea, and keep our foes without ;
Our privilege upon the seas we bravely do maintain,
And can enlarge it when we please in Royal Charles his reign.

*   *   *   *   *

We kiss our wives when we return, who long for us did wait,
And he that's single need not mourn, he cannot want a mate :
Young women still are wondrous kind to sea-men in their need ;
And sure it shows a courteous minde to do a friendly deed.

In the Pepys Collection there is a ballad entitled " The Sea Martyrs ; or, The Seamen's Sad Lamentation for their Faithful Service, Bad pay, and Cruel Usage ; being a Woful Relation how some of them were unmercifully put to death for Pressing for their Pay, when their Families were like to Starve." It was written at a time when the sailors were indeed badly treated in the reign of Charles II, but it would seem to have been quite as appropriate to the times of his father, and more truthful than the picture drawn by Laurence Price. A variant of " Saylors for My Money," with a somewhat similar refrain, possibly adapted by some seaman who knew the real condition of things, is entitled " Neptune's Raging Fury ; or, The Gallant Sailor's Sufferings." We quote a few of the fourteen verses of one of the finest of all our sea ballads, which is, indeed, an epitome of the sailor's sufferings, hardships, courage, endurance, resignation, and cheerfulness :—

> You gentlemen of England, that live at home at ease,
> Full little do you think upon the dangers of the seas ;
> Give ear unto the mariners, and they will plainly show,
> The cares, and the fears, when the stormy winds do blow.
>
>   *   *   *   *   *
>
> Sometimes in Neptune's bosom our ship is tost in waves
> And every man expecting the sea to be their graves :
> Then up aloft she mounteth and down again so low ;
> 'Tis with waves, oh ! with waves, when the stormy winds do blow.
>
> Then down again we fall to prayer with all our might and thought ;
> When refuge all doth fail us 'tis that must bear us out ;
> To God we call for succour, for He it is, we know,
> That must aid us, and save us, when the stormy winds do blow.
>
>   *   *   *   *   *
>
> If enemies oppose us, when England is at wars
> With any foreign nations we fear not wounds and scars ;
> Our roaring guns shall teach 'em our valour for to know,
> Whilst they reel in the keel, when the stormy winds do blow.

In the stormy swing of these lines we hear the voice of the sea and the thunders of the heavens ; we feel the bitter contrast between the lives of those who live the life of the sea, and those who pass their pampered

days and live at home at ease; we know the touch
of scorn with which the mariner, "sure to endure,"
regards those who live in the lap of luxury. Another
version of this song, entitled "The New Mariners,"
to distinguish it from the older version, was largely
borrowed from by Campbell, a circumstance which the
poet candidly acknowledged when he sent his verses
to the editor of the "Morning Chronicle," in which
they were published on 18th March, 1801, with the title
"On the Prospect of a Russian War," the title being
afterwards changed to that we know it by now.

It will have been noticed that in one of the songs just
quoted it is remarked that our land would be liable to
invasion if it were not for the seamen, and the same
idea finds expression in one of the ballads in the Rawlin-
son Collection in the Bodleian Library, called "The
Seaman's Compass," from the pen of the same author.
Here Laurence Price sings :—

> Thus for rich and poor men,
>   The Sea-man does good,
> And sometimes comes off with
>   loss of much blood.
> If they were not a guard
>   And defence for our Land,
> Our Enemies soon would
>   get the upper hand ;
> And then in a woful case
>   straight should we be.

If, however, the extent to which the State relied upon
its seamen was appreciated in Charles I's reign, it was
not so later on, when the pamphleteers and the song
writers had but one subject, the grievances of the sailors.
"The Sea Martyrs" has already been referred to, their
principal complaint having reference to the difficulty
they experienced in getting their wages and the treatment of those who pressed for payment. Here are a
couple of verses from another ballad to the same effect,
this being taken from the same garland which contains
"The Jolly Sailor's True Description of a Man-of-War."

The writer is describing the difficulty he has found in getting his just due :—

> Dear shipmate, I've been here a month,
>   And cannot get mine for the truth ;
> On board a man-of-war I went
>   When I was a frolicsome youth.
> My king and my country to serve
>   I fought like a sailor so bold.
> Now that the wars are all over
>   I really cannot get my gold.
>
> To the navy office each day I did go ;
>   I've been both hungry and dry.
> My money I then did demand.
>   "You cannot have it," they cry.
> My life I have ventur'd for gold,
>   My king and my country to serve.
> Now that the wars are all over
>   Brave sailors may perish and starve.

Later on there are the ballads expressing the complaints of the seamen who mutinied in 1797. And then, towards the end of the Great War, we find that this class of ballad describes the troubles and discomforts of the seamen's life in a taut ship with a captain who was a bit of a martinet. The following extracts from " The Flash Frigate " and " The Saucy Scylla " are of this description, while a slightly different complaint is the subject of the ditty which Jemmy Ducks sings in Marryat's " Snarleyyow."

Here is the grievance of the songster of the *Flash* frigate :—

> But now, my brave boys, comes the best of the fun :
> "All hands about ship and reef topsails," in one
> O it's "lay aloft topmen," as the hellem goes down,
> And it's "clew down your topsails," as the mainyard swings round.
>
> "Trice up, and lay out, and take two reefs in one,"
> And all in a moment this work must be done.
> Then man your head-braces, topsail-halliards, and all,
> And it's "hoist away topsails," as you "let go and haul."
>
> Our senior lieutenant, you all know him well,
> He comes upon deck, and he cuts a great swell.
> O, it's "bear a hand here, boys," and "mind what you're at,
> And at the lee gangway he serves out the cat.

While the moan from the *Saucy Scylla* is :—

> At four in the morning the work it came on,
> For sand and for holy stones loud was the song ;
> For fore and main topmen loud was the call,
> For sand and for holy stones both great and small.
>
> The next thing to divisions your hammocks you bring,
> You must have them as snug and as round as a ring ;
> With your lanyards and lacings, all made up so neat,
> Or to carry 'em all day on your shoulders your fate.
>
>   *   *   *   *   *
>
> In less than two minutes top sail's must be reef'd,
> All sail set above them so snug and complete ;
> For black-list and drilling grieved us to the heart,
> And our six-watered grog it just measured one quart.

But it was the ladies of Mutton Cove and Mount Wise who complained of the action of the Port Admiral :—

> Who ever heard in the sarvice of a frigate made to sail
> On Christmas Day, it blowing hard, with sleet, and snow, and hail ?
> I wish I had the fishing of your back that is so bent,
> I'd use the galley poker hot unto your heart's content.
> > Here Bet and Sue
> > Are with me too,
> > > A-shivering by my side,
> > They both are dumb,
> > And both look glum,
> > > And watch the ebbing tide.
> > Poll put her arms a-kimbo :
> > > At the admiral's house looked she ;
> > To thoughts that were in limbo,
> > > She now a vent gave free.
> > You've got a roaring fire, I'll bet,
> > In it your toes are jammed ;
> > Let's give him a piece of our mind, my Bet :
> > Port Admiral, you be d——d !

CHAPTER XX

NAVAL HISTORY IN VERSE AND SONG

I N Tudor and Stuart times the ballads and broadsheets were the cheap literature of the period, the source from which the public got its news. The professional writers in prose or poetry described the most dramatic incidents of their day, or those they thought best calculated to interest, amuse, or instruct the people. When, then, the sailors were playing a very prominent part in the national history, when their victorious achievements were ringing through the world, it would have been strange indeed if these had not been utilised by the ballad writers, or if sometimes they did not receive even more elaborate poetic treatment. At a later date the party satirists, or the writers of verse for the favourite singers in the theatres or assembly halls, also saw in these subjects opportunities for poetical treatment. While the former dealt with the subject from a political point of view, the latter illustrated the trend of popular opinion. All these forms of verse, therefore, possess a certain value for historical purposes, because while some illustrate the occurrences of naval history, the others supply evidence of the relative estimate in which those who acted in them were held by the people. The recital of brave deeds by Laurence Minot or John Dryden, the satirical treatment of similar events by Sir John Denham and Richard Glover, no less than the ballads written by the sailors themselves, or the songs about the seamen by lyrists like Purcell, Gay, and Dibdin, furnished material which the historian cannot afford to overlook or despise. This, at all events, is our view, and in this chapter we propose to indicate how from all these kinds of verse it is made manifest that, as a forgotten laureate sings :—*

'Tis not the oak whose hardy branches wave
O'er Britain's cliffs, and all her tempests brave ;
'Tis not the ore her iron bowels yield,
The cordage growing on her fertile field,
That form her naval strength.—'Tis the bold race
Laughing at toil, and gay in danger's face,
Who quit with joy, when fame and glory lead,
Their richest pasture and their greenest mead,
The perils of the stormy deep to dare,
And jocund own their dearest pleasures there.
One common zeal the manly race inspires,
One common cause each ardent bosom fires,
From the bold youth whose agile limbs ascend
The giddy mast when angry winds contend,
And while the yard dips low its pointed arm,
Clings to the cord, and sings amid the Storm,
To the experienc'd Chief, who knows to guide
The labouring Vessel thro' the rolling tide ;
Or when contending Squadrons fierce engage,
Direct the battle's thunder where to rage :—
All, all alike with cool unfeign'd delight
Brave the tempestuous gale, and court the fight.
Britain ! with jealous industry maintain
The sacred sources of this generous train,
Daring beyond what fable sings of old,
Yet mild in conquest, and humane as bold ;
Now rushing on the foe with frown severe,
Now mov'd to mercy by compassion's tear—
Fierce as the ruthless elements they brave
When their wronged country calls them to the wave ;
Mild as the softest breeze that fans thy isle,
When sooth'd by peace and wooing beauty's smile.
A race peculiar to thy happy coast,
But lost by folly once, for ever lost.
Ne'er from the lap of luxury and ease
Shall spring the hardy Warrior of the Seas—
A toilsome youth the Mariner must form,
Nurs'd on the Wave, and cradled in the Storm.

The prowess of Englishmen on the sea received recognition in the metrical narratives of the time as early as the reign of Richard I, the great battle fought by

* H. J. Pye, 1798.

the English fleet on its voyage to the Holy Land in
1191 off the coast of Syria being very fully set forth.
The enemy's vessel, described as a marvellous ship,
carrying among other things in her armament, Greek
fire and "two hundred most deadly serpents," was full
of soldiers, and was proceeding to the relief of Acre,
then besieged by the Crusaders. Richard, with his
galleys, attacked her, but was at first driven off, as her
height out of the water prevented boarding. Then a
tactical move on the part of the British seaman saved
the situation, for the King, using his vessels as rams,
drove their iron beaks into the hull of the enemy, so that
her sides were stove in and she foundered. Peter de
Langtoft thus describes the fight :—

> The Kynges owen galeie, he called it Trencthemere,
> That was first on weie, and com the schip fulle nere.
> Other were ther inowe, that ther after drouh,
> Bot he com with a suowe, that the schip to rof.
> The schip cast trokes out, the galeie to tham drouh,
> The Kyng stode fulle stout, and many of tham slouh ;
> Wilde fire thei kast, the Kyng to confound ;
> His schipmen were fulle wrask, els had he gone to ground.
> The Kyng abaist him nouht, bot stalworthly fauht,
> Alle to dede he brouht, that his galeie over rauht.
> The galeie ther thorght schete, and the Kyng was gode,
> The schip that was so grete, it dronkled in the flode.

The result of this battle was that Richard, with his
forces, was able to land at Acre without further trouble,
and the aid he brought to the besiegers was such that
the town surrendered almost immediately afterwards.
Richard's flagship, the *Trenchmer*, or, as we should call
her, the *Shearwater*, is one of the earliest vessels in the
English Navy of which we know the name.

The great battle in the Dover Straits in 1217, in which
again the English seamen won by their tactical skill,
does not appear to have inspired a poet, although it
certainly merited this distinction. On the other hand,
it is the first of our English sea fights of which we possess
a picture. Two representations of the battle are given
with the description by Matthew Paris, which, if not very

accurate, are probably at least as near the truth as many more modern pictures of engagements at sea.

The next naval battles of importance occurred in the reign of Edward III, and were sung by Laurence Minot. Two of Minot's poems describe respectively the battle of Sluys in June, 1340, and the battle known as Les Espagnols sur Mer, which was fought off Winchelsea in August, 1350. Minot describes the method of warfare, and the desperate fighting. The enemy's ships were moored in line, so that King Edward's vessels with a fair wind, and the sun at their backs, sailed in under cover of clouds of arrows, when the men-at-arms boarded and drove the enemy into the sea. No quarter was given and no prisoners were taken, unless of high rank for ransom. Upwards of two thousand of the enemy are said to have perished. The second fight took place at sea, and the Spaniards had better vessels and the weather gage, so that they tried ramming, but again the good shooting of the English archers and the intrepidity and daring of the men-at-arms in the hand-to-hand fighting that ensued gave the English the victory. Not only were the chief nobility and knights of England present, says the historian, but they were led by their Sovereign and the Prince of Wales in person, who both so completely shared the danger of the day that they fought until their ships actually sank under them. Here are three specimen verses from Minot's first poem, somewhat modernised :—

> Listen, and the battle I shall begin,
> Of Englishmen and Normans in the Swyn.
>
>   *   *   *   *
>
> Sore it them smarted that fared out of France ;
> Englishmen learnèd them there a new dance.
>
>   *   *   *   *
>
> King Edward unto sail full soon was dight (ready),
> With earls and barons and many a bold knight
> They came before Blankenberghe on St. John's night ;
> That was to the Normans a wretched sight.
> Yet trumped they and dancèd, with torches full bright,
> In the wild waning (moon) were their hearts light.
>
>   *   *   *   *

Two hundred and more ships on the sands
Had our Englishmen won with their hands ;
The cogs of England were brought out of bands,
And also the Christopher that in the stream stands ;
In that stound (time) they stood, with streamers full still,
Till they wist full well King Edward's will.

In the reign of Henry V the victory of the Duke of
Bedford and Sir Walter Hungerford in August, 1416,
off the mouth of the Seine, was described in his metrical
chronicle by Hardyng. The fleet was despatched for
the purpose of relieving Barfleur, and was entirely
successful after severe fighting. Sir Harris Nicolas
questions the accuracy of the poet's figures, but admits
that his account of the fighting, of the tactics of the
French, and of the bravery displayed on both sides,
is fully deserving of credence. As was customary, the
ships ran alongside one another, grappled, and the
fighting was hand-to-hand, but the attempt of the galleys
to take advantage of the calm which fell after the battle
is an interesting circumstance. Here are Hardyng's
spirited verses :—

They fought full sore afore the water of Séyn,
With carrikes many, well stored and arrayed ;
And many other shippes great of Hispayne,
Barges, balyngers, and galleys, unaffrayed,
Which proudly came upon our ships unprayed :
And by the even their sails avaled were set,
The enemies slain in battle, and sore bet.

And many drownèd were that day in the sea,
That as our fleet rode there then still alway,
Unto the feast next of her Nativity,
The bodies flote among our ships each day ;
Full piteous was and foul to see them aye,
That thousands were—twenty as they then told—
That taken were in that same battle bold.

In which meantime, while as our ships there lay,
It was so calm, withouten any wind,
We might not sail, nor fro thence pass away,
Wherefore their galleys each day there gan us find,
With oars many about us did they wind,
With wild fire oft assayled us day and night,
To burn our ships in that they could or might.

In a ballad descriptive of an event which took place in 1511, but which may have been written later, we get the first detailed account of an engagement which was not settled by hand-to-hand fighting. In the early years of Henry VIII the English Channel and the North Sea were virtually at the command of the foreigners. Piratical craft swarmed along the coasts, and even picked up prizes in our harbours, until their depredations led to the fitting out of fleets for the protection of our shores. This ballad tells of a fight between Sir Edward Howard and a Scotch pirate, Sir Andrew Barton, and although the latter's ship was eventually captured by boarding, it was not until after she had been beaten at long bowls and her captain slain. When Sir Edward volunteered to go in search of the pirate he first of all chose his gunner, Peter Simon.

> "My lord," sais hee, "if you have chosen mee
> Of a hundred gunners to be the head,
> Hange mee att your maine-mast tree
> If I misse my marke past three pence bread."

Then Sir Edward selected a first-rate archer, William Horsley, who was to command a hundred bowmen. After which, having put to sea, he meets with a Newcastle ship, the captain of which, Henry Hunt, agrees to accompany him as pilot and to join in the fight. Hunt is acquainted with the pirate, and describes his ship.

> "Hee is brasse within, and steele without,
> And beames hee carres in his topcastle stronge;
> His shipp hath ordinance cleane round about;
> Besids, my lord, hee is verry well mand."

Presently they sight the Scotch vessel, and Howard determines to disguise his ship.

> "Take in your ancyents and your standards,
> Yea that no man shall them see,
> And put me fforth a white willow wand,
> As merchants use who sayle the sea."

As the result of this diplomacy, Sir Andrew Barton is enticed within range, and Simon shoots away his mast. Then the archer is sent for, and he shoots Sir Andrew

through the brain. The Scotch seaman, however, dies
game.

> " Fight on, my men," says Sir Andrew Barton,
> " These English doggs they bite soe loe ;
> Fight on for Scotland and Saint Andrew
> Till you heare my whistle blowe ! "

> But when they cold not heare his whistle blowe,
> Says Harry Hunt, " I'll lay my head
> You may board yonder noble shipp, my lord,
> For I know Sir Andrew, hee is dead."

They then boarded and captured the ship, and brought
her into the Thames as a New Year gift for the King.
All the principal people were rewarded, Simon Hunt
and Horsley, as well as Sir Edward Howard.

In some other verses written in the reign of Henry VIII,
or perhaps a little later, there is clearly an indication of
the Imperial spirit due to the expansion of the maritime
resources of the country, and to the desire for an extended dominion, which grew with the voyages and discoveries of the seamen. The verses are entitled " Neptune to England," and are printed in Halliwell's Early
Naval Ballads. We quote the concluding stanzas :—

> Goe on, great State, and make it knowne,
> Thou never wilt forsake thine owne
>   Nor from thy purpose start :
> But that thou wilt thy power dilate,
> Since narrow seas are found too straight
>   For thy capacious heart.
> So shall thy rule, and mine, have large extent :
> Yet not so large, as just and permanent.

The influence which the daring adventures and the
successful enterprises of the Elizabethan mariners and
explorers had upon the literature of the period has
already been referred to in other sections of this work.
Just as the courage, skill, and hardihood of the English
seamen impressed the public mind, so also it exercised
a lively fascination upon the imagination of the poets.
The patriotic pride of the nation was deeply stirred by
that movement which in giving to the country the dominion of the seas ultimately gave her dominion over

a considerable portion of the world. Many elaborate poems and many more popularly written ballads describe the exploits of the Elizabethan sailors, or eulogise with pardonable pride the character of their great leaders. The imperishable fame of Sir Richard Grenville, and the famous fight of the *Revenge* off the Azores, was cele- brated by Gervase Markham, who makes the great sea captain say :—

> Since losing, we unlost keep strong our praise,
> And make our glories gainers by our ends,
> Let not the hope of hours (for tedious days
> Unto our lives no longer circuit lends),
> Confound our wondered actions and assays,
> Whereon the sweet of mortal ears depends,
> But as we live by wills victorious,
> So let us die victors of them and us.

The expedition to Lisbon of Drake and Norreys in 1589 was described by George Peele, while Charles FitzGeffery in elaborate poems extolled the exploits of many of the adventurous mariners of Tudor times, from Sebastian Cabot onwards. In a poem narrating the last voyage of Drake and Hawkins, FitzGeffery says of the latter :—

> Nestor in wisdom, art, and policy,
> Nestor in knowledge, skill, and prudency,
> Nestor in counsel, and in gravity,
> Nestor in wit, foresight, and modesty,
> Nestor in might, and magnanimity :
> O would he had (as he had Nestor's hairs)
> Enjoyèd Nestor's age and Nestor's years.

Thomas Greepe, in " The True and Perfect News of the Worthy and Valiant Exploits of Sir Francis Drake," narrates in rhyme the taking of Cartagena, an expedition at which he may well have been present. Here is a specimen of his verse :—

> Their yards across, hoist at the top,
> Their anchors weighed them presently ;
> Their sails displayed, their good ships lope,
> The mariners stand their tacklings by,
> Each rope belayed, with good respect
> As skilful masters did direct.

Other poets who should be mentioned in this connection are Michael Drayton, who in his "Ode to the Virginia Voyage" refers to the illustrious Hakluyt; William Warner, who in "Albion's England" describes the defeat of the Spanish Armada and the worthy feats of "Lord Charles, our Admiral," Gilbert, Fenton, Davis, Cavendish, and others; and Thomas Deloney, who deals with the destruction of the great galleon *St. Laurence* on Calais Bar, and the death of her admiral, Don Hugo de Monçada. No less than three poets found in Martin Frobisher a subject for panegyric, John Kirkham, Thomas Ellis, and Abraham Fleming, the last-named calling him "a right heroicall heart of Britainne blood." The expedition to Cadiz under Howard and Essex in the year of Drake's death also found an anonymous commemorator, the details in whose verses lead one to suppose that he may have made one in the adventure. As a description of the thorough way in which the sailors went to work at the sacking of a captured town, there is no equal to this lively ballad.

The naval decay which fell upon the country in the course of the next two reigns, with the lack of enterprise and want of vigour that characterised the few expeditions which were undertaken, finds reflection in a picturesque passage by William Browne, of Tavistock, in the second book of his "Britannia's Pastorals." Browne was justly proud of his native Devonshire and the race she had produced. He sings of her "sea ruling men":—

> Time never can produce men to o'ertake
> The fames of Grenville, Davis, Gilbert, Drake,
> Or worthy Hawkins, or of thousands more
> That by their power made the Devonian shore
> Mock the proud Tagus; for whose richest spoil
> The boasting Spaniard left the Indian soil
> Bankrupt of store, knowing it would quit cost
> By winning this, though all the rest were lost.

And then comparing the stirring times when the ships these worthies commanded repelled the Armada with the

condition of those ships in the reign of Elizabeth's
successor :—

> Those vessels lie,
> Rotting like houses through ill-husbandry ;
> And on their masts, where oft the ship-boy stood,
> Or silver trumpets charm'd the brackish flood,
> Some wearied crow is set ; and daily seen
> Their sides instead of pitch caulked o'er with green :
>
> *   *   *   *   *
>
> Upon their hatches where half pikes were borne,
> In every chink rise stems of bearded corn :
> Mocking our idle times that so have wrought us,
> Or putting us in mind what once they brought us.

Browne's sorrowful reflections present a more faithful
picture of the state of affairs than any of the panegyrics
by professional writers, or the verses in which the ships
built by Charles to enforce his claim to the sovereignty
of the seas were glorified.

The naval victories of the Commonwealth, although
few ballads on the subject have survived, supplied the
inspiration to Edmund Waller and Andrew Marvell for
more than one important poem. Blake's victory at
Santa Cruz in 1657, and Stainer's capture of the Spanish
galleons off Cadiz in the previous year, were fittingly
commemorated in verses which breathe the spirit of
the time, the national exultation in the triumphs by
sea, and that conviction that England's greatness lay
afloat, which so obviously inspired many of the Parlia-
mentary leaders, including Cromwell.   Marvell writes of
Blake :—

> For your resistless genius there did reign,
> By which we laurels reaped e'en on the main :
> So prosperous stars, though absent to the sense,
> Bless those they shine for by their influence.

And Waller, in his poem, has the significant lines :—

> Others may use the ocean as their road,
> Only the English make it their abode,
> Our oaks secure, as if they there took root,
> We tread on billows with a steady foot.

It was not long, however, before the tone of exultation,

so apparent in the Commonwealth poems, was to be changed by the unfortunate reverses to the fleet in the Second Dutch War. Not, indeed, that there were wanting poems on the other side, for, on the Duke of York's victory in June, 1665, John Dryden wrote some verses, and the event was celebrated by Waller in his poem entitled " Instructions to a Painter for the Drawing of the Posture and Progress of His Majesty's Forces at Sea under the Command of His Highness Royal ; together with the Battle and Victory obtained over the Dutch, June 3rd, 1665." In the guise of instructions to a painter Waller described the incidents to appear upon the canvas, and the " valiant Duke," whose dress was bespattered with the blood of those who fell near him, was in the forefront of the picture. This poem was the forerunner of many satires when the British victories were turned to defeats. Sir John Denham, in a parody on the " Instructions to a Painter," dealt with the later episodes of the war, and Pepys, writing on 14th September, 1667, says : " I met with a ' Fourth Advice to a Painter upon the coming in of the Dutch to the River, and end of the War ' that made my heart ache to read, it being too sharp, and so true."

Andrew Marvell also, in " The Last Instructions to a Painter about the Dutch Wars," satirised the neglect of the Navy, and described the burning of the ships in the Medway. He blamed the Government because :—

> Meantime through all the yards their orders run,
> To lay the ships up, cease the keels begun.
> The timber rots, the useless axe does rust ;
> The unpractised saw lies buried in its dust ;
> The busy hammer sleeps, the ropes untwine ;
> The stores and wages, all are mine and thine ;
> Along the coasts and harbours they take care
> That money lacks, nor forts be in repair.
>
> * * * *
>
> Our seamen, whom no danger's shape could fright,
> Unpaid, refuse to mount their ships for spite.

And he describes the grief and chagrin of Monk at the dismal sight :—

He finds, where'er he succour might expect,
Confusion, folly, treachery, fear, neglect.
But when the Royal Charles (what rage! what grief!)
He saw seized, and could give her no relief;
That sacred keel that had, as he, restored
Its exiled Sovereign on its happy board,
And thence the British Admiral became,
Crowned for that merit with her master's name;
That pleasure-boat of war, in whose dear side,
Secure, as oft he had this foe defied,
Now a cheap spoil, and the mean victor's slave,
Taught the Dutch colours from its top to wave.

Marvell also commemorated the heroism of Captain Douglas, a land officer who with a party of soldiers endeavoured to defend the *Royal Oak* against the attack of the Dutch. He had no orders to retire, and declined to leave the ship until he was told to do so.

Down on the deck he laid himself and died,
With his dear sword reposing at his side,
And on the flaming plank he rests his head,
As one that warmed himself and went to bed;
His ship burns down, and with his relics sinks,
And the sad stream beneath his ashes drink.

In the ballads, those which were inspired by the Four Days' Fight and the Fight of St. James's Day, equally with those which describe the actions of the Third Dutch War, contain many references to the character of the naval commanders. In " England's Triumph and Holland's Downfall," the Four Days' Fight, we read how :—

The first and second day of June,
Put Holland's trumpets out of tune;
Prince Rupert and the Duke to boot,
Have given the Dutch-men all the rout :
So bloudily they cut their coats,
And bruis'd and bang'd and burn'd their boats,
They ne're will offer to displease,
King Charles their Soveraign of the seas.

In " England's Royall Conquest," a ballad to the same tune on the St. James's Day Fight, Rupert, Monk, and Penn are mentioned, and :—

> Sir Jeremy Smith did roughly greet,
> The Admiral of the Zealand fleet,
> With fire and ball he made them run,
> Untill the victory he had won,
>
>   *   *   *   *
>
> Brave Allen and Holmes fought like men,
> And chas'd the Dutch with five to ten,
>
>   *   *   *   *
>
> 'Tis said, de Ruyter and Trump are slain,
> And never will face their foes again.
>   Then Butter-boxes all lament,
>   For now you are paid to your own content.

Another ballad on this fight, with a rousing chorus, entitled " A Famous German Prince and a Renowned English Duke," by Sir John Birkenhead, tells how " brave Tom Allen led the van, stout Utber and bold Tiddiman," " that Jordan (Heart of Oak) was there," and gallant Holmes, while :—

> Our rere was Smith, with other two
> (Spragge and Kempthorn) both true blew,
>
>   *   *   *   *
>
> His chaplain fell to his wonted work,
> Cryed, " Now for the King and the Duke of York ! "
> He prayed like a Christian and fought like a Turk.
>   With a thump, thump, thump, thump, thump,
>   Thump, thump, thump-upon-thump.

Of course, there is a ballad on Holmes's bonfire, in which due credit is given to Sir William Jennings as well, and " the Solebay Fight," the battle off the coast of Suffolk on May 28th, 1672, is described by an eye-witness of the battle from the shore, whose sympathies are manifest from the verse we quote below :—

> Of all the battles gain'd at sea
> This was the rarest victory
> Since Philip's Grand Armado.
> I will not name the rebel Blake ;
> He fought for horson Cromwell's sake,
> And yet was forced three days to take
> To quell the Dutch bravado.

The last naval engagement of the war, that between Prince Rupert and Sir Edward Spragge on the one side with their French allies under the Comte d'Estrées, and on the other the Dutch under De Ruyter, Cornelis Tromp, and Banckers, is also commemorated, with special reference to the intrepidity of Sir Edward Spragge, Lord Ossory, and Sir John Kempthorne. In this battle, the *London* man-of-war carried the flag of Vice-Admiral Sir John Harman, who had fought under Blake, and of whom an elegy was written, in which, after recording his previous exploits, it is said " in '72, Vice-Admiral of the Blue, he like a Tyger 'mongst the Dutchmen flew," and his character is described as valiant, just, humble, patient, and sincere. Elegies on the officers who fell in the battles of the Dutch wars were common, and amongst others so commemorated were Lord Maidstone, Sir Edward Spragge, Henry Terne, Francis Digby, and Thomas Harman, the man who broke the boom in Sir Edward Spragge's expedition against the Algerines in May, 1671.

The actions of the principal sea commanders in the reigns of William III and Queen Anne have all received commemoration in naval ballads, but it cannot be said that any of these are of very high merit. Sir Cloudesley Shovell appears to have been the most popular of the naval officers, as Narborough and Myngs, other Norfolk men, had been before him. A sailor gives an account of a cutting-out affair which took place in 1690 under the title of "The Courageous Commander; or, a Brief Relation of that most noble Adventure of Sir Cloudesly Shovell, in the Bay of Dublin, on Good Fryday, in bringing the *Pellican* Frigat out of their harbour in triumph and victory " :—

> Now, noble brave boys, let the sweet trumpet sound,
> While seamen with trophies of honour are crown'd ;
> For gracious King William they'll fight till they dye,
> And scorn from the face of a Tory to flye.
> Sir brave Cloudesly Shovell sail'd to Dublin Bay,
> And brought the brave Pellican frigat away.

Herbert of Torrington's conduct of the Beachy Head battle was, on the other hand, a theme to the taste of the satirical songsters, who made quite clear their view of his strategy :—

> The Dutch to the enemy boldly drew near,
> But th' admiral o' th' English m ɔre wisely did steer,
> For he thought it was safer to keep in the rear,
>   Which nobody can deny.

The Duke of Grafton, John Tyrrel, and Robert Dorrell, all of whom commanded ships in the battle, are commended, but the courage and conduct of the " wise Herbert " are derided for the benefit of " the melancholy widows of Wapping." Russell's cruise in the Channel in the following year was made the occasion for an attack by the same political poet upon Torrington's successor, who sings :—

> But Russell, the cherry-cheekt Russell, is chose
> His fine self and his fleet at sea to expose ;
> But he will take care how he meets with his foes,
>   Which nobody can deny.

This view did not last long, for Barfleur and La Hogue made the poetasters change their tune, and " valiant " Ashby, " brave " Delaval, " glorious " Shovell, with " renowned " Russell, and Rooke, " that brave heroic soul," are all praised as :—

> True sons of thunder, that will not retreat
> Till they see that their foes are destroyèd and beat.

Lord Danby, Thomas Heath, James Greenaway, Thomas Foulis, and Rear-Admiral Richard Carter (who was killed in the action at La Hogue), are all mentioned in another ballad ; while yet a third, extolling the valiant seamen's courage, concludes :—

> Boys, the work we'll compleat, with a most royal fleet,
> For we valiant tarpollians do scorn to retreat ;
> Not a Frenchman we'll spare ; let them come if they dare ;
> On the ocean, brave Russell will fight with them fair.
>   This is but a beginning of what he intends
>   To show them before the brave summer it ends.

With the accession of Anne and the War of Succession we have the ballads in praise of Benbow, another popular hero. The cowardice of the captains who refused to

support him is pilloried, while the memory of their unfortunate victim is perpetuated in the toast :—

> Come, all you brave fellows, wherever you've been,
> Let us drink to the health of our King and our Queen ;
> And another good health to the girls that we know,
> And a third in remembrance of brave Admiral Benbow.

Sir George Rooke at Vigo and Malaga, with Lord
Dursley, who commanded the *Boyne*, Sir John Jennings,
the *St. George*, and Sir William Jumper, the *Lenox*, in
the last-named battle, all receive mention in the commemorative ballads. Of Jumper, who was wounded at
Malaga, it was said that when he met a French ship
" he bravely would thump her " ; while Sir John Leake,
whose flag was in the *Prince George*, had a ballad all to
himself.

In the reigns of the first two Georges we have the war
with Spain that broke out in 1718, and that associated
with " the fable of Jenkins's ear." Byng's battle off
Cape Passaro was the only action in the first war to
elicit a ballad, but in the second, Vernon's exploit at
Portobello receives due recognition :—

> All their brass guns he took away, the iron ones he nailed
> And threw them in the sea before from thence he sailed.
> Many a jolly sailor's pouch was cram'd with white and yellow,
> From plunder they could not be kept in the town of Portobello.

His taking of Cartagena was also the subject of a
couple of ballads ; and then the engagement of Mathews
in February, 1744, which led to the trial of Mathews
himself, Lestock, and others, is the subject of verses
by a sailor who reflects the popular favour in which
Mathews was held. The victories of Anson in May,
1747, and of Hawke in October of the same year, were
naturally the cause of great rejoicing. The wagon-loads
of money taken by Anson particularly stirred the imagination of the poets ; Hawke's remark that the enemy took
" a good deal of drubbing " also attracted their notice,
and in a sailor's song on the latter event entitled " A Sea
Kick for a Land Cuff," the nation is advised that :—

> While our salt water walls so begird us about,
> And our cruisers, and bruisers, keep good looking out,
> What force need old England to fear can offend her,
> From France, or from Spain, or a Popish Pretender?
> So, Huzzah! to King George, boys; long, long may he reign,
> By the right of old England, long lord of the main.

In the Seven Years' War, the unfortunate behaviour of Byng in the conduct of his action with La Galissonière in 1755 produced a crop of satirical poems and epigrams. A collection of many of these, under the title of " Bungiana ; or, An assemblage of What-d'ye-call-ems in prose and verse that have occasionally appeared relative to the conduct of a certain naval commander, 1756," was published that year, and included parodies of the Admiral's despatch, accusations of treachery, and other squibs and lampoons, the cruelty and injustice of which doubtless reflected the popular feeling. The country, indeed, was lashed to madness by the politicians who made the unhappy Admiral their scapegoat. The King was thoroughly frightened, and, in spite of indignant protests and feeling appeals, the Admiral was sacrificed.

> For behaving so well in the ocean,
>   At least he deserves well a string ;
> And if he wou'd sue for promotion,
>   I hope they will give him his swing.
>   Swing, swing, O rare Admiral Byng !

Four years later the victories of Boscawen and Hawke, with the successful labours of Saunders in Canada, were the theme of many ballads of triumph, some by sailors and others by landsmen. Garrick wrote " Heart of Oak " at this time, and Beard sang it at Covent Garden in " The Reprisal." The following from a more pretentious poem by I. Wignell, entitled " Neptune's Resignation," reflects the change of opinion :—

> " Ye Winds, go forth and make it known
> Who dares to shake my coral throne,
> And fill my realms with smoke!"
>   *   *   *   *

2 D

The Winds reply—"In distant lands
There reigns a king who Hawke commands
    He scorns all foreign force ;
And when his floating castles roll
From sea to sea, from pole to pole,
    Great Hawke directs their course !

     *   *   *   *

Boscawen's deeds, and Saunders' fame,
Join'd with brave Wolfe's immortal name "—
    Then cried, "Can this be true ?—

"A king ! he sure must be a god,
Who has such heroes at his nod
    To govern earth and sea :
I yield my trident and my crown
A tribute due to such renown,—
    Great George shall rule for me."

It would be tedious to quote from the innumerable
ballads commemorative of the battles fought during the
era of the American Revolution or those of the Great
War from 1793 to 1815. The victories of Keppel,
Barrington, Byron, Rodney, Hood, Parker, Graves, and
Hughes, in the first period, and among others those of
Hotham, Howe, Bridport, Jervis, Duncan, Collingwood,
and Nelson in the second, were made the subjects of
verses of all kinds and values from whatever point of view
they are regarded. As it does not appear to be generally
known, it may be mentioned here that in December,
1805, Warren Hastings, writing to a friend about the
pleasure he had derived from reading "The Lay of the
Last Minstrel," expressed the wish that "Mr. Scott would
compose a poem in the nature of the old minstrelsy, and
make our gallant Nelson the subject of it. He would
indeed weave into it, by episode and digression, all the
naval achievements of this and the last war, and make it
not only the most interesting, but if set to appropriate
airs adapted to common capacity, the most useful incentive to national ardour." This letter of Hastings
appears to have been sent through a mutual friend to
the poet and novelist, for in the same month Sir Walter,
as he was yet to become, wrote that he would be utterly
devoid of the feelings of an author if he were not highly

flattered by the approbation of Mr. Hastings, "to whose
genius and talent we owe the preservation of the British
Empire in the East." He pointed out, however, "one
great and insurmountable obstacle to my profiting by
a hint derived from a quarter of such high authority."
It seemed to him indispensable that to attempt such
a task the poet should have enough knowledge of seafaring matters to be able to select circumstances which,
though individual and so trivial as to escape general
observation, were precisely those which in poetry give
life, spirit, and above all truth to the description.
"Now, my total and absolute ignorance of everything
of and belonging to the sea would lay me under the
necessity of either generalising my descriptions so much
as to render them absolutely tame, or of substituting
some fantastic and, very probably, erroneous whims of
my own for the natural touches of reality which ought to
enliven and authenticate the poem." He added that the
same objection applied with double force to his ever
being a useful instrument in the patriotic plan of writing
songs for sailors, and that he was of opinion that in all
probability Dibdin's songs, with their professional allusions and apt sea phrases, would be preferred by the
honest tars "to the effusions of a mere landlubber
like myself." In concluding this chapter we will pick
out a few specimens of the verse in which were chronicled
single-ship engagements, the disasters of peace and war,
and such other notorious events as the mutinies of 1797.

The ballads descriptive of single-ship engagements
were almost wholly cast in the same mould as those
which were mainly concerned with actions between
merchantmen and pirates in the fifteenth and sixteenth
centuries and the frigate actions of the wars in the seventeenth and eighteenth. The same phrases, indeed, were
constantly repeated, and so far as the framework was
concerned, one ballad was built up upon another. Many
were doubtless written by the sailor poets, and these
have more of the professional flavour about them, while
nearly all are spirited and obviously intended to be

sung. As an example we will quote one of these songs written on the capture of the French 64-gun ship *Mars* by the *Nottingham*, Captain Philip Saumarez, on 11th October, 1746, as this does not appear in any of the more recent anthologies of sea songs and ballads :—

Come all ye jolly seamen, a tough old Tar I am.
I'll sing ye of a fight, my boys, fought in the Nottingham.
'Twas by a brisk young Captain, Phil Saumarez was his name,
bis. And he was bent, with bold intent, old England's foes to tame.

On the 5th day of October our anchor we did weigh,
And from old Plymouth Sound, my boys, we shaped our course away.
Along the coast of Ireland, our orders were to go,
bis. The seas to cruise, and none refuse, but boldly fight the foe.

We had not been out many days before we chanc'd to spy
A sail all to the westward which drew to us full nigh.
She hail'd us loud in French, my boys, and ask'd from whence we came,
bis. "From Plymouth Sound, we've just come round, and the Nottingham's our name."

"Are you a man-of-war," they said, "or a privateer maybe?"
"We are a man-of-war," said we, "and that you soon shall see.
So haul up smart your courses, and let your ship lie to :
bis. If you stand out, or put about, we'll sink you ship and crew."

The first broadside we let them have, we made the rascals quail :
The next their yards and topmas'es came rattling down like hail.
We drove them from their quarters, their Captain frantic grew,
bis. He curs'd our shot, it came so hot, "Mille diables ! Sacré bleu !"

We fought them seven glasses when, to add to all their fears,
The shout was raised for "Boarders !" and we gave three ringing cheers ;
Down came her flag, we took her ; her name it was the Mars.
bis. The French be d——d, they ne'er can stand and fight with British Tars.

Amongst the poetry recording great disasters, the most famous, or the best known, is Cowper's dirge on " The Loss of the Royal George."

Toll for the brave—
   Brave Kempenfelt is gone,
His last sea-fight is fought,
   His work of glory done.

The three earlier disasters of Queen Anne's reign, the
storm of November, 1703, when four men-of-war were
lost; the casting away of Sir Cloudesley Shovell, with
four vessels, including his flagship, on the rocks of Scilly,
in October, 1707; and the blowing up of the *Edgar* at
Spithead on 11th October, 1711, were all the subjects of
descriptive ballads or commemorative verse. In an
elegy on the lamented death of Sir Cloudesley Shovell,
which is in the British Museum, we are reminded :—

> At Bantry, Beachy, and at Malaga
> The French too well his dauntless conduct saw ;
> There you might see the British glory shine,
> And Shovell break th' impenetrable line.

But perhaps the most typical ballad of this kind is that
on the loss of the *Victory*, the flagship of Sir John Balchen, on the Caskets, in 1744, which we find in a collection of slip songs, and which was reprinted by Ashton.
It begins in characteristic fashion :—

> Good people all, pray give attention, to this fatal tragedy,
> Which I am bound to mention of the gallant Victory :
> Fourteen hundred souls did perish, and are to the bottom gone,
> Oh ! the dismal grief and horror of their widows left alone.

Then, after a description of the sailing of the ship, and
her probable fate, we are told :—

> The brave gallant Admiral Balchen with fourteen hundred men beside,
> If she's lost, went to the bottom, and all at once together died :
> Oh ! the dismal grief and horror, if one had been there to see,
> How they all were struck with horror, when sunk down the Victory.

The ballad concludes :—

> Children crying for their fathers, widows weeping in distress,
> God will surely be their comfort, and protect the fatherless.
> He'll be a husband to the widow, that loves honest industry,
> And does give them His protection : farewell, fatal Victory.

This ballad was written more than a century ago, and
it is interesting to note that in two modern ballads, one
of which was descriptive of a boiler accident on board the
Thistle gunboat, in November, 1869, and another of the
loss of the *Captain* in September, 1870, similar phrases

to those used in it were again employed. In the latter we find this verse :—

O ! such a tale as this was seldom told, five hundred jovial young sailors bold—
Have been engulfed in the briny sea ! which has caused the greatest of anxiety.
The fathers weeping all in despair ; the mothers tearing their snow-white hair ;
The orphans weep, and the widow sighs, and the pretty maiden for her lover cries.

Chorus : The Captain sailed from old England's shore
With five hundred men to return no more.

The mutinies at Spithead and the Nore produced several ballads and more than one play. The views of the seamen at Spithead, the cause of their action and its result, thus find expression in verse :—

The reason unto you I now will relate:
We resolved to refuse the purser's short weight ;
Our humble petition to Lord Howe we sent,
That he to the Admiralty write to present
Our provisions and wages that they might augment.

* * * * *

But at length from our king Lord Howe he was sent
To redress our grievance to our full content ;
We received the old hero with joy as our friend,
And the Act being passed, we will cheerfully sing
" Confusion to France, and long live our King !"

The mutiny at the Nore was of a different character, and there were ballads in which the deeds of Parker and his companions are applauded, while in others the chief mutineers were held up to execration as traitors of the worst description. The other mutinies which at this time disgraced the Fleet do not appear to have been made the subject of poetry. We will close this chapter with a quotation from the only poem we have discovered commemorative of a naval review at Spithead. The poem was written by the Rev. Robert English, late chaplain of the *Royal George*, who also wrote a piece of verse on Hawke's victory at Quiberon Bay. His poem, entitled " The Naval Review," was illustrated with a pretty little line engraving by P. C. Canot after a drawing by Dominic Serres.

> The warlike drums, and sprightly trumpets sound,
> While bursting shouts from Hantia's Tow'rs rebound ;
> A thousand banners float in wanton play ;
> A thousand hands with flow'rets strew the way ;
> The gath'ring crowd impetuous throng before,
> Hailing their Monarch to the happy shore,
> Where the proud Argo deck'd, in royal state,
> 'Midst the loud cannons' roar embarks th' imperial freight.
>
>   *   *   *   *
>
> Here gallant fleets in awful order lie,
> Whose waving flags the world combin'd defy.

Not, however, in heroic ballads of battle, nor in glowing appeals to the glamour of glory, do we touch the heart of the seaman. The proud praise of an admiral or captain, whose deeds and services are better appraised by the historian, leaves the humanity of officer and man undiscovered. By inference and allusion, indeed, we may picture to ourselves what manner of men these seamen were. Beneath the jollity of their seeming thoughtless lives ran the undertone of a recognised sorrow. The very mention of the press-gang evokes the picture of a whole world of anguish—of men torn from homes bereft, to labour in toil and peril for their country's weal, sometimes to die, and sometimes to experience the joy of a happy return. We have seen something in the last chapter of their temperament and character as the balladists depict them, and now we have to follow them in the execution of some of their duties, and to enter into the story of their love and devotion for sweetheart and wife.

CHAPTER XXI

THE SAILOR'S LIFE AND LOVES

And oh, the little warlike world within !
The well-reeved guns, the netted canopy,
The hoarse command, the busy humming din,
When at a word, the tops are manned on high :
Hark to the Boatswain's call, the cheering cry !
While through the seaman's hand the tackle glides ;
Or schoolboy Midshipman that, standing by,
Strains his shrill pipe as good or ill betides,
And well the docile crew that skilful urchin guides.

 * * * * *

White is the glassy deck, without a stain,
Where on the watch the staid Lieutenant walks :
Look on that part which sacred doth remain
For the lone chieftain, who majestic stalks,
Silent and fear'd by all—not oft he talks
With aught beneath him, if he would preserve
That strict restraint, which broken, ever balks
Conquest and fame : but Britons rarely swerve
From law, however stern, which tends their strength to nerve.

IT is proposed in this chapter to quote from the national poetry some descriptions of the various grades of seamen, both those who walked the quarter-deck and those who served " before the mast." The object is to determine how they were regarded at different periods of history by their shipmates, by the ladies, and by the poets and rhymesters who were sufficiently interested in them to endeavour to relate their actions and thoughts in verse.

It was the midshipman among the officers who seems to have secured the greatest amount of attention :—

A ship-boy high upon the giddy mast.

His pranks, his courage, his woes, even his loves have all
been made the burden of songs and ballads. That at
times he exercised the authority with which he was invested in a somewhat arbitrary manner is shown by a
lower-deck complaint in " The Jolly Sailor's True Description of a Man-of-War," a copy of which, with a
delightful woodcut, is in our possession.

> There are snotty boys of midshipmen
> Who cry with shrilly bellow ;
> As to their age, some hardly ten
> Strike many a brave fellow,
> Who dare not prate at any rate,
> Nor seem in the least to mumble ;
> They'll frap you still, do what you will ;
> 'Tis but a folly to grumble.

At the date this ballad was written the midshipman
had hardly come by his own. The title was originally
given to the seamen who acted as messengers and carried
orders from the officers on the quarter-deck to those
on the forecastle, and thus worked amidships or between
these two stations ; it was from this class that master's
mates were generally chosen, as they were active, smart,
young men, whose conduct was always under the eye
of their superiors, to whom they frequently owed their
introduction to a sea life. At that time the midshipmen
messed with the ship's company, but on the after part
of the lower deck, the wardroom being then allotted
to the sick, and the gunroom being the repository for
small arms and the gunner's stores. Later on the position
of the midshipmen was improved with a view to their
supplying officers for the quarter-deck, and they were
then berthed in the cockpit, and various regulations for
their entry were issued. Their training was also regulated
with a view to their fitting themselves for the higher
position, but it was not until the middle of the eighteenth
century that the midshipmen were recognised as " young
gentlemen," and given a uniform. If, however, they
lacked interest, or an opportunity for the display of
their talents, the midshipmen might never rise above

that grade, and "young gentlemen" of venerable appearance and grey hairs were not unknown. Billy Culmer is the traditional example of the ancient midshipman. He is a familiar character in naval memoirs, and many are the anecdotes told about him. He was proud of being the oldest midshipman in the Navy, and is said to have served in that capacity under Lord Hood about 1765, and to have been still serving in the same rank towards the end of the Great War. Mr. Flexible Grummet, in "Leaves from My Log-book," published in the "United Service Journal" in 1839, thus refers to this character when reflecting on the contrast presented by the days of his youth and the Service as it was at that date :—

I will not believe it! What! because I am laid upon the shelf, and shall never more behold the brightness of England's naval glory, is every youngster to vex my spirit with his yarns of the degradation of that Service which my soul so ardently loved? Is it not enough to torture my sight with scarlet patches and facings, but I must also be told that the Middies of the present day use rose-water to wash their hands, and scent their handkerchiefs (a luxury but little known when I was a "young gentleman") with bergamot and perfumes of mille fleurs? The handkerchiefs, too, are made of cambric. Oh, spirit of my revered friend, Billy Culmer, look down with pious indignation upon such enormities as cambric handkerchiefs in a Midshipman's berth. In our days two of dubious complexion were considered quite enough for the whole mess, and these were transferred, not from nose to nose, but from pocket to pocket, as in regular turn we took our seats at the Captain's dinner-table; and woe, or rather a cobbing, betided the offender who dared to use them with indignity on such occasions. Billy, my boy, where are you now? Oh! that I could "parley with your ghost," if it was only to see how comical you would look at overhauling a midshipman's chest in 1839, with three dozen of cambric—white cambric—handkerchiefs to his own cheek! Then there's silk stockings, and frilled night-caps! Oh! Billy, where are you now?—what an innovation!—silk stockings and frilled night-caps!—when, at the period when

Midshipmen were really men-of-war, both stockings and
night-caps were in requisition—the former for a dog's-body
bag, and the latter for a plum-duff, but who on earth, or on
the ocean, could cook a dog's-body in a silk stocking, or a
plum-duff in a frilled night-cap? They call their silk stockings hose! Ah! Billy, the only hose you and I ever knew
was the hose to fill the water-casks in the hold; but now the
Midshipmen case their lower stancheons in silk stockings,
and call them hose! Can anything be more unnatural! Our
worthy, kind-hearted, and industrious old mothers, Billy,
made our shirts themselves—scanty enough it is true, for
there was

> "Thrift, thrift, Horatio,"

and it must be admitted that no lawyer, however clever his
pretensions to legal knowledge, could "seize them entail;"
but still they were home-made—the work of a mother or of
sisters, occasionally aided by the taper fingers of some sweet
little nymph, whose soft blue eyes were melting into tears as

> ". . . she would sit and weep
> At what a sailor suffers."

In the "Memoirs of James Hardy Vaux" are some
verses said to have been written by the younger midshipman of the *Astræa*, frigate, in 1798, from which three
verses may be quoted. The young gentleman begins
his moan by regretting that he entered the Service, for
had he "in the country stay'd, I might have learnt some
useful trade, and scorn'd the white lapelle."

> When first on board the ship I went,
> My belly full, my mind content,—
>   No sorrows touched my heart:
> I view'd my coat, so flash and new,
> My gay cockade, my hanger too,
>   And thought them wondrous smart.
>
> But now, alas! my coat is rent;
> My hanger's pawned; my money spent;
>   My former friends I've missed;
> And when of hardships I complain,
> My messmates swear 'tis all in vain,
>   And cry, "What made you list?"
>
> *   *   *   *

> Shiv'ring he walks the quarter-deck,
> Dreading the stern lieutenant's check,
>   Who struts the weather side ;
> With glass and trumpet in his hand,
> He bellows forth his harsh command,
>   With arrogance and pride.

With the prospect of peace, the midshipman's position, if he was without influence, became a dismal one, for he was liable to be turned ashore, and in 1763 we find one disconsolately facing the problem thus :—

> Says the midshipman, " I have no trade ; I have got my trade for to
>   chuse :
> I will go to St. James Park gate, and there I'll set blacking of shoes."

An amusing caricature by W. Heath, published about 1827, showed a midshipman on half-pay engaged as a bootblack on Tower Hill, and the following verses, entitled " A Sketch from the Cockpit," were written about the same time :—

> I do remember well a midshipman,—
> In cockpit's gloom he messed—in berth enscreen'd
> Made up of dirty hammocks, cobbling a boot :
> Desponding were his looks—his rigging shy ;
> Promotion, long-deferred, had soured his phiz—
> An empty bottle on an old chest stood,
> Wherein was stuck a wasting candle-end,
> Which glimmered round a solitary ray ;—
> The pendent shelf was garnished out with junk,
> Some biscuits, and the fragments of a pipe.
> Hamilton Moore, Steel's Lists, with day's-works soiled
> And tailors' bills *not paid* made up the score.
> Noting this misery, to my self I said,—
> " Now, if Lord Melville had a spare commission,
> And wished to make a son of Neptune happy,
> He here might find an object to his mind ! "

Nevertheless, these groans and sorrowful reflections do not present the popular view of the midshipman, whose courage, bravery, and warmth of feeling have been the theme of scores of poets down to our own time.

> He was one who, in youth, on the stormy seas,
>   Was a far and a fearless stranger ;
> Who, borne on the billow, and blown by the breeze,
>   Had deemed lightly of death and of danger.

*   *   *   *

Yet in this rude school had his heart still kept
All the freshness of gentlest feeling ;
Not in woman's warm eye hath a tear ever slept
More of softness and kindness revealing.

Here are some verses which present another phase of his character :—

I'm here or there a jolly dog,
At land or sea I'm all a-gog,
To fight, or kiss, or touch the grog,
　For I'm a jovial midshipman,
　A smart young midshipman,
　A little midshipman !
To fight, or kiss, or touch the grog,
　O, I'm a jovial midshipman.

And about the time of Trafalgar another rhymester tells us :—

When tossing on old ocean's foam,
Perhaps, a thousand leagues from home,
No danger can his mind o'ercome,
　Or daunt the dashing midshipman.

All this expresses a certain truth with regard to the midshipman, but it is only a partial truth. The balladists who sought to catch more than the humours of the hours of ease were few. Those who have read what precedes in this volume will know how the gay burden of song falls into the harmony of our literary picture. The midshipman, like every one else on board, had hard and serious work to do—to do with the cheery enthusiasm expressed in the ballad—and it was done with the professional keenness which made seamen what they were. In the great war especially a vivid zest was in all of them for the life of the sea. Its excitements and dangers were the salt of endeavour and the joy of existence. The letters which young officers wrote to their parents and friends show that the flame of zealous seamanhood and high patriotism burned within them. Therefore, when we read even of the jollity of the midshipman we must remember that other side of the sea character which has been described elsewhere.

A ballad that seems to breathe the very air of the Restoration period is one published by D'Urfey in his " Wit and Mirth ; or, Pills to Purge Melancholy." It is a regular carousing song, such as, no doubt, was sung by the tarpaulins under Sandwich and Narborough, or privateersmen like Woodes Rogers and Dampier. It was an officers' song by the allusion to the punch-clubbers in the coach, the cabin of the captain, and appears to have been a favourite well into the eighteenth century :—

> All Hands up aloft,
> Swab the Coach fore and aft,
> For the Punch Clubbers strait will be sitting ;
> For fear the Ship rowl,
> Sling off a full Bowl,
> For our Honour let all things be fitting :
>
> * * * *
>
> The Winds veering aft,
> Then loose ev'ry Sail,
> She'll bear all her Topsails a'trip :
> Heave the Logg from the Poop,
> It blows a fresh Gale,
> And a just Account on the Board keep :
>
> * * * *
>
> The Quartier must Cun,
> Whilst the foremast-man steers ;
> Here's a Health to each Port where'er bound,
> Who delays 'tis a Bumper,
> Shall be drubb'd at the Geers ;
> The Depth of each Cup therefore sound :
>
> Chorus: To our noble Commander,
> To his Honour and Wealth,
> May he drown and be damn'd,
> That refuses the Health :
> Here's to thee honest Harry,
> Thanks honest Will,
> Old true Penny still,
> Whilst the one is a drinking,
> The other shall fill.

The captain and lieutenant do not make any great figure in nautical song. Both of them were, perhaps, too serious a subject for the balladist, except sometimes by way of gibe. The lieutenant might, indeed, in some of his tribulations, have won the songster's tuneful sympathy, for when peace came the occupation of many of them was gone. Thus "An officer of the Royal Navy" in a curious booklet, "The Story of the Learned Pig," 1786, exclaims: "Our parents had much better have made barbers and tailors of us than to have given us a profession which only taught us to look high to make us more sensible of our fall."

The quartier or quartermaster (the contraction being common in pamphlets, plays, and songs of the time) had his station at the " cun " or " conn," as it was spelt later, on the quarter-deck, that is, he stood in the weather netting when the ship was close hauled, or by the compass when she was running free, and directed the helmsman. Master's mates were sometimes chosen from the quartiers, and these steady, reliable, petty officers were deemed to belong to the master's gang, and specially attached to the navigation and pilotage of the ship, as the boatswain's mates were to the officers charged with the internal economy and equipment of the vessel.

After the midshipmen, the officers most prominent in the ballads, and especially the earlier ones, are the master, the purser, and the boatswain. In "The Mariners' Song," from the " Comedy of Common Conditions," the seamen sing of their officers and their vessel :—

> And here is a maister excelleth in skill,
>   And our maister's mate he is not to seeke ;
> And here is a boteswaine will do his good will,
>   And here is a ship, boy, we never had leak.

But another Tudor seaman, who gives " Cordial Advice to Rash Young Men who think to advance their decaying fortunes by navigation, showing them the many dangers and hardships that sailors endure," explains what form the " goodwill " of the boatswain may take at times, presumably from sad experience. Readers of what precedes will know exactly how to appreciate the things to which the songster alludes.

For if we faint or faulter,
    to ply our cruel work,
The Boatswain with the halter
    does beat us like a Turk:

*   *   *

A cursed cat with thrice three tails,
    does much increase our woe.

The feeling of the men towards both the purser and
the boatswain is indicated in the musical piece written
by Sir William Davenant, where the helmsman of Sir
Francis Drake sings :—

Oh, how the purser shortly will wonder,
    When he sums in his book
    All the wealth we have took,
And finds that we'll give him none of the plunder ;

*   *   *   *

At sight of our gold the boatswain will bristle,
    But not finding his part
    He will break his proud heart,
And hang himself strait i' the chain of his whistle.

The purser was perhaps the best-abused of the officers,
but not altogether with justice, since his supposed mal-
practices were frequently a consequence of the regulations of the time.   He was, in fact, made the scapegoat
of " Ye gent behind ye curtaine," and other harpies
who battened on the seamen.   The mistake was one
into which the landsman might easily fall, and the more
ignorant among the seamen doubtless believed it.   Thus
we find the ballad entitled " The Sailor's Complaint ; or,
The True Character of the Purser of a Ship."

As his name foully stinks, so his butter rank doth smell,
Both hateful to sailors, scarce good enough for hell :
The nation allows men what's fitting to eat,
But he, curse attend him, gives to us musty meat ;
But bisket that's mouldy, hard stinking Suffolk cheese,
And pork cut in pounds, and pork cut in pounds,
    for to eat with our pease.

This was probably written by a landsman like Ned
Ward, at a seaman's suggestion, in the reign of Queen

Anne, and the purser is described as " the worst of all
plagues that e'er fate did decree to vex and to punish
poor sailors at sea." It was published later on as a
broadside with a rough woodcut of a ship such as may
often be seen reproduced on Liverpool or Newcastle ware.
The popularity of some of the verses may be gauged by
the circumstance that they are also to be found on jugs
and mugs made for the seafaring classes. But a real
sailor puts the matter somewhat differently, and it should
be noted that at the time of the mutiny in 1797, when the
victualling was a most serious ground of dissatisfaction,
it was the system and the regulations, and not the
officer whose duty it was to put the latter into execution,
that were complained of.

> Not winds to voyagers at sea,
> Nor showers to earth more necessary be,
> Nor to the thirsty boatswain flip,
> Than is a purser to a ship.

Before we leave this phase of the subject we may
quote one more song which has been ascribed to Gabriel
Harvey, and in which all the officers are mentioned.
It is entitled "In Praise of Sailors ; the hard fortunes
which do befall them on the seas when landmen sleep
upon their beds."

> When as the raging Seas do fome,
>   and lofty winds do blow,
> The Saylors they go to the top,
>   then Landmen stay below.
>
> Our Masters mate takes helm in hand,
>   his course he steers full well,
> When as the lofty winds do blow
>   and raging Seas do swell.
>
> Our Master to his Compass goes,
>   so well he plies his charge,
>   *   *   *
> The Boatson he's under the Deck,
>   a man of courage bold,
>   *   *   *

2 E

The Pylot he stands on the Chain,
  with a line and a lead to sound,

          *   *   *

Our Captain he is on the Poop,
  a man of might and power,

          *   *   *

The Quarter-Master is a man,
  so well his charge plies he,
He calls them to the Pomp amain,
  to keep their leakt Ship free.

Now let us look at the character of the foremast man,
his views of life and duty. His creed, one rhymester
tells us, was thus :—

    . . . Manliness, merit, mirth, friendship, and love,
      All in that gallant sailor unite,
  Who, while doing his duty below or above,
    Is as ready to pardon as willing to fight.

And Dibdin, who sang " Content's this life's best weather
gage," lost no opportunity of inculcating a similar
standard :—

          Love honour as thy life,
            Never do a paltry thing ;
          Protect thy friend and wife,
            Spare foes, and serve thy king.

Charles Dibdin appears to have come to London
just about the time when the country was terribly cast
down by the disaster which led to Byng's execution.
As we have pointed out elsewhere, attempts were made
in the theatres to revive the national spirit and patriotism,
and the impressions Dibdin then received gave fruit in
his after life. As he says himself, " the character of
the British tar, plain, manly, honest, and patriotic,
had not very pointedly been put forward. I thought,
therefore, the subject honourable, and commendable,
and in some degree novel ; especially as it would give
an opportunity through public duty of expressing private
affection." He appears to have been sincerely and
deeply attached to his brother, a captain in the mer-

chant service, and, when the sailor died, to have
translated his sympathy and sorrow into verse in the
favourite song :—

> Here, a sheer hulk, lies poor Tom Bowling.

Dibdin himself was fond of the sea, and made three
voyages, as he says, to learn the sea phrases. He appears also to have taken every opportunity of making
himself acquainted with the character of seafaring
people, and in his ballads, which it should be remembered
were many of them written for the theatre, he never
fails to place the sailor in a good light, or to try to raise
him in his own estimation and that of the public. The
first sailor song he ever wrote was addressed to " The
Friendly Tars " :—

> While up the shrouds the sailor goes,
>   Or ventures on the yard,
> The landsman, who no better knows,
>   Believes his lot is hard.
>
> But Jack with smiles each danger meets,
>   Casts anchor, heaves the log,
> Trims all the sails, belays the sheets,
>   And drinks his can of grog.

At another time he sings :—

> A Sailor's life's a life of woe,
>   He works now late, now early ;
> Now up and down, now to and fro ;
>   What then ? he takes it cheerly.

And again :—

> Why should the hardy tar complain !
> 'Tis certain true he weathers more,
> From dangers on the roaring main,
> Than lazy lubbers do ashore.

It may be a little difficult to understand, but there
can be no question that many of the prime sailors,
perhaps the older men in particular, had a real liking
for weather the very thought of which to those who
have lived their lives on shore is discomforting. Captain
Mahan, in his reminiscences, is inclined to admit that
there were some sailors who actually enjoyed what they

would themselves describe as dirty weather, and he says, of the song from which we quote a verse below, " This ditty does grotesquely reproduce the lazy satisfaction and security of the old-timers under the conditions :—

> One night came on a hurricane, the sea was mountains rolling,
> When Barney Buntline turned his quid, and said to Billy Bowling,
> A strong sow-wester's blowing, Billy, can't you hear it roar now ?
> Lord help 'em, how I pities all unhappy folks on shore now !

The true seaman, indeed, entertained a sovereign contempt for those he was pleased to call landlubbers, but this feeling had in it a strong element of pity for what he regarded as the unfortunate condition of those who were unable to share his views of the benefits of salt-water experience. His scornful attitude towards the soldier also finds frequent expression in the ballads. We have in our collection a very curious pictorial broadsheet, in which three sailors of woebegone appearance, with Greenwich Hospital in the background, are chanting a ditty in which the following lines occur :—

> We care not for those Martial-men that do our states disdain ;
> But we care for those Merchant-men that do our states maintain.

As was always the case, the mariner's heart and hand were ever open to his brother seaman, or, indeed, to any one in distress, although the comradeship of the sea has ever the strongest of all calls upon his sympathy and benevolence.

> But seamen, you know, are inur'd to hard gales,
> Determin'd to stand by each other ;
> And the boast of a tar, wheresoever he sails,
> Is the heart that can feel for another.

And Thomas Dibdin tells us :—

> 'Tisn't the jacket and trousers blue,
> The song or the grog so cheerly,
> That show us the heart of a seaman true,
> Or tell us his manners sincerely ;

> * * * * *

'Tis the hour of distress, when misfortunes oppress,
　And virtue finds sorrow assail her,
'Tis the bosom of grief, made glad by relief,
　That pictures the heart of a sailor.

While the seaman's courage, his generosity, chivalry,
and cheerful devotion to duty are unquestioned in the
ballads, very serious doubts are raised about his constancy.　He is believed, indeed, to have absorbed something of the fickleness and instability of the element
upon which he passed his life.　The view taken of him
by one poet is expressed in the lines :—

A sailor's life's a pleasant life,
　He freely roams from shore to shore ;
In ev'ry port he finds a wife ;
　What can a sailor wish for more ?

And this was probably a paraphrase of some earlier
verses which we find in a musical play in the middle
of the eighteenth century :—

How happy is the sailor's life,
　From coast to coast to roam ;
In every port he finds a wife,
　In every land a home.
　　He loves to range,
　　He's nowhere strange ;
　He never will turn his back
　　To friend or foe ;
　　No, masters, no ;
　My life for honest Jack.

But John Gay puts into the mouth of Black-eyed
Susan's lover the sailor's own view and his refutation of
this charge :—

Believe not what the landmen say,
　Who tempt with doubts thy constant mind :
They'll tell thee sailors, when away,
　In every port a mistress find :
Yes, yes, believe them, when they tell thee so,
For thou art present wheresoe'er I go !

And Lieut. H. B. Gascoigne of the Marines, in his "Path
to Naval Fame" writes :—

> Much I lament that fate still bids me roam,
> O'er stormy seas, far distant from my home ;
> Yet this believe, that wheresoe'er I go,
> No change of sentiment my heart can know.

Of the fact that the seaman at all times found moments in the intervals of his duty to think of those he had left behind there is ample evidence. It may be as Arnold wrote, that when the enemy was in sight, none " thought of home or beauty," but we have Lord Dorset's whimsical song, written on the eve of the battle of Solebay, to prove that there were times when thoughts of the dear ones far away stirred the heart and the imagination :—

> To all you ladies now at land
>   We men at sea indite ;
> But first would have you understand
>   How hard it is to write ;
> The Muses now, and Neptune too,
> We must implore to write to you.
>
> Then if we write not by each post,
>   Think not we are unkind,
> Nor yet conclude our ships are lost
>   By Dutchmen, or by wind ;
> Our tears we'll send a speedier way,
> The tide shall waft them twice a day.
>
> In justice you cannot refuse
>   To think of our distress,
> When we for hopes of honour lose
>   Our certain happiness ;
> All those designs are but to prove
> Ourselves more worthy of your love.
>   *   *   *   *
> In hopes this declaration moves
>   Some pity for our tears ;
> Let's hear of no inconstancy,
> We have too much of that at sea.

Richard Lovelace, too, leaving his sweetheart and going beyond the seas, shares this sentiment :—

> Though seas and land betwixt us both,
>   Our faith and troth,
>   Like separated souls,
>   All time and space controls ;
> Above the highest sphere we meet
> Unseen, unknown ; and greet as Angels greet.

Nor did his sweetheart leave the sailor without some keepsake as a reminder of her he had left behind. Sometimes the souvenir took the form of a broken coin, but in " The Gallant Seaman's Resolution," a slip song, the tar is presented with a more costly memento, since the lady sings :—

If I should hear, in any case, that thou abroad should married be,
Then would I weep, lament and grieve, and break my heart for love
    of thee.
            Turn to thy love and take a kiss,
            This gold about thy wrist I'll tie,
            And always when thou look'st on this,
            Think on thy loving landlady.

Charles Dibdin probably hit upon the more likely keepsake, and the subject of his verse has been illustrated over and over again :—

            Upon his 'bacco-box he views
            Nancy the poet, Love the muse :
            " If you loves I as I loves you,
            No pair so happy as we two."

Sometimes the lady was not content with giving her sweetheart a keepsake, but she felt that she could take better care of him if she went too, and, braving the perils of the ocean, shared his discomforts and dangers. In a curious old ballad—which with some alterations was long a favourite with the groups round the forebitts in the evening at sea, the unhappy result to two faithful lovers is related. The following verses tell the story :—

            Farewel, my Heart's Delight,
                Lady adue ;
            I now must take my flight,
                What e're insue.
            My Country-men I see,
                Cannot yet agree,
            Since it will no better be.
                England farewel !

            *   *   *

Then let me with you go,
    Heart, Love, and Joy,
I will attend on you,
    And be your Boy;
If you will go to Sea,
I'le serve you night and day,
    For here I will not stay,
        If you go hence.

*   *   *

The Seas are dangerous,
    Strangers unkind;
The Rocks are perillous,
    So is the Wind;
My care is all for thee,
As thou mayest plainly see,
Dear Heart go not with me,
    But stay behind.

*   *   *

In man's Apparrel she
    To Sea now went,
Because with him she'd be,
    Her Heart's Content.
She cut her lovely hair,
And no mistrust was there,
That she a Maiden fair
    Was at that time.

*   *   *

The Ship being cast away,
    Fortune so frown'd:
He swum to shore that day,
    But she was drown'd;
O his true Love was drown'd,
And never after found,
He was incompast round
    With grief and care.

It was not always that the result of the lady's escapade
terminated so tragically. Sometimes, as in the case of
" The Undaunted Seaman," who set out under Sir
John Ashby to fight the French foe, the tar eventually
persuaded his sweetheart to stay ashore, although :—

With sighs and tears this damsel said, " If you resolve to go to sea,
In sailor's robes I'll be array'd and freely go along with thee;
Life and fortune I will venture rather than to stay on shore:
Grief will oppress me, and possess me, that I ne'er shall see thee
    more."

Then, again, there is the comforting ballad of " Con-
stance and Anthony," in which the lady, by leave of
her sweetheart, who could not part with her, entered,
and, " drest in man's array, she seem'd the blithest lad,
seen on a summer's day."

> In the Ship 'twas her lot
>   To be the Under-Cook ;
> And at the Fire hot,
>   Great Pains she ever took ;
> She serv'd every one
>   Fitting to their degree ;
> And now and then alone
>   She kissed Anthony.

This loving couple, after many adventures, in which
they suffered the chances of wreck and battle, presently
returned to their own county of Westmorland, there to
live in mirth and glee.

> Still she cries, Anthony,
>   My bonny Anthony,
> Good Providence we see,
>   Hath guarded thee and me.

And then, again, there is the story of " The Valiant
Mayde," who, when her father was slain, took command
of the vessel and beat off the enemy :—

> There was a gallant damsel, a damsel of fame,
> She was daughter of the captain, and Nancy was her name ;
> She stood upon the deck, and gallantly she calls,
> "O stand to your guns, boys, and load with cannon-balls."
> 　　　*　　　*　　　*　　　*
> We fought for a watch, for a watch so severe,
> We scarcely had a man left was able for to steer,
> We scarcely had a man left could fire off a gun,
> And the blood from our deck like a river it did run.
>
> For quarter, for quarter, the Spanish lads did cry,
> "No quarter, no quarter," this damsel did reply ;
> "You've had the best of quarter that I can well afford,
> You must fight, sink, or swim, boys, or jump overboard."

Indeed, in the romantic ballads of the eighteenth
century, and in the early nineteenth, the maid who,

disguised as a sailor, accompanies her lover, or if he is faithless, pursues him to sea, is a most prominent character. Sometimes her sweetheart is torn from her arms by the press-gang, and then she sings :—

> Aboard of my true love's ship I'll go,
> And brave each blowing gale ;
> I'll splice, I'll tack, I'll reef, I'll row,
> And haul with him the sail :
>   In jacket blue,
>   And trousers, too,
> With him I'll cruise afar,
>   There shall not be a smarter chap
> Aboard of a man-of-war.

Of the young lady who pursued her faithless lover to sea, the female lieutenant was probably the favourite ; she is to be found in many versions in the illustrated slip songs, and has been made the heroine of more than one play. We read how when Billy Taylor was about to be married the press-gang carried him away :—

> Soon his true love followed after,
> Under the name of William Carr;
> Her soft hands and milk-white fingers
> Were daub'd all over with the nasty pitch and tar.
>
> Now behold the first engagement,
> Bold she fought among the rest ;
> Her jacket open, void of danger,
> All exposed her lily-white breast.
>
> When the captain came for to hear of it,
> He said, " What wind has blown you here ? "
> " Kind sir, I came to find my true love,
> Him you prest and I love so dear."
>
> *   *   *   *
>
> Then she call'd quick for a pistol,
> Which was brought at her command ;
> Strait she shot the bold deceiver,
> With the fair one in his hand.
>
> When the captain saw the wonder
> Which the maiden fair had done,
> He quickly made her the first lieutenant
> Of the gallant Thunder Bomb.

By far the best song of this class, and a favourite one
among the junior officers forty years ago, is that entitled
"Harry Grady and Miss Elinor Ford," to be sung to the
tune of "Banks of the Dee."   It is printed among some
nautical sketches by Hamilton Moore, junior, published
in 1840.   These are three of the five verses :—

> In Cawsand Bay lying,
> The Blue Peter flying,
> The hands all turn'd up for the anchor to weigh ;
> There came off a lady,
> As fresh as a May day,
> Who looking up modestly, these words did say :

> "I wants a young man, there,
> So do what you can there,
> To hoist me aboard, or to send him to me ;
> His name's Harry Grady,
> And I am a lady
> Come off for to save him from going to sea."

>   *   *   *   *

> "Avast," says the lady,
> "Don't mind him, Hal Grady,
> He once was your captain, but now you're at large ;
> You shan't stay aboard her,
> In spite that man's order " ;
> Then out of her bosom she lugg'd his discharge !

> Says the captain, says he now :
> "I'm blowed, but he's free now " ;
> Hal sings out, "Let Weatherface have all my clothes ";
> For the shore then he steer'd her,
> And all the hands cheer'd her,
> But the captain was jealous, and look'd down his nose !

>   *   *   *   *

> Their house it was greater
> Nor e'er a first-rater,
> With servants in uniform handing the drink;
> And a garden to go in
> Where flowers was blowin',
> Sunflower, jessamine, lily and pink.

> Then he got eddication
> Just fit for his station,
> For you know we are never too old for to larn ;
> And his shipmates soon found him,
> With young uns around him,
> All "chips of the old block," from stem to the starn.

There is no lack, indeed, among the sentimental ballads of those which indicated the preference of the ladies :—

> O praise ye the jovial sailor O,
> No red-coat, tinker, or tailor O,
>   Can e'er with him compare,
>   For liveliness and air,
> And all we enjoys through his labour O.

And this in its way is but a variant of a much older song attributed to the time of the Commonwealth, in which a fair maid sings " a pleasant Song made of a Saylor, Who excells a Miller, Weaver, and a Taylor, Likewise brave gallants that goes fine and rare, None of them with a Seaman can compare " :—

> The gallant brave Seaman God bless him I say,
> He is a great pains-taker both night and day,
> When he's on the Ocean so hard worketh he
> Then of all sorts of tradesmen a Seaman for me.
>
>   *   *   *   *
>
> Here's a health to my dear, come pledge me who please,
> To all gallant Seamen that sail on the seas,
> Pray God bless and keep them from all dangers free,
> So of all sorts of tradesmen a Seaman for me.

And this, again, is not unlike some verses of Laurence Price, which he entitles " A dainty new ditty composed and penned, the deeds of brave seamen to praise and commend, 'twas made by a maid that to Gravesend did pass, now mark and you quickly shall hear how it was." The first verse reads :—

> As lately I travelled
>   Towards Gravesend,
> I heard a fair Damsel,
>   A Sea-man commend,
> And as in a Tilt-boat
>   We passéd along,
> In praise of brave Sea-men
>   She sung this new Song,
> Come Tradesman or Merchant,
>   Whoever he be,
> There's none but a Seaman shall marry with me.

The songs in which the maiden, after due consideration

of all other callings, decides that " of all sorts of tradesmen, a Seaman for me," must have been popular with
the people on the waterside when Congreve wrote " Love
for Love," and Doggett helped him, for it was a song
with this refrain that Ben sang in the comedy. This
song, again, was afterwards made the plot of a boisterous
farce played at the fairs. That there was a difference
of opinion upon the trustworthiness of the seaman as a
lover has been already shown, and here are a couple
of verses which exhibit the contrast very clearly. The
first is from a garland published in the reign of Queen
Anne :—

> Besides the many dangers that are upon the seas,
> Whenever they are on the shore they ramble where they please ;
> For up and down in sea-port town they court both old and young ;
> They will deceive ; do not believe the sailor's flattering tongue.

And this from one of Charles Dibdin's earlier songs :—

> That girl who fain would choose a mate
> Should ne'er in fondness fail her,
> May thank her lucky stars if fate
> Should splice her to a sailor.

Of all the sentimental ballads dealing with a sailor's
life, those which depict the joys of his return to the shore
are the most numerous, and there are more illustrations
of his departure—" Sweet Love, take heart, For we but
part, In joy to meet again "—and of his happy return,
than of all the other episodes connected with the vicissitudes of his career. Songs of this character date back to
the seventeenth century, as " a pleasant new song betwixt a sailor and his love," of which there is a version
in Halliwell's " Early Naval Ballads."

> *He:* Smile on me, be not offended,
> Pardon grant for my amiss,
> Let thy favour so befriend me,
> As to seal it with a kiss.
> To me I swear,
> Thou art my Dear,

That for thy sake I'le fancy none ;
  Then do not frown,
  But sit thee down,
Sweet, kiss and bid me welcome home.

*   *   *   *

She : Seeing thou art home returnèd,
  Thou shalt not go againe in haste,
But lovingly come sit down by me,
  Let my arms imbrace thy waist :
    Farewell annoy,
    Welcome my Joy,
Now lullaby shall be the song,
    For now my Heart
    Sings "loath to depart"
Then kiss, I bid thee welcome home.

It is not unlikely that this is the song referred to by Chaplain Teonge as sung by the men of the *Assistance* in 1675 when they parted with their wives and sweethearts at the mouth of the Thames (see p. 109). Boteler also seems to refer to this song or to the air to which it was sung. There is another ballad, in which the sailor, returning and finding his mistress bewailing his absence, puts her constancy to the test by pretending that he is some one else and has heard of her lover's death, when, finding that she is still true, he reveals himself :—

Unto this maid I stept,
  Asking what grieved her,
She answered me and wept,
  Fates had deceived her :
"My love is prest," quoth she,
  "To cross the ocean,
Proud waves do make the ship
  Ever in motion."

*   *   *

Under one banner bright
  For England's glory,
Your love and I did fight—
  Mark well my story :
By an unhappy shot
  We too were parted ;
His death's wound then he got,
  Though valiant-hearted.

*   *   *

She, raging, fled away,
  Like one distracted,
Not knowing what to say,
  Nor what she acted.
At last she curst her fate,
  And showed her anger,
Saying, "Friend, you come too late,
  I'll have no stranger."

* * *

He, hearing what she said,
  Made his love stronger,
Off his disguise he laid,
  And staid no longer.
When her dear love she knew
  In wanton fashion
Into his arms she flew,—
  Such is love's passion.

* * *

Then hand in hand they walk,
  With mirth and pleasure,
They laugh, they kiss, they talk
  —Love knows no measure.
Now both do sit and sing—
  But she sings clearest ;
Like nightingale in Spring,
  Welcome my dearest.

A later song illustrates the custom which ruled for
so long of permitting the girls to come on board the ship
when she returned to port, in order to compensate Jack
for lack of liberty :—

No more of waves and winds the sport,
Our vessel is arrived in port ;
At anchor, see, she safely rides,
And gay red ropes adorn her sides ;
The sails are furled, the sheets belayed,
The crimson petticoats displayed—
Deserted are the useless shrouds,
And wenches come aboard in crowds ;
Then, come, my lads, the flip put round,
While safely moored on English ground.

And then, again, there was that not altogether unusual
experience of the sailor, when flying to the arms of his
dear, he discovered that she had been faithless. The
philosophy of the sailor and the characteristic nonchalance

with which he received the news find expression in Hudson's hornpipe ditty, " Jack Robinson " :—

> The perils and the dangers of the voyage were past,
> And the ship at Portsmouth arrived at last,
> The sails all furled, and the anchor cast,
> The happiest of the crew was Jack Robinson.
>
>   ✱   ✱   ✱   ✱   ✱
>
> Says the lady, says she, " I've changed my state,"
> " Why, you don't mean," says Jack, " that you've got a mate ;
> You know you promised me." Says she, " I couldn't wait,
> For no tidings could I gain of you, Jack Robinson."
>
> " But to fret and to stew about it's all in vain,
> I'll get a ship and go to Holland, France, or Spain,
> No matter where ; to Portsmouth I'll ne'er come again,"
> And he was off afore you could say Jack Robinson.

This, however, was the exception, and a far better ending was that when the dauntless sailor could sing :—

> Now, all the toils and dangers past,
> And Susan's love remains ;
> The honest tar is blest at last,
> Her smiles reward his pains.

There was another inducement to the sailor to be faithful, an important one, since if he should prove faithless or unkind, the fact might soon be revealed to his shipmates. In the night-watches at sea strange sights appeared to the superstitious seamen, and presently the faithless one who had treated his sweetheart badly might share the fate of William Grismond :—

> There is some wicked person
> The shipmen they did say,
> Within the ship we know it,
> That cannot pass away ;
> We must return to land here,
> And make no more delay.

And then, moreover, if his crime had been of a particularly heinous nature, the ghost of " his deserted Dearie " might come for him as Nan of Wapping's did for Jack Oakum, and, accompanied by diabolical imps, demand his carcase, lest evil befell the ship and those that sailed in her.

> Then, to preserve both ship and men,
> Into the boat they forced him then ;
> The boat sunk down in a flame of fire,
> Which made the sailors all admire.

Ballads of this character, fruitful of warning for the faithless and fickle, usually wound up in this fashion :—

> All you young men and maidens pray learn by my song,
> To be true to your sweethearts and do them no wrong ;
> Prove constant and just, and not false-hearted be,
> And so I will now conclude my new Ditty.

There is one other class of sailor's song that must be referred to, the so-called chanty. Something has already been said on the subject. We are not able to agree either with the statement that the chanty is a modern form of sailor song, or that it was the invention of the merchant service. We have already given an example of the use of the verb to chant in a song dating back to the early eighteenth century, but the chanty itself is much more ancient. Luiz de Camoens, in his " Lusiadas," originally published in 1572, tells us, in his description of Vasco da Gama's voyage to India, that it was the custom, when getting the ship under way, or making sail, for the mariners to sing songs and catches to lighten their work. Such is the custom of foreign sailors to this day, and it is more than probable that it was also the custom in English ships, since the form of many of the older songs is that of the chanty. It was not until towards the end of the eighteenth century that the introduction of some form of instrumental music, the fiddle or the bagpipes, made the chanty unnecessary as an accompaniment to the work of the sailors in the men-of-war. That even then it was used at times is also capable of proof. For example, Gascoigne, who commanded the Marines on board the *Melpomene* frigate in 1805, in describing the evolution of beating the ship to windward, distinctly refers to a chanty :—

> " Now with a song the bowlines well they haul."

2 F

In the same poem he tells us how in the evening at sea:—

> On the forecastle a cheerful ring
> Sit at their ease, and ship-made verses sing,
> Of pot-house scenes, and girls they left on shore,
> Or husbands tame, whose wives the breeches wore.

But although it was no longer the practice in the larger men-of-war to sing on every occasion to lighten the work, that it was so still in the small craft we have the evidence of a naval officer in the " United Service Journal " for January, 1834, who, describing the work in a revenue cruiser, writes as follows : " On board a well-disciplined man-of-war no person except the officers is allowed to speak during the performance of the various evolutions. When a great many men are employed together, a fifer or a fiddler usually plays some of their favourite tunes : and it is quite delightful to see the glee with which Jack will ' stamp and go,' keeping exact time to ' Jack's the Lad,' or ' The College Hornpipe.' On board a revenue cruiser, for want of music, it is customary for one of the men to give them a song, which makes the crew unite their strength and pull together. The following is a specimen of this species of composition :—

> " O, haul pulley, yoe.
> (*Chorus, piano.*)
> Cheerly men.
> O, long and strong, yoe, O.
> Cheerly men.
> O, yoe, and with a will,
> Cheerly men.
> (*Grand Chorus, forte.*)
> Cheerly, cheerly, cheerly, O.

> " A long haul for widow Skinner,
> Cheerly men.
> Kiss her well before dinner,
> Cheerly men.
> At her, boys, and win her,
> Cheerly men.
> Cheerly, cheerly, cheerly, O.

" A strong pull for Mrs. Bell,
    Cheerly men.
Who likes a lark right well,
    Cheerly men.
And, what's more, will never tell,
    Cheerly men.
Cheerly, cheerly, cheerly, O.

" O haul and split the blocks,
    Cheerly men.
O haul and stretch her luff,
    Cheerly men.
Young Lovelies, sweat her up,
    Cheerly men.
Cheerly, cheerly, cheerly, O."

Much has been written of late about the old sea
chanties, but we have not seen this one referred to, and
it is the earliest example we have found in which specific
reference is made to the purpose for which it was used. It is
apparently often forgotten in these days, when the difference between the man-of-war's man and the merchant
seaman is obvious to every one, that until about fifty
years ago such a difference hardly existed. Fifty years
before that, the sailor, whether officer or man, passed
and repassed from the national service to that of the
mercantile marine so frequently and so easily as to make
it impossible that there could have been any great
difference in the habits and tastes of those who followed
the sea in either calling. The two great lines of demarcation lay in the stricter discipline of the man-of-war
and the larger pay of the merchant service. For several
years after the Russian War, when the lower decks in
the Navy still contained a large quota of men from the
Mercantile Marine, many of the so-called chanties were
sung by the groups round the forebitts in the evening or
by the men when away on boat duty or seining. It was
most likely after the peace in 1815, when the silent
system became the rule in the Navy, that songs as an
accompaniment to work were prohibited. There are
several indications, too, that chantying was not permitted
in later days in the ships of the East India Company, in

which service the officers wore uniform and carried side arms, and the gun drills, discipline, and routine of the ships were assimilated to those of the Royal Navy.

It will be noticed that the song quoted above was not called a chanty in 1834, nor is there any evidence that the term was applied to its present use until very recently. It is probable, moreover, that although the words of the chanties in use in the Merchant Service during the last fifty years are comparatively modern, the airs in many cases in their original form are of great antiquity. Certainly the words seldom look well in print. What Mr. Masefield has said about them is perfectly true :—

They are songs to be sung under certain conditions, and where those conditions do not exist they appear out of place. At sea, when they are sung in the quiet dog watch, or over the rope, they are the most beautiful of all songs. It is difficult to write them down without emotion; for they are a part of life. One cannot detach them from life. One cannot write a word of them without thinking of days that are over, of comrades who have long been coral, and old beautiful ships, once so stately, which are now old iron.

In concluding this part of our quest for light upon the character of the British sailor we cannot do better than quote the memorandum which the Admiralty addressed to the Fleet at the termination of the Great War. It is a fine tribute to all the serious qualities of the seaman which we have illustrated from the pages of our literature :—

The patience, perseverance, and discipline, the skill, courage, and devotion with which the seamen and marines have upheld the best interests and achieved the noblest triumphs of their country entitle them to the gratitude, not only of their native land, which they have preserved inviolate, but of the other nations of Europe, of whose ultimate deliverance their successes maintained the hope and accelerated the accomplishment.

FAMILY FELICITY.

R. POLLARD, 1785.

Now, all the toils and dangers past,
And Susan's love remains;
The honest tar is blest at last,
And smiles reward his pains.

To face page 436.

on doubtful points must be warned to use great caution
and circumspection. The sense of artistic propriety
is not always on the same plane as the standard of un-
swerving fidelity demanded of the historian. It is
reasonable to expect that the painter will not sacrifice
effect to minutiæ of detail, and the fact must be reckoned
with. It may obviously be necessary sometimes, in order
to obtain a pleasing picture, to omit some particulars,
but the absence of these must not be taken as testimony
that such things were not there, that they did not exist,
or were not in use at the time. And then again the
painter's fancy must have fair play, and it was often
impossible for the artist to reproduce the depicted scene
exactly as it appeared at any given moment, such as we
catch, for example, in the camera. In addition to
judicious elimination, then, the artist will sometimes
have had occasion to introduce features which were not
present, or at least visible conspicuously, but the inclusion of which was necessary to make the scene representative, and to bring home to the spectator a generally
truthful idea of the actual occurrence. We may be
sure that where it was possible to be perfectly correct
and equally effective the artist would not go out of his
way to create a false impression, since to do so would
be entirely foreign to his object.

Nevertheless it is expedient to assume, and, indeed, it
will be found almost invariably that the artistic merits of
a composition bear no relation to its value as historical
evidence, some of the crudest attempts at drawing
yielding more important results by reason of their
actuality as a record of the things seen. As Mr. J. R.
Planché says, in speaking of the invariable practice of
the early illuminators of portraying every person in
the dress of the artist's own time, "had they indulged
their fancy in the invention of costumes, instead of
faithfully copying that which they daily saw, our task
would have been almost impracticable ; for it is seldom,
if ever, that the most minute description can convey
to the mind an object as successfully as the rudest

drawing, and the impression received by the eye is as lasting as it is vivid."

It is not intended here to deal with pictorial effort from the point of view of the art critic, our principal purpose being to regard each illustration as a document to be drawn upon and utilised in so much as it may help to throw light upon the character, the habits, and the customs of the seamen. But of equal importance it has been deemed to indicate to the student of naval life and manners where he may chance to find that of which he is in search; and while no claim is made to have supplied anything like a complete iconography, it is hoped that the selection will be found comprehensive enough for the purpose. Not only have the pictures actually reproduced in the book been described, but our aim has been to give a general reference to the illustrations of naval life and seamen, in whatever form they may be found. It has often been complained, indeed, that no work on naval art, or pictorial art as applied to the Navy, exists, and that information on this subject is difficult to discover. There is foundation for the complaint, but much has been done of late, especially in public institutions such as the Print Room of the British Museum and the Art Department at South Kensington, to remove the reproach. There are also a few chapters here and there in naval books and books upon costume to which the searcher may turn with advantage, while the catalogues of the printsellers who especially deal in this line will often be found of considerable value. Considering, however, the innumerable sources to be searched, it is not surprising that no general work on naval iconography exists, and it is highly probable that the time and labour needed for adequate research would be ill repaid by the demand for such a volume. Nevertheless, an attempt has been made here to indicate the nature of the material that exists, and the various kinds of illustrations that may be obtained and should be found useful. It has been thought best to treat the subject chronologically ; to deal with the illustrations contemporary to the subject depicted only ; and to omit all but the briefest reference to recent work of the kind, since the scope of this volume does not include the modern man-o'-war's man.

The reader will, it is hoped, pardon the digressions which relate to costume apart from illustration, in a time when there were scarcely any illustrations except on stone. Indeed, it may be questioned whether any pictorial representation of a seaman as such can be found before the tenth century, if then. Certainly as regards the inhabitants at the beginning of the history of Britain, such scanty information as exists is not of a pictorial character. But in all the invasions —wave upon wave that passed over these islands of which we have any record up to the beginning of the twelfth century—Celts, Jutes, Saxon, Angles, the newcomers must all have possessed some sea aptitude. It may be assumed, therefore, that their dress was that of men who used the sea, and although these rovers and pirates gradually settled down into some system of society, it is not likely that in the matter of their attire there was any marked distinction between those who turned to agricultural pursuits and those who still followed their original calling. A sleeved jacket or tunic, tight trousers, fastened below the knee with strips of cloth, a conical head-covering, and some form of boot, constituted the garments of all, although in the case of the men of rank these were frequently decorated, and to them in cold or wintry weather a cloak was added. The clothing was made of skins or leather more or less treated, or of cloth, which a Roman writer describes as a coarse felt made of coloured wool, and so thick as to be a protection against the sword. When, however, he went into battle, it was the practice of the warrior to discard the greater portion of his clothing, and from this circumstance may have originated the idea that the islanders were originally without any garments whatever.

In the National Museum of the Society of Antiquaries of Scotland is a portion of sculptured sandstone

which shows a mounted Roman soldier in combat with
four Calèdonians, two of whom he has slain. They
are naked, but armed with spear, sword, and shield.
But on the other side some husbandmen are shown in
wearing apparel such as we have described. During
the period of the Roman dominion the dress, manners,
and language of the conquerors were introduced, and
while the wealthier classes copied the Roman fashions,
the seafarers naturally adopted their weapons and armour.
During this period the sculptor's art comes to our aid,
and there are, perhaps, useful indications to be found
on coins, pottery, tombstones, and even from such unlikely objects as the votive offering of the crew of a
trireme which has been preserved in the Museum at
Boulogne. But from about the fifth century onward
we begin to get the testimony of illuminated manuscripts,
the work of monastic scriptoria, by men whose known
skill and fidelity of delineation prompted them to reproduce that which they themselves had seen.

But in dealing with all pictorial work up to about
the tenth century, it cannot often be said with any
certainty that the subject represented belongs to a fixed
date. In the case of dress, manners, weapons, the
equipment of ships, etc., the old fashion or style always
existed alongside the new, and this was especially the
case with the sailors and all that concerned them, for
although they were to some extent cosmopolitan, and
acquired much from the other nations they visited, they
were at the same time very conservative and jealous of
innovation. Thus it is necessary to exercise great caution
before accepting anything in the shape of naval architecture, or the furniture of a vessel, first, because the
pictures were not executed by seamen, and, secondly, they
were probably the work of men ignorant of all that concerned shipping. It is possible, of course, that in some
cases the heraldic craftsmen or seal engravers may have
been inspired by seamen, particularly where the work was
done for the seaports, but such is scarcely likely in the
case of the pictures which embellish the churchmen's

writings, whether these were of an ecclesiastical or of a lay character. But although this caution applies to the vessels and their equipment, it does not, at any rate to the same extent, apply to the seamen and their costume, and since we have no intention of dealing with such vexed questions as concern the evolution of rigging and the fitment of ships, we may pass from the matter with a warning which applies equally to the Bayeux Tapestry, worked by women with no knowledge of ships, but who doubtless tried to reproduce with their needlework the dress of their time.

From the period when the Roman power was declining until the coming of the Normans there is ample proof that under the various rulers who succeeded in establishing their sovereignty over portions of the island there always existed a professional class of seamen, the Butsecarls or naval bodyguard of the Saxon and Danish chieftains. Their dress must have been such as was suitable for sea wear, and since they were paid, provisioned, and supplied with their garments by the leader whose fortunes they followed, there must needs have been some kind of uniformity in their appearance. We know, indeed, that while the Saxons affected blue or red, the Danes were dressed in black. The invaders, moreover, were better equipped than the hasty levies of countrymen who assembled round a nucleus of professional fighting men to resist them. There is a bronze plaque in the National Museum at Stockholm which shows the Vikings with helmets and armour. From the various sources which have been mentioned it may be assumed that the dress and equipment of the fighting seamen consisted of a tunic, quilted or protected either with rings of metal or scales of leather, shoes, stockings, and drawers, some kind of head protection, and a shield, with, as arms, swords, daggers, spears, and axes. Moreover, as on the sea might was right, every seaman was bound to be ready to fight for his own.

Nothing, however, appears to have been yet discovered in the shape of sculpture or pictures which throws any light upon the methods of the seamen in following their avocation. There are a few figures in the ships of the Bayeux Tapestry which may be meant for seamen, but what they are supposed to be doing is not clear. As William the Conqueror is said to have burnt his vessels, and the crews in all probability accompanied him to the battle of Hastings and in his subsequent movements, we might expect to find some trace of the seamen in the illustrations of these events, but there is nothing of the kind, and they are indistinguishable from the other military men. In the Colloquy of Ælfric, which is preserved in the British Museum, nearly all the different classes of workmen and professional callings are referred to, as the fisher who says, " It is a far row for me to the sea," and the merchant who speaks of going on board his ship and oversea to sell his goods, but no allusion is made to the deep-sea mariner who already, inured to the discipline of the ship and energised by the perils of his environment, must have been a marked man in any assembly. That the personnel of the Navy received its training and support from a commercial marine is more than probable, and that its officers made it an hereditary calling derives a certain amount of support from the fact that it was a son or grandson of Stephen FitzErard, who was captain of the *Mora*, which brought William across, who commanded the *Blanche* on the occasion when the son of Henry I was drowned with many other persons in the wreck of that ship in 1120. Even in the battle scenes by sea, which after the fifth century begin to appear in the decorated manuscripts or on the seals of which we then get examples, there are what are evidently conventional representations of ships, but the sailors as such are unrecognisable. It is noticeable, too, that Strutt, Fairholt, and other writers on costume, either barely mention or omit any reference to the seamen of the Middle Ages. Remembering the very distant relations of the seaman and the artist who was engaged on descriptive work, it is perhaps not strange that until

the sixteenth century we fail to get any satisfactory picture
distinctly labelled as that of a seaman, although pre-
viously there had been an abundance of illustrated
histories, chronicles, and romances, such as those of
Geoffrey of Monmouth and Matthew Paris, with ecclesiastical manuscripts of all kinds, embroidery, tapestry,
and even many official documents, all embellished with
drawings.

After the first few years under the Normans the
missal and other paintings show an increased knowledge
of drawing; there were painters, too, such as those who
were employed by Henry III, probably to paint frescoes
in the Palaces of Windsor and Westminster, and the
stained - glass windows exhibited great improvement.
Yet in spite of all this artistic development only a very
incidental light, and that of the slightest, is thrown upon
our subject. Among all the seals, only that of Pevensey
in the thirteenth century can be said to give an indication of the dress of the Cinque Ports seamen, whom
we know from other sources to have worn white quilted
cotton jacks with the cognisance of the ports emblazoned
upon them before and behind. Even the Black Book
of the Admiralty, dating probably from the early part of
the fifteenth century, although dealing with the manners
and customs of the seamen, contains no scenes of nautical
life among those which embellished its illuminated initials.
The nautical illustrations, of which there are many, are
of the type of those showing a ship attacking a fort
in 1218, and a sea fight, reproduced by Sir Harris
Nicolas in his "Naval History," which, it has been
conjectured, were from the pencil of Matthew Paris, and
afford some idea of the methods of sea fighting in the
thirteenth century.

In Queen Mary's Psalter, which contains a variety
of drawings of secular subjects, there is a picture
of tilting on the water, a kind of tournament which
can only have found favour with men at home in
boats. In the Ellesmere MSS. of the fifteenth century
there is a picture of Chaucer's Shipman, and in a con-

temporary history of Richard II is an illustration of a
fleet, with figures of the characters on board the ships
in the costume of that period. The drawings in the
manuscript of John Rous, which were reproduced by
Strutt in his " Manners and Customs of the Inhabitants
of England," give the ships of the Earl of Warwick,
and are among the very best examples, as they show
clearly the crossbowmen, the archers with longbows,
and even the cannons with which the ships were armed, as
well as the dress of the combatants. These wear iron
morions or leather helmets, and quilted jacks, either of
cotton or leather, but the armour seems to be restricted
to the headpiece and to something like a breastplate.
The jack is in some cases worn loose and in others is
belted, a dagger and pouch being suspended from the
waist. There are also in the British Museum several
French or Flemish manuscripts, in which occur some
pretty little pictures of warships and sea battles. There
is, indeed, an ample field for further investigation, for
it is very doubtful if all the manuscripts which have
been preserved have ever been carefully overhauled
with a view to obtaining accurate knowledge of how the
mariners of the Middle Ages were dressed and armed.

The next step forward is the introduction of printing,
woodcuts, and engraving. The early woodcuts used in
England were probably of foreign origin, even those
made in this country being copied from the work of
foreigners, and therefore entirely useless as illustrations of contemporary English life. When a little later,
or about the beginning of the sixteenth century, we do
find the printed books illustrated by cuts, the figures,
which are represented in a conventional manner, are
those of almost every calling except that of the sea.
How it came about may be explained by experts, but
all kinds of publications, prayer-books, books of hours,
ballads, dramas, and the like, when they were illustrated
or were given frontispieces, almost invariably had for
their cuts those of foreign origin. Apparently the English
printers or publishers either bought, borrowed, or an-

nexed the blocks or the designs they used from France or Holland. In any case, these have nothing to teach us, and unless in some at present unexplored quarter there is a surprise in store, the lack of contemporary pictures of seamen from this source appears to be irreparable. What would we not give for a sixteenth-century illustrated edition of Hakluyt or Purchas ?

To attempt to explain why, in view of the high standard of drawing which distinguishes the illustrated work in the later manuscripts, England was much behind other countries in the matter of artistic wood engraving is beyond our purpose, but we look in vain for any entirely satisfactory native pictorial reproduction of the mariners of Tudor times. Still, as we said before, it is not artistic merit, but its actuality as an illustration, that gives to us value in a picture. For this reason we must not despise even those rude drawings of seamen observing with cross-staves or other primitive nautical instruments which are to be found in the old works on navigation and seamanship in the Library of the Royal Geographical Society and elsewhere. There are such pictures, too, in the old engravings, as in some of the little insets to the maps of the circumnavigators' voyages, in the large woodcut of the *Ark Ralegh*, and in similar works, in which sailors are figured; but these wear no dress appreciably different from that of the landsman, and if it were not for the frequency of such remarks as that of Essex in 1597, when he referred to the men who had been pressed " in mariners' clothes," and who yet did not know one rope from another, we might be inclined to suspect that no difference existed. It is, however, beyond question that in the reign of Henry VIII the ancient custom still prevailed of providing some sort of uniform in the shape of " coats " or " jackets " to the officers and men of the Navy, the colours and materials of which are given by Mr. Oppenheim from " Letters and Papers " of that time. The same writer also refers to a sketch in a contemporary treatise on navigation of a seaman, apparently an officer, wearing a Monmouth cap, a small ruff round the neck, a close-fitting vest, and long, bell-mouthed trousers. Furthermore, we have the direct evidence of the second edition of a book on costume by Cesare Vecellio, " Habiti Antichi et Moderni di Tutto il Mundo," published in Venice and printed by Sessa in 1598, in which there is a woodcut of a full-length figure of an English mariner, thus proving that at the time the book was issued our seamen were regarded as a distinct type, with a characteristic dress of their own. The following description appears with the cut :—

"Del marinario Inglese. Queste marinari sono molto valorosi et arischiati in ogni sorte di fortuna, et navigano di continuo per grā vento contrario che essi habbiano : il loro vestire e di panni biavi, bianchi, et altri colori ; costumano certe vestine curte, braghesse larghe, sgonfrie, piene di falde, et latughe, il capello e peloso a modo di schiavina.

"Anglus navclerus. Navite angli, non modo sunt in maritimus rebus peretissimi, sed etiam in omnibus periculis audacissimi, atque intrepidi ; nec unquam ob ventorum rabiem a navigatione desistunt ; horum vestes lane, femoralia oblonga, lata, inflata, et plicis plena, pileus est villosus, et gan sapinus."

Of which this is a free translation :—

"They are brave fellows, ready for any danger, and do not run to port because of stormy contrary winds. They wear short coats, sky blue, white, or some other colour, wide baggy breeches with many folds, and collars. Their caps are hairy like those that pilgrims wear."

It is noteworthy that in the first edition of the work, published in 1590, the English costumes did not include that of the mariner. In the second edition of 1598 it appears, and also another, that of a merchant, is introduced, these additions being due doubtless to the renown and stir which the exploits of the English seamen and voyagers were making at the time. In the third edition, issued in 1664, the mariner disappeared. The second edition was republished, with engravings, by Huyot, in Paris in 1859, and the representation of

2 G

the sailor is also reproduced by J. R. Planché in the
second volume of his "Cyclopædia of Costume," 1876-9.
It is characteristic of Planché that although he has included this picture, and also refers to the warrants by
which uniform was granted to the Principal Masters of
the Navy in the reigns of Queen Elizabeth and James I,
he remarks that the Navy was distinguished by no
particular costume from that of the Army till the time
of George II.

Even more curious and interesting are the pictures of
officers and men of the reign of Henry VIII, which
appear in the vellum rolls containing coloured drawings,
compiled by Anthony Anthony, presented to the King
in 1546. One of these rolls is in the British Museum,
and was exhibited there at the time of the Nelson Centenary in 1905. This roll is 16 feet 8 inches long, and
contains fifteen vessels, ranging from the *Graunde
Masterys* and *Anne Gallante*, of 450 tons, to the *Lyon* and
Dragon, of 140 tons. The part of the roll which was
displayed at the exhibition showed the *Swallowe*, of 240
tons, and the galley *Subtille*, of 200 tons. On the deck
of the *Subtille* is a sea officer directing the rowers, possibly
a boatswain. He is dressed in a "jack" or coat of
livery, made of some white material, hanging as low as
his knees. It has on the breast a circular badge, containing a crest or cognisance, either national or royal;
a red cross on a white ground, with four blue patches, or
roundels, between the arms of the cross. The badge bears
an extraordinary resemblance to the Union flag, and that
it is not merely a fortuitous arrangement of colours is
proved by its repetition in more than one place on the
vessel herself. We know that in 1513 Henry VIII
reassigned to the seamen of the Cinque Ports as their
uniform "a cote of white cotyn, with a red crosse, and
the armes of the portes underneathe," and it seems
possible that these red, white, and blue badges on a
coat of white cotton were distinctive of some uniform or
livery of that time.

In several of the French illuminated manuscripts about

this period there are pictures of sailors, and from these
we gather that the French mariner was dressed very
differently from the English. There is, for example, an
illustration of the burning of the *Cordelière* and the
Regent in the Bibliothèque Nationale, which is reproduced in the tenth volume of the publications of
the Navy Records Society, and in which the men in
the shrouds of the French vessel are shown wearing red
jackets and black or blue breeches. In another French
MS. describing the reception of Mary Tudor, the sister of
Henry VIII, when she went to Paris to marry Louis XII,
one of the devices displayed in her honour was a ship
with sailors in the rigging. These sailors wear tunics
open at the throat, with hoods attached for covering the
head, while their breeches are very tight at the ankle.
Half of the sailors are in dark tunics and light breeches,
and the other half in light tunics and dark breeches.
Two other men, who may be sailors, wear morions and
carry spears. But although these illuminations and
woodcuts may throw a little light upon costume, they
are not the pictures of social life or professional work
for which we look. We are not shown the men on board
the ships, fighting the guns, keel-hauling malefactors, or
in their hours of recreation, nor do we see them on shore
at their pastimes or roistering in the streets, although
from the written descriptions we know that such things
must have been.

There is one other source from which we might
have hoped to obtain information. There is a painting
representative of the embarkation of Henry VIII at
Dover on May 31st, 1520, by Vincent Volpe, the Painter
in Ordinary to the King, which is in Hampton Court
Palace. This picture was engraved as the frontispiece
to the second volume of Sir Nicholas Harris Nicolas's
" History of the Royal Navy." It may be of some
value for naval architecture, but the sailors are indistinguishable from the other characters depicted. There
is also a painting of the encampment of the English
forces near Portsmouth, with a view of the English and

French fleets, at the beginning of the action on July 19th, 1545, probably by the same artist. This picture shows the loss of the *Mary Rose*, but the same remark applies to it as to the previous one. It is interesting from many points of view, but not in the aspect from which we would regard it. Nor do we get any help from the Dutch pictures, such as that of the arrival at Flushing of Leicester, painted by Vrume in 1586. Even at the date of the defeat of the Armada the artists and engravers of the time appear to have thought those who followed the calling of the sea, unless they were distinguished among the commanders, beneath their notice. And yet there were playing cards depicting the series of fights in the Channel between the English and the Spaniards. We could wish that the artists had been more inspired by the exploits of the seamen.

Passing on to the seventeenth century, it might surely be expected that, with the great advance which was made in all illustrative art, we should find ourselves on firmer ground. Painters, etchers, and engravers were at work everywhere, a very large proportion of the books were illustrated, broadsheets and ballads were adorned with woodcuts, and towards the close of the century emblematical and satirical prints abounded. Yet a prolonged search, extending over five-and-twenty years, has failed to reveal anything which can be distinctly characterised as a picture of sailor life. There is a dearth of the right material even in the Dutch etchings by Romeyn de Hooghe and others, illustrating the Dutch and English naval wars, and when now and again the searcher is rewarded for his trouble by coming across such a title as " The Sailors at the Gate of Lambeth," during the first Civil War, his joy is quenched by the discovery that the illustration depicting this incident also does duty for the Scots Army invading England, and that the little figures shown as seamen are identical with those used for many other purposes.

There are some interesting pictures and prints of nautical spectacles, such as, for example, the visit of King

Charles II to Portsmouth in May, 1662, a Dutch print
showing the embarkation of the King at the Point
preparatory to his visit to the fleet at Spithead. We
have here confirmatory evidence of the practical uniformity of dress among the watermen, since all the rowers
in the boats are attired alike, and similar uniformity
in the costume of the boatmen is shown in a pageant on
the Thames at Whitehall in the same year. The ancient
custom of providing uniform for the seamen of the Navy
had now died out, but in its place a practice had risen
of providing slop clothing for sale on board the ships,
and as this clothing was of a prescribed pattern it resulted
in a certain amount of uniformity. On the other hand,
the King's watermen on the Thames appear from medieval times to have been dressed uniformly, and until
well into the nineteenth century a number of these
watermen always accompanied the King to Portsmouth
or other seaports on such an occasion as we have referred
to, for the purpose of manning his barge, so that the
rowers in the barges which are taking Charles II and his
Court to the ships need not necessarily have been man-
of-war's men. In the illustrated account of the funeral
of George Monk, Duke of Albemarle, by Francis Sandford,
Lancaster Herald, there are pictures of the Duke's watermen and Master of the Barge in 1670. These men are
uniformly dressed, and wear badges on the left arm.
Their doublets have the full skirt, associated with the
dress of the watermen at a very much later age.

While there is much other proof that the sailors and
watermen of the seventeenth century wore a distinctive
dress, it must be admitted that there is not much to rely
upon in the pictorial evidence to that effect. There is,
however, no lack of odd bits of testimony which may
be accepted as conclusive of the fact. One of these is
to be found in a ballad called the "Cunning Northern
Beggar," and adorned with woodcuts. Here we are told
that the beggar disguised himself as a sailor wounded in
the wars, which he could not very well have done unless
the costume to some extent supported his tale. On the

stage, too, as already shown, it was not unusual to adopt
the seaman's dress as a disguise. Pepys, on May 11th,
1668, after a visit to the Duke of York's Theatre, where
he had been to see " The Tempest," records that between
the acts he went, as we should say, behind the scenes,
and there " had the pleasure to see the actors in their
several dresses, especially the seamen and the monster,
which were very droll; so into the play again."   Other
diarists, like Teonge, refer to the issue on board ship of
slops, detailed instructions for the material and nature
of which clothing were issued by the Duke of York in
1663.   Then from a poem on the death of Lord Maidstone by J. W., published in 1674, we get hints that the
seaman's rig was provided for him by the King, and
that it was mainly made of canvas.

> Though the bold sailor's arm'd 'gainst wind and weather,
>   Whose nerves like cordage knit his limbs together,
> Whose joynts like pulleys, and his callous hand
>   Like the ship's helm, can its vaste bulk command ;
> And legs and arms, as yards and masts, whilst he
>   Vaunts with his strength, the ship's epitome :
> Rigg'd by his king, he fears not to prevail,
>   Tallow'd in smells, and when cloath'd under sail,
> Such a sea-man-of-war by 's own broadside,
>   Not by the ship's, thinks himself fortified.

Again, in the engraved print in the Sutherland Collection, of Judge Jeffreys arrested at Wapping in 1688,
it is stated that he was disguised as a sailor, and he is
certainly depicted in a dress which differs from that of
the men who have seized him. This is the earliest line
engraving in which the seafaring population is distinctly
shown, and marks the end of that period which may be
said to have begun when Humphrey Cole was embellishing
his maps with little figures, and Augustine Ryther his
plans to illustrate the defeat of the Spanish Armada
about 1590. The other early line engravers, like Remigius
Hogenberg, William Rogers, De Bry, and Elstracke,
right down to William Faithorne, devoted themselves
mainly to portraiture or frontispieces, and for illustrations of social life the woodcut was not ousted in popular

favour by the engraver on copper or other soft metals until the beginning of the next century.   Reynier, Zee-man, Bakhuysen, and other Dutch etchers did, indeed, produce many battle pieces and views of shipping which form historical records, and Wenceslaus Hollar, a most industrious etcher and engraver, has left many accurate pictures of shipping among his other works, but we have been unable to find anything distinctive of seamanhood.

From now onwards through the eighteenth century the period of obscure and imperfect art as applied to the illustration of naval life is left behind, and although for some few years yet there is not as much material as one could wish for, and what there is exhibits a strong Dutch flavour, yet it very soon becomes difficult to lay down any clear principle for selection among such a mass of matter, or to avoid making a mere catalogue of the artists and their work.   We shall not, however, merely describe the pictures chosen to illustrate this work, but at the same time endeavour to indicate sources which may be useful to the collector, without at the same time making the chapter tedious to other readers.   It should be remembered, too, that from our point of view the interest in the portraits is mainly biographical and per-sonal, until after the middle of the century, when they become valuable also for details of uniform, while the battle pieces and pictures of shipping, useful as they are to the naval archæologist and as memorials of our naval history, cannot compare, in their relation to our subject, with illustrations of the social life of the seamen, however crude and inartistic.

CHAPTER II

THE NAVY ILLUSTRATED

THE story of the Navy, as it presented itself to the
artist, has never been shown to better advantage
than at the great Naval Exhibition at Chelsea in 1891.
Nearly all the chief artists and many of lesser note
who have painted portraits, engagements, or other
notable events in our naval annals were represented on
its walls. The naval commanders were there mirrored
from Elizabeth's time to Victoria's, and although naturally all the achievements of our seamen were not as
the painters depicted them in fact or fancy, the galleries
were in a large measure an epitome of naval history.
The arrangement of the pictures in chronological order
enabled the spectator to obtain a fairly complete view
of the war services of the fleet from the time of Henry
VIII. What was wanting in the galleries devoted to
oil paintings was to a large extent made up for in those
in which engravings and water-colours were exhibited.
There was further shown a selection, more valuable in
quality than in quantity, of the humorous representations and caricatures of the social life of the Navy and
its political interest.

The catalogue of the Naval Exhibition is invaluable
to all who would study pictorial art as applied to naval
life, and those who take this as the basis of their study
of the subject cannot go far wrong. There are, however,
numerous other sources which the student, the collector,
or the extra-illustrator will desire to draw upon, and we
will here endeavour to indicate some of those sources.

They are, indeed, manifold, and the enthusiast may pick up a clue in many an unexpected quarter. Quite recently, for example, in turning over the pages of the latest edition of Bryan's " Dictionary of Painters and Engravers," issued by Messrs. George Bell and Sons, we came across the reproduction of a painting by Zoffany, entitled " In the Cabin of the *Norfolk*." Of the three figures represented in the picture, two were evidently naval officers, by their dress. A comparison of dates with the history of the *Norfolk* made it fairly clear that one of the persons represented was either Captain Cook, the circumnavigator, or Kempenfelt, who was lost in the *Royal George*. Being put in communication with the owner of the picture, Sir C. Hubert H. Parry, we received a courteous reply, from which the following is an extract :—

" The views you express about the Zoffany picture in your second letter are correct. The officer seated is Admiral Cornish ; the officer standing is Kempenfelt, who was the flag-captain at the siege of Manila, in connection with which the picture was painted. The civilian in the centre is Thomas Parry, who was acting as secretary to the expedition, and the picture was painted for him. Zoffany was in India for some years about the time of the expedition, and this afforded the opportunity for painting the picture. Thomas Parry was my great-grandfather, and I suppose the picture has been in the possession of the family ever since it was painted."

It was a great pleasure to have thus discovered another portrait of Kempenfelt, the only one shown at the Exhibition having been painted by Tilly Kettle at a much later date. Kettle's picture was engraved by Earlom, and is not uncommonly met with, but Zoffany's portrait appears never to have been engraved as such.

Originally this section of the work was projected on a much larger scale than our space will permit, and the subject was divided into the following categories : portraits, battle pieces and naval occurrences, such as shipwrecks, etc., satirical prints and caricatures, hu-

morous and pathetic pictures of social life, drawings of
uniform and outfitters' patterns, and miscellaneous
works. Under the last-named heading there is a very
wide field indeed, for it includes not only book illustrations, but masonic summonses, tradesmen's cards, tickets
of admission to places of entertainment, lottery tickets,
book plates, theatrical posters, pictures on pottery,
and many other curious and unlikely sources of illustration. Of each of these divisions there is much to tell,
and the chapter on portraits alone ran easily up to five
thousand words, and was then anything but exhaustive.
It is essential, however, to condense and to devote the
remaining part of our space mainly to the illustrations
in the book itself.

There is room for a volume on naval art alone, and if
any one should take this work in hand he should have
no difficulty in finding ample materials. It is unnecessary
to go to the original paintings, which very often are not
best adapted for the purposes of reproduction. There
are many collectors of prints and engravings who have
either devoted themselves to one division of the subject,
as Admiral Sir Wilmot Fawkes, who possesses a magnificent gallery of naval portraits, or others, whose tastes
are more catholic, as Captain Sir Charles Cust, who
allowed a part of his splendid collection of genre pictures
to be exhibited at the Whitechapel Art Galleries in
1903. It is a matter, perhaps, for some regret that
at the British Museum, at South Kensington, and at
similar public institutions, the subject indices to the
prints leave something to be desired in the way of assisting
the searcher. But in 1905, in connection with the celebration of the Centenary of Trafalgar, the British Museum
authorities published a catalogue of the naval engravings
on exhibition, which, in its way and within its scope,
is a model of concise and valuable information on the
subject. Next to this we would put the catalogue of the
Royal United Service Institution, compiled by Mr. B. E.
Sergeaunt, the Assistant Curator, and the official guide
to the collection in the Painted Hall at Greenwich should

not be overlooked, nor the catalogue of the Naval Exhibition held at Earl's Court in 1905. Some useful hints,
too, we have obtained from the sale catalogues of the collections of marine artists like those of Mr. W. H. Overend
and Sir Oswald Brierly, while that of Mr. Joseph Grego
(and this gentleman's books also) should be consulted
on the subject of caricatures. In a note we give the
names and addresses of print and book sellers who have
published or issue from time to time catalogues of naval
engravings and the like. To many of these we are indebted for useful advice and information.* Still more
are we indebted to Mr. A. M. Broadley, of The Knapp,
Bradpole, whose extra-illustrated lives of Nelson, Byng,
Hardy, and other naval worthies literally teem with
scarce and curious prints, autographs, aud rariora
of all kinds, most interesting to the collector. Although
with only a few exceptions the illustrations to this work
are from our own collection, we desire to acknowledge
our indebtedness to Mr. Broadley for some of the quaintest
of those which originally formed the frontispieces to jest-
books and similar out-of-the-way publications.

It may be interesting to mention that the most ancient
contemporary portrait of a sea officer known to us is
that of Thomas Howard, Earl of Surrey, who in May,
1514, when his brother, Edward Howard, had been
killed in action with the French off Brest, became Lord
High Admiral. This painting, and that of a portrait
of Lord Howard of Effingham, who commanded the
English fleet against the Spanish Armada in 1588, are
by Holbein. They have been engraved by Jacob Hou-
braken, who with George Vertue engraved in line a
very large series of "heads of illustrious persons" for
their royal and other patrons. In the gallery of engravings by these two artists will be found a long series
of naval commanders, extending from the time of Drake

* Messrs. T. H. Parker, 7 Spur Street, Leicester Square, W.C.;
Alfred Davis, 17 King's Road, Chelsea, S.W.; Francis Harvey, 4 St.
James Street, S.W.; E. Parsons and Sons, 45 Brompton Road, S.W.;
James Rimell and Son, 53 Shaftesbury Avenue, W.; Maggs Brothers,
109 Strand, W.C.; and Robson and Co., 23 Coventry Street, W.

to that of Anson. Many other naval worthies of Tudor times will be found in the " Herœologia Anglica " of Compton Holland, the plates for which were engraved by the members of the Van de Passe family of Dutch engravers, who were working in England from 1613 to 1637. William Rogers and Thomas Cockson should be mentioned as among our first native line engravers who reproduced portraits of distinguished seamen. John Payne, who will also be remembered as the engraver of the great plate of the " Sovereign of the Seas," engraved a portrait of the Earl of Warwick after Van Dyke, and there are several engraved portraits of Blake, but perhaps the finest is that in mezzotint by T. Preston. Of two of Blake's fellow-generals at sea, there are engraved portraits by Peter Lombart and William Faithorne after paintings by Robert Walker, a favourite of Oliver Cromwell.

From this time onwards almost all the important seamen had their portraits painted, and engravings of these are not difficult to obtain. The cheaper ex-amples have naturally been reproduced for book illus-tration, but anything like a complete set of the Admirals would contain specimens of the principal English en-gravers in line, mezzotint, and stipple. Nearly all the most distinguished sailors of the first half of the eighteenth century may be found among the prints by the two Fabers, father and son, and with them also begins in this connection the use of mezzotint for reproduction. Portraits of many of the men who became notable during the reign of George II were engraved by James McArdell, Richard Houston, Edward Fisher, and Richard Purcell. Among the masterpieces of Valentine Green are many portraits of naval officers, while those remarkable artists in mezzotint, Richard Earlom, J. R. Smith, and the brothers Ward, are all represented in any fairly complete gallery of naval worthies. A few of the more celebrated engravings in stipple of naval officers are those of Hawke, by Bartolozzi after Cotes ; Nelson, by Burke after Savage; Collingwood, by Gaugain after Scriven ; Sir Edward Berry, by Keating after Singleton ; and Captain Cook,

by J. K. Sherwin after Dance. A book which can now
generally be obtained at a moderate price is Locker's
" Naval Gallery of Greenwich Hospital," which contains
many excellent portraits. There were, moreover, several
commemorative groups of naval portraits engraved in
connection with celebrated battles. After Jervis's victory
off Cape St. Vincent the portraits of twenty-one commanders were done on one sheet by Parker and Worthing-
ton. Similar commemorative engravings were executed
for the battles of the Nile, Camperdown, and Trafalgar.

Turning to naval actions and battle pieces, we may
pass over as already sufficiently dealt with, the Tudor
period in the persons of Antony Antony, who painted
the ships of the Navy Royal ; Ryther, who illustrated
the defeat of the Spanish Armada ; and a few other line
engravers or etchers of historical subjects. Nor do we
know of any contemporary paintings of the battles of
Blake and Penn, while for the incidents of the earlier
Dutch wars we are indebted to Reynier, Zeeman, Rudolf
Bakhuysen, and other Dutch etchers, whose battle
pieces and views of shipping are works of art as well as
historical records of the period. The earliest English
sea painter we have been able to discover was Isaac
Sailmaker. He is said to have painted for Oliver Cromwell a series of Blake's victories, but none of his pictures
appear to be now in existence, and we only find him
represented by an engraving of the battle of Malaga,
fought in August, 1704. Wenceslaus Hollar, who came
to England in 1637, and died here in 1677, was a
most versatile artist, and there is no end to the
subjects which he has interpreted and left as historical
documents. Most of the sea fights with the Dutch
were reproduced by his etching needle, and a very
spirited picture of the fleets off Deal. In 1673 he was
sent to Tangier in the suite of Lord Henry Howard to
draw and engrave plans of the city and its fortifications,
then newly an English possession. On the return journey
the vessel in which he took passage was attacked by
Algerine corsairs, and Hollar took a sketch of the en-

gagement, in which the English came off victorious. This etching was published by E. Kirkall, who was also an engraver, and who reproduced many of Van de Velde's pictures. Kirkall is also remarkable for the early use of tinted paper and coloured inks.

Willem Van de Velde was born at Leyden a few years after Hollar, and in his early life was a sailor. Developing a taste for painting, he was sent to sea by the States of Holland to illustrate their sea fights pictorially. Becoming known to Charles II, he accompanied the King to England in 1675, and became marine painter to that monarch, and afterwards to James II. His paintings are particularly interesting for their accuracy in all that pertains to sea life, as well as for the importance of the incidents he placed upon canvas. His son, the younger Van de Velde, accompanied his father to England, and many hundreds of his pictures and drawings have been catalogued. In his pictures he frequently wrote the names of the ship and her commander over the drawing of a vessel, and the notification " V. Velde's gallijodt " indicates the ship from which he witnessed the action and took his sketch. The figures in his pictures are said to have been put in by his brother, Adriaan Van de Velde, and add not a little to their historical value. A fourth Van de Velde, Kornelis, copied the works of his father and grandfather, and even, it is reported, added their signatures. Engravings from the paintings of these artists depict most of the battles in our wars with the Dutch. Two other Dutch artists should be mentioned whose pictures have been engraved, Willem Schellinks, who painted the Dutch burning the ships in the Medway and the destruction of Sheerness, while E. Koster painted the embarkation of William III at Helvetsluys for England in 1688, and the same monarch reviewing his fleet at Beachy Head after the battle in 1691.

The principal marine painters who followed one another in succession from this time were Peter Monamy, who was at his best about 1726, Thomas Baston, and Charles Brooking, painting in the reign of George II, John Hood,

Francis Swaine, Monamy Swaine, Richard Paton, and Dominic Serres, who carry us down to the end of the eighteenth century. Then there were J. F. Serres, P. J. de Loutherbourg, Thomas Luny, Nicholas Pocock, Robert Dodd, Anderson, Cartwright, and the Cleveleys, who, beginning their work in the eighteenth, painted on into the nineteenth century, most of them being represented by the principal actions in the reign of George III. Examples of the work of many of these marine artists were reproduced in "The British Fleet," and in an appendix to that book some additional information will be found about them, and others of lesser note, with the men who engraved from their pictures.

To come to our more immediate purpose, a description of the illustrations in this volume. Such notes are given as may be of assistance to those who wish to form a similar gallery, either of the originals or of photographs of them, and by expert amateur users of the camera the latter comparatively inexpensive method is not to be despised. It will be a fair generalisation, although not strictly accurate, if we classify the pictures which give us glimpses of naval life and manners during the eighteenth century into three groups, those of political satire, social humour, and grotesque caricature. Of course, these overlap, for in the political satire of the century there is not a little humour, and the vagaries of society were the subject of much caricature, if by this word we mean a grotesque exaggeration of fact. In the first class, however, the sailor is introduced incidentally, and merely as an indication of his importance as a factor in the political situation, or because he was a common object in the scenes of daily life.

In the very comprehensive collection of satirical and emblematic engravings in the Print Room of the British Museum, not a few sailors of the reigns of William and Mary, of Queen Anne and the early Georges, may be found in the pictures, and these are particularly useful for costume. Many are by Dutch hands, but later on we have Sandby, Sayer, Gillray, Rowlandson, and Isaac

Cruikshank. In their political caricatures these talented
artists give us, not so much a mirror of the passing world
on its lighter side, as momentary impressions of the sordid
or tragic aspects of party or international political strife.
At the same time naval matters were so closely woven
with the phase of contemporary history they chronicle
that it is more often than not that a sailor may be found
in their pictures. Particularly is this the case when
we arrive at that period when the French revolutionary
movement loomed so large in the public imagination,
and when the sinister form of Bonaparte hovered, an
ever-present menace, on the horizon. In the marvellous
series of Napoleonic satires of Gillray, and in the political
caricatures of Rowlandson, there are, indeed, plenty of
sketches of sailors, but this source has not been drawn
upon to any large extent as it presents an interesting
aspect of history which deserves more detailed attention.

Nor, for obvious reasons, has that grosser kind of
caricature which was supplied by Rowlandson, Woodward
and others of lesser note, been included. Here again the
sailor life is very much to the fore, but depicted in a vulgar
atmosphere, often carried so far as to be indefensible.
But Rowlandson, whose line was much wider in scope
and less brutal than Gillray, was not seen at his best in
caricature, and it is sometimes difficult to believe that
the same artist executed the beautiful work published
by Ackermann. Moreover, Rowlandson actually knew
something of the Navy personally. He had visited
Portsmouth to see the wreck of the *Royal George* in
1782, and from no complete collection of naval genre
pictures could his work be entirely omitted. Some day,
perhaps, a volume on naval history as it was burlesqued
by June, Boitard, Mosley, Sandby, Gillray, Rowlandson,
and others, will appear. In that work the caricatures
of Boscawen and Byng, of Hawke and Hood and Howe,
of St. Vincent, Nelson, and Gambier, with many other
naval commanders, viewed as they were from the political
or patriotic standpoint of the hour, will find their proper
place.

In the pictures of naval life here reproduced there is intentionally more comedy than satire, and the aim has been to present the sailor in general as his contemporaries saw him at work and play. Many of the prints are generically described as humorous mezzotints, and choice impressions of these examples of the art are not now easily obtained, while even the retouched reprints and copies are far from common. The vogue of the humorous mezzotint seems to have begun with John Collet, who painted in the style of Hogarth, and the circumstance that his father was in the employment of the Admiralty may have given him a special interest in the seamen, whose exploits on shore he so frequently depicted. Naturally, among the great mass of the humorous mezzotints turned out by the many publishers and printsellers only a small proportion dealt with the life of the sailors, a far greater number being devoted to representing in a genial spirit of fun the follies and fashions, the pleasures and pastimes of the people.

This form of social travesty is a fascinating subject, whether regarded from the artistic standpoint, the collector's point of view, or in its aspect as evidence for costume and character. No subject of a similar kind is richer in material, none more varied, nor relatively is there any so little exploited, especially if we reject that which is rather pictorial satire than pictorial humour. The artists who executed this kind of work were not unknown men, but among the most celebrated in their calling, although the humorous mezzotint was usually an anonymous production both in respect to the painter and the engraver. For this reason the publishers' names only will be found on most of the reproductions of the mezzotints, which have been selected from a much larger number in order to exhibit the style of subject which most appealed to the patrons of the more famous of the print publishers. These may be said to have begun with John Bowles, who had a shop in Cornhill in 1710, and they include among others Edward Cooper, Carington Bowles, Bowles and Carver, Robert Sayer,

2 H

who afterwards went into partnership with Bennett, R. Pollard, Haines, Ryland, Hurles, and, at the end of the century, Laurie and Whittle, and Fairburn. Of the draughtsmen Collet has already been mentioned, and in addition Morland, Singleton, Wheatley, Dighton, and other well-known artists supplied sketches, while among the scrapers of the plates were such celebrated workers in mezzotint as Earlom, Houston, J. R. Smith, and both James and William Ward. Not infrequently the artist was himself the engraver, and sometimes the publisher too.

Of earlier date than the humorous mezzotints, and following closely upon the satirical and emblematical prints already referred to, were the line engravings, here represented by the work of Mosley and Boitard. It is from the accession of George II that it is usual to date the regeneration of English art, and it is also from about that period that the earlier illustrations in this volume date. As has been shown, there were plenty of portraits and sea pieces of great merit and interest to the naval student from a much earlier time, but it was then that the period of satirical and humorous genre began with Hogarth, who was the founder of a school, the influence of which may be traced through Collet, Gillray, Rowlandson, and the Cruikshanks to the satirical and comic artists of later times.

The best example of the sailor of his period to be found in Hogarth's moral dramas in pictorial form, is the figure seen on the top of a coach in " The Stage Coach in a Country Inn Yard." This sailor has just returned to England in the *Centurion*. He has been round the world with Anson, and is on his way home. The subject is a favourite one, and in the two pictures of the sailor's farewell and return by Boitard we have it treated in a more popular fashion. In the second picture, where the fortunate tar is shown presenting his sweetheart with doubloons and pieces of eight, the background is filled in by the wagons laden with treasure captured in the Acapulco galleon, the *Nuestra Señora de Cavadonga*, on their way to the Mint in London under a guard of seamen and soldiers.

Naturally the departure and return of the sailor is the theme most likely to appeal to his audience, and therefore most frequently chosen by the artist. It is somewhat differently treated by John Simon and by C. Mosley, a little earlier than Boitard. These painters appear to have had their eyes on the privateersman rather than on the man-of-war's-man, since Mosley introduces the word on the seaman's box in one of his pictures, and Simon in the verses appended to his. Simon, it may be mentioned, though originally a line engraver, began to practise mezzotint early in the century, and he continued to work quite up to the period with which we are now dealing. The plates here reproduced were originally printed from in 1737, and are said to be still in existence. Anyway, they were republished fifty years after he had scraped them with another print-seller's name and with the figure " 3 " in the date trans-formed into an " 8." Mosley's print of the sailor's parting is particularly interesting both for costume and the details of the ship in which the scene is supposed to occur.

Attwold's picture is a little later, and is believed to be the earliest humorous print of the officers in the new uniform authorised in 1748. It is quite possible that it may originally have formed the frontispiece to one of the many editions of Ned Ward's scurrilous little tract, " The Wooden World Dissected." We have here a very early representation of the captain's cabin of a man-of-war. The captain is a little whipper-snapper with spindleshanks, taking his ease in an arm-chair. His quadrant, telescope, and pistols hang upon the wall, while a pipe, bottle, and half-emptied wine-glass on the table indicate his tastes. Above his head is a swing-ing compass, and through the stern windows we see another vessel putting to sea. The first lieutenant, a great contrast to his commander, is bowing obsequiously and from his mouth proceeds the legend, " Sir, your

commands ? " while the captain replies : " See, Jack
Spritsail, have another dozen, dame 'e ! "

Of quite a different class of picture are those by the
group of painters which includes Bunbury, Stothard,
Singleton, and Wheatley, to mention only the better
known. Their work is only at times illustrative of naval
life, but when this is the case it is most valuable. Henry
William Bunbury drew humorous pictures of life like
Collet ; but whereas the latter selected his material from
the lower orders of society, Bunbury satirised the extravagant side of life in a higher grade. Moreover,
a good deal of his work was not at all in the nature of
caricature, as in the case of those charming colour prints
illustrative of the ballads of " Black-eyed Susan " and
" Auld Robin Gray," and in the sketch here reproduced,
which was engraved by J. R. Smith, and was drawn by
Bunbury when he visited Portsmouth in 1785. The
sailors by the dockyard wall waiting to go off to their
vessel belonged to the *Edgar*, Captain Adam Duncan,
then the guardship in the harbour. Two comic sketches
of a different class, published by James Bretheton, are
" Sweet Poll of Plymouth " and " The Amorous Rivals."

Thomas Stothard was commissioned by George III
in 1779 to go down to Portsmouth and paint a picture
of Prince William Henry, afterwards William IV, on
board the *Prince George*, the vessel in which His Royal
Highness first went to sea as a midshipman. The
particular picture Stothard painted was reproduced in
Hervey's Naval History, but at the same time he painted
four others representing respectively the sailors carousing
on the forecastle, fighting a gun, exercising their calling
in a storm, and Jack's return from sea. Stothard, who
was a most prolific artist, and whose book illustrations
are said to have run into thousands, was quite at home
with naval life, and his graceful work dealing with this
subject may be found in magazines, pocket-books,
keepsakes, costume plates, and children's books. A
circular plate engraved by C. Knight in stipple, " Sweet
Poll of Plymouth," is a favourite one with the collectors

of coloured prints, and "The British Naval Hero," engraved by J. Young, representing a joyful middy saying good-bye to his family, was painted as a contrast to the French conscript dragged to his duty from the arms of his sorrowing friends.

Henry Singleton also did a number of pictures in which we get glimpses of sailor life. Like Stothard, he painted several large canvases for exhibition in the Academy of naval incidents, including Nelson boarding the *San Josef*, but it is in the picture here reproduced of "The Sailor's Return," in "The East End of the Town," and in that well-known pair, "British Plenty" and "Scarcity in India," that he depicts the seaman in a more social aspect. Francis Wheatley, like De Louther-bourg, originally a theatrical scene-painter, is justly admired for his graceful women and pretty children, as well as for the delicacy and beauty of his rustic genre. One of his favourite pictures shows a sailor with two girls on Tower Hill, but he is here represented by "The Seaman's Return" engraved by Hübner. The most celebrated of the genre painters is George Morland, who, if his career was morally a failure and a disastrous one, was a realist in his art, and his pictures of life are almost always true to nature and enjoyable from every point of view. Two popular specimens of his work, "Jack in the Bilboes" and "The Contented Water-man" are here reproduced from pretty little stipple prints by W. Clamp. They illustrate, of course, Charles Dibdin's song, "My Poll and My Partner Joe." Many of the pictures of Morland were connected with the sea and sea life, and two much prized by connoisseurs are those which were engraved in mezzotint by Dawe en-titled "Anxiety, or the Ship at Sea," and "Mutual Joy, or the Ship in Harbour," while another pretty coloured print is that of "Black-eyed Susan."

Other work from the same school is represented by pictures after Julius Cæsar Ibbetson, who gained a knowledge of naval life and marine subjects as draughts-man to the Cathcart Embassy to China in 1788. His

" Sailors Carousing in the Long Room at Portsmouth "
was painted for William IV, and among other incidents
depicted is that of the sailors frying their watches.
" The Sailor's Farewell " is a companion to " The Sailor
Shipwrecked," but the latter is not nearly such a pretty
work of art as the former.   J. H. Ramberg, who also
gives us " The Sailor's Farewell," studied painting under
Sir Joshua Reynolds, and engraving under Bartolozzi.
The companion picture is " The Soldier's Return."
He was also an historical painter and caricaturist.   As
Bartolozzi has been mentioned, this famous artist's
work should be noticed in the reproduction of a picture
by F. Vivares, which has been supposed to have some
connection with a musical trifle written by Andrew
Cherry.   Bartolozzi is remarkable for the variety as
well as the excellence of his work, much of which was
of a fanciful character.   He engraved many of his own
designs, among them one of a British sailor in landing
kit, illustrating a poem on the slave trade.   Another
example of his work is seen in the stipple print after H.
Walton of " The Young Maid and the Old Sailor,"
these figures, it may be said, being, it is supposed, portraits of the artist and his daughter.   J. G. Huck, who,
as he came to England from Hanover in 1780, must
have seen something of sea life, is responsible for the
pretty little oval engraved in stipple by T. Ryder of
the officer parting from his sweetheart, which was used
as another illustration to the ever-popular " Sweet Poll
of Plymouth."   Robert Sayer, who is better known as
a political caricaturist, is represented by two mezzotints
illustrating the ballad of " Auld Robin Gray " by Lady
Anne Barnard ; and other men who did work in this
school were Robert Pollard, W. Bigg, the painter of " The
Shipwrecked Boy," and Henry Corbould.   From two
very scarce coloured stipple prints, possibly after Lady
Diana Beauclerc, we have " The Royal Seaman's Farewell " and " The Sailor's Wife's Farewell."

Towards the end of the eighteenth century the firm
of printsellers, Laurie and Whittle, were responsible for

the issue of what were known as drolls, a specimen of which may be seen in "Pretty Poll and Honest Jack." But the output of this firm was enormous, particularly as they reissued a large number of the older plates retouched, as well as many new ones. Isaac Cruikshank, the father of the more famous George, worked for Laurie and Whittle, as well as in the more absorbing business of political caricature. He was a contemporary of Gillray and Rowlandson, and one of his earliest etchings was dated 1796. Of his two sons, Isaac Robert Cruikshank, who was originally a midshipman in the East India Company's service, appears to have been attracted to the calling of his father by the success of his brother George. He frequently deals with naval subjects, and for illustrations of nautical melodrama the collector should look through Cumberland's "British Theatre" and "Minor Theatre," for both of which works Robert Cruikshank did many frontispieces. Of George Cruikshank it will not be necessary to say much, as his work is so well known. Some of his earliest efforts may be found in the coloured sheets and children's books sold by W. Belch, Newington Butts, London. In the plates represented in this volume, for that of "The Sailor's Progress" he had the assistance of Captain Marryat, and for "A Sailor's Description of a Chase and Capture" he was indebted to hints by Lieutenant John Sheringham, R.N. A. H. Forrester, who used the pseudonym "Alfred Crowquill," was another caricaturist of the same date as George Cruikshank. He generally etched his own designs, and two of his books are a "Comic English Grammar" and "Comic Arithmetic." Naval subjects will also be found in the work of the Dightons, John Doyle ("H. B."), Hablot K. Browne ("Phiz"), and Leech.

To return to the class of work published by Laurie and Whittle, it is impossible to mention all the artists who were engaged in the eighteenth and the early nineteenth century in the illustration of song heads, chap books, broadsheets, lottery tickets, and various other forms of pictorial art which illustrated sailors and sea life. The chap book, indeed, dates from the reign of Queen Elizabeth. It became uncommon in the seventeenth century, and then again was poured forth in shoals mainly consisting of an abridgment of larger works, with a frontispiece sometimes coloured. In the Pepys Collection at Magdalene College, Cambridge, there are a number of these little volumes bound up under the titles of " Penny Merriments " and " Penny Godlinesses." As a rule the paper used was very coarse, the type poor, and the woodcuts were rough. At a later date, however, there was a great improvement in the class of illustration, even such men as Bewick and Blake, Clennell and George Baxter, with many others of equal note, supplying the frontispieces. Perhaps the most delightful specimens of the chap books are the garlands, collections of songs and ballads, mostly by various hands, and almost always illustrated. Of a similar character to the chap books are the broadsides and song slips of which specimens will be found in this volume. The song slip, or ballad on one sheet, dates back to the sixteenth century, and later on the same form was used by many persons for announcing prospectuses of their businesses and the like. Tradesmen's circulars, especially those of the naval outfitters, and mathematical instrument makers, announcements of lotteries, and the summonses of freemasons and similar orders, are often full of interest from the naval point of view. Then again old music and old plays afford instructive plates illustrating the subject. From almost all these sources specimens are given in this volume.

Book illustration is naturally extremely important, especially in the old magazines, such as the " Town and Country Magazine," the " Britannic Magazine," the " Naval Magazine ; or, Nautical Miscellany," and, in the early part of the nineteenth century, the " Naval Chronicle." In the " Oxford Magazine " of 1770 there is a curious print of the press-gang, and another illustration of the same subject has been taken from the " Attic Miscellany " of 1790. How common a spectacle of the time was the working of the press is shown by the little mezzotint representing children playing at it as a game. The many publications of Fairburn, song books, chap books, etc., are full of pictures of sailors. Fairburn issued a monthly journal of naval occurrences, from which we give two pictures, illustrating little dramatic sketches of a nautical character. A very scarce little book, entitled "Whims of the Day," in four volumes, contains several naval illustrations of character. Oddly enough, the same picture is used to represent more than one subject. Thus the plate which in one volume represents Jamie's return to his sweetheart after the battle of Camperdown also serves in another for Willie's return to his lass after the battle of the Nile. The pictures are much in the style of those which appear in Fairburn's publications, and are possibly by one of the Cruikshanks. In "The Flowers of Anecdote, Wit, Humour, Gaiety, and Genius," with eighteen plates by Landseer and Heath, published by Charles Tilt in 1831, and in "The Humourist," with eighty engravings by W. H. Brook, published by Ackermann in 1832, there are several illustrations of sailors.

The class of naval illustration which is found in the older histories is shown by the engravings illustrative of the capture of Judge Jeffreys and the death of Lord Robert Manners. From the "Newgate Calendar" and the "Tyburn Chronicle" we have pictures of the execution of a pirate at Wapping and the murder of Daniel Chater by smugglers, who believed that he had given information to the excisemen. Historical incidents sometimes formed the subject of the humorous mezzotints, as in the case of the one published by Sayer of "An English Jack Tar Giving Monsieur a Drubbing," which is to be found in two states, the names over the public-house door being changed from Keppel and Harland to Rodney and Hood; and also in those published by Laurie and Whittle of the "Glorious First of June" and the "Mutiny at the Nore." The illustrations of a special class of chap book are represented by "The Mutiny of the Bounty," from the "Mariner's Marvellous Magazine," and " The Loss of the Guardian " from Duncan's " Mariner's Chronicle."

Next must be mentioned the books with illustrations in colour issued early in the nineteenth century, the principal publisher being Rudolf Ackermann, to whose commercial enterprise and artistic instinct we owe so much in this connection. Most of the pictures were reproduced in aquatint, or an imitation of drawing in water colours. Paul Sandby much earlier was one of the first artists to utilise this process, which was gradually improved until there is nothing which beats it for reproducing the delicacy of the water colour or the drawing in Indian ink. In almost every case, however, the coloured aquatints were finished by hand. One of the earliest of Ackermann's publications was " The Microcosm of London ; or, London in Miniature," by Pugin and Rowlandson, the latter supplying the spirited figures to the former's backgrounds. Among the interesting pictures from a naval point of view in this work are " The Admiralty Board Room " and " The Nelson Car " in the Painted Hall at Greenwich. John Boydell, printseller and Lord Mayor of London, published in 1808 views in the South Seas, with sixteen plates drawn and engraved by J. Webber, who was draughtsman in Captain James Cook's expedition round the world, the original drawings for which book are said to be still at the Admiralty. Edward Orme, the publisher to George III and the Prince Regent, issued several remarkable books, including " A Picturesque Voyage to India by the Way of China," by Thomas and William Daniel. Both these artists, uncle and nephew, utilised the knowledge of sea life they had picked up during the voyage to India in illustrations which are now comparatively scarce. Among these may be mentioned " Reefing Topsails," " Crossing the Line," and " Landing Through the Surf," the actual occurrences, no doubt, having been witnessed while on board the *Hannibal*. Orme also issued " A History of the Life, Exploits, and Death of Horatio Nelson," in which there are sixteen

plates, four being in colours, one showing Nelson as a
midshipman attacking a bear, and the others the funeral
procession and ceremonial at St. Paul's. H. Merke, who
worked on these plates, also aquatinted a set of naval
figures by Rowlandson showing the uniforms worn in
1799. Another book of Orme's is entitled "Historic
Military and Naval Anecdotes of Personal Valour, etc.,
which occured to the Armies of Great Britain and her
Allies in the last long-contested War terminating with
the Battle of Waterloo." This book contained forty
coloured aquatints from drawings by J. A. Atkinson,
W. Heath, George Scharf, and others, and the plates include "Nelson in the Cockpit," "The Capture of the
Chesapeake," and "British Sailors Boarding a Man-of-
War." The last-named is reproduced as a specimen of
the spirited work of John Augustus Atkinson, and shows
him to have been a most capable workman, although it
is not possible to reproduce the brilliant colouring of
the original pictures. William Heath, mentioned above,
was also a caricaturist who did a good deal of naval
work, some of which will be found in his "Omnium
Gatherum" and "Nautical Dictionary." A book of
a similar character to that published by Orme is "The
Naval Achievements of Great Britain from the years
1793 to 1817," but the coloured aquatints in this book
and in J. Ralfe's "Naval Chronology of Great Britain"
are of naval engagements, and contain no figure subjects.

It is beyond our scope to deal with the many costume
books published at this period, but there are some books
with illustrations of a humorous character in colours which
must be mentioned. Two of Rowlandson's drawings
illustrating an edition of Smollett deserve special attention, because the artist has dressed Bowling in the
uniform of his period, and not in the dress given him by
the author at a period when no such uniform existed.
Similar mistakes are frequently met with in book illustration, and overlooking the anachronism are most useful
to the student of the cult of clothes. Two other pictures
by Rowlandson are from "The Adventures of Johnny

Newcome in the Navy," by Alfred Burton, published by Simpkin and Marshall. This book produced another one with a similar title, the work of John Mitford, who at one time served as a midshipman of the *Zealous* under Sir Samuel Hood. He was dismissed the Service when a master's mate as being unaccountable for his actions. He is said to have written his adventures of Johnny Newcome while he hid in the gravel pits at Bayswater from the bailiffs, and received a shilling daily in return for his copy. He afterwards edited " The Scourge," illustrated by George Cruikshank, and died a hopeless drunkard in the workhouse. A third book of the kind is " The Post Captain ; or, The Adventures of a True British Tar," written by a naval officer and illustrated by C. Williams. Mitford's book contains twenty plates, and that of Williams twenty-five. They are of very unequal merit. We have also reproduced a plate from Westmacott's " English Spy," in which Rowlandson did some work, but Robert Cruikshank the greater part. Henry Alken did one or two humorous pictures of a nautical character for McLean, the publisher, but his principal work was in the sporting line. Before leaving this class of book illustration we must mention " Greenwich Hospital," a series of naval sketches descriptive of the life of a man-of-war's-man, written by Barker (The Old Sailor), and adorned with twelve hand-coloured etchings by George Cruikshank besides numerous woodcuts. The original illustrations to this book were in a collection sold in 1903.

We have left ourselves very little space to refer to some other sources of illustration, the theatrical prints in line, mezzotint, stipple, and lithograph ; the pretty little watch plates, of which a couple of specimens are given ; the book plates, interesting to students of costume ; the curious frontispieces to jest books ; the valentines, which in their early days, with lottery tickets, were produced by the brothers Cruikshank ; and the penny plain and twopence coloured theatrical characters issued by Messrs. Bailey, West, Clarke and Hodgson, from 1802 to 1820,

and later as the Skelt's " Juvenile Drama," which had
such a fascination for Robert Louis Stevenson. It has
been mentioned that in his early days George Cruikshank
illustrated children's books, and this source deserves con-
sideration. A few examples may be given: " Proverbs
Exemplified, and Illustrated by Pictures from Real Life
—Teaching Morality and a Knowledge of the World;
With prints, Designed as a succession book to Æsop's
Fables, after the manner, and by the author, of Hogarth
Moralised; printed for and published by the Rev. J.
Trusler, and sold at the Literary Press, No. 62 Wardour
Street, Soho, and by all booksellers. Entered at
Stationers' Hall (price 3s. half-bound, London, 1st May,
1790)." This little book contains a picture of a sailor
and a lady, with the following note :—

A Faint Heart Never Won Fair Lady. This proverb
figuratively implies that courage and perseverance are absolutely necessary to effect any end we may have in view, and
is by no means confined to the literal sense; for as a faint
heart never won fair lady, so cowardice and supineness will
infallibly produce a failure in the accomplishment of any
other purpose we may aim at. Before, however, we determine to persevere, we should maturely consider the object
of our attention, and how far it may tend (if successful) to
our honour, our interest, and our happiness. The Tar in our
print, like the element on which he gains his livelihood, has
his calm and boisterous moments; but in the most violent of
the latter he acts with prudence; and in the smoothest even
of the former, carefully avoids everything that is indiscreet.
A wife is the object of his wishes. He meets with a woman
whom he fancies he should like, attacks her with boldness,
accosts her under the consciousness of acting honourably, and
declares his passion for her with his natural bluntness and
honesty. She listens to his proposals, and crowns his wishes
by accepting his offers.

Three other publishers of children's books in which
naval officers, sailors, and ships frequently occur were
J. Harris, of St. Paul's Churchyard; B. Tabart and Co.,
The Juvenile Library, 157 New Bond Street; and S. and

J. Fuller, The Temple of Fancy, Rathbone Place. The following specimens of the inscriptions to the pictures in two little arithmetic books will give an idea of the illustrations. In "Marmaduke Multiply's Merry Method of Making Minor Mathematicians" (1816), we have:—

> Four times five are twenty,
> Jack Tar says his purse is empty.
>
> *   *   *
>
> Seven times ten are seventy,
> Now we're sailing very pleasantly.
>
> *   *   *
>
> Nine times twelve are a hundred and eight,
> See what a noble fine first-rate!

The first-rate ship of war in the last-named picture represents, of course, the *Victory;* and in the other book, entitled "The Mint, or shillings transformed into pounds, by Peregrine Proteus the younger, a near relation of that celebrated character Marmaduke Multiply" (1818), we find:—

> Ninety shillings is four pounds ten,
> The bounty given to Nelson's men.

There were also children's toys of a naval character which the collector should look for, though he may seldom be successful in his search. One of these, played with a pool, counters, and a tee-totum, like the renowned game of "Goose," was called "The Log Book of a Midshipman," and was illustrative of the voyages and travels of Captain Basil Hall. The scenes on the board, twenty in number, are representations of cockpit adventures, described by Captain Hall. An earlier toy was entitled "The Protean Figure and Metamorphic Costumes," in which by a supply of various articles of costume the figure might be attired to represent a number of persons, including a British naval officer. But as in every other field, the nursery literature of long ago will well repay search by the curious collector of illustrations of naval life.

PLATES OF NAVAL UNIFORM, 1748–1848

Nov., 1777. Drawn and published by Dominic Serres, Warwick Street, Golden Square.
(Illustrating uniform regulations, 1748, as amended in 1767 and 1774. See Schomberg's "Naval Chronology" and "The British Fleet.")

Nov., 1779. Drawn by I. P., and published by Wm. Richardson, 68 High Holborn.
(Illustrating dress of officers and men at the period.)

Feb., 1799. Drawn by Rowlandson, aquatinted by H. Merke, and published by R. Ackermann, Strand.
(Illustrating uniform regulations of 1787–1795. See "Annual Register" and Falconer's "Marine Dictionary.")

June–Aug., 1800. "The Naval Magazine or Miscellany," published monthly by Harrison, Cluse and Co., 78 Fleet Street.
(Four plates illustrating changes made about 1797.)

Jan., 1805. "The Costume of Great Britain," aquatinted and coloured by hand by W. H. Pyne, published by Miller, 49 Albemarle Street.
(A flag officer only, often incorrectly coloured.)

June, 1805. "A Book explaining the Ranks and Dignities of British Society," published by Tabart and Co., 157 New Bond Street, in 1809.
(Two plates dated June, 1805.)

Jan., 1807–1808. "A Picturesque Representation of the Naval, Military, and Miscellaneous Costume of Great Britain," soft ground etchings by J. A. Atkinson, published by Miller, 49 Albemarle Street.
(Illustrating uniform regulations of 1797, often incorrectly coloured.)

Jan., 1813. "A Picturesque Representation of the Dress and Manners of the English," drawn by J. A. Atkinson, published by John Murray, Albemarle Street.
(A flag officer only, often incorrectly coloured. No other plates have been traced illustrating uniform regulations of 1812.)

1825. "Description of the Uniform which in pursuance of His Majesty's Pleasure is to be worn by Officers of the Royal Navy," dated from the Admiralty Office, January 1st, 1825, and signed by J. W. Croker, Secretary of the Admiralty.
(Eleven pages letterpress and fifteen plates. These Dress Regulations were the first published in the official Navy List. The plates were reproduced in "The Cyclopædia of British Costume" from "The Metropolitan Repository of Fashions," published by W. Hearn, 20 Southampton Street, Holborn.)

1828. Drawn by W. Alais and published in "The Gentleman's Magazine of Fashion," May to December, 1828.
(One plate only, illustrating regulations of 1828.)

1829. "The Costume of the British Navy as ordered by His Royal Highness the Lord High Admiral in 1828," drawn and lithographed by M. Gauci (some of the drawings are ascribed to E. Hull). Printed and published by Engelmann, Graf, Condel and Co., lithographers to the Duke of Clarence.
(Twelve plates dated 1828–1829 and so numbered; three plates dated 1829-30 and numbered 16 to 18. It is doubtful if plates numbered 13, 14, and 15 ever existed. Although dated earlier, the facings to the uniform in the plates 16, 17, 18 are often found coloured red, a change not made until 1833.)

1839. "Costumes of the Royal Navy and Royal Marines in the reign of William IV," drawn by L. Mansion and St. Eschanzier, coloured by C. H. Martin, and printed by Leferre and Co. Published by Andrews and Co.
(His Majesty in the uniform of the Lord High Admiral and fifteen other plates, dedicated to Queen Adelaide, illustrating uniform regulations of 1833.)

1848. Drawn by R. C. Ulsdell, engraved by J. Harris, and published by J. Ackermann, Strand.
(Six plates illustrating changes in regulations, 1843–1847.)

1854. Drawn by W. Sharpe and published by E. Gambart.
(Illustrating the uniform regulations of 1847–1853.)

1859. Drawn and lithographed by W. Sharpe, printed by M. and N. Hanhart, and published June 1, 1859, by E. Gambart and Co., 35 Berners Street.
(Illustrating uniform regulations of 1856, with portrait of Duke of Edinburgh as a midshipman.)

INDEX

Sea power, Shakespeare and, 149
" Sea Voyage, The," by D'Urfey, 191
" Seafardingers describing Evill Fortune," ballad, 378
Seahorse, 332
" Seaman's Compass, The," ballad by Laurence Price, 382
" Seaman's Return, The," picture by Francis Wheatley, 469
" Seaman's Secrets, The," 64
Sea, Language of, 45, 162
Seamanship and Navigation, Early, 47, 49, 50, 52
Seamen's Protestation, The, 100, 101
Seasickness, 7, 96, 179, 253, 279, 300, 367
Sea Serpent, 153
" Seathrift," character in Mayne's " The City Match," 178
" Seaward, Sir Edward," novel by Miss Porter (1831), 302-3
Seaward Islands, The, 303
" Seawit, Captain," character in Davenant's " The News from Plimouth," 186
Secretary of the Navy, Smollett and bribes to, 268
Sedgemoor, Battle of, Defoe at, 259
Seine, Battle of the (1416), 389
Selden's " Mare Clausum," quoted, 14 n.
Selkirk, Alexander, 112
" Seraglio, The," musical extravaganza by Dibdin, 236
" Serious Reflections on . . . Robinson Crusoe " (Defoe), 261
Serres, Dominic, and J. F., marine painters, 407, 463
Settle, Dionese, old writer, 52 n.
Settle, Elkanah, city laureate and author of " The Empress of Morocco," 228
Seven Years' War, The, 119; ballads on, 401; farce on, 237
Shadwell, Charles, dramatist, 119, 149, 204-22, 273, 275
Shakespeare, 134, 137, 149, 163, 164, 167, 169-71, 175, 181, 225, 241, 250; on the Pole Star, 177; inspiration of " As You Like It," 252; allusion in Marryat's " King's Own," 312
" Shandy, Tristram," character of Laurence Sterne, 277, 284
Shannon and the *Chesapeake*, 37, 38, 307

Shearwater, 387
Sheerness, Dutch destruction of (1667), illustrated, 462
" Shelen-a-gigg," music played by " Mizen's " crew, 211
Shem, character of, in the mystery plays, 156
Sheridan, R. B., dramatist, " The Critic " (1779), 235; play on the Glorious First of June, 239; song by, 361
Sheringham, Lieutenant John, R.N., and Cruikshank's pictures, 471
Sherwin, J. K., engraver, 461
" Ship, The," play at the Fortune Theatre, 179
" Shipman, The," of Chaucer, 47-8, 148, 155, 165, 367; illustrated, 446
Ship-money fleet, The, 9
" Shipwreck, The," poem by Falconer, 370-3
" Shipwrecked Boy, The," picture by W. Bigg, 470
Shipwrecks, ballads on, 405
Shirley, dramatist, author of "The Young Admiral," 191
Shooter's Hill, 163
Shovell, Sir Cloudesley, 15, 20, 78, 85, 111; monument of in Westminster Abbey, 258; ballads on, 398-9, 405
" Shyp of Folys, The " (1509), 290
Sidney, Sir Philip, production of " Arcadia," 252
Sidney, Sir Robert, 58
Signals and Flags, 24, 27, 30, 101, 169, 176, 181
" Siege of Rhodes, The," Davenant, 187
Sierra Leone, Hawkins and, 51
" Silent Woman, The " (Ben Jonson), 174
Simon, Howard's gunner in the battle with Sir Andrew Barton, 390-1
Simon, John, artist, 467
Simonides, Don, " Travels and Adventures of," 251
" Simony " and " Simplicity," characters in " The Pleasant and Stately Moral," 178
Sinbad, Stories of, 227
Sinclair, Captain Archibald, author of " The Discipline, Customs, etc., of the Navy about 1815," 322-4

2 L

WILLIAM BRENDON AND SON, LTD.
PRINTERS, PLYMOUTH

Printed in the United States
102858LV00002B/22/A